CULTURAL CITIZENSHIP

TOBY MILLER

CULTURAL
CITIZENSHIP

*Cosmopolitanism, Consumerism,
and Television in a Neoliberal Age*

TEMPLE UNIVERSITY PRESS
Philadelphia ocm68373500

Temple University Press
1601 North Broad Street
Philadelphia PA 19122
www.temple.edu/tempress

Copyright © 2007 by Temple University
All rights reserved
Published 2007
Printed in the United States of America

⊗ The paper used in this publication meets the requirements of the American
National Standard for Information Sciences—Permanence of Paper for Printed
Library Materials, ANSI Z39.48-1992

Library of Congress Cataloging-in-Publication Data

Miller, Toby.
    Cultural citizenship : cosmopolitanism, consumerism, and television in a
neoliberal age / Toby Miller.
        p. cm.
    Includes bibliographical references and index.
    ISBN-13: 978-1-59213-560-8   ISBN-10: 1-59213-560-9   (cloth: alk. paper)
    ISBN-13: 978-1-59213-561-5   ISBN-10: 1-59213-561-7   (pbk.: alk. paper)
    1. Culture—Study and teaching—United States. 2. Consumption
(Economics)—United States. 3. Mass media—United States. 4. United
States—Politics and government. I. Title.

    HM623.M54 2007
    306.0973—dc22   2006045603

2   4   6   8   9   7   5   3   1

CONTENTS

ACKNOWLEDGMENTS

T HANKS FOR COMMENTS, forums, information, labor, shelter, and technology to Barbara Abrash, Pal Ahluwalia, Mona Ahmad Ali, Amy Aidman, Manuel Alvarado, Sarah Banet-Weiser, Rebecca Barden, Carlos Barrera, Ira Bhaskar and her family, Sarah Berry, William Boddy, Göran Bolin, Elizabeth Botta, Edward Buscombe, Ed Butler, Ann Chisholm, Jim Clifford, Jim Collins, Marilyn Davis, Patrick Deer, Robyn Donahue, Ana Dopico, Susan Douglas, Emory Elliott, Liz Ferrier, Tracy Fisher, James Friedman, David Theo Goldberg, Larry Gross, Sara Gwenllian-Jones, Robert Hamilton, John Hartley, Gail Hershatter, John Hill, Natalie Hirniak, Pierrette Hondagneu-Sotelo, Drew Hubbell, Tina Andersen Huey, Engin Isin, Aparna John, Mariana John-son, Tanius Karam, Noel King, Micah Kleit, Amitava Kumar, Josh Kun, Mariam Beevi Lam, Geoffrey Lawrence, Marie Leger, Justin Lewis, Laura Lora Lozon, Reymond Levy, Nick Lowe, Anna McCarthy, Alec McHoul, Martin McLoone, Eric Kit-Wai Ma, Randy Martin, Daniel Mato, Rick Maxwell, Ranjani Mazumdar, Margareta Melin-Higgins, Mike Messner, Arturo Mier y Teran, Silke Morgenroth, Monica Narula, Rebecca O'Con-nor, Rune Ottosen, Laurie Ouellette, Dana Polan, Arvind Rajagopal, Ellen Reese, Kristina Riegert, Andrew Ross, Lawrence Schehr, Anna Scott, the editorial staff at Scribe, Ellen Seiter, Christie Slade, Marita Sturken, Ravi Sundaram, Ken Sweeney, the Temple University Press workforce, Doug

Thomas, Antonette Toney, Leshu Torchin, Paula Treichler, William Uric-chio, Ravi Vasudevan, Cecilia Vilchis Schondube, Jane Ward, Allen Weiss, Chuck Whitney, Rosalía Winocur, Ken Wissoker, Cynthia Young, George Yúdice, Caitlin Zaloom, Barbie Zelizer, Alicia Ziccardi, Diane Zimmerman, and Vera Zolberg. Having received some very incisive criticisms of the project from anonymous and known readers, I removed three chapters and redrafted the "full catastrophe," as Zorba might have put it. Toward the project's conclusion, Dana P., Rick M., John H., and Micah K. offered very helpful advice based on their close readings of the manuscript. It is leaner and less mean as a consequence.

The ideas also benefited from feedback via my interviews and talks for CNN, All-India Radio, New York 1, George Yúdice's Privatization of Culture Project on Cultural Policy, *Consoling Passions*, *Media in Transition 3*, the National Communication Association, the Department of Communications at the University of California, San Diego, Sarai at the Centre for the Study of Developing Societies in Delhi, the International Association for Media and Communication Research, the Department of Sociology at Central Queensland University, the Department of Culture and Communication at New York University, the Program in American Studies & Ethnicity, plus the School of Cinema-Television and the Gender Studies Program at the University of Southern California, the Department of Film, Television, and Digital Media at the University of California, Los Angeles, the Annenberg School for Communication at the University of Southern California, the *New Economy, Creativity and Consumption Symposium* at the Queensland University of Technology, the Center for Ideas & Society at the University of California, Riverside, the Seminario de Formación Docente: Ciudad, Cultura y Comunicación at the Universidad de la Ciudad de México, Susquehanna University, the Cultural Policy Seminar at the University of Illinois, Champaign-Urbana, *Crossroads*, the Centre for Media Research at the University of Ulster, the Department of Sociology at the University of Southern California, the School of the Art Institute of Chicago, the Western Humanities Alliance, the Institute for the Study of Women and Gender at the University of Michigan, and a senior-citizens' group in Riverside.

I also wish to express my appreciation to everyone at Sarai for stimulating me to rethink "the contemporary"—*acha*. Much of this was done at Riverside, thanks to my opportunity to be its Distinguished Faculty Visitor in the first half of 2003. I had never worked at a place where adequate facilities and resources were available to scholars. And I had fine intellectual and dining companions. Then the project received a great boost from time in Mexico City, where I enjoyed perfect working conditions in a wonderful casa amidst the stimulating but relaxing environs of Coyoacán.

Parts of this book appeared elsewhere, as I developed my thinking about cultural citizenship. All previously published sections have been extensively rewritten and articulated against one another, with much new material included. Original sites of publication for some of these ideas include the *Handbook of Citizenship Studies*. Ed. Engin F. Isin and Bryan S. Turner. London: Sage, 2002; *International Journal of Cultural Studies* 5, no. 1 (2002); *M/C: A Journal of Media and Culture* 5, no. 1 (2002); *The Sarai Reader 02: The Cities of Everyday Life*. Ed. Ravi S. Vasudevan, Jeebesh Bagchi, Ravi Sundaram, Monica Narula, Geert Lovink, and Shuddhabrata Segupta. New Delhi: Sarai—The New Media Initiative/Amsterdam: Society for Old and New Media, 2002; *French Food: On the Table, On the Page, and in French Culture*. Ed. Lawrence R. Schehr and Allen S. Weiss. New York: Routledge, 2001; *High-Pop: Making Culture into Popular Entertainment*. Ed. Jim Collins. Oxford: Blackwell, 2002; *Reality Squared: Televisual Discourse on the Real*. Ed. James Friedman. New Brunswick: Rutgers University Press, 2002; *Sarai Reader 04: Crisis/Media*. Ed. Monica Narula, Shuddhabrata Sengupta, Ravi Sundaram, Ravi S. Vasudevan, Jeebesh Bagchi, and Geert Lovink. Delhi: Sarai, Center for the Study of Developing Societies, 2004; *U.S. and the Others: Global Media Images on "The War on Terror,"* ed. Stig A. Nohrstedt and Rune Ottosen. Göteborg: NORDICOM, 2004; *Politics and Culture* 5, no. 2 (2005); and *Global Wars—Local Views: Media Images of the Iraq War*. Ed. Stig A. Nohrstedt and Rune Ottosen. Göteborg: NORDICOM, 2005.

INTRODUCTION

"While Europe was tensely watching the crisis over Czechoslovakia, Herr Hitler, accompanied by eight of his generals, paid a surprise visit to the French frontier to-day."

That is the way the newspapers talk about the world. These actual words were splashed across the Star on August 29, 1938. . . .

Of course, that is assuming that Britain, and the rest of Europe, really were at that time "tensely watching." But were they? How many were more tensely watching the racing news and daily horoscope?
—Mass-Observation (1939, 8)

QUESTION—who attracted most U.S. press coverage in 1938?
a) Seabiscuit
b) Roosevelt
c) Hitler; or
d) Mussolini
ANSWER—the racehorse
—Jaroslav Pelikan (2005, xviii)

Beginning with Generation X (people in their 20s to early 40s) and all the generations that follow, multicultural is normal. . . . Their friends are all races, sexual preferences. They walk the walk of a nation.
—Ann Fishman, President of Generational Targeted Marketing (quoted in El Nasser and Grant, 2005a)

The disarray and disinterest of our mass media towards fulfilling its crucial democratic commitments gives me serious pause.
—William E. Kennard, Chair of the Federal Communications Commission (FCC) (2000)

W E ARE IN A CRISIS of belonging, a population crisis, of who, what, when, and where. More and more people feel as though they *do not* belong. More and more people are *seeking* to belong, and more and more people are not *counted* as belonging. *Cultural Citizenship* is concerned with the way this crisis is both registered and held in check in the United States, through practices of government, consumption, risk, and moral panic in popular culture, specifically television. With economic welfare disowned as a responsibility of the sovereign state, and pushed onto individuals and communities, governing at a distance is the norm (Donzelot 1991). Traditional means of state control, via instruction or restraint, have been added to by a project of neoliberalism, which seeks to manage subjectivity through culture—ironically, the very thing supposedly imperiled by threats to belonging.

The term "culture" has earthy connotations. It derives from the Latin "colare," which implied tending and developing agriculture as part of subsistence. With the emergence of capitalism's division of labor, culture came both to *embody* instrumentalism and to *abjure* it, via the industrialization of farming, on the one hand, and the cultivation of individual taste, on the other. In keeping with this distinction, culture has usually been understood in two registers, via the social sciences and the humanities—truth versus beauty. This was a heuristic distinction in the sixteenth century, but it became substantive over time. Eighteenth-century German, French, and Spanish dictionaries bear witness to a metaphorical shift into spiritual cultivation. As the spread of literacy and printing saw customs and laws passed on, governed, and adjudicated through the written word, cultural texts supplemented and supplanted physical force as guarantors of authority. With the Industrial Revolution, populations became urban dwellers. Food was imported, cultures developed textual forms that could be exchanged, and consumer society emerged through horse racing, opera, art exhibits, masquerades, and balls. Cultural labor indexed the impact of this shift. *Poligrafi* in fifteenth-century Venice, and hacks in eighteenth-century London, wrote popular and influential conduct books, works of instruction on everyday life that marked the textualization of custom and the appearance of new occupational identities. Anxieties about "cultural invasion" also date from this period, via Islamic debates over Western domination.

Culture became a marker of differences and similarities in taste and status. The corollary in academia is that in the humanities, it is judged by criteria of quality and meaning, as practiced critically and historically. In the social sciences, the focus is on sociopolitical norms, as explored psychologically or statistically. So, whereas the humanities articulates population differences through *symbolic* means (for example, which class has the cultural capital to appreciate high culture and which does not), the social sciences articulates population differences through *social* ones (for example, which people are affected by TV messages and which are not) (Williams 1983, 38; Benhabib 2002, 2; de Pedro 1999, 61–62, 78n1; Briggs and Burke 2003, 10, 38, 60, 57; Mowlana 2000, 107; Wallerstein 1989).

Combining these two disciplines, I take my bearings from several sources. I am indebted most of all to cultural studies. By attending to inequality and identity, cultural studies' reintegration of the humanities and the social sciences under the sign of popular democracy has provided "a riposte to the mandarin prejudice of high cultural journalism and the facile classifications of market researchers" (Maxwell 2002). In the context of moribund disciplines adrift in the detritus of Cold War professionalism, it offers "una salida de emergencia" [an emergency exit] (García Canclini 2004, 122).

Despite the dominant U.S. critique of cultural studies, it is not just about literature departments engaging in a partial makeover. Historical and contemporary analyses of slaves, crowds, pirates, bandits, audiences, minorities, women, and the working class have utilized archival, ethnographic, and textual methods to emphasize day-to-day noncompliance with authority, via practices of consumption that frequently turn into practices of production. For example, British research on the contemporary has lit upon Teddy Boys, Mods, bikers, skinheads, punks, school students, teen girls, Rastas, truants, dropouts, and magazine readers as its magical agents of history—groups who deviated from the norms of schooling and the transition to work. Scholar-activists examine the structural underpinnings to collective style, investigating how bricolage subverts the achievement-oriented, materialistic, educationally driven values and appearance of the middle class. The working assumption has often been that subordinate groups adopt and adapt signs and objects of the dominant culture, reorganizing them to manufacture new meanings. Consumption is thought to be the epicenter of such subcultures. Paradoxically, it has also reversed their members' status as consumers. The oppressed become producers of new fashions, inscribing alienation, difference, and powerlessness on their bodies (Leong 1992).

Virginia Postrel, then editor of the libertarian *Reason* magazine, and later a *New York Times* economics journalist, wrote a 1999 op-ed piece for the *Wall Street Journal* in which she described cultural studies as "deeply threatening to traditional leftist views of commerce," because its notions of active consumption are close to those of the Right. "The cultural-studies mavens are betraying the leftist cause, lending support to the corporate enemy and even training graduate students who wind up doing market research." Consumption seemed to be the key to this mantra, with production discounted, labor forgotten, the consumer sovereign, and government there to protect that sovereign (Frank 2000).

Of course, for some 1960s mass-society theorists, and many of us in cultural studies, commercial culture does indeed represent the apex of modernity. Far from being supremely alienating, it stands for the expansion of civil society, the first moment in history when central political and commercial organs and agendas became receptive to, and part of, the broader community.

New forms of life were necessitated by industrialization and aided by mass communication, and the population became part of the social, rather than excluded from political-economic, calculation. The number of people classed as outsiders diminished in mass society, along with a lessening of authority, the promulgation of individual rights and respect, and the simultaneous development of intensely interpersonal and large-scale human interaction. The spread of advertising broke down social barriers between high and low culture (Shils 1966, 505–6, 511; Hartley 1998), paradoxically preparing the way for niche-targeted "citizens of the future," who "don't wear conformist jumpsuits, live in utilitarian high-rises, or get [their] food in pills" (Postrel 2003, 4–5). But the change toward a popularly available array of stylistic choices and forms of social participation is accompanied by a shift from building and acknowledging a national popular culture to technologizing and privatizing it. For once all classes have been incorporated into society, technical forms of knowledge and systems of commodification must govern the problems and promises these masses bring with them (Martín-Barbero 2003, 38).

If we follow Postrel (and certain textual reductionists), the dominant strand of U.S. cultural studies lost political economy as its animator, in favor of some ghastly, scholarly mirror of the post-welfare state. The substructural corollary would be the way in which gentrification guts working life for proletarians and minorities, as it creates a space of safety, entitlement, and groove for corporate gays, white liberal feminists, frat boys and sorority girls who are keen to wear black clothes and eschew suburbia until the children arrive, and people like my friends and me (to the extent we are not covered by any or all of the above categories). Does this mean cultural studies is now the handservant of capital?

No, it does not. Many leading practitioners have always blended political economy with cultural studies.* And much has changed since the Simple-Simon, academic-reader-as-hegemon narcissism that plagued U.S. cultural studies through much of the 1980s and 1990s, via professors earnestly spying on young people at the mall, or obsessively staring at them in virtual communities. Political economy has reasserted itself, as it always does. Sociologist Vincent Mosco starts from the power of cultural myths, then "builds a bridge

---

*I am thinking of such U.S.-based writers as Dave Andrews, Stanley Aronowitz, Michael Bérubé, Ben Carrington, Paula Chakravartty, C. L. Cole, Michael Curtin, Susan G. Davis, Susan Douglas, John Downing, Philomena Essed, Rosa-Linda Fregoso, Faye Ginsburg, David Theo Goldberg, Herman Gray, Larry Gross, Lawrence Grossberg, Ed Guerrero, Michael Hanchard, Robin D. G. Kelly, Doug Kellner, Laura Kipnis, Mariam Beevi Lam, George Lipsitz, Cameron McCarthy, Anne McClintock, Lisa McLaughlin, George Marcus, Jorge Mariscal, Randy Martin, Rick Maxwell, Rob Nixon, Vorris Nunley, Constance Penley, Dana Polan, Andrew Ross, Dan Schiller, Ellen Seiter, Ella Shohat, Lynn Spigel, Bob Stam, Tom Streeter, and George Yúdice. Despite their prominence, their work is often taken to be apolitical-economic, or not to stand for cultural studies in dominant public characterizations. Hmm.

to political economy" in his excoriation of neoliberal fantasies about empowerment, insisting on "the mutually constitutive relationship" between political economy and cultural studies as each mounts "a critique of the other" (2004, 6–7). In the words of media studies critic Richard Maxwell, we must

> identify ways to link a critique of neo-liberalism and a cultural studies approach to consumption . . . not by issuing nostrums against the pleasures of shopping[,]but by paying attention to the politics of resource allocation that brings a consumption infrastructure into the built environment (2002).

This has already been achieved in cultural studies beyond Britain, the United States, and their white-settler academic satellites (Israel, Australia, Canada, and Aotearoa/New Zealand). The sociologist Arvind Rajagopal notes that because television, the telephone, the Internet, and the neoliberal are all new to India, "markets and media generate new kinds of rights and new kinds of imagination . . . novel ways of exercising citizenship rights and conceiving politics" (2002). We see the evidence in media-activism-scholarship organizations such as sarai.net in New Delhi. Anthropologist Rosalía Winocur has noticed that since the fall of U.S.-backed dictatorships, talk radio in Latin America has offered a simultaneously individual and social forum for new expressions of citizenship. In the context of decentered politics, emergent identities, minority rights, and gender issues, the radio has created a public space that transcends old ideas subordinating difference and privileging élite experience (2002, 15, 91–93). These are exemplary instances of the work that understands the importance of material conditions in the formation of subjectivity.

This book poses questions of political economy. The United States has become the least socially mobile advanced Western economy. Frankly, it is not a First World country for a fifth of its inhabitants. Although income inequality gradually decreased between the Great War and Vietnam, the process went into reverse, starting with Jimmy Carter's Presidency. Thanks to a gigantic clumping of wealth at the apex of the nation, there is now a poor, unskilled, and ill base: forty-six million residents are indigent, fifty-two million are functionally analphabetic, and forty-four million lack health insurance. By contrast with European welfare systems, the capacity to exit poverty for good has diminished over the last two decades of neoliberalism, and the proportion of national income held by the extremely rich is two to three times the level in France or Britain. Race and gender massively stratify access to money and net worth, and the gaps are widening. Black men earn 73 percent of the hourly wage rate for white people, and women fifty-six cents on the male dollar. In the two decades from Carter to Bill Clinton, the wealthiest 1 percent doubled their share of national pretax income, to 18 percent. From 1979 to 2000, the top 1 percent of incomes increased by 194 percent, the top 20 percent by 70 percent, and the bottom 20 percent by 6.4 percent. In 1967, chief executive officers of corporations were paid twenty-four times the average wage of employees. In 1990, they received 107 times that amount. By 2005, the ratio was 431 to 1—up from 301 to 1 just the year before. The national minimal wage in 2005 was US$5.15 an hour. Had it risen at the same rate as executive pay over the previous fifteen years, the hourly rate would have been US$23.03! The Congressional Budget Office reports that across the late 1990s, the wealthiest 1 percent of U.S. households had a greater combined income than the poorest 40 percent. Over George Bush Minor's first term, profits rose by 60 percent, and wages by just 10 percent. In 2004, after-tax profits for corporations grew to their highest proportion of Gross Domestic Product (GDP) since the Depression (Skocpol 2004; Thelen 2000, 552; Freeman 2004; *Economist*, 2005h; Talvi 2005a, 10; "Breaking" 2005; Jeffery 2006; Yates 2005; Anderson et al. 2005, 1–2; Hutton 2003b, 133, 148; Taibo 2003, 24).*

This bizarre reconcentration of wealth in the hands of the ruling class is unprecedented in world history since the advent of adult electoral franchises. No wonder the *Economist* captioned a photo of the Queen of England greeting Bush Minor and his wife as "Liz, meet the royals" (*Economist*, 2005h). Even those bastions of bourgeois comfort and onanism, the *Wall Street Journal* and the *New York Times*, run repeated, sizeable stories on the new Gilded Age of the twenty-first century and its reorganized class relations (Lexington 2005, 32). Those with the highest levels of income and education are most likely to participate in lobby groups and vote in Presidential elections, while those with the lowest are least likely to do so. This is in accordance with the positive salience of the state in their lives. The role of government has been redefined, at least rhetorically, from a sometimes feisty agent stabilizing labor and capital via redistribution, to a mendicant servant of capital with some residual duty of care to the citizenry (American Political Science Association Task Force on Inequality and American Democracy 2004, 3–5; Jencks 2004; Crouch 2004, 23, 40).

Yet, many residents embrace the United States ideologically. Why? Demographic change, public-policy fashion, and the political economy of the media have altered U.S. citizenship. Sectarian allegiances below and across the level

---

*Of course, the United States has a massive and efficient welfare state. It's called Israel, and its citizens are subsidized by an average of US$500 a year from the United States (Mann 2003, 54).

of the sovereign state have displaced models of national unity, while managerialist and neoclassical discourses of scarcity have deregulated the social, recasting the population as consumers and believers in a way that differentiates between social groups via a fine, culturally precise grain. These reactionary forces have borrowed the categories and tactics of progressive cultural politics, and trumped it in the process. We said we were cultural citizens, so they said they were, too.

Commodities have been a key to this process. They elicit desire by wooing consumers, glancing at them sexually, and smelling and looking nice in ways that are borrowed from romantic love, but reverse that relationship. People learn about correct forms of romantic love from commodities. Sociologist Wolfgang Haug's term "commodity aesthetics" captures this division between what commodities *promise*, by way of seduction, and what they are *actually about*, as signs of production (1986, 17, 19, 35). For the public, this is "the *promesse du bonheur* that advanced capitalism always holds before them, but never quite delivers" (Benhabib 2002, 3). In media terms, the price paid for subscribing to cable or satellite access (exchange value) takes over from the programs being watched (use value). The sociologist Jean Baudrillard maintains that all products purchased within capitalist societies involve the consumption of advertising, rather than objects themselves. Such is the contest for newness. The culture industries are central to the compulsion to buy, through the double-sided nature of advertising and "the good life" of luxury: they encourage competition between consumers, at the same time as they standardize processes to manufacture unity in the face of diversity. For all the pleasurable affluence suggested by material goods, the idea of transcendence has been articulated to objects. Commodities dominate the human and natural landscape. The corollary is the simultaneous triumph and emptiness of the sign as a source and measure of value. Baudrillard discerns four "successive phases of the image." It begins as a reflection of reality that is transformed when false information displaces a representation of the truth. Then these two, delineable phases of truth and lies become indistinct. The sign comes to refer to itself, with no residual need of correspondence with the real. It simulates itself (Baudrillard 1988, 10–11, 29, 170), as "human needs, relationships and fears, the deepest recesses of the human psyche, become mere means for the expansion of the commodity universe" (McChesney and Foster 2003, 1). Commodities hide not only the work of their own creation, but their postpurchase existence as well. Designated with human characteristics (beauty, taste, serenity, and so on) they compensate for the absence of these qualities in everyday capitalism via a "permanent opium war" (Debord 1995, 26–27, 29–30).

But the commodity form cannot be dismissed out of hand. Clearly, alternative models of citizenship and consumption must go beyond standard critiques of, say, cultural imperialism (watching U.S. drama will turn rural people around the world into Idaho potato farmers) or feel-good invectives about socially responsible shopping (purchasing environmentally sound toilet paper and free-range chicken will transform the world, one roll/wing at a time). At certain moments, even leftists resisting authoritarian politics embrace ideologies of liberal individualism and free choice via consumer preference. At other times, they may foreground work rather than consumption in a struggle for collective justice. Consumption can threaten the Right when it is tied to radical social change, linking issues of labor and circulation across industries and in public debate. Production and consumption must be understood as equal parts of an enterprise—the enterprise of social justice.

Journalist Naomi Klein's remarkable chronicle of corporate malfeasance in marketing, and activism against it, wagers "that as more people discover the brand-name secrets of the global logo web, their outrage will fuel the next big political movement, a vast wave of opposition squarely targeting transnational corporations" (1999, xviii). The liberal governance model *can* be progressive when it operates in the interests of human needs rather than individual satisfaction, quickening the breath of anxious conservatives and neoliberals in the face of collective consumer action. The decline of the British economy and state across the 1970s was exemplified in punk's use of rubbish as an adornment: bag liners, lavatory appliances, and ripped and torn clothing. But capitalism has appropriated the appropriator. Even as the media set in train various moral panics about punk, and cultural studies responded by valorizing it as a subculture, the fashion and music industries were sending out spies in search of trends to market. The contemporary equivalent is Coca-Cola hiring African Americans to drive through the inner city selling soda and playing hip-hop; AT&T paying San Francisco buskers to mention the company in their songs; performance poets rhyming about Nissan cars for cash, simultaneously hawking, entertaining, and researching; and Subway sandwich commercials supposedly "shot by real teenagers." This is the delightfully named "viral" or "peer-to-peer" marketing, characteristic of such campaigns as McDonalds' "365Black." It associates the company with civil rights via African American athletes endorsing its products in commercials, and hip-hop musicians receiving remuneration each time one of their songs referring to the company is played on radio, emulating Kanye West "mentioning" nineteen brands on four singles in 2004. Such campaigns are meant to distinguish McDonalds from the tokenism of Black History Month, in concert with new uniforms designed in the hope that young African American employees will wear them socially and make them stylish (McChesney and Foster 2003, 12; Piccalo 2004; Ouellette and Murray 2004, 9; Ford 2005; Graser 2005a and b; MacArthur 2005b).

There has been relatively little survey research into consumer boycotts and their opposite, buycotts, but a 2002 study revealed that half the U.S. population engaged in such practices—higher numbers than for other forms of civic participation like churchgoing or volunteerism. After the 2004 Presidential election, Buy Blue emerged as an online advisory bureau for progressives anxious to patronize companies that were pro-environment and anti-conservative. The coyBOTt software package has revealed interesting correlations between boycotts, brand popularity, and corporate cultural sponsorship (BuyBlue.org 2004; Keeter et al. 2002, 8–9, 20–21; Costanza-Chock 2002). Examples include the ecoconsumerism of Greenpeace, chronicled in *Ethical Consumer* magazine as an "economic vote" via "shareholder activism," whereby social movements purchase a financial stake in polluters and change corporate conduct (Newell 2001, 92, 99). This induces apoplexy in fossil-fuel capitalists and their political and intellectual allies. Similarly, because of racist hiring practices, Denny's restaurant chain has been boycotted by leftists in the United States, some of whom, conversely, buycott the Working Assets long-distance telephone service, which donates a portion of its proceeds to left-wing causes. Clearly, with consumers targeted by a culture-driven economy, their identities come to be points of sociopolitical and commercial organization. The desire of capital to sell to major U.S. minorities over the past hundred and fifty years has both enabled and *been* enabled *by* the hyphenated political-economic actions of Jewish, African, Mexican, Central and Northern European Americans. These actors are simultaneously interest groups and customers. As the first African American major-league baseball player, Jackie Robinson, put it: "Every human has a vote every time he makes a purchase" (quoted in Glickman 1999, 8).

The turn of the twenty-first century saw the uptake of ethical principles by International Shareholder Services (ISS). ISS acts as the proxy advisor for many large institutional investors, such as mutual and pension funds. It exerts major influence on votes at over twenty thousand shareholder meetings a year. Previously a stalwart of the Right on issues of social responsibility, in 2002 ISS changed its position, astonishing outsiders by recommending votes in favor of renewal-fuel research and anti-sexual-discrimination policies by ExxonMobil stockholders, and against child labor in Marriott hotels. ISS did so because it had determined that "being perceived as a good corporate citizen might affect shareholder value" by appealing to socially concerned investors. Put another way, for the first time, ISS judged that being on the same side as environmentalists and unions made sense and cents, in keeping with studies that correlate high stock valuations of companies with strong pro-environmental programs. Whereas growth in professionally managed assets in the United States is about 15 percent annually, the figure is 40 percent for those with mandates for "social responsibility." Trillions of dollars are at stake (Cordasco 2002, 9; Keeler 2002). Corporations are aware that mutual funds serving academics and unionists want to see social as well as financial value flowing from their investments. For example, the California Public Employees' Retirement System controls more than US$186 billion in pension funds for nearly one and a half million people, many of whom are educators and unionists (Keeler 2002; Alperovitz 2005). This imperative became urgent with the multiple disgraces of U.S. big business under Bush Minor, and Third World issues such as child labor and pharmaceutical pricing (Maitland 2002, 10). When some public pension funds lost US$300 billion to the Enron scandal, they grew more interventionist about their investments, leading to aggressive criticism from business front organizations as part of the Republican Party's "shadow civil society" (Greider 2005; Schell 2005, 6).

But more than 90 percent of Fortune 500 companies appear in "socially responsible" investing portfolios, which use the Dow Jones Industrial Average as their metric! From worthy origins in opposition to apartheid, the American War in Vietnam, and polluting firms, many of these entities have turned into corporate shills whose massive secrecy belies their claim to ethical conduct. The World Economic Forum's list of the "100 Most Sustainable Companies in the World" includes corporations that bribe officials, provide false accounts, and are mass polluters, but are sold as appropriate for progressive investors (Hawken 2004 and 2005). Even relatively responsible firms elude any critique of capitalism. Consider the 2004 holiday season pitch made by the outdoor equipment company, Patagonia, based on the fact that it allocates 1 percent of revenue to conservation:

> There's no such thing as a free lunch. The air we breathe in big gulps. The snow we slide on every chance we get. We can't take any of it for granted. This holiday season, when you give the gift of Patagonia to your near and dear ones, you'll also be giving back to the environment. Since 1985, we've donated 1% of our sales to grassroots enviro groups. Shop Patagonia and give back (Patagonia 2004).

The Right's glorification of consumers rarely endorses organized political action by them. When the *Economist* proudly announces that consumers "are kings" because of new technology and transparent costs (does that mean see-through price tags?) it is referring to an "All-seeing, All-knowing," surveillant, selfish, shopper—not a socially engaged collective force (Markillie 2005, 3). Eulogies to public opinion and rational choice do not carry over to endorsements of social activism. People are sovereign when they purchase, but magically transmogrify into "special interests" when they lobby; hence the formation of the Business Roundtable in the 1970s to combat consumer movements from the very top levels of executive action, rather than through discrete trade associations. Absent an ongoing fabric of democratic control, consumer activism will always be an irritant rather than a systemic counter to corporate destructiveness. For one thing, "consumer democracy" gives the wealthy more votes than the poor. Most U.S. activists are affluent and highly educated, so the practice ironically mirrors the unrepresentative plutocracies of the International Monetary Fund (IMF) and the World Bank. The impact on, and inclusion of, working people in such actions is frequently problematic. And ethical consumption is difficult to sustain when, for example, numerous items with distinct production histories are bundled together, as in electrical equipment. Boycotts and buycotts require high levels of organization and sustained commitment, and they often end with apparent success, only for corporations to resume their nefarious activities in a quietly efficient manner (Baudrillard 1999, 55; Micheletti 2003; Hutton 2003b, 84; Hutton in Giddens and Hutton 2000b, 47; Keeter et al. 2002, 21; Frank 2003; Monbiot 2003, 56–58; Shaw 1999, 111).

It seems to me that the neoliberal Right is winning struggles enacted over culture, sometimes in concert with the cultural studies Left—when valorizing difference as a marketing concept; and sometimes in concert with the reactionary Right—when making nationalism into a cultural and commercial norm. This is possible because while there are superficial differences between a collectivist ethos and individualistic utilitarianism, they share the precept that ethico-aesthetic exercises are necessary to develop the responsible individual, amenable to both self-governance and niche cultural commodification (Lloyd and Thomas 1998, 121). "Good taste" becomes a sign of, and a means toward, better citizenship. Ethico-aesthetic exercises favor bourgeois manners for a circumscribed set of individuals in one period, and stratified access to resources on the basis of divers demographics slicing at one another. Pan-ethnic categories characterize the U.S. census, media and consumer markets, and political voting blocs. They efficiently clump people into five "American" types— European, African, Latino, Native, and Asian—as state and capital embark on the colonizing and policing of territory and subjectivity, of space and historiography (Shapiro 2001, 118). This is done in the *service* of capital accumulation; under the *sign* of national protection and individual choice; and via the *technology* of television.

The anthropologist Néstor García Canclini places a particular focus on the media as *loci* of problems such as insecurity and pollution, and practices such as difference and development. He examines culture in terms of difference, inequality, exclusion, and exploitation as much as similarity, equality, inclusion, and justice (2001b, 12 and 2004, 43). As the cultural historian Ravi Vasudevan eloquently explains, through the media, via regulating and stimulating access, content, and conduct, the state frequently exercises duty of care and control (2001, 62). The U.S. government began regulating the media's audiovisual output because Congress feared that radio amateurs had interfered with messages from the *Titanic* calling for aid (Cook 2005, 255). An *"actuarial gaze,"* a visual management of threats and responses, characterizes the contemporary "cultural political agenda," with the media simultaneously a mirror and a site of creation, reflection, policy, and action, which binds the everyday to spectacle, the private to the public (Feldman 2005, 206–7). Citizenship is effectively incarnated in an array of sites across the media, via such techniques as vox populi, demonstrations, public-opinion polls, and magical incantations (for example, "the American public *is* . . .") (Lewis et al. 2005, 19). Today, the most important "site of the world risk society is not the street[,]but *television*" (Beck 1999, 44).

TELEVISION

The word is half Greek, half Latin. No good can come of it.
—*Guardian* editor, CP Scott (quoted in Wasko 2005, 1)

TV is king.
—Title of song by The Tubes

[T]hat terrible turning inward, which means the less you know about the world, the less you want to know about it, and therefore the less a ratings-obsessed industry decides to tell you
—BBC journalist John Simpson on U.S. television news (2005)

Since its inception, TV has been regarded principally as a means of profiting and legitimizing its controllers, and entertaining and civilizing its viewers. In the words of the famous BBC executive Huw Wheldon, its mission is "To make the good popular, and the popular good" (quoted in Airey 2004). A nice phrase, but the sociologist Pierre Bourdieu sees these as competing rather than consistent imperatives. He refers to a duel between "populist spontaneism and demagogic capitulation to popular tastes" and "paternalistic-pedagogic television" (1998, 48). As the philosopher Theodor Adorno said, while there are problems with "cultured snobbism," populist TV disempowers audience knowledge in the key areas of public life affected by politics. Half a century ago, he moaned that viewers were discerning when it came to high technology, which they regarded as a sign of their power as consumers, but were not exercised by public affairs (1996, 89, 139).

When veteran newsman Edward R. Murrow addressed the Radio-Television News Directors Association in 1958, he used the description/metaphor that television needed to "illuminate" and "inspire," or it would be "merely wires and light in a box." In a famous speech to the National Association of Broadcasters three years later, John F. Kennedy's chair of the FCC, Newton Minow, called U.S. TV a "vast wasteland" (1971). He was urging broadcasters to embark on enlightened Cold War leadership, to prove that the United States was not the mindless consumer world that the Soviets claimed. The networks would thereby live up to their legislative responsibilities to act in the public interest by informing and entertaining, and go beyond what he later recognized as "white suburbia's Dick-and-Jane world" (Minow 2001). They responded by doubling the time devoted to news each evening, and quickly became the dominant source of current affairs (Schudson and Tifft 2005, 32). Twenty years later, Ronald Reagan's FCC head, Mark Fowler, celebrated the reduction of the "box" to "transistors and tubes." He argued in an interview with *Reason* magazine that "television is just another appliance—it's a toaster with pictures," and hence, in no need of regulation, beyond ensuring its safety as an electrical appliance (1981).*

Minow's and Fowler's expressions gave their vocalists instant and undimmed celebrity (Murrow already had it as the most heralded audiovisual journalist in U.S. history). Minow was named "top newsmaker" of 1961 in an Associated Press survey, and he was on TV and radio more than any other Kennedy official. In an irony of ironies, the phrase "vast wasteland" has provided raw material for the wasteland's parthenogenesis, as the answer to questions posed on numerous game shows, from *Jeopardy!* to *Who Wants to Be a Millionaire?* (Minow and Cate 2003, 408). The "toaster with pictures" is less celebrated, but it has been more efficacious as a slogan for deregulation across successive administrations, and remains in *Reason's* pantheon of famous libertarian quotations, alongside Reagan and others of his ilk. Where Minow supports public culture's restraining and ultimately conserving function for capitalism, Fowler represents capitalism's brooding arrogance, its neoliberal lust to redefine use value via exchange value. Minow decries

---

*Not surprisingly, Alfred Hitchcock had said it earlier and better: "Television is like the American toaster, you push the button and the same thing pops up every time" (quoted in Wasko 2005, 10).

Fowler's vision, arguing that television "is not an ordinary business" because of its "public responsibilities" (Minow and Cate 2003, 415). But Fowler's phrase has won the day, at least to this point. Minow's phrase lives on as a recalcitrant moral irritant, rather than a central policy technology.

Fowler has had many fellow travelers. Both the free-cable, free-video social movements of the 1960s and 1970s, and the neoclassical, deregulatory intellectual movements of the 1970s and 1980s, saw a people's technology allegedly emerging from the wasteland of broadcast television. Portapak equipment, localism, and unrestrained markets would supposedly provide an alternative to the numbing nationwide commercialism of network television. The social movement vision saw this occurring overnight; the technocratic vision imagined it in the "long run." One began with folksy culturalism, the other with technophilic futurism; both claimed in the name of diversity. These visions even merged in the depoliticized "Californian ideology" of community media, which quickly embraced market forms (Mullen 2002; Barbrook and Cameron 1996). Neither formation started with economic reality. Together, they established the preconditions for unsettling a cozy, patriarchal, and quite competent television system that had combined what was good for you and what made you feel good, all on the one set of stations—a comprehensive service. The enabling legislation that birthed and still governs the FCC promised this service, supposedly guaranteeing citizens that broadcasters serve "the public interest, convenience and necessity." This promise was part of a tradition that began when CBS set up a radio network in the 1920s founded on news rather than its rival NBC's predilection for entertainment (Scardino 2005). Yet, in place of the universalism of the old networks, where sport, weather, news, lifestyle, and drama programming had a comfortable and appropriate frottage, highly centralized but profoundly targeted consumer networks emerged in the 1990s that fetishized lifestyle and consumption over a blend of purchase and politics, of fun and foreign policy.

Similarly, cybertarian technophiles, struck by the "digital sublime," attribute magical properties to communication and cultural technologies that supposedly obliterate geography, sovereignty, and hierarchy—a new truth-and-beauty combination that will heal the wound of the division of labor. Thousands, perhaps millions, of flowers bloom in this libertarian cornucopia. Or, at least, that is what some analysts and businesses project from the amnesia and awe occasioned by the fog of hot air between them and reality (Mosco 2004). As ever, these ahistorical celebrants have not investigated equivalent claims from the past that the print medium would educate the entire population, that radio's ethereal qualities would cure cancer and contact the dead, or that TV would unite the world—fantasies associated with new communications

1	Yahoo! News	24.9 million
2	MSNBC.com	23.8 million
3	CNN.com	21.3 million
4	AOL News	17.4 million
5	Gannett Newspapers	11.3 million
6	NYTimes.com	11.2 million
7	Internet Broadcasting	10.9 million
8	Knight Ridder Digital	9.9 million
9	Tribune Newspapers	9.0 million
10	USAToday.com	8.6 million
11	Washingtonpost.com	8.5 million
12	ABC News Digital	7.7 million
13	Google News	7.2 million
14	Hearst Newspapers Digital	6.9 million
15	WorldNow.com	6.2 million
16	Fox News	6.0 million
17	CBSnews.com	5.9 million
18	BBC News	5.1 million
19	Advance Internet	4.5 million
20	McClatchy Newspapers	3.6 million

FIGURE 1. Top 20 online news Web sites, June 2005. *Source: U.S. Home & Work*, Nielsen/Net Ratings

technologies, from positive as well as negative sides. Each one of these new technologies became increasingly empty commodities in the United States, hollowed out by the wider political economy. So when Yanquis go online in search of news, they visit sites owned by major conglomerates (see Figure 1).

Fowler's footprint has left a large space. He introduced a system whereby broadcasters could renew their licenses by mailing him a postcard, thus avoiding the unpleasantness and bother of meeting their critics in open session before the FCC. And self-regulation? In 1982, the networks agreed to screen fewer than ten minutes of commercials per hour during prime time and on children's shows. Twenty years later, neoliberal dogma diminished that sense of social responsibility, such that fourteen to seventeen minutes of advertising each hour became the norm. Doctrines of Fairness and Right of Reply, local evaluation of stations, laws to encourage racial equality in hiring—all have been deemed unnecessary, as diversity and debate are measured not by personnel, texts, or interpretations, but by numbers of outlets and varieties of technology. Even the National Association of Broadcasters' Code of Conduct has been held to violate antitrust legislation. Meanwhile, the craven 1996 Telecommunications Act allowed unprecedented consolidation of ownership across media until Bush's FCC began its dread work. The last ten years have seen the U.S. media go from being controlled by fifty competing companies to five. The environment is oligopolistic, with 90 percent of top cable stations owned by the firms that run the networks and cable systems (Copps 2003).

Many of these institutions are corporate conglomerates for whom the traditions of journalism are incidental to their core business. After arms manufacturer General Electric purchased NBC in 1986, and tobacco beneficiary Lawrence Tisch bought CBS the following year, these stations commenced programs of disinvestment and disemployment, with news divisions subjected to similar profit expectations as entertainment sectors. NBC eliminated 30 percent of news employees in the five years to 1992. Overall, there has been a decrease in network news correspondents by a third since Tisch and his ilk appeared on the scene. The drive for a Tayloristic, scientifically managed control of input has caused topics to be tested in advance on advertisers, rather than being spontaneous reactions to stories of import. Currently, there is also an unprecedented interpenetration of corporate and media power, via overlapping directorates. The notion that the media perform a special function of critique by virtue of their commitment to the public interest is thoroughly compromised when as at mid-2005, the 118 people sitting on the boards of the top media companies were directors of 288 other national and global corporations. The impact on diversity has been predictable. On-camera, current-affairs appearances by adults are largely restricted to white men and "right-wing blondes," apart from anti–affirmative action or Beltway-*servidor* minorities. The notion of audience sovereignty is equally compromised. Seventy-seven percent of the United States public wants the Fairness Doctrine—which the FCC abjures—reinstated, while of the people writing in to complain about sex on television—which the FCC regards as crucial—almost 100 percent come from one group, the Far Right moral panicker, the Parents Television Council. And the new populism has not been a success with audiences. Ratings have plummeted during the era of "soft" news. As Andrew Heyward, then President of CBS News, put it after the 2003 invasion of Iraq, the networks are in a struggle for "survival of the samest" and are "uncannily similar," because news has become "a commodity." Unprecedentedly, CBS and ABC lost viewers at that time of crisis, so quickly did they return to game-show programming, entertainment news, and other genres. It's all about cutting the cost of production, not satisfying viewers (Barkin 2003, 89; Schechter 2003a; Phillips 2005; Lloyd 2005, 74; Benton Foundation 2005; McChesney and Foster 2003, 2; Douglas

2005; *EXTRA!* 2005a, 5; Heyward quoted in Elkin 2003; Boyd-Barrett 2005; Smith 2003).

> Rather than acknowledge that changes in news format and content have been driven by business priorities, U.S. network TV personnel invoke the audience. In former CBS news anchor Dan Rather's 2002 words: "if you lead foreign you die," because "the public has lost interest in international reporting" (quoted in Schechter 2003b, xl). For his part, media mogul Rupert Murdoch proclaims that "Internacional no vende" [The international doesn't sell] (quoted in Leguineche 2002, 16). Leaders of the industry bemoan the fact that a "shorter attention span among the public forces reporters to make the news fast and exciting" (Carnegie Corporation 2005, 4) without backing this up empirically, or indicating why foreign news is slow and boring, even as they continue to assume that the US is "a beacon of good journalistic practice" (Carnegie Corporation and John S. and James L. Knight Foundation, 2005).

In this book, I am concerned especially with citizens' knowledge of US foreign/military policy and corporate/governmental conduct in areas of basic needs and the environment. In lamenting the state of the news media, I am adding to a long and rather repetitive complaint about journalism in terms of quality and theme, a strain that goes back to seventeenth-century Western Europe. Also, I am buying into the gendered reactions against lifestyle programming of antediluvian TV executives, such as muscular British Conservatives Alasdair Milne and Lord Taylor of Warwick (Briggs and Burke 2003, 3; *BBC News Online* 2004; Leonard 2001). The recursive and sexist nature of these concerns inevitably posits some better, other time, a utopic moment when the media were free from nationalism, statism, commodification, or the everyday. I am all too aware that there never was a time of adequate U.S. reportage of the questions that animate my work, but the democratic deficit run up by the contemporary U.S. media transcends anything in my lifetime, or what I have found in other countries and language groups I have lived in, visited, and studied. It may be an old moral panic, but the risks are different when we are talking about the impact of U.S. power over and ignorance regarding peace, militarism, and the environment.

Consider foreign policy and international relations. The international political content of news has diminished significantly since Fowler, excusing and excluding U.S. citizens from a vital part of the policy process—informed public comment, dissent, and consent. Given the expansion of U.S. power over the last quarter of a century, and the decline in political participation by its citizens, it is noteworthy that TV coverage of governmental, military, and international affairs dropped from 70 percent of network news in 1977, to 60 percent in 1987, and 40 percent in 1997. In 1988, each network dedicated approximately two thousand minutes to international news. A decade later, the figure had halved, with about 9 percent of the average newscast covering anything "foreign." Between May 2000 and August 2001, just 22 percent of network news was international—ten points below, for example, its British and South African equivalents, and twenty points below the German. Of that U.S. coverage, just 3 percent addressed U.S. foreign policy. In 2000, three stories from beyond the United States, apart from the Olympics, made it into the networks' twenty most-covered items, and all were directly concerned with domestic issues: the Miami-Cuba custody dispute over Élian Gonzales, the second Intifada, and the bombing of the USS Cole off Yemen (*On the Media* 2002; Project for Excellence in Journalism 2002; *New Yorker* 2001; Pew Research Center 2005, 43; Calabrese 2005b).

As NBC news producer Steve Friedman notoriously intoned after the Cold War, "there isn't anything geopolitical left" (quoted in Calabrese 2005b, 272). The main broadcast networks have closed most investigative sections and foreign bureaus—other than, of course, in Israel. Where ABC News once maintained seventeen overseas posts, now it has seven. CBS has one journalist covering Asia, and seven others for the rest of the world. Parochialism is the watchword. Numerous academic studies have found the networks incapable of devoting attention to other countries other than as dysfunctional or threatening to the United States, even when covering successful democratic elections. It should be no surprise that a 2002 analysis of U.S. newspapers with circulation over a hundred thousand found that 80 percent of their editors had negative views of TV network coverage of international stories. Meanwhile, Australia's national broadcaster, the Australian Broadcasting Corporation, has offices in London, New York, Port Moresby, Singapore, Jakarta, Kuala Lumpur, New Delhi, Tokyo, Washington, Bangkok, Amman, Beijing, Brussels, Hong Kong, Johannesburg, Moscow, and Nicosia (Chester 2002, 106; Project for Excellence in Journalism 2002; Compton 2004; Higham 2001; Golan and Wanta 2003; Pew International Journalism Program 2002; Australian Broadcasting Corporation 2001). Last I looked, Australia had a population of nineteen million people, but they seem to think it's worth knowing about billions of others.

When the Yanqui media elect to venture beyond the fifty states, it becomes abundantly clear that some people's problems matter more than others. In 2003, Médecins sans Frontières [Doctors Without Borders] listed ten humanitarian disasters that barely rated a mention on network television, such as famine in Angola, and civil war in Somalia, Liberia, Colombia, and Sudan. In 2003, two million people died from AIDS in Africa; total coverage of the disease on network news that year amounted to thirty-nine minutes (Lobe 2003a and 2004). Nicolas de Torrente, director of the U.S. branch of the Médecins, put it this way: "Silence is the best ally of violence, impunity and contempt . . . these enormous catastrophes don't seem to exist for most Americans" (quoted in Rotzer 2003). In place of such coverage, we are offered reality television, a strange hybrid of cost-cutting devices, game shows taken into the community, cinéma vérité conceits, scripts that are written in postproduction, and ethics of Social Darwinism, surveillance, and gossip (Ouellette and Murray 2004, 8–9). To repeat, all this is a direct response to deregulation and conglomerate takeovers — *not* consumer sovereignty.

Don Hewitt was the originator of *60 Minutes*, which began in 1968 and quickly drew the highest ratings on television, making CBS News profitable for the first time. Decades later, Hewitt admitted that his creation had "single-handedly ruined television," by establishing the expectation that news reporting be profitable through an entertainment-based cult of personality. News divisions have been fetishized as individual profit centers, rather than their previous function as loss leaders that gave networks a character and "endorsed" other genres. The celebrity aspects of contemporary newsgathering derive from decisions to air *Inside Edition* and *Entertainment Tonight* against network news in the late 1980s. By 1990, the latter had doubled coverage of star gossip. Across the fifteen years since, executives in charge of network news have increasingly lacked any serious background in journalism, and have focused on stories that look like Hollywood productions, promote the network's programs almost as much as they report on nonmedia events, and follow strict binary oppositions between good and bad — when they bother to stride beyond midtown Manhattan and Botox Beverly Hills for stories. The epithet once used to deride local news television in the United States ("if it bleeds, it leads") today applies to network news, where the correlation between national crime statistics and crime coverage shows no rational linkage. The drive to create "human interest" stories from blood has become a key means of generating belief in a risk society through moral panics about personal safety, which occupied 16 percent of network news in 1997, up from 8 percent in 1977. Pondering coverage of Michael Jackson's child-molestation trial in 2005, horror novelist Stephen King argued for a divide within popular culture, telling journalists that he and they had different duties to the public: "My job is to give them what they want. . . . Your job is to give the people what they need." Disobeying his dictum, by 2005, local TV news was basking in 50 percent profit margins, while national news continued to lose ground in a vainglorious attempt to make money (Schudson and Tifft 2005, 32, 38; Hewitt quoted in Barkin 2003, 53; Barkin 2003, 9, 51; Smith 2003; Calabrese 2005b, 271–72; Carter 2005; *New Yorker* 2001; Lowry et al. 2003; Thussu 2003, 123; King quoted in *EXTRA!* 2005b, 5; Project for Excellence in Journalism 2005).

The old commercial television networks have survived, still delivering advertisers the closest approximation to a national audience, and doggedly offering a mix of programming. The only change is now they account for less than a fifth of the time Yanquis spend watching television, and have lost the commitment to thorough journalism that developed their newsgathering reputations of old. TV matters as much as ever, but increasingly via cable. During the 2004 U.S. presidential election, of the 78 percent of U.S. citizens who followed the campaign on television, 47 percent did so via cable news (the respective figures for the 2000 contest were 70 percent using television, of whom 36 percent relied on cable). But the claim from the 1990s that twenty-four-hour news channels would compromise the capacity of corporations and governments to obfuscate is now laughable. Rather, cable news has pioneered nonunionized, multitasked, low-wage news labor, with workers required to write, speak, and appear in multifarious formats and genres, without increases in numbers, resources, or pay scales. Low budgets meet fragmented audiences, and money can be made from small numbers of viewers. Web journalism has not led to originality, because of intense recycling, with wire services rapidly displacing primary reportage as sources. Web newsrooms are experiencing massive staff cutbacks despite improved readership numbers, such that they now rewrite copy rather than generating it. There is concern amongst U.S. reporters that the quality of their work is diminishing as a result of corporate pressure to increase revenue (Webster 2005, 378; Pew Research Center for the People & the Press 2005; Robinson 2004, 99; Project for Excellence in Journalism 2005; Schechter 2005b; Barkin 2003, 85; Calabrese 2005b, 273–74; Raphael 2004, 123–24; Schatz 2003, xvii; Project for Excellence in Journalism 2005; Pew Research Center 2005, 43; Carnegie Corporation 2005, 3). Laurie Garrett, a Pulitzer, Polk, and Peabody prizewinner, left U.S. journalism in 2005 with a stinging memo:

> All across America news organizations have been devoured by massive corporations, and allegiance to stockholders, the drive for higher share prices, and push for larger dividend returns trumps everything that the grunts in the newsrooms consider their missions (quoted in *Editor & Publisher* 2005).

Even Roger Ailes, head of the Fox News Network, admits that "journalism in cable sometimes is light because the depth of investigative research isn't there" (quoted in Atkinson and Klaassen 2005). His own journalists offer opinions without any sources to back them up in 70 percent of their reports (Moisy 1997). A narcissistic ignorance is dominant even though transnational news is available as never before. The proliferation of computing, satellites, fiber optics, and the Internet should make for an efflorescence of reportage in the same way that the advent of the 707 airplane did. But it hasn't (Höijer et al. 2004, 16; Robinson et al. 2005, 952).

Ideology is also important here. There has been a campaign by the Right over four decades to discredit the bourgeois media, on the ground that they are liberal fiefdoms. The Center for Media and Public Affairs, underwritten by the Olin and Scaife foundations, has circulated fanciful but effectively waspish material for two decades, alleging that the mainstream media are leftist bigots—virtually the only media studies' topic that gets any attention *from* the bourgeois media! New outlets for these positions include fissiparous Web sites appealing to Christians, and Weblogs assiduously promoted by the *National Review* (Clark and Van Slyke 2005; Massing 2005). The principal beneficiary of this well-funded cycle of venom and caution, Bush Minor, continues to complain that the mainstream media "are biased against conservative thought" (quoted in Alterman 2003, 2). These same media react like lackeys to critiques of putative liberalism, covering reactionary complaints with an assiduous self-loathing, despite the fact that such complaints only surface when public opinion reacts against Republican positions, and that there has been no progressive host on network TV since Disney fired Jim Hightower upon buying ABC in 1995. How do dozens of conservatives protest liberal bias from regular positions of expert commentary if they are the victims of savage exclusion? And how can the empirically disproven claim, that the bourgeois press opposed the war in Vietnam, be taken up again and again (Smolkin 2003; Domke et al. 1999; Herman 1999, 1; Robinson 2004, 97)? As Studs Terkel says, "liberal media" is "an obscene phrase . . . burlesque" (2003). To give just one example, the *Washington Post*, bizarrely accused of progressiveness by many on the right, ran four hundred and thirty opinion pieces between June and August 2001, of which ten came from the Left. To do so, it excluded expertise in favor of bluster. Studies of the two major cable news channels, CNN and Fox, reveal that despite the latter's claim that it is less liberal, each delivers a pro-Bush position on foreign policy as if it were an organ of the Pentagon. CNN markets itself to urban and suburban, educated viewers, whereas Fox targets suburban and rural, uneducated viewers. One functions like a broadsheet, the other a tabloid, with CNN punditry coming mostly from outsiders, and Fox punditry delivered by presenters as well as guests. CNN costs more to produce and attracts fewer routine viewers but many more occasional ones. It brings in much higher advertising revenue because of the composition of its audience, and because its fawning and trite business coverage addresses and valorizes high-profile investors and corporations in ways that Fox's down-market populism does not (Schechter 2003b, 8; Pew Charitable Trusts 2002a; Farhi 2003; Alterman 2003, 136–37). Otherwise their coverage is remarkably similar. Reaction will be televised.

THE BOOK YOU HOLD IN YOUR HANDS

> Warmly socialist.
> —Anne Cooper-Chen (2002)

> From the time the term "politics" was invented, every type of politics has been defined by its relation to nature, whose every feature, property, and function depends on the polemical will to limit, reform, establish, short-circuit, or enlighten public life.
> —Bruno Latour (2004, 1)

> Because my job as a private investigator lent itself more toward the mundane and realistic, I didn't have much use for theory.
> —James Crumley (2005, 24)

This book takes its frames of reference from cultural studies, but without neoliberal or reactionary *rapprochements*. We simply must address the destructive implications of the fact that "consumption is now virtually out of control in the richest countries"—that the wealthiest 20 percent of the world consumes over five times more food, water, fuel, minerals, and transport than their parents did, and that annual expenditure on advertising in the United States alone is heading toward US$275 billion, close to half the global total. In the last two centuries, the world's population has increased by a factor of five and goods and services by a factor of fifty (Beck 1999, 6; Klaasen 2005; Sanders 2005b; Sattar 2001, 12).

Of course I am not arguing for an absolute choice between pleasure and politics, leisure and labor, or consumption and citizenship. It is as absurd to *ignore* markets as it is to reduce society to them (Martín-Barbero 2001b, 26). In pondering communications scholar Liesbet van Zoonen's productive provocation, "Can citizenship be pleasurable?" (2005, 1), I endorse the stress on freedom to choose, and the use of commodities to build culture. Yet, I abjure the model of the consumer, audience member, or artist as the center of politics and theory, in favor of a commitment to difference, understood through disability, religion, class, gender, race, and sexuality.

Unlike many within cultural studies, I do not focus primarily on fictional media. Instead, I concentrate on the factual deficit that neoliberal deregulation and its associated moral panics have generated. Clearly, popular art is enormously important in the world constructed for citizens; both in the themes it investigates and the formal and stylistic tropes it pioneers. But my intention is to shed light on who owns the knowledge that animates society, how they define and communicate that knowledge, and the complex imbrication of politics, economics, and culture that colors our *barrio*. This is a work of tendency, designed to assist leftist politics via the reassertion of a democratic, internationalist state that ensures citizens know enough to comprehend and change relations with others, by reducing the risks of everyday life and their distortion as moral panics.

It is obvious that media coverage of terrorism and militarism poses key questions for citizens, and that media deregulation has led to a consolidation and rationalization of ownership and practice that militate against adequate public knowledge about foreign policy—hence the centrality of terrorism and war to Chapter Two. But why are food (Chapter Three) and weather (Chapter Four) here? They concern the problems identified by the first demographers, and listed by the economic critic Will Hutton as our "great global public goods—peace, trade, aid, health, the environment, and security" (2003b: 3). *Cultural Citizenship* uncovers how these goods are privatized, transforming the citizen into a consumer governed via cultural niches, and the cost of such developments to progressive politics. Utilizing Hutton's categories:

- Under peace and security, I look into terrorism and war—how the media and the state externalize and export risk.
- Under trade, aid, and health, I consider food—how the media and the state regulate and corporatize risk.
- Under the environment, I turn to weather—how the media and the state govern and commodify risk.

The world of a comprehensive television service, with occasional forays into dinners and downpours, has been displaced by niche stations like the Food Network and the Weather Channel, bizarre blends of "tabloid journalism, documentary television, and popular entertainment" (Hill 2005, 15). In terms of giving the public a voice in the media, U.S. TV uses vox populi to cover consumerism (Lewis et al. 2005, 79, 126). Food and weather are here because, as the dogged amateur ethnographers of Britain's Mass-Observation (M-O) movement of the 1930s and 1940s noted in the quotation beginning this Introduction, somewhere below and beyond foreign policy swirls a diurnal citizenship that is closely aligned with consumption and other practices of making do.

M-O started in the late 1930s as an antidote to grandiose state-of-the-nation diagnostics. The movement's founders, a bizarre blend of surrealist artists and empiricist sociologists, enlisted fifteen hundred "amateur Observers" to go about Britain "observing and analysing the ordinary," compensating for the blind spots of their academic counterparts, who were thought to "have contributed literally nothing to the anthropology of ourselves" (Mass-Observation 1939, 10, 12). During the War, despite the value of this work for various state projects, MI5 raided the offices of M-O on instructions from Prime Minister Winston Churchill, who believed the observers were "criminally liable" for asking ordinary Britons their opinions on the conflict (Crossland 1997, 6). M-O went on to be commodified, and sold as a tool of market research. Of course, since that time, the study of the everyday has become important in ethnomethodology, anthropology, and cultural studies, both for its own significance, and as a way to understand societies through popular struggles for legitimacy. That paradox, whereby commodities carry potential metacritiques, is not lost on me.

In today's climate, capital is well aware of the importance of everyday culture, and how to fetishize it away from politics. Rather than a media-policy metric that focuses exclusively on ownership, control, and morality, the shared obsessions of Right and Left in U.S. regulation, we need to look at all the genres that help give life meaning. We need to interrogate the absences that commercial dictates produce, even as we acknowledge the importance of the quotidian to the lived experience of citizenship. To understand Latino/a popular culture in the United States, for example, it is necessary to understand the part television commercials play in it. And of the top twenty-five advertisers in Latino/a media, a quarter sell food and drink: McDonald's, Burger King, Coca-Cola, Pepsi, Wendy's, and Miller Lite (*Hispanic* 2005, 20). There is as strong a nexus between the electronic media and weather and food as there is to foreign policy. The word "broadcasting" has agricultural roots. It originally described spreading seeds in a field, and while that origin has become metaphoric, its linguistic shift has not lost an important referent. A glance back at the earliest days of Australian national radio, in the 1930s, finds weather and cooking to the fore (Australian Broadcasting Corporation 2001).

These everyday concerns become especially crucial in the new U.S. reality. Successive population waves—no longer just white ones—have fled the inner city, and the nation has just become the first in the world with more than half its people living in suburbia (a quarter of whom are minorities) with 75 percent of new office space constructed there (*Economist* 2005e). As this historic demographic shift from a rural to an urban to a suburaban country continues, people are increasingly disarticulated from both subsistence and the state. Finally, food gives neoliberalism its urge to acquire—there is allegedly no purer marketplace than fruit and vegetables—while weather presents neoliberalism with a limit case—how do you commodify climate?

This book is quite different from most work on citizenship, which tends to be either very theoretical, focusing on ideal-typical reasoning and a history-of-ideas approach from political theory and philosophy (this-freedom-begat-that-freedom, this theory-begat-that-theory); or very empirical, concentrating on the status of certain classic entitlements from the perspectives of sociology and political science (this is the condition of social security, this is the level of voter participation). Theoretical work is vital, but not when it amounts to the citational masturbation of one U.S.-based author tenured at a research university after another. Empirical work is vital, except when it is a tiresome deployment of one U.S.-based form of methodological individualism tended at a research university after another.* For these reasons, I blend theorization with grounded study, and my topics are directly related to culture, rather than the predilections of "normal" social science. Both theories of sovereignty and empirical practices must be analyzed in equal measure, since the "problem of the central soul" of the state is immanent in "multiple peripheral bodies" and the messy labor of controlling them. Therefore we need to undertake research "not at the level of political theory, but rather at the level of the mechanisms, techniques, and technologies of power" (Foucault 2003a, 37, 29, 241). This necessitates allocating equal and semi-autonomous significance to natural phenomena, social forces, and texts in the analysis of contemporary life. Just as objects of scientific knowledge only come to us in hybrid forms that are coevally affected by social power and textual meaning, so the latter two domains are themselves affected by the natural world (Latour 1993, 5–6). Readers will therefore be moving rapidly and repeatedly between theory and fact, speculation and setting. I know of no other way to write.

To repeat, each topic in this book derives from longstanding concerns of demography, consumption, and citizenship—security, subsistence, and ecology—with a stress on their cultural and media components. The United States is a prime zone for such analysis, for three reasons. First, its population, polity, consumption, and culture are massively influential on international relations, agriculture, and the environment. Second, its factor endowments fit capitalism so well—natural harbors, oceanic links, superabundant raw materials, and crops that vary between the tropics and the snows. And third, the United States has always been subject to fissures, because of its origins as a simultaneously immigrant and individualistic, Calvinist and consumerist nation, and the fact

*Why enter 'a crazed bibliographic gallop' (Downing and Husband 2005, 25)?

that collectivity and heritage continue their duel with choice and futurity (hence the overarching logic of cultural citizenship).

I argue in this book that far from being undermined by leftist identity politics, as some maintain, contemporary threats to national unity are a consequence of the deregulation created by and for the very right-wing sources that rail at a loss of oneness, in a country of widening gaps in subsistence and pleasure, gaps that yawn even as neoliberalism smiles. Chapter Two illustrates the severe limits to unregulated capital's ability to provide adequate foreign-affairs coverage, because it produces an uncritical press that shines and basks in the heat and light of empire. Chapters Three and Four illuminate its frailties and fallacies in other spheres of self-governed risk, assessing the limits of a consumer address for an effective citizen politics, and arguing against the contention that choice through purchase guarantees the democratic workings of a market-driven society, with the culture industries providing what the public desires. These Chapters demonstrate how the media are crucial in building and guiding consumers. In the First World, the imperative of generating consumption through spectacle favors culture determined by quantity and regularity in ways that deny the conditions of production that make objects for sale through labor power. By tracking the life of the TV commodity sign (whether journalistic, culinary, or climatic) we can identify the material shocks and circuits that bring culture to consumers, and not as a market mechanism that identifies people's desires and meets them. Kathy Lane, a spokesperson for the Weather Channel, says it "created a need" (quoted in Miles 2004, 22). *Cultural Citizenship* examines such "needs" inside the cable box and satellite, twin scions and suppliers.

For now, a project of government at a distance is well and truly in place, via a complex web of consumerist politics that sees the popular media avoiding the fascinating politics at the heart of the everyday, in favor of a trivial, exploitative focus: "At stake, the primal American right of free speech, the freedom, without fear of censor, to beguile, confuse, and otherwise distract the people into plodding obeisance of pop" (Whitehead 2001, 47). Hence the necessity to look at the apparent margins of public debate (food and weather), as well as its center (militarism) I wish to seek out popular and everyday energies and problems. The realities of the contemporary media must animate cultural studies, as we explain to the public how neoliberalism operates, and help to create a society of equality, difference, and pleasure, rather than stratification, conformity, and religiosity. TV can "ignite . . . the cultural citizen" (Mohanty and Bhabha 2005). But for now, something is rotten at the heart of cultural citizenship.

1

WHAT IS CULTURAL CITIZENSHIP?

> Increasing numbers of citizens . . . *do not belong.* This in turn
> undermines the basis of the nation-state as the central site of
> democracy.
> —Stephen Castles and Alistair Davidson, *Citizenship and*
> *Migration: Globalization and the Politics of Belonging*

> We have no idea, now, of who or what the inhabitants of our future
> might be. In that sense, we have no future. Not in the sense that our
> grandparents had a future, or thought they did. Fully imagined
> cultural futures were the luxury of another day, one in which "now"
> was of some greater duration. For us, of course, things can change so
> abruptly, so violently, so profoundly, that futures like our grandparents'
> have insufficient "now" to stand on. We have no future because our
> present is so volatile.
> —Hubertus Bigend, founder of the Blue Ant advertising agency*

> I'm a citizen of nowhere and sometimes I feel mighty homesick.
> —Joshua Logan, *Paint Your Wagon* (1969)

W HY CITIZENSHIP, and why now? When I started talking
about citizenship to people interested in cultural and
social movement activism twenty years ago, they often
seemed either disturbed or bored. "What is this rapprochement with the state?" "Why refer to universal concepts when there
should be a focus on specific forms of oppression and rights?" and "Is this
about social control achieved through civics?" were representative—and
bowdlerized—responses. Within a decade, such talk had passed, because
the term had gained currency in political discussion and academic
research. This happened for two main reasons: First, various oppositional
formations had splintered. Marxists were criticized by feminists, Global
Southists, and others who questioned class position as the principal axis of
social suffering and critical agency. The collapse of dictatorship in Latin

*William Gibson, *Pattern Recognition* (New York: GP Putnam's Sons, 2003).

America and state socialism in Europe, and the emergence of capitalism in China, compromised existing fascism and leftism, and explanations of them. Feminists who posited a uniform female experience confronted critiques from women of color, lesbians, the Global South, and the working class, who pointed to differentiated gender relations, strategic alliances with subjugated men, and multiperspectival notions of oppression. Paradoxically, identity politics had sometimes referenced the very difference-crushing machine of universalism that it was designed to counter, because its claims downplayed or denied particular traits of conduct or whole categories of person (Mouffe 1992 and 1993). For example, cultural studies maven Stuart Hall notes both the utility of the word "black" in the U.K. context, as a reversed, renewing trope against racism, but also its more negative coefficients, such as the exclusion of Asian people of color, and black people who have other coordinates of collective identification. As queer littérateur Eve Kosofsky Sedgwick insists, even social movements founded on difference seem to be bounded by exclusion (1990, 61). United fronts, adopted for the purposes of external conflicts, conceal "differences . . . raging behind" (Hall 1991, 56); frequently economic ones. And the valorization of specificity over generality in oppositional movements has often been a misnomer. It would be a bizarre rendering of history and anthropology to argue that only "Western" ideas are universalist, that the "West" is homogeneous, or that universal ideas are a "Western" invention, magically sequestered from other influences (Benhabib 2002, 24). Cultures generalize obsessively, and the "West" has drawn many such tendencies from elsewhere.

Second, the intensification of neoliberal globalization via a global division of labor, regional trading blocs, globally oriented cities with supranational ambitions, international TV markets, and the spread of conflictual religious relations, has taken citizenship out of the narrow confines of the sovereign state and linked it to universal rights. In Michel Foucault's words, the market has become "a 'test,' a locus of privileged experience where one . . . [can] identify the effects of excessive governmentality" (1997, 76). Deregulation accompanies social movements on their ride to self-assertion, where they duel with the Janus face of modernity—the risks of progress and the loss of meaning—which in turn become conditions of existence for reenchantment (Murdock 1997). Many of these movements are, of course, opposed to economic deregulation; nevertheless their cultural sides provide useful information to new markets, and they like the state to keep its hands off their bodies. Thus, the understanding that both social movements and forces of deregulation have of consumption as sovereignty, challenges citizenship. In keeping with that environment, this chapter begins with an examination of the uneasy interdependence of citizenship, consumption, and politics, then moves on to look at competing definitions and theories of citizenship in general, and cultural citizenship in particular. Throughout, the media are essentially offscreen, because they tend to be viewed as epiphenomena of citizenship, rather than purposive components of it. But the issues emerging here are crucial to the ensuing chapters, which focus primarily on the media .

CITIZENSHIP, CONSUMPTION, AND POLITICS

> Hairy-backed swamp developers and corporate shills, faith-based economists, fundamentalist bullies with Bibles, Christians of convenience, freelance racists, misanthropic frat boys, shrieking midgets of AM radio, tax cheats, nihilists in golf pants, brownshirts in pinstripes, sweatshop tycoons, hacks, fakirs, aggressive dorks, Lamborghini libertarians, people who believe Neil Armstrong's moonwalk was filmed in Roswell, New Mexico, little honkers out to diminish the rest of us. . . . Republicans: The No. 1 reason the rest of the world thinks we're deaf, dumb and dangerous.
> —Garrison Keillor (2004)

> Faced with anomalies in human decision-making, economists prefer cognitive psychology to cultural anthropology; how much easier to incorporate into one's models decision heuristics that are invariant and hard-wired rather than to deal with perturbations caused by culturally varying schemes of perception and value.
> —Paul DiMaggio (1994, 29)

The first epigraph, a party-political critique, reads like the irritated rant of an urban hipster, mercilessly mocking people beyond the world of downtown lofts and polymorphous pleasure, with words effortlessly dropped from a laptop while hurtling above the flyover states. In fact, it comes from a true son of the Midwest, whose career derives from a folksy relationship to harsh winters and hardy residents. The second epigraph is a critique of neoliberal academia's methodological individualism and favors a more interdisciplinary and empirical approach. It derives from the cautious but slightly arch vocabulary of Ivy League sociology. The two epigraphs encapsulate the contradictions that color the complicated relationship between the citizen and its logocentric double, the consumer (García Canclini 2001a).

The citizen is a wizened figure from the ancient past. In Aristotle's words, "man is by nature a political animal," who gathers with others to form a state for their mutual benefit (1963, 61). Through such processes, rational discourse can produce good outcomes. Knowledge informs opinion, *pace* Plato's pessimism about the irrationality of the popular classes (Lewis 2001, 22). The consumer, by contrast, is naïve, a relatively precocious creature. Derided as a wastrel of natural resources in the fourteenth century, and stereotyped by Immanuel Kant ("I need not think, so long as I can pay" [1991, 54]), the consumer was understood by Karl Marx as "man separated from man" (1994, 139). Consumption was first conceived as a legitimate practice in the nineteenth century, with the advent of bourgeois political economy, the Industrial Revolution, and the Knights of Labor, followed in the twentieth century by the National Consumers' League, African Americans' "Don't Buy Where You Can't Work" campaigns, and the United Farm Workers (Frank 2003; Williams 1983, 78; Glickman 1999, 1, 3).

The citizen and the consumer have shadowed each other as the *national* subject versus the *rational* subject—with politics rendered artificial and consumption natural, a means of legitimizing social arrangements (Marx 1994, 140). Adopting the tenets of the consumer, the citizen becomes a desirous, self-actualizing subject who still conforms to general patterns of *controlled* behavior. Adopting the tenets of the citizen, the consumer becomes a self-limiting, self-controlling subject who still conforms to general patterns of *purchasing* behavior. Sometimes, both sides fail to see what is "good" for them, (as when citizens resist financial globalization or consumers shop erratically). In an era that abjures the graceless antinomies of "paternalism and consumerism" (Miliband 2004, 11), the lines between the two categories are less sharply drawn than ever.

The popularity of consumers with the neoclassical economists and policy wonks who make plans for citizens is well known: The market is said to operate in response to ratiocinative agents, who, endowed with perfect knowledge, negotiate between alternative suppliers, such that an appropriate price is paid for desired commodities. The assertion of neoclassical economics as an absolute truth has guided public policy toward a business orientation over the past thirty years. In the purview of this historically contingent reading, prima facie, anything done in the name of the market is good and efficient, and anything done in the name of government is bad and inefficient (other than standing armies, which magically provide models for corporate endeavor).

The extraordinary permeation of neoclassical economics throughout liberal discourse over the past three decades ironically incarnated the economist in public policy, to stand for antistatist positions; hence the latter's hypocritical dependence on the heaviest of state interventions in order to remodel *previous* state interventions (Hindess 1993, 315). In one sense, we are embarked on a centralized project of anticentralization. If we create a market to deal with a problem of public policy, the outcome is said to be flexible and transparent, necessarily derived from the desires of ordinary people. The "isolated and private expression of preferences" (Elster 2003, 143) displaces "open and public activity"—or rather, they come together in an intermittently uncomfortable frottage. This has created a rapprochement between awkward neighbors, such that consumption and citizenship have become mutually constitutive. For example, foreigners who invest US$1 million in a business project, and give jobs to ten people or more, can become Yanqui citizens. This has led to the proposal that U.S. citizenship be put on sale—US$50,000 at 2002 prices—to ensure that those arriving are entrepreneurial and will boost tax revenue and capital, rather than seek welfare (Borna and Stearns 2002).*

The consumer has become the classless, raceless, sexless, ageless, unprincipled, magical agent of social value in a multitude of discourses and institutions, animated by the drive to realize individual desires. Rather than existing "naturally," the consumer is endowed with a metaphysical presence through public- and private-sector discourses and policies, as the state imposes Kant's Enlightenment on its subjects. Kant envisaged *"man's emergence from his self-incurred immaturity"* as independence from religious or governmental direction (1991, 54). The development of complex economies has both enabled and restricted that fantasy. The notion of the free individual suits it, and the statistical imagination delimits it. Consider political scientist Barry Hindess' gloss of the current moment:

> the liberal gaze perceives settings in which individuals left to their own devices can normally be trusted to conduct themselves as autonomous rational agents and other settings—ranging from imperial domains to areas of inner city poverty—in which they cannot be trusted (2001, 366).

In India, the Planning Commission, a key instrument of Nehruvian secularism and modernization in the early years of nationhood, was unfashionable by the 1990s. It gave way to such euphemisms for neoliberal projects as "empowerment" (Beteille 1999). The nation's Central Board of Film Certification promulgates a *Citizen's Charter* that calls on the public to engage in a form of citizen censorship. The *Charter* begins with the query "Who will bell the cat?" avowing that "do it yourself!" is the best means of acting against movie theaters showing materials that audiences dislike. It lays out tasks that consumers should undertake when entering cinemas, such as looking for certification, categorization, deletions as per a state "cut list," and so on—all in the name of "your fellow citizens" (2004). In Mexico, this neoliberal trend reached its apogee when President Vicente Fox repeatedly and notoriously challenged reporters querying the record of neoliberalism with: *"¿Yo por qué? . . . ¿Qué*

---

*The class, race, and gender impact of the proposal is not, of course, discussed.

no somos 100 millones de mexicanos?" [Why ask me. . . . Aren't there 100 million other Mexicans?] (quoted in Venegas 2003). The burden of his words—offered in such delightful company as business leeches like Carlos Slim—was that each person must assume responsibility for his or her material fortunes. The fact that not every one of those Mexicans has control over the country's money supply, tariff policy, trade, labor law, and exchange rate might have given him pause. For the consumer is not a "king, as the culture industry would have us believe, not its subject but its object" (Adorno 1996, 85). So how was this form of government over subjects or objects achieved?

The 1940s and 1950s were marked by Washington exporting ideas of citizenship to the rest of the world, with the intention of building strong national political and legal institutions and robust civil societies, opposed to Maoism and Marxism-Leninism, in Western Europe and the decolonizing world. That export seemed compromised by critiques in the 1960s and 1970s that the policy was narcissistic, dangerous, and blind to the history of imperial and commercial powers annexing states and their labor forces—not to mention its Pollyannaish misrecognition of life in the United States itself. But another, related development was underway. Domestic economic policy during the 1950s sought to link practices of production to habits of consumption. Each was to be a way of life, and this prescription, too, was exported to the rest of the world. Bourgeois economic theory posited a strong correlation between increases in productivity and lower prices for consumer items. As the ruling class was treated to expensive goods and services, the cost of these pleasures would go down, such that low-income households could afford them. In turn, price reduction would help the ruling class cut its costs and afford new innovations. The resultant so-called "virtuous cycle" paradoxically relied on income *inequality* to ensure a critical mass of wealth as new technologies were marketed, but also a certain income *equality*, to ensure a critical mass of consumption once prices fell (Matsuyama 2002).

The contemporary state continues to forge two kinds of cross-pollinating subjectivities; practices of consumption have not entirely superseded practices of civics. Sometimes the selfish/selfless couplet is exposed as logocentrically interdependent—the consumer who purchases products to favor the environment and labor, versus the citizen who endorses aerial bombardment.* Each is of course an ideal type. The selfless, active citizen, who cares for others and favors a political regime that compensates people for losses in the financial domain, still operates in an uneasy dialectic with the selfish, active consumer, who favors a financial regime that compensates people for losses

---

*I owe this point to John Hartley.

in the political domain. Hence the British Government's active-citizen.org.uk claims that "active citizenship is about taking part! . . . Creating a better society through a direct and positive contribution to . . . communities," via an alchemy of "democratic self-determination with mutuality and solidarity" (Accuweather.com 2005). This leads to the latest fetish of neoliberalism lite, exemplified by the British Labour Party's "personalisation" thesis, whereby public services allegedly animated by consumer choice simultaneously impose the disciplines of the market onto the delivery of public services and the discipline of public goods onto private initiatives—a magic elixir of timely service and orderly self-control (Tempest 2004; Surowiecki 2004; Leadbeater 2004). The Yanqui equivalent is Bush Minor's puerile "ownership society" (2005).

The individual at the bottom of this theory is the consumer making rational choices about personal expenditure, not the citizen concerned about the nation or other members of the polity. Neoliberalism is opposed to any politics of labor, culture, or welfare, and is essentially agnostic about congressional politics, other than when governmental outlays are at stake. It can enlist philosophical liberals and conservatives, but some, for example, prayer-and-care communitarians, feel queasy about its rampant individualism and faith in the market, fearing that these may overrun church, family, community, and nation. Neoliberalism has ties to liberal philosophy at two levels—first, that the rule of law can be applied as a privatized domain of corporate activity, both nationally and internationally, with minimal democratic accountability; and second, that liberal individuals can govern themselves (Newell 2001: 91). Citizenship is basically conceived by neoliberalism as "voluntary actions of the people in managing their lives" (Vigoda and Golembiewski 2001: 274). Neoliberal mavens claim the paradox that the "standard of living people in the West enjoy today is due to little else but the selfish pursuit of profit" and the way it binds groups together in mutual dependency (Crook 2005) via a division of labor. And all this directly relates to governing at a distance. For example, in 1996, Bill Clinton outlined five policy precepts: a family orientation for workers; health-care and retirement systems; safety on the job; training for productivity; and employee participation. His administration introduced numerous incentives for industry in the name of citizenship (Hemphill 2004, 343–44).

Two additional political and theoretical positions dominate the relationship between self-interest and collaboration, consumption and citizenship in the United States. The first is the "Beltway binary"—the division offered again and again in Congress and the bourgeois media between seemingly liberal and conservative policies. In this context, "liberalism" signifies D-Worders, from the Democratic Party, and "conservatism" signifies R-Worders, from the

Republican Party. Needless to say, D-Worders and R-Worders have much in common. They share commitments to neoclassical economics and the development of U.S. commercial and military power. For example, in the Congressional campaign of 2000, Republicans ran in support of prescription-drug benefits, education, and a patients' bill of rights, while Democrats ran in support of measured tax cuts (Dionne, Jr. 2003, 227). The parties were barely distinguishable in their reactions to the events of September 11, 2001, and subsequent decisions to invade and remodel the Middle East, if not over the precise way the makeover was managed. Since the news media are full of this bipartisan neoliberalism and "hys-terrorism," it is no wonder that less than half the U.S. population characterizes the Republican Party as more reactionary than the Democrats (Keeter et al. 2002, 15). The sociologist Immanuel Wallerstein helpfully historicizes this hideous bricolage: Just as "conservative forces . . . attempted to portray themselves as wiser liberals" from the 1860s to the 1970s, today's "centrist liberals [seem] compelled to argue that they . . . [are] more effective conservatives" (2003, 20). Such proclivities are equally a product of the U.S. bourgeois media's tendency to diminish the legitimacy of ideological commitment (and the significance of material motivation) by deriding party-political debate as a kind of childish squabble that mature subjects of reason must rise above, as they float across ideologies in search of the magic middle (Lewis et al. 2005, 4–5).

The second position derives from philosophy. Liberal philosophy posits a Whiggish historical development of civic activism and democracy in three successive stages: a clique of oligarchs, followed by the emergence of political parties, and finally, the rule of law, which operates regardless of personal or collective affinities (Schudson 1998, 8). This form of thought is extrapolated from the idea of the individual as a sovereign, reasoning subject who relies on the rule of law and transparent ideology and governance to create a just society. Thus, the state is a device for umpiring disputes between parties that cannot be resolved through the market, or for rectifying problems in areas where markets fail to clear — that is, where there is systematic, ongoing inequality. A government must preserve individual freedom by negotiating its own need for control against its citizens' rights to be silent, loud, or anything else that does not impinge on others' rights to the same conduct. One of the best means of doing so is to police a boundary that distinguishes private life from public power. Responsibilities and rights are decoupled from racial, ethnic, gender, religious, linguistic, and other collective identities, which are set aside from the public realm in the name of "neutral justice and formal equality" (Cowan et al. 2001, 2). Liberal philosophy is related to republican ideals of virtue, whereby individuals loosen or drop their originary affiliations in the interests of a nonsectarian, secular, national good. This idealized good tolerates diversity in private, but calls for unity in public, thereby assuring citizens that their government treats all equally (Williams 2001, 93; Barry 2001; Castles and Davidson 2000, 12). In its U.S. incarnation, this is what that bitter opponent of multiculturalism, journalist Richard Bernstein, proclaims with typical modesty as "the genius of Americanization": a device for permitting the private retention of culture in return for its loss in public (2003, 66).

DEFINING CITIZENSHIP

> If the Western citizen of the nineteenth century was a member of a consolidating nation, the contemporary citizen of the twenty-first century is a member of a deterritorializing state.
> —Katharyne Mitchell (2003, 387)

Classical political theory accorded representation to the citizen through the state. The modern, economic addendum was that the state promised a minimal standard of living. The postmodern, cultural guarantee is access to the technologies of communication. The latter promise derives its force from a sense that political institutions need to relearn what sovereignty is about in polymorphous sovereign states that are diminishingly homogeneous in demographic terms. Heteroglossic populations complicate the executive government's expectation that "its" people will be faithful to the state, while claiming their support as the grounds for its own existence (Miller 1993). This third turn to communications is clearly open to commodification by corporations, and appropriation by far-right Christian fundamentalists, as much as expressive protest by social movements, especially in an era of deregulation.

Put another way, the last two hundred years of modernity have produced three zones of citizenship, with partially overlapping but also distinct historicities. These zones of citizenship are:

- The political (the right to reside and vote)
- The economic (the right to work and prosper)
- The cultural (the right to know and speak)

They correspond to the French Revolution's cry *"liberté, égalité, fraternité"* [liberty, equality, solidarity] and the Argentine Left's contemporary version *"ser ciudadano, tener trabajo, y ser alfabetizado"* [citizenship, employment, and literacy] (Martín-Barbero 2001a, 9). The first category concerns political rights; the second, material interests; and the third, cultural representation (Rawls

1971, 61). The *U.S. Citizenship Test* draws on all three categories. It requires a political understanding of the structure of governance and judicial review, an economic understanding of the history of slavery, and a cultural understanding of the signification of the Stars and Stripes. All in all, the *Test* asks many questions about flags, and many others to which the answer is "Washington." We see something similar in contemporary schooling, where the trilogy is participation via civic service, self-governance via individuated responsibility, and justice via affiliation with equality (Westheimer and Kahne 2004a and b).

Political citizenship—the *liberté* or *ser ciudadano*—emerged from the English Revolution. It locates sovereignty in "relations between the general will and its representative organs" (Foucault 2003b, 152). Political citizenship gives the right to vote, to be represented in government, and to enjoy physical security, in return for ceding violence to the state (although the United States is contradictory about this issue, because of the putative Constitutional right of private citizens to bear arms). Despite its focus on the nation and the state, the founding assumption of political citizenship is that personal freedom is both the wellspring of good government *and* the source of its authority over individuals. In Jean-Jacques Rousseau's paradox, this involves "making men free by making them subject" (1975, 123). Democracy is conventionally said to arise and thrive in the interactions of governments and populations, its models being the French and American Revolutions. Inhabitants who recognize one another as political citizens, and use that status to invoke the greater good, bound the polity. An oft-quoted example of the primacy of political citizenship is that Western women's gains in economic and cultural areas generally followed their acquisition of political rights (Bosniak 2000, 447–49; Fallon 2003, 525–26).

It has long been held that the preconditions and functions of political citizenship are largely "dependent on [the] internal development" of the sovereign states that emerged from the necessity to deal with European religious conflicts of the sixteenth and seventeenth centuries (Halliday 2001, 86; Barry 2001, 21). Ignoring the fact that citizenship was forged in relation to bellicose encounters of West and East, nineteenth and early twentieth-century liberal philosophers postulated it as the outcome of "fixed identities, unproblematic nationhood, indivisible sovereignty, ethnic homogeneity, and exclusive citizenship" (Mahmud 1997, 633; also see Hindess 1998). Effortlessly linking nationalism with political rights, they largely failed to abjure imperialism or affirm the equal legitimacy of different cultures, and justified extraterritorial subjugation on the grounds that sovereignty was only legitimate if it was economically dynamic and led to individual autonomy, not social diversity (Falk 2004, 1011; Jaggi 2000; Parekh 2000, 45). Colonial conquest was a "complement" to "positivist nation-building at home," with bloodletting legitimized by capitalism and nationalism (Asad 2005, 2). The linkage between capitalism and nationalism differentiated imperial forms of political organization from prior and alternative styles of governing:

> the rise of democracy *within* the developed world was accompanied by a very contrasted history *without*, the export of liberalism to the less advanced part of the world, be this through colonial rule and its coercive maintenance on the one hand, or the sustaining, in the cold war, of authoritarian regimes on the other (Halliday 2001, 87).

Nor can this be read as a Whiggish narrative at the core, a happily unfurling welcome carpet of inclusiveness. To give just two instances, African American men won, lost, and regained suffrage between the 1860s and the 1960s, while poll taxes have often been used to disenfranchise the poor. Today, unlike 108 other democracies, including Afghanistan and Iraq, the U.S. Constitution does not guarantee the right to vote, which remains subject to antediluvian state legislation in many instances. A million ballots were thrown out in the 2004 presidential election due to these jurisdictional inconsistencies, while nine million citizens are permanently disenfranchised for reasons such as felony convictions (Thelen 2000, 551; Jackson 2005).

As it has developed through capitalism, slavery, colonialism, and liberalism, political citizenship has expanded its reach and definition. Although spread unevenly across space and time, the Enlightenment model is critical to every sovereign state. In 2000, 120 countries were democracies, representing 63 percent of the world's population (Chua 2003, 124). For philosophers dedicated to the procedural ratification of governmental decisions through conversation, the model can be recast from its origins in imperialism and nationalism to offer a "constitutional patriotism" that surpasses bigotry (Habermas 1998). For example, women in countries undergoing democratization frequently rely on predemocratic systems for protection and enlargement of their economic and cultural rights because they doubt the efficacy and safety of electoral participation; but ultimately, they also look to political guarantees (Fallon 2003).

Of course, this apparently pacific, participatory system can equally benefit imperialism. The U.S. government spent US$1 billion throughout the 1990s to encourage democratization in Eastern and Central Europe, Africa, Latin America, Southeast Asia, and the Caribbean—but not in the Middle East, where its oil interests were implicated with the fortunes of existing oligarchies (Chua 2003, 123–24). Its latter-day discovery of the virtues of democracy in that region was restricted to noncompliant states in need of violent instruction, or client states with demonstrably restive populations whose lack of freedom might become articulated to anti-Yanqui sentiment.

The harsh link of soil to blood has remained central to citizenship. Most states confer rights through *ius sanguinis*, based on parentage. The United States is unusual, in that it only uses ius sanguinis for children born overseas to its own citizens. A much older, medieval concept is dominant here: *ius soli*, a right of the soil that is based on residence, but frequently discriminates along racial and gender lines.* Ius soli derives from the Fourteenth and Fifteenth Amendments' antiracist guarantees of citizenship to those born or naturalized in the United States. Until 1865, native-born women and people of color were not allowed to vote, but white male immigrants could do so without being naturalized. In 1855, the U.S. Congress allowed foreign women who married U.S. men to become citizens, but in 1907, new legislation expatriated locally born women who married foreigners. It took decades of concerted struggle before women gained the right to vote in 1920, followed by inalienable citizenship in 1931. For much of the first half of the twentieth century, Asian men were excluded from citizenship and their wives could not enter the United States. The 1946 War Brides Act permitted these men to send for their relatives. But again, this is no Whiggish triumph with an inclusive telos. The 1996 Defense of Marriage Act codified court-sanctioned immigration practices that disqualified people from citizenship because of polygamy or same-sex marriage. This sexual obsession is also expressed in recent antiabortion movements, which declare that fetuses are citizens, and promote legislation granting them rights (Stevens 1999, 135–36; Casper and Morgan 2004).

What about those of us who are in between countries? The 1932 Hague Convention on nationality states that "every person should have a nationality and should have one nationality only." This was endorsed by the Council of Europe's 1963 Convention on Reduction of Cases of Multiple Nationality (Aleinikoff 2000, 137; also see Bauböck 2005, 6). But recent changes in global demography have compromised the intensity of state-based ethnonationalism. The economic realities of departure, and the cultural ones of memory, militate against maintaining a pure citizenship of the kind envisaged at The Hague. Global remittances are valued at US$100 billion a year (Schweder et al. 2002, 27). As a consequence, in 1998, fifty countries recognized dual citizenship, up from twenty just a few years earlier; by 2005, one hundred nations did so. In return for their economic support, foreign-based nationals of twenty states,

---

*Germany, for long an especially dubious subscriber to ius sanguinis, added ius soli in 2000 (Benhabib 2002, 159).

including the Philippines, the Dominican Republic, Cape Verde, Croatia, Eritrea, Armenia, and Turkey have recently gained the vote. The Dominican Republic enacted arrangements in 1994 such that a Dominican American could act as a politician in both Santo Domingo and Washington Heights. Exiled nationalists essentially bought Croatia's 1990 election, and two years later were rewarded with guaranteed parliamentary participation, when 10 percent of seats were allocated to the diaspora, which was more than resident minorities rated. As for long-term foreign residents, they may vote in Aotearoa/New Zealand and Britain, in the latter case, if they hail from former colonies (Cohen 2003, 65; *Economist* 2003b; Wucker 2005; Levitt 2001, 204–5; Bauböck 2005, 16, 24 and 2000, 306–7; Aleinikoff 2000, 138–39, 142, 144, 162–63; *Economist* 2005s).

This unity is not always easily managed. The idea of loyalties split through hybrid cultural identifications has long been difficult for citizenship theory and practice, which tend to require unity rather than diversity. Multiple citizenship institutionalizes split subjectivity. The impact goes further than matters of voting, military service, and diplomatic assistance. It gets to the heart of an affective relationship to the sovereign state, and generates contradictions in even the most chauvinistic of countries, providing a clue to the fragility of citizenship.

Thomas Hobbes says that human nature is constructed around differentiation. Therefore "*man is made fit for Society not by nature, but by training*" (2002, 25). Rousseau insists that "it is not enough to say to the citizens, *be good*, they must be taught to be so" (1975, 130) by a normalizing power that sets an ideal. Consider Massimo D'Azeglio's apocryphal but influential claim after the wars of unification that "Italy has been made; now we must make Italians" (quoted in Thelen 2000, 557). In France, the Third Republic made secular education mandatory for six- to thirteen-year-olds in order to forge citizens who would generate responsible public opinion, a term that spread across Western Europe in the latter half of the eighteenth century. Allied to this reform were a statistical system covering human conduct, a Declaration of Human Rights, and a form of "leveling" to counter social inequality (Asad 2005, 2; Briggs and Burke 2003, 72; Mattelart 2003, 19). Horace Mann's promotion of universal public schooling in the United States was predicated on the need to manufacture citizens: "It is a very laborious thing to make Republicans [not R-Worders—they are generated by the lord's work, presumably]; and woe to the republic that rests upon no better foundations than ignorance, selfishness, and passion" (quoted in Thelen 2000, 552)

Ideal citizenship can never quite be attained, but the drive toward perfection as the best possible consumer, patriot, or ideologue, enjoins the subject to strive for it by the instillation of ethical incompleteness (Miller 1993).

Ethical incompleteness inscribes a radical indeterminacy in the subject in the name of loyalty to a more complete entity through educational and other cultural regimes. These regimes assume an insufficiency of the individual against the benevolent historical backdrop of the nation and form a collective public subjectivity, via what John Stuart Mill termed "the departments of human interests amenable to governmental control" (1974, 68). Citizens are supposedly "abstracted from cultural characteristics," in keeping with ideals of unity— e pluribus unum. But as a country's nationals, citizens are meant to share "common cultural values" (Castles and Davidson 2000, 12) rather than be "cultural outlaws without taste," as U.S. officials of state described immigrants a century ago (quoted in Portes 2001, 185). In that vein, the President General of the Daughters of the American Revolution, Sarah Mitchell Guernsey, argued in 1919 that "[y]ou can never grow an American soul so long as you use a hyphen" (quoted in Negra 2002, 75).

Twenty-two territories and states of the United States once gave the vote to immigrants who were not citizens, but by the mid-nineteenth century, these rights were diminished, and entirely eroded with the Americanization campaigns of the 1920s. Workplace training, propaganda, and cultural policies pushed new arrivals to discard their heritages in return for legal advances. The United States has long preferred that citizens belong to just one polity, but the Supreme Court invalidated the prohibition of dual citizenship in 1967, and the State Department finally acknowledged its legitimacy in 1990. Multiple nationalities can now be attained here via four methods: naturalization as a U.S. citizen and renunciation of one's original citizenship followed by its reclamation, with the United States none the wiser; naturalization, with renunciation not recognized by one's country of origin; birth in the United States to immigrant parents from a country that recognizes ius sanguinis; and birth outside the United States to a U.S. citizen. Some progressive municipalities have recently reintroduced local voting rights to permanent residents. Robust nationalists like the Federal Bureau of Investigation, however, will not employ dual citizens (Wucker 2005; *Economist* 2005j).

There is a tie between dual nationality and cultural citizenship. The *Fresno Bee* endorses cultural citizenship as "a concept sweeping America's universities" that eschews assimilation but demands rights, including the maintenance of immigrant cultures. In support of this, the paper argues that a "Salvadoran family . . . is Salvadoran whether they live in Washington, D.C., or San Salvador" (Rodriguez and Gonzales 1995). Perhaps, but what would happen to that family in the event of a military conflict between El Salvador and the United States, when members might be called on to fight for one side or both; or less spectacularly, which set of national laws should apply to them? The

United States has had a long history of harboring and abetting enemies of other states, starting with Irish rebels in 1798, moving on through José Marti in the 1880s, its support of Salvadoran death squads during the Ronald Reagan and George H. W. Bush administrations, to Cuban anti-Marxists of today. Consider the mythologization of Irish Americans, many of whom have been financial supporters of violent parastatal activity for decades, and who stand ready to vote in Ulster. If, as the *Fresno Bee* asserts, this dualism is a matter of "basic human rights," what if El Salvador and the United States adopt different positions on human rights, or similar ones, but they are infractions of the very concept as parlayed through the UN? The recent history of the two nations makes this debate far from abstract (Wucker 2005).

Other nations have dealt with recently expanded immigration in a variety of ways. Mexico has been protectionist on this question, not surprisingly, since its land was expropriated. As a young Chicano/a poet quoted by Renato Rosaldo says, "*No crucé la frontera, la frontera cruzó a mí*" [I didn't cross the border, it crossed me] (1997, 31). To own land in Mexico, foreigners have long had to renounce the right to diplomatic protection by their countries of citizenship. Property in coastal and border territories was subject to additional restrictions. Since the North American Free Trade Agreement/*Tratado de Libre Comercio* (NAFTA/TLC) and California's Proposition 187, however, Mexico has had to deal with increased immigration to the United States, and ensure that its nationals have political power over the border whilst retaining economic status "at home." Now that so much money is held by transnationals, and annual remittances from the United States to Mexico are double the value of farm exports and roughly equal to that of tourism (García Canclini 2002, 19), the government has adopted a different position. The Mexican state even has a Hispanic Fund, which encourages Latin firms in the United States to engage in partnerships with Mexican companies. And the state of Zacatecas reserves two congressional seats for U.S.-based citizens. In Mexico, as in the United States, all persons born in the country are nationals, and naturalizing aliens must renounce their citizenship of origin. Mexico used to require citizens to renounce their citizenship in order to become a citizen of another nation, although ius sanguinis made the latter genetically inalienable—adults could lose their own Mexican citizenship, but still transmit it to their progeny. Since 1997, dual nationality is permitted by Mexico. And, although only residents may vote, since 1996 expatriates can do so if they return for the event. Mexican politicians campaign vigorously inside the United States, while newspapers on the Mexican side endorse U.S. political candidates. With perhaps five million Mexican citizens now residing north of the border, 2005 legislation paved the way to establish polling centers in the United States. Though the politics of voting were complex in 2006, there was the precedent of the expatriate Iraqi vote.

The Indian Citizenship Act of 1955 does not allow for dual citizenship, but a nonresident South Asian naturalized in the United States can own a Pennsylvania hotel chain, then expand to Mumbai. Today, the government operates remittance incentive schemes for nonresident citizens that see US$14 billion sent home each year. In 2002, Delhi announced its intention to permit many of the twenty million Indians living elsewhere to become dual nationals and embark on direct investment of their collective income, which amounted to 35 percent of the GDP of their billion countryfolk. The new status would, of course, be available to Indians from the First World's bourgeoisie and salariat! Person-of-Indian-Origin identification cards are very costly, and dual citizenship may set high passport fees as a class barrier. How else to deal with moral panics over the possibility of Pakistanis claiming this right in order to destabilize the polity (Shah 2002; Srinivas 2002)?

That brings us to the second citizenship type, economic citizenship—the *égalité/tener trabajo* model. Economic citizenship has been alive for a very long time, via the collection and dissemination of information about the public, its ways and means, through the census and related statistical devices. This became an interventionist category with what the economic historian Karl Polanyi called "the discovery of society"—that moment in the nineteenth-century transformation of capitalism when paupers came to be marked as part of the social sphere, and hence deserving of aid and inclusion. Their well-being was incorporated into collective subjectivity as a right, a problem, a statistic, and a law, and juxtaposed to the self-governing worker or owner. Society was held to be simultaneously more and less than the promises and precepts of the market. Then came public education, mothers' pensions, U.S. Civil War benefits, and overseas business travel (Polanyi 2001, 89, 82–85; Watts 2000, 197; Skocpol 2003; Robertson 2003).

Welfarist economic citizenship really took off in the First World during the Great Depression and in the Global South during decolonization. It addressed employment, health, and retirement security through the redistribution of capitalist gains. At the same time, the state came to act as an investor to assist capitalist innovation in areas of market malfunction. For Franklin Delano Roosevelt, the great task of the New Deal was "to find through government the instrument of our united purpose" against "blind economic forces and blindly selfish men," via "a new chapter in our book of self government" that would "make every American citizen the subject of his country's interest and concern" (Roosevelt 1937). In the words of his Australian equivalent, Prime

Minister John Curtin, government was the means "whereby the masses should be lifted up" (quoted in Van Creveld 1999, 35).

In 1945, when both Roosevelt and Curtin died, two historic promises were made by established and emergent governments: to secure the political sovereignty of citizens and to secure their economic welfare. At the end of World War II, the promise of universal sovereignty required concerted international action to be fulfilled. Extant colonial powers (principally Britain, the Netherlands, Belgium, France, and Portugal) had to be convinced that the peoples whom they had enslaved should be given the right of self-determination, with nationalism, a powerful ideology of political mobilization, as a supposed precursor to liberation. When this promise was made good, the resulting postcolonial governments then began to undertake efforts to deliver on the economy. Economic welfare seemed locally deliverable by state-based management of supply and demand and the creation of industries that would substitute imports with domestically produced items. Most followed "capitalism in one country," known as import-substitution industrialization (ISI), frequently via state enterprises or on the coattails of multinational corporations (MNCs) that established local presences. But Global South states suffered underdevelopment because of their dependent relations with the core, and thus, were unable to grow economically. Public-private partnerships intervened around the world to destabilize threats to U.S. economic dominance, via clandestine and overt funding from agencies such as the perversely named National Endowment for Democracy and "Economic Hit Men," who tied developing countries to improbable infrastructural investments and debt regimes (Quaccia 2004; Perkins 2004).* Formal *political* postcoloniality rarely became *economic*, apart from some Asian states that pursued "permanent capitalism," known as Export-Oriented Industrialization (EOI), and service-based expansion. After the capitalist economic crises of the 1970s, even those Western states that had bourgeoisies with sufficient capital formation to permit a welfare system found that stagflation undermined their capacity to hedge employment against inflation. So they selectively turned away from ISI, and required less-developed countries to do the same. Development policies of the 1950s and 1960s were problematized and dismantled starting in the 1970s, a tendency that grew in velocity and scope with the erosion of state socialism.

---

*It should come as no surprise that the National Endowment for Democracy, a front organization with an International Republican Institute staffed by R-Word mavens, worked to destabilize Jean-Bertrand Aristide in Haiti in 2004, leading to perhaps the greatest chaos in that state's sorry history (Kurlantzick 2004).

When Britain's neoliberal Prime Minister Margaret Thatcher countered Polanyi by claiming there was no such thing as "society," her remark signified a massive shift toward the legitimation not of the poor, but of the wealthy. A new priority—swelling the coffers of the latter through redistribution—was justified by the notion that society was "a figment of the collectivist and bureaucratic imagination" (Meek 1998, 2). Economic citizenship has been turned on its head since that time through historic policy renegotiations conducted by capital, the state, and their rent-seeking intellectual servants in political science and economics. Anxieties over unemployment have been trumped by anxieties over profits, with labor pieties displaced by capital pieties, and workers called upon to identify as stakeholders in business or as consumers, rather than combatants with capital (Martin 2002, 21; Miller and O'Leary 2002, 97–99). These reforms have redistributed income back to bourgeoisies and First World metropoles. Today's privileged economic citizens are corporations, and individual citizens are increasingly conceived of as self-governing consumers. For Bush Minor, the mantra is "making every citizen an agent of his or her own destiny" (2005). Reactionaries favor individual rights in the economic sphere of investment, but not in other social spheres (*Economist* 2004h, 14).

Thanks to the neoliberal agenda, financial and managerial decisions made in one part of the world increasingly take rapid effect elsewhere. New international currency markets have proliferated since the decline of a fixed exchange rate, matching regulated systems with piratical financial institutions that cross borders. Speculation brings greater rewards than production, as the trade in securities and debts outstrips profits from selling cars or building houses. The world circulation of money creates the conditions for imposing international credit tests on all countries. At a policy level, this has put an end to ISI and the very legitimacy of national economies, which have been supplanted by EOI and the idea of an international economy. In the words of the economist Samir Amin, "the space of economic management of capital accumulation" no longer coincides with "its political and social dimensions" (1997, xi). Currently, governments are supposed to deliver formal sovereignty and controlled financial markets, but neoclassical orthodoxy and business priorities call for privately managed international capital. The *Economist* calls this "[i]mpossible" (*Economist* 1999, 4). With productive investment less profitable than financial investment, and companies rationalizing production, the worlds of marketing, labor, and administration have been reconceived on an international scale. Of course, these neoliberal positions are highly contingent. When it suits U.S. steel or farm subsidies, market moralists become unrepentant protectionists, and corporate welfare services continue (Stiglitz 2002). And no doubt the minute that retirement savings fall prey to major shifts and shocks in health, macroeconomics, climate, and stock-price irrationality, R-Worders will abandon their fantasies about privatizing Social Security. But the notion of indoctrinating citizens into the dogma of self-governance continues unabated.

The corollary of open markets is that national governments cannot guarantee the economic well-being of their citizens. The loan-granting power of the World Bank and the International Monetary Fund (IMF) has forced a shift away from the local provision of basic needs, redirecting public investment toward sectors supposedly endowed with comparative advantage. Globalization does not offer an end to center-periphery inequalities, competition between states, or macro-decision-making by corporations. Instead, this power just cuts the capacity of the state system to control such transactions, and relegates responsibility for the protection and welfare of the workforce to multinational corporate entities and financial institutions.

These revisions to economic citizenship have generated an extraordinary redistribution of global income. In the two decades from 1960 to 1980, most of the Global South was state socialist, or had a significant welfare system and followed ISI. Per capita income during that period increased by 34 percent in Africa and 73 percent in Latin America, while the standard deviation of growth rates amongst developing economies was 1.8 from 1950 to 1973. In the quarter century since these political economies shifted to EOI, the corollary numbers disclose a drop in income across Africa of 23 percent and an increase in Latin America of just 6 percent, while the standard deviation of growth has climbed to 3.0, because of China and India's successes. In 1998, the richest 20 percent of the world's people earned seventy-four times the amount of the world's poorest, up from sixty times in 1990 and thirty times in 1960, while 56 percent of the global population made less than US$2 a day. In 2001, every child born in Latin America immediately "owed" US$1500 to foreign banks. For a tiny number, that would amount to a few hours of work once they had attained their majority. For most, it would represent a decade's salary (Palast 2003a, 151; Ocampo 2005, 12–14; UNESCO Institute for Education 1999, 3; Sutcliffe 2003a, 3; García Canclini 2002, 26–27).

Meanwhile, the U.S. Government's 2002 *National Security Strategy* fancifully refers to a "single sustainable model for national success: freedom, democracy, and free enterprise" (The White House 2002). This model, elegantly simple and seductively meritocratic in its pure form, has never been applied, and never could be, outside the inequalities and struggles of time and place (which it avoids by using the outlier categories *"ceteris paribus"* — other things being equal — and "the long run"). For example, at the World Trade Organization (WTO) meeting in 2001, U.S. Trade Representative Robert

Zoellick announced to the Global South that compliance with trade liberalization would be seen as an litmus test of attitudes toward terrorism. Clearly, rather than sitting comfortably alongside democracy and equality, neoclassical economics has been a tool of domination. In countries accustomed to colonial occupation, these developments amount to one more sign that political participation is pointless (Mukhia 2002; Nandy 1998, 48; Holland 2005).

The United States' great early achievement was establishing the state as an abstraction beyond its embodiment in a monarch or group. But this move that made rights available to citizens also made rights available to other non-human actors, such as corporations. U.S. corporations began life as the creatures of state governments, to conduct business in the public interest, such as building canals. They were quickly transformed into private concerns (Drutman and Cray 2005). By 1884, President Rutherford Hayes sorrowfully declared that the country had become "a government of corporations, by corporations, and for corporations" (quoted in Ferguson and Henderson 2003). Two years later, as if to mock and confirm this remark simultaneously, the Supreme Court decreed that corporations were entitled to Constitutional protections that had been designed for human beings. Since that time, MNCs have developed their economic reach and legal stature, and attained the national and international status that was once only available to governments. So the Multilateral Agreement on Investment of 1995–98 sought to generate citizenship status for global economic actors, to the exclusion of all others. Similar attempts are likely to follow. Fortunately, strong echoes of Hayes' concerns can still be heard. In the 1960s, about a third of the U.S. population thought that governments catered to corporate interests; by the 1990s, three-quarters realized this fact, as support for MNCs plummeted. Seventy-seven percent of people believe that large companies wield too much power, though this is barely, if ever, reported by the bourgeois press (Allen 2001; McMichael 1996, 27–29; Wallerstein 1989, 10–11; Van Creveld 1999, 415–16; Egan and Levy 2001, 75; Lewis 2001, 61–62; Pew Research Center 2005, 17).

The consumer activism mentioned in the Introduction tends to occur in struggles with the most successful companies. Their response often includes the assiduous cultivation of "corporate social responsibility" (CSR) projects, notably support of major and minor cultural institutions to show they are good global, national, and local corporate citizens—effectively appropriating avant-garde practices previously used against them by activists. CSR is sometimes said to be foreign to U.S. and British business norms (Davis 2005) but this is as ahistorical and unsupportable as one would expect from its author—McKinsey & Company's worldwide managing director. Some date CSR-like practices to the early twentieth century in the United States. It has really developed as a discourse since the 1960s, covering economic, ethical, legal, and philanthropic practices (Hemphill 2004; Logsdon 2004, 68). With the solidification of civil-rights discourses and the advent of Friends of the Earth and Greenpeace in 1970, companies felt the need to respond to emergent public concern over pollution and civil strife. Shareholders of Eastman Kodak prevented its executives from funding a black civil rights group in 1972. But the following year, the Interfaith Center for Corporate Responsibility began ushering in a new shareholder activism, and as Shell invested more and more in the Middle East, it began to factor social responsibility into its analyses of risk. By the mid-1970s, activists were pressing MNCs to disinvest in South Africa, and General Motors adopted a code of principles for dealing with apartheid in 1977 (Ferguson and Henderson 2003).

These trends have gathered force since their inception. In the U.K., the Prince of Wales' Trust links companies and social problems on the premise that it is "good business sense" (V. Matthews 2003). In 2000, the UN announced a Global Compact on Corporate Accountability regarding human and labor rights, signed by fifty companies and twelve unions. The following year saw a charter on environmental risks called the London Principles, followed by an Extractive Industries Transparency Initiative, and participation by the Office of the High Commissioner for Human Rights (Ferguson and Henderson 2003; World Economic Forum 2004, 113; Business for Social Responsibility 2004). The World Economic Forum's *Global Governance Initiative* argues that the private sector must be integrally involved in the UN's Millennium Declaration and its goals of diminished poverty and suffering, by following "the global public interest" as "core business strategy and practice" (2004, vi, xv). Brazil's Instituto Ethos specializes in national CSR, and estimates that eight hundred firms are involved in purportedly prosocial activities. Across Latin America, Forum Empresa provides a CSR umbrella for companies engaged in "Responsibilidad Social Empresarial," and 87 percent of large corporations believe CSR aids their image, with 58 percent deeming it "a major competitive advantage" (Guevara 2004). Such rhetoric is now virtually universal in the annual reports and executive suites of major multinationals, alongside the mantra of growth and profit (Crook 2005). Merely abiding by the law and making money seems "so *passé*" (Crook 2005, 11) to groups such as the International Business Leaders Forum, with its resolute "CSR Roadmap" (2004). A European Research Working Group on Corporate Citizenship encourages business executives to look into "social investment, corporate responsibility, sustainability, and CSR issues," (Conference Board 2002) and Business for

Social Responsibility, a nongovernmental organization (NGO), argues that model citizenship and prosocial interventions manifest enlightened self-interest for corporations.

CSR is said to generate new markets, massage labor, deliver positive public relations, and heighten brand recognition—it engages contemporary economic citizenship. Following the CSR pathway, MNCs not only obtain free rides from host nations, but also cultivate the image of responsible international subjects whose exemplary liberal self-governance means they do not need regulating. So selfless are these corporations that they even participate in social planning and private welfare, helping to define policy issues and managing public programs alongside NGOs. Through foundation donations, corporate sponsorship, and executive largesse, multinationals have become bigger sources of global aid than states—a fact they remorselessly promote, along with their compliance with voluntary codes of restraint. This movement into the public sector parallels their takeover of natural state monopolies through the neoliberal privatization of water, power, telecommunications, incarceration, the military, and so on.

Consider the Ford Motor Company, which claims that in order "to become a leading contributor to a more sustainable world, corporate citizenship has become an integral part of every decision and action we take" (2002b). To back up this assertion, it brings out annual CSR reports, participates in partnerships around the world to "provide for those in need," sponsors the arts and humanities, and runs "Employee and Community Enrichment Programs" under the rubric of "Sustainable Mobility" (Keeler 2002). Ford's "Employee Resource Groups" include a "Middle Eastern Community," which is designed to bring workers together and make the firm a preferred option for U.S.-based customers from that region, as well as raise money for victims of terrorism (Ford Motor Company 2002a, 25). Ford also runs a series of magazine advertisements promoting the "Race for the Cure," an NGO-sponsored series of actions against breast cancer. Stars such as Helen Hunt are depicted in advertisements wearing the 2003 Ford breast cancer awareness scarf, which is described as a "social statement." The company joined the Susan G. Komen Breast Cancer Foundation's million dollar council as part of this "breast cancer marketing" (King 2001).

Ford parades its dedication to human rights and its ethical policing of subcontractors' treatment of workers as "an expression of our deep commitment to people around the world." But within a few carriage returns, it insists on the need for such policies because a bad reputation will alienate consumers, whereas being pro–human rights "is an important advantage in today's challenging marketplace." The promise is a mythic simultaneous orgasm: "our company more profitable and the world more equitable and sustainable." This may seem like a happy confluence of principle and profit, but when the company is losing market share to General Motors' vile sport utility vehicles, it reacts by indulging in the same eco-violence to win back customers, because "'corporate citizenship can only be achieved in the context of a strong and profitable business." Chair Bill Ford even has a defense of this: "If we were to withdraw from that market, customers would be forced to buy the competitive vehicle, with a truly negative impact on the environment" (Ford Motor Company 2002a, 3, 6, 10–11). Meanwhile, the Union of Concerned Scientists identifies Ford as responsible for the worst gas emissions of all major car manufacturers (Corpwatch 2005).

Needless to say, many business leeches worry about the value of CSR. As *Global Finance* put it, "one question remains, perhaps the most important of all: Does it pay?" The magazine found a particularly delightful CSR consultant who replied that "qualitatively you can show how issues like child labor will impact on, say, brand and image. Quantifying it is trickier" (Keeler 2002). It is just as well this character didn't have to think about what was ethical, or consider labor justice. But he or she needn't have worried. Academic studies of the contemporary UN/NGO corporate-citizenship "partnerships" between civil society and MNCs in the Global South show that they are dominated by corporate methods and interests—romantically deterritorialized and decentralized in accordance with the shared fantasy structure of social movements and corporations (Rondinelli 2002, 391–92, 404, 405; Dagnino 2003, 10, Dummett 2004).

Observant political scientists note that domestic U.S. politics "ha[ve] become the affair of professionally run, top-down advocacy groups," with parastatal bodies that specialize in "faking civil society" (Schell 2005, 6; Skocpol 2003, 197). In the words of Clive Crook: "The human face that CSR applies to capitalism goes on each morning, gets increasingly smeared by day and washes off at night" (2005, 4). And CSR charity is often capriciously withdrawn, so it is notoriously difficult to plan around. This establishes a power dynamic that rarely lets up, especially when twinned with homilies of the kind so common to U.S. giving. The CSR/NGO fetish is no substitute for compensation derived from justice, whereby wrongs are adjudicated and compensated responsibly, with the parties on an equal footing (Dobson 2003, 27). No wonder Bush's first Secretary of State, Colin Powell, regarded NGOs as "a force multiplier for us, such an important part of our combat team" (quoted in Mann 2003, 119).

CULTURAL CITIZENSHIP

> The European liberal constitutions of the nineteenth century were
> political constitutions. . . . The constitutions of the first third of the
> twentieth century . . . were devoted to economic and social issues. . . .
> another stage is evidenced in the decade of the 1970s in the eruption of
> cultural concerns: this generates lexical forms and doctrinal categories
> such as "cultural rights" . . . the free existence of culture, cultural
> pluralism, and the access of citizens to culture are guaranteed in
> intensified forms.
> —Jesús Prieto de Pedro (1999, 63)

The requirement to drop ISI in favor of EOI has stimulated U.S. cultural
production as its economy slowly changes from a farming and manufactur-
ing-based economy to an ideological one. This development can be traced
back a long way, but perhaps its contemporary incarnation is best tied to a
1971 report for Presidential advisors that referred glowingly to "the development of flexible citizens who, as many people have already realized, are
the kind of citizen the twenty-first century is going to need" (quoted in Mattelart 2003, 109). The United States now sells feelings, ideas, money, health,
laws, religion, and risk—niche forms of identity, also known as culture. The
significance of this for the United State's image abroad is immense, while
the domestic correlatives are important in terms of wealth, job creation, and
ideology. Under EOI, with manufacturing going offshore in search of cheap
labor, culture has become a crucial sector of First World production and foreign exchange. In 2000, services created one dollar in seven of total world
production. U.S. services exported US$295 billion, and eighty-six million pri-
vate sector service jobs generated an US$80 billion surplus in balance of pay-
ments, at a time when the country relied on trade to sustain its society and
economy (Office of the United States Trade Representative 2001). The trade
in services is facilitated by a New International Division of Cultural Labor
(the NICL). U.S. sport, film and television production, and computing have
gone global in search of locations, labor, and audiences. This expansion provides an economic base for the making and selling of personhood—U.S.
subjectivity on export. Some romantic souls see it as a cosmopolitan
exchange between cultures that occurs without obliterating difference. In
reality, this change is based on class discrimination, with the free movement
of labor restricted to managerial levels (Miller et al. 2001 and 2005; Burawoy et al. 2000; Freeman 2000; Sharma 2003, 28; *Non Resident Indians
Online* 2001; Abu-Laban 2000, 512), and ideas dominated by an unequal distribution of culture.

This is the substructural reality to the "New Economy." Significantly, the idea of a "creative class" drawn to cities that cultivate "the arts, music, night life and quaint historical districts" has been quantified by two indexes: the Technological Index and the Gay Index. These are said to measure technical innovation, entrepreneurship, and the avant-garde, effortlessly blending Big Blue with Big Bohemian in a shared search for knowledge infrastructures and "lifestyle amenities." Newness meets diversity via "technology, talent and tolerance" (Dreher 2002) — a grand middle-class melting pot of corporate cybertarianism and multiculturalism that generates a civic gold rush (Stevenson 2004). In Britain, the Association for the Business Sponsorship of the Arts highlights the corporate fascination with "how they can benefit from the arts, how new experiences, values and skills can unlock 'creativity'." Organizational argot aside, this is a bee's knee away from the Royal Society of the Arts opining that "creativity and innovation are the lifeblood of any organization concerned with survival and prosperity" and the Arts and Humanities Research Board announcing that the work it funds must make "the transition from creativity into productivity" (Day 2002; Curtis 2002). So, The Body Shop asks its executives to practice body painting, Mars puts on a musical, *Henry V* becomes a management text, and *Sandalistas* is simultaneously an advertisement for sandals on sale at Barney's and *Condé Nast's* term for Yanquis buying real estate in postrevolutionary Nicaragua — a mocking reverse trope of the Sandinistas. The economic turn to services is a crucial link to this cultural citizenship — *fraternité/ser alfabetizado*. A broader meaning of civic identity is increasingly addressed through popular journalism that engages the everyday world of risk and panic, often transcending these weighty topics of national significance (Day 2002, 38; Babb 2004; Meijer 2001).

Citizenship has always been cultural. For instance, the Ottoman Empire offered non-Muslims "extensive cultural but few political rights" (Parekh 2000, 7). The first constitutional guarantees of culture appear in Switzerland in 1874. Today, cultural provisions are standard in postdictatorship charters, for example those of Mexico, South Africa, Brazil, Portugal, Guatemala, Nicaragua, Paraguay, Perú, and Spain. The meaning is generally a double one, blending artistry and ethnicity. Concerns with language, heritage, religion, and identity are responses to histories structured in dominance through cultural power and the postcolonial incorporation of the periphery into an international system of "free" labor: The NICL. Malaysia, for instance, has been a predominantly Islamic area for centuries. Colonialism brought large numbers of South Asian and Chinese settlers, along with their religions. The postcolonial Constitution asserts a special status for ethnic Malays and Islam, while protecting the cultural rights of others. Muslims are the only people who can evangelize, and they have religious courts. Other religions are tolerated, but may not proselytize, and are governed by secular rule. In the Netherlands, Sudan, Yemen, Slovenia, Bahrain, and Portugal, citizenship rests on language skills. In Sweden and Sudan, it depends on leading "a respectable life" and having "good moral character," respectively. "Attachment" to local culture is a criterion in Croatia, and knowledge of culture and history in Romania. Liberia requires that citizens "preserve, foster, and maintain the positive Liberian culture," something it avows can only be done by "persons who are Negroes or of Negro descent." This racialization also applies in Sierra Leone, and Israel restricts citizenship to Jews plus Arabs who lived there prior to 1948 and their descendants. Partial racial and religious preferences also rule in Bahrain and Yemen. No wonder the British government's 2002 decision to impose an English, Welsh, or Scottish Gaelic-speaking requirement on those seeking citizenship quickly drew fire from the people of color it was clearly designed to exclude, even as its defenders regarded it as a test of fitness for everyday life. Likewise, the Argentine state's attempt to suppress non-Euro cultural formations by a variety of bizarre cultural technologies, from requiring all school pupils to cover their clothes with white dustcoats to prohibiting indigenous languages, has failed (de Pedro 1991, 1551 and 1999; Mahmud 1999, 1223; *Economist* 2005v; Pollard 2003, 72–81; *Economic Times New Delhi* 2002, 13; Crick 2003; Grimson 2005).

The model liberal citizen is a clear-headed, cool subject who knows when to set aside individual and sectarian preferences in search of the greater good. This sounds acultural and neutral, even neutered. But historically, it has frequently corresponded, in both rhetorical and legal terms, to male, property owning subjects protecting their interests from the general population by requiring the public renunciation of other loyalties, an unquestioning embrace of national ideologies, and an apparent self-control over personal desire. This has caused the U.S. government, a putatively culture-free zone, to have profoundly cultural qualifications for citizenship. Many philosophical liberals insist on a common language and nation as prerequisites for effective citizenship (Lister 1997, 52; Zacharias 2001; Abizadeh 2002). But in nations split by a migrant population's languages, religions, and senses of self, cultural differences bring into doubt what a "properly ordered life" might mean. As the political theorist Will Kymlicka says, it "is not that traditional human rights doctrines give us the wrong answer to these questions. It is rather that they often give no answer at all. The right to free speech does not tell us what an appropriate language policy is" (1995, 5). Theodore Roosevelt's insistence on a "swift assimilation of aliens" via the "language and culture that has come down to us from the builders of the republic" (quoted in

Parekh 2000, 5) looks impractical, an ill-advised, ideological furphy. Force or fiat cannot decide these issues any longer. The United States is unable to sustain the cultural nationalism of a "Monolingual Eden" (Fuentes 2004, 79).

When the United States sought to prevent Chinese Americans from obtaining passports a century ago, applicants were required to speak English, follow "American customs and dress," and demonstrate a knowledge of national geography and history (Robertson 2003). Today, to become a citizen of the United States other than by birth or blood, in addition to never having murdered anyone or having more pot than for immediate personal use, one must meet certain cultural requirements:

- Reside here
- Renounce allegiance to other states
- "Support the Constitution"
- Know the country's basic political history
- "Read, write, and speak words in ordinary usage in the English language"
- Eschew polygamy
- Only gamble legally; and
- Neither consort with sex workers nor be repeatedly drunk in public

To join the U.S. military it is not necessary to be a citizen—obtaining citizenship is a potential benefit that attracts recruits but there are several cultural requirements, such as no tattoos on the hand or face, no children out of wedlock, and no more than two within it. Only recently did no convictions for domestic violence join the list.* The Citizenship and Immigration Service utilizes these tests to determine "whether an applicant has established good moral character" (Immigration and Naturalization Service, 2001). Just as well I'm content with my Green Card.

It is clear that just as globalization and the NICL impose and invite mobility, so cultural practices proliferate, split, and cross-pollinate. With little time for "processes of acculturation and assimilation" (Castles and Davidson 2000, vii), a volatile mix of hybridity and primordiality emerges. It would be excessive to claim this as entirely new—the rebel pragmatist philosopher Randolph Bourne coined the phrase "Transnational America" in 1916 (Portes 2001,

*This marks a return to the Civil War, when entire units of the Union Army communicated in Scandinavian languages and German. Neoconservatives now call for the military to recruit undocumented residents and people who have never even visited the U.S., under the rubric of a "Freedom Legion." The reward for service would be citizenship, following similar gifts to anticommunist East Europeans in the 1950s. Killing and dying are already culturally transterritorial, with eight thousand British and thirty-eight thousand U.S. soldiers being aliens (*Economist* 2004g; Boot 2005; *Economist* 2004i). This latest proposal would turn the domestic poverty draft into a global one.

182–83, 185), and blends of the modern and the traditional are constitutive of Latin America (García Canclini 1995). But it *does* appear as though more and more transnational people and organizations now exist, weaving political, economic, and cultural links between places of origin and domiciles. There is a crucial difference between the Early Modern period in which contemporary citizenship was forged, when the West provided unwelcome, warlike migrants to the Global South, and the post-1950s period, when the process went into reverse, largely minus belligerent intentions. Traditional views of naturalized citizenship have been thrown into confusion by late twentieth-century immigration and multiculturalism (Feldblum 1997, 103). This is a matter of cultural belonging and material inequality.

The "history of individual peoples, and indeed of whole continents such as 'Europe,' is now being written in terms of a cultural formation defined by something outside, 'the other'" (Halliday 2001, 113). A global, postnational, or transnational citizenship is emergent; and unlike the longstanding utopias of world citizenship, these terms are heuristic devices to describe actually existing formations. Transnational cultural rights have emerged as a terrain of struggle. The framers of the Universal Declaration of Human Rights were riven over the topic, with the United States and Canada virulently opposed to enshrining minority rights. Now a developing discourse of national and international human rights transcends borders, with the Commission on Human Rights recognizing the cultural sphere in 2002 (Bosniak 2000, 449; United Nations Development Programme 2004, 28; Chase-Dunn and Boswell 2004; Purcell 2003).

Most migrant workers around the world are not in the capitalist class or the salariat. They are "temporary" or "undocumented" employees, neither citizens nor immigrants. Again, culture is critical. These workers' identities are quite separate from both their domiciles and their sources of sustenance. They are frequently guaranteed equitable treatment not by sovereign states, but through the supranational discourse of human rights and everyday customs and beliefs that supplement the legal obligations of conventional citizenship (Shafir 1998, 19, 20). The new conditions of citizenship do not necessarily articulate with democracy, because subjects of the international trade in labor frequently lack access to the power bases of native-born sons and daughters (Preuss 1998, 310). In Argentina, for example, which has a migrant workforce from Bolivia and Perú to do menial jobs, Leftists seek protection for "guest workers" by arguing that rights achieved in the aftermath of dictatorship should be extended to all residents, even as the state blames these guest workers for the recrudescence of embarrassing "premodern" diseases such as tuberculosis and measles. In the European Union, the creation of "supranational citizenship" in 1992 problematized the coupling of citizenship to a national culture. At the same time that this recognized a new international division of labor, similar processes limited the rights of guest workers from non-E.U. nations, who have long represented the vast majority of international labor within the Union (García Canclini 1999, 32; Abu-Laban 2000, 511).

While both conservative critics and culturalist celebrants explain cultural citizenship as the outcome of social movements, it must also be understood as an adjustment to economic transformation; the right wing's project of deregulation has played a role in creating and sustaining cultural citizenship. It is no surprise that the EOI push for the Global South to constitute itself as a diverting heritage site and decadent playground for the West has seen the emergence of sex tourism and terrorism (Downey and Murdock 2003, 01). Consequently, there can be no room for a leftist cultural politics that decenters the role of capital. Globally, cultural citizenship is a response to an increasingly mobile middle-class, culture-industry workforce generated by the NICL, which favors North over South and capital over labor. Domestically, cultural citizenship and media deregulation are coefficients of globalization, offering both raw material for foreign sales, and a means of local control.

Where is the idea of national belonging, as exemplified by the U.S. motto, e pluribus unum, in all this? There is an intense irony in that motto since it necessitates a complex triple-declutching between the distinctly different experiences of hitherto discrete or conflictual cultural groups, the requirements of nationalism and state obedience, and the individualism that underpins laws of personhood and property, otherwise known as the Constitution and the Bill of Rights (Hutton 2003b, 56–57). To control the forces unleashed by such changes, neoliberalism posits that the rational calculator inside each person—whose only motivation is to maximize individual utility—must moderate his or her desires in the interests of harmony, blending consumerism with citizenship. Such contradictions are at play when almost two-thirds of the U.S. population, a self-declared caring nation, place the pursuit of personal ambition over the state protection of those in need (Pew Research Center for the People & the Press 2003b; Keeter et al. 2002, 4).

E pluribus unum can simultaneously be articulated to commercial, national, and multicultural CSR purposes, with the ideology of obliterating difference. After September 11, 2001, DKNY offered images of its clothing draped in the Stars and Stripes, along with a weeping model and the upscale clothing and accessories chain Kenneth Cole distributed a free postcard that read, "WHAT WE STAND FOR IS MORE IMPORTANT THAN WHAT WE STAND IN—KENNETH COLE," superimposed over the U.S. flag. This seeming corporate self-abnegation suggested that the very items that gave the store its profile were insignificant, but putting the company's name there gave the lie to the mantra. The lie was revealed on the reverse side of the card, which advised that only participating NYC outlets would donate 10 percent of every US$100 spent there to the "Kenneth Cole World Trade Center Relief Fund." Coca-Cola offered Atlanta billboard readers the slogan "We live as many. We stand as one," accompanied by an image of three headless, legless, multiracial torsos with their hands on their hearts (Hassell 2001; Lewis et al. 2005, 126). Meanwhile, the AdCouncil (2002) trumpeted e pluribus unum in TV spots made immediately after the 9/11 attacks, as part of a nation binding campaign, operating via polyethnic commercial targeting. Called "I Am An American," the commercial was born from the desire to say, in the creators' words, "Up yours, bin Laden" (quoted in Gunther 2001). The campaign was mediated through the state's desire to sell democracy and capitalism, and the AdCouncil's wish to claim commodified diversity as a founding and sustaining precept of Yanqui life that achieves its best expression in marketing. Ordinary people, from firefighters and police officers to playground frolickers and pseudo–gang members, were filmed on the streets of seven U.S. cities, staring into the camera and intoning "I am an American." The commercial was distributed to three thousand media outlets across the nation, many of which aired it without charge. Such moves were in keeping with a rash of "'institutional' or 'public relations' advertising" that effortlessly twinned sympathy and shill (Kinnick 2004).

Many who join today's throng of plaintiffs lamenting a lost citizenship are encouraged by multiculturalism. Although it was founded out of a respect for difference, many on the left regard multiculturalism as a means of integration, and reactionaries accuse it of furthering a "racial particularism" that threatens liberalism (Alexander 2001, 238) through the assiduous efforts of "ethnocultural political entrepreneurs," who mobilize constituencies devoted to "sectional demands" (Barry 2001, 21). Journalist Peter Brimelow of the Center for American Unity says U.S. Latinos comprise "a strange anti-nation," and the Center for Immigration Studies, a right-wing think tank, bemoans the advent of "post-Americans," who have "a casual relationship" with the United States rather than a love affair (1996). They are citizens "of nowhere in particular" (Krikorian, 2004). John F. Kennedy staffer, pop historian, and pundit Arthur Schlesinger, Jr. diagnoses a "disuniting of America" through the revival of "ancient prejudices" by academic multiculturalists, who imagine then institutionalize social divisions that had barely existed beforehand (1991). Reagan bureaucrat, pop ethicist, and serial gambler William J. Bennett calls for a "cultural war" that will reinforce "traditional" values. He opposes counter histories that threaten previously dominant Whiggish narratives of a nation led by great men guided by the beacon of democracy to do great things for all (1992). By supposedly pandering to difference and establishing codes of conduct that are politically correct, inimical to free speech, supportive of identity politics and contemptuous of patriotism, universities have compromised these afore-mentioned critics' historic missions of innovation, quality, and heritage. The outcome is a threat to the golden heritage of Jeffersonian democracy, when propertied men were voters, women were emotional and physical servants, African Americans were slaves, and native peoples fought to survive. The liv-ing white male writers referenced above embody a phobia that women, work-ers, slaves, queers, and racial minorities are attaining places at the center of the nation's past and present. Such fears have a long heritage. A century ago, reactionaries railed against Progressives in universities who called for modern languages to join classical ones, for U.S. literature to be read alongside Euro-pean writing, and for a revised history of the nation's birth (Rosaldo 1994, 404–5). So as a consequence of this really rather mundane, traditional process of curricular reform and reactionary moral panic, the nation is said—by suc-cessive thought-disordered, anxious critics of the nineteenth, twentieth, and twenty-first centuries—to have lost its oneness. The contemporary version is troubled by the supposedly desirable aspects of laissez-faire coupled with the supposedly undesirable aspects of cultural relativisms siege on normativity. Put another way, "the ethics and politics of the unregulated will" (Parekh 2000, 2) are thought to be in play as never before.

These "professors lite" and media pundits warn of increasing public polar-ization, constantly invoking popular sentiment in their media appearances. Again and again, highly impressionistic and reactionary claims are made about threats to and triumphs of e pluribus unum—threats and triumphs based on nothing. The two clearest expressions of citizen opinion, polls and protests, are systematically distorted in media coverage to support right-wing politics and suppress radical tendencies. But no credible public opinion research instru-ment, from the National Election Study to the General Social Survey, discerns increasingly polarized attitudes in the United States—the alibi of this e pluribus unum moral panic. Instead, opinions on racial and sexual difference, schooling, the environment, and public prayer show significant harmonization over time—in a liberal direction. The main exception is abortion (Lewis 2001, 44; Lewis et al. 2004b; DiMaggio 2003).

Here again, Yanqui notions of citizenship seem very cultural indeed. The United States is supposedly the apotheosis of the secular rule of law. The Con-stitution does not mention a god, and the 1797 Treaty of Tripoli specifies that the country "is not in any sense founded on the Christian religion" (quoted in Allen 2005). Yet, the force of its faith matches its economy and military.

The population's radical embrace of religion places it alone amongst nations with advanced economies and educational systems. Citizens that believe in a higher power number 96 percent, and 59 percent state that religion is crucial to their life; more than twice the proportion for Japan, South Korea, Western Europe, and the former Soviet bloc. U.S. Christians number 79 percent, with 41 percent belonging to fundamentalist evangelism and 18 percent aligned with the religious Right. Evangelicals speak of an almost physical transformation, from a faith based in ideas to something that resembles transubstantiation via a trancelike condition of intimacy. One must seriously ponder an avowedly pragmatic and instrumentalist nation of which the vast majority attests to the existence of a devil and individuated angels, 45 percent of its citizens think aliens have visited Earth, 64 percent of its adult Internet users (i.e., 82 million Yanquis) go online in search of spiritual information, three times more people believe in ghosts than was the case a quarter of a century ago, and 84 percent credit the posthumous survival of the soul, up 24 percent since 1972 (Luhrmann 2004, 520; Pew Research Center for the People & the Press 2002b; Newport and Carroll 2003; Hutton 2003a; Mann 2003, 103; Pew Internet & American Life Project 2004; Gallup 2002–03).

Regardless of their varied beliefs, these people are certainly very cultural. The avowedly acultural sphere of liberalism has been trumped by cultural politics from Left and Right, as the world's largest technocracy has re-enchanted its world, turning capitalism and statecraft into magic. To the contrary of the liberal leaning survey results listed earlier, the New Protestantism is a key participant in politics because of vigorous links between the 18 percent religious Right and R-Word funding and activism. In this context, what began in the 1980s is the latest of several Great Awakenings in the United States. This time it's a consumerist one, with selfishness and chauvinism characterizing a revocation of traditional Christianity, as if the latter were the embodiment of Great Society liberalism. There is an organic link today between apparent logocentric opposites—new churches and new markets. Perhaps these far-right Christian fundamentalists hear a famous tag line from San Diego televangelism ringing in their ears: "Remember, prosperity is your divine right" (quoted in Murdock 1997, 96). The corollary is opposition to secular income redistribution, environmental reclamation, and penological rehabilitation. Literary critic Tiffany Ana Lopez describes the attendant shift "from an emphasis on reform to a near obsession with retribution" (2003, 26). These retributive attitudes exist in what purports to be the citadel of individual liberty and redemption. Consider the words of John J DiIulio, Jr., Bush's first director of the White House Office of Faith-Based and Community Initiatives:

True conservatism flows from a singular unifying belief: God. In private life and in the public square good liberals can take Him or leave Him, but true conservatives must always seek Him and strive to heed Him. In the conservative creed human beings are moral and spiritual beings. Each of us has God-given personal rights and God-given social duties, God-given individual liberties and God-given moral responsibilities. (2003: 218)

The Homeland Security Act (U.S. Congress, HR 5005, 2002), which set up the Bureau of Citizenship and Immigration Services (USCIS), specified a mandate to work with "faith-based" groups to further "civic engagement and integration." Needless to say, all such support went to Christian organizations, and not a brass tack to Sikhs, Jews, Muslims, or Buddhists. In its first five years, the administration gave away US$600 million to abstinence-only sex education, delivered by organizations such as the Several Sources Foundation Center, which gives chastity training to women (Kaplan 2004, 22; Talvi 2005b, 10). MentorKids USA, which also received USCIS funds, required volunteers to sign a pledge avowing that "the Bible is God's authoritative and inspired word that is without error . . . including creation, history, its origins and salvation" (quoted in Freedom From Religion 2004).

Signs of religiosity and nationalism seem to satisfy the nervy mavens of the Right. A high priest of contemporary antisectarianism, the political sociologist Robert Putnam pronounced himself well pleased with the patriotic unity in evidence post–September 11, 2001. His pleas for church membership and amateurish meddling in other people's lives were vestigial cries for a united population that reworked antimulticultural citizenship, favoring "volunteerism and kindness" over "politics and policy" (Westheimer and Kahne 2004b, 241). In a notorious *New York Times* op-ed piece, Putnam reminisced about the reaction to 1941 and Pearl Harbor, rhapsodizing "victory gardens in nearly everyone's backyard, Boy Scouts at filling stations collecting floor mats for scrap rubber, affordable war bonds, and giving rides to hitchhiking soldiers and war workers." All these practices supposedly taught "the greatest generation" an enduring lesson in civic involvement that was evident from the "sacrifice" on view in that era's "popular culture from radio shows to comic strips" (2001). He was delighted by increases in religious attendance and blood donations after September 11 (most of the latter wasted, a failure that led in part to the departure of the Red Cross director) and encouraged by Bush Minor's call for U.S. youth to rake yards and wash cars to raise funds for Afghan children after U.S. planes had bombed what remained of the country to bits.

A few people disputed Putnam's version of history, drawing attention to the one hundred thousand Japanese Americans interned during World War II, the abundant racist stereotypes of wartime U.S. popular culture, the horrendous firebomb and atomic attacks by the government, and hypermasculinist, racist, anti-immigrant sentiments amongst "the greatest generation," let alone its shameful profit-making role for latter-day U.S. anchormen turned historians (Sanbonmatsu 2001). Journalist Katha Pollitt, in particular, had the bad taste to inquire whether Putnam was referring to "certified heterosexual, Supreme-Being-believing Scouts . . . and certified harmless and chivalrous hitchhiking GIs, too—not some weirdo in uniform who cuts you to bits on a dark road" (2001, 10). But the federal government heeded Putnam more than these critics, and established the USA Freedom Corps and the Corporation for National and Community Service to tie patriotism and homeland defense to volunteerism (Westheimer and Kahne 2004a, 244).

Putnam dates the moment when things began unraveling in his suburban idyll to 1965, but does not stress the treble significance of that period: the dramatic buildup of U.S. troops in Vietnam, the opening of U.S. borders to migrants of color via amendments to the Immigration and Nationality Act, and inner-city race rebellions. In his halcyon early 1960s era, 75 percent of the immigrant U.S. population was white. Four decades on, 15 percent is white, as a consequence of the imperial war in Vietnam and attendant refugee relocation; Europe becoming a destination rather than a source of migration; and NAFTA/TLC devastating the Mexican economy (Mosisa 2002, 4; Massey 2003, 144–45).

Immigration is surely the key to the disquiet expressed by Putnam and the other professors lite. Political theorist Bonnie Honig (1998) has shown that immigrants have long been *the* limit case for loyalty, as per Ruth the Moabite in the Torah/Old Testament. Such figures are both perilous for the sovereign state (where does their fealty lie?) and symbolically essential (as the only citizens who make a deliberate decision to swear allegiance to an otherwise mythic social contract). In the United States, immigrants are crucial to the nation's foundational ethos of consent, for they represent alienation from origins and endorsement of destinations. This makes achieving and sustaining national culture all the more fraught. The memory of what has been lost, even if by choice, is strong and so is the necessity to shore up "preferences" expressed for U.S. norms.

Rights accorded to the citizen are designed to generate popular assent to governance—"everybody is meant to belong" (Castles and Davidson 2000, vii). But within the NICL, cosmopolitans search for "flexible citizenship" (Ong 1999, 112–13), acting as, according to the Right, "defiant refusniks"

(Rieder 2003: 39). This strategic making-do seeks access to rights while evading responsibilities. Instrumental migration frequently alienates those who expect citizens to have an affective, nonsectarian relationship with the state, rather than what neoliberalism derides as free riding. Alternatively, such actions might be regarded by institutionalist political science as exemplary instances of interest-group pluralism, or lauded by neoclassical economics as market-style shopping! Capital and the state may embrace in equal measure the footloose neoliberal subject who is flexible, and the mobile multicultural subject who is tolerant; but both can become very panicky about loss of national fealty. This is an increasing tension between neoconservatives and paleoconservatives versus neoliberals (Aleinikoff 2000, 132, 145; Vigoda and Golembiewski 2001, 276; Mitchell 2003).

Another possibility is that immigrants lack affective investment because "they cannot take control of the levers" to change host societies (Seaford 2001, 107). Consider the situation of those who, because of changed socioeconomic conditions, shift from the status of pariahs to migrant citizens. For example, excluding and brutalizing Asians was critical to white Australian citizenship and national identity throughout the twentieth century until Asian economic power emerged in the 1970s. Asian Australians' latter-day take on citizenship is, not surprisingly, instrumental. Many are concerned with rights, and do not feel patriotic (Ip et al. 1997), while the Association of Southeast Asian Nations (ASEAN) refuses Australia membership. In the U.K., a third of minority citizens "do not think of themselves as British" (Seaford 2001, 107), and the United States continues to wrestle with having denied most people in the world the chance to become citizens for three-quarters of its history because of their race, gender, and nationality. This differentiation continues today, along ideological lines. Cuban refugees are urged to use U.S. public institutions, but Mexican immigrants are discouraged from doing so. The alibi is the notion of the deserving versus the undeserving, manifested in terms of those who are determined escapees from tyranny versus poor managers of desire. One gets welfare and love, the other exile and loathing (Tienda 2002; Horton 2004; Downing and Husband 2005, 26).

Liberal philosophy has long held that the integration of migrants would follow from the acquisition of citizenship and a nondiscriminatory, culture-blind application of the law, once successive generations mastered the dominant language and entered the labor market as equals with the majority. The patent failure to achieve this outcome has seen governments recognizing cultural difference, intervening to counter discrimination in the private sector, and imposing quotas for minority hiring (Kymlicka 2000, 725). This produces a reaction from neoliberalism and conservatism against such state participation, on economic and nationalist grounds. The backlash was evident in opposition to affirmative action across the 1990s, and a rejection even of the idea of citizens as consumers of government services. Instead, they should be taught to serve the nation for free (Vigoda and Golembiewski 2001). This is a case where the model of self-governance through intelligent consumption and a properly ordered life encounters the idea of service to the nation and the unequal distribution of rights. An example is New-Labour socio-lapdog Anthony Giddens' claim that "ethnic divisions and identity conflicts" characterize locales where "civil society is too strong," and that increased racism correlates with increased migrant labor (Giddens and Hutton 2000b, 18; Back et al. 2002, 445).

Trevor Phillips warns against hyperrelativism from his position as head of Britain's Commission for Racial Equality. He rejects the idea that "we tolerate any old nonsense because it's part of their culture," while Chancellor of the Exchequer Gordon Brown has announced that there is no need to keep apologizing for colonialism (quoted in *Economist* 2004k, 26; Ahmed 2005). In similar vein, the Malaysian Government forces teenage Indians, Malays, and Chinese to intermingle, via a National Service program designed to make summer camp racially integrative (*Economist* 2004c, 44). The United Nations Development Programme allows that "cultural liberty" necessitates "choosing one's own identity" as part of "leading a full life," and thereby embarking on a complex dialectic between the maintenance of tradition and the invention of consumerism. These forms of relativism and liberalism inexorably buy into market-based selfhood, in that lonely hour of the last purchase (2004, 1, 4–5, 11).

Cultural studies scholar David Birch maintains that the discourse of pan-Asian "values" was invented by authoritarian leaders in Southeast Asia across the 1970s and 1980s to protect oligarchies threatened by the popular cultural corollaries of international capitalism and their message of social transcendence (1998a and 1998b). This explains why ASEAN calls for "a united response to the phenomenon of cultural globalization in order to protect and advance cherished Asian values and traditions which are being threatened by the proliferation of Western media content" in its Bangkok Declaration, arguing that human rights can only be applied with reference to "history, culture and religious backgrounds" (quoted in Chadha and Kavoori 2000, 417 and Parekh 2000, 136). For states caught between the desire to manage representations and languages along national, racial, and religious lines, *pace* financial commitments to internationalism, "Asian values" became a distinctive means of policing the populace. The U.S. support for human execution is similar. Human execution is considered barbaric in virtually every democracy in the world and its advocacy in the U.S. is clearly part of religious fundamentalism and racial aggression given its inefficacy as a deterrent, its spurious constitutionality, and its racially marked application (Sarat 2001).

Consider the Salman Rushdie case. Rushdie was sentenced to death in absentia by Iran, a country of which he was not a citizen and in which he had not been tried for any crime, because of *The Satanic Verses*, a book he had written and published elsewhere. Should Iran respect the universalist claims of individualistic human rights discourse? Should liberals respect the universalist claims of collectivist Islamic dignity discourse? The problems multiply with religions such as Buddhism, Confucianism, and Hinduism, which are atextual and nontranscendent by contrast with Islam, Christianity, and Judaism, because reincarnation and family values trump the notion of life as an individual project (Brown 2000, 200, 206).

Beyond bizarre superstitions, a crucial issue, for both ghost-fearing, god-bothering Gringos and simpler, secular souls, is the practical management of differences within populations. In other words, can they refuse what ethnomethodologists call Membership Categorization Devices (MCDs) such as "we" or "everyone"? The appearance in multiracial societies of people who operate like code switchers brings into question the power of MCDs to describe people in their totality. The idea that culture is a private realm that can and should be set aside in public, other than through commodities, seems impractical, while an absolute opposition between cultural and individual rights is untenable (Roy 2001). Consider these examples that control or channel difference:

- Sikhs object to British school-uniform rules and legislation against the carrying of concealed knives, and British and Canadian laws regarding motorcycle helmets and construction-industry hard hats, because of their ritual requirement to wear turbans and bear arms, and their claim that turbans provide protection from head injuries. They also protest French prohibitions on distinctive religious signage, on the grounds that the ban is cultural whereas headgear is spiritual.
- Jewish men in the U.S. military demand exemptions from dress codes and don the yarmulke in obeisance to god.
- British Muslims, Jews, and U.S. Santerias seek permission to slaughter animals by bleeding them to death, thereby adhering to ancient lore and violating laws that apply to others.
- The French NGO Soulidarieta provides pork soup to the homeless because it only wants to aid "compatriots and European homeless people."

- U.S. Afghanis claim that kissing the genitals of children is customary.
- Gypsies/Romas/Travelers/Gitanos/the Tzigane/the Rom insist that their children spend less time in school than other U.K. residents, because of the group's peripatetic norms.
- Indian women's groups and orthodox Hindus call on the courts to decide between struggles over the practice of Sati, whereby women are burnt to death at the funerals of their husbands.
- Amish in the United States and Mennonites in Canada school their own children from puberty to restrain intercultural sex, and the Supreme Court and Congress exempt the Amish from child labor laws.
- Native Americans limit their own access to Supreme Court redress against tribal decisions under the Bill of Rights, out of respect for native-council patriarchy.
- British Hindus request the authority to immerse the ashes of their dead in rivers
- Ethiopian Zionist Copts claim an exemption from U.S. antimarijuana laws on the grounds of ceremonial obligations.
- French Muslim girls protest being sent home for wearing *foulards* to school, which they regard as a dereliction of duty.
- Citizens donate their organs exclusively to people of a particular race.
- Expatriates from Gambia, Egypt, Mali, Sierra Leone, Sudan, and Somalia continue female circumcision in host nations that ban it (but may allow male circumcision).
- The Nisga'a of British Columbia petition the Canadian state to disenfranchise non-Nisga'a from voting there.*

Here is the double bind: should cultures be protected from *external* oppression *and* their members protected from *internal* oppression when fundamental human rights are compromised in the name of culture, religion, or whatever? Grand narratives of collectivity and individualism collide. The state must double-declutch between support for "a community of individuals and a community of communities" (James Johnson 2000, 406, 408; Runnymede Trust Commission 2000, 176–77, 240). In place of MCD compulsion, we find "voluntary self-ascription," whereby people can opt out of des-

*Kymlicka 1995, 31, 38–39, 41; Barry 2001, 38, 40–41, 60–61; Das 2002, 107–17; *Economist* 2004a; Benhabib 2002, 12; Sandford 2005; Tripathi 2003, 129; Asad 2005; Winthrop 2002; Parekh 2000, 243, 245; Schweder et al. 2002; Jenson and Papillon 2001.

ignations that they find oppressive. The retention of a norm may become a means of preventing cultural change and individual autonomy. This leads to many complex limit cases. For example, a British woman rejects her Muslim parents' plans for an arranged marriage, and her parents seek intervention by the state in the name of cultural maintenance, citing Sikh helmet-safety exemptions as a precedent. Here is a case where measures designed to protect minorities from outside harassment in fact insulate them from internal dissent, with the state policing religious observance and familial power dynamics (Benhabib 2002, 19; Kymlicka 1995, 2, 35–36). How can the *New York Times* reconcile its seemingly absolute support for protecting indigenous people from "cultural extinction" with its ringing denunciations of ritualized West African female slavery in religious shrines? To do so, it must place a premium on individual freedom over cultural maintenance, problematizing its faith in MCDs. Similar quandaries are evoked when the National Rifle Association takes up the cudgels (or whatever weapons are at hand) on behalf of resident aliens when Congress proposes limiting the right to own guns to citizens. Minority discourse is not always used for progressive ends. South African apartheid was justified as a defense of minorities, while Nazi Germany said it invaded Czechoslovakia and Poland to protect the rights of ethnic Germans living there. The Nazi claim was a key reason for human rights advocates of the 1940s basing new international covenants on individualism rather than collective identity. More recently, as states have crumpled and multiplied in the wake of the Cold War, identity politics in favor of cultural difference have become key resources for such right-wing formations as the *Front National* in France, *Vlaams Blok* in Belgium, the Danish People's Party, Italy's *Lega Nord*, the People's Party of Austria, and Northern Irish ultra-Unionists. Right-wingers have appropriated calls from U.S. and Australian native peoples for their respective governments to evaluate public policy proposals via cultural-impact statements, as per their environmental-impact equivalents. So where progressives seek an assessment of what impact marine bases or observatories might have on their lives, reactionaries seek an assessment of what same-sex marriage or politicized art might have on theirs. Cultural defenses have been mobilized to exonerate a Chinese American man who murdered his wife for adultery, a Japanese American woman who murdered her children, also for adultery, and a Hmong man who abducted and raped a Laotian American woman. In each case, the assailants argued they were acting in accordance with their cultures of origin (James Johnson 2000, 405, 410; Aleinikoff 2000, 161; Thio 2002; Downey and Murdock 2003, 71; Downing and Husband 2005, 76; Benhabib 2002, 87–89; Sproat 1998; Nakai 2003). Cultures make trouble when they collide.

THE SEVEN FORMATIONS

> Although marches, religious services, and political advocacy were
> important aspects of [César] Chávez's work, such activities do not
> constitute allowable activities under this grant. . . . Prohibited activities
> include: lobbying, marches, petitions, participating in events or activities
> that include advocacy legislation or party platforms.
>   —California state guidelines for support of community service to mark
>   César Chávez Day (quoted in Westheimer and Kahne 2004a, 244)

These complex politics form the backdrop to cultural citizenship. The following are seven key formations that have theorized the phenomenon, each with strong links to the public sphere.

First, cultural studies sociologist Tony Bennett and colleagues in the Anglo-Australian cultural-policy studies movement focus on a guaranteed set of competences that governments should give citizens through "both the provision of cultural facilities and the regulation of cultural industries," across all aspects of artistic capital (Chaney 2002, 168). Bennett favors an uplift and dissemination that respects popular knowledge, borrowing from the liberal *donnée* that the most effective form of government rules via free individuals, who are given the skills to live both autonomously and socially. His primary interlocutors are the cultural bureaucracies of Australia and the Council of Europe, and his admirers include progressives in search of influence beyond effective protest and critique (Meredyth and Minson 2000; Bennett 1998 and 2001; Miller and Yúdice 2004). Skeptical of ludic protest against the state and capital, Bennett nevertheless recognizes that social-movement identities must be acknowledged by the modern liberal state. This line buys into the economic opportunities delivered by globalization *and* the need for local heritage to both counter and participate in it.

Second, Chicano anthropologist Renato Rosaldo and colleagues in Californian, Texan, and New York Chicano/a, Tejano/a, ethnic, and Latino/a studies seek vernacular rights for U.S. minorities, in order to "establish a distinct social space" through a combination of self-incorporation into the United States, and the maintenance and development of a separate heritage and identity (Flores and Benmayor 1997b, 1–2). Their primary interlocutors are Chicano/a and Latino/a social movements, their admirers include the *Fresno Bee*, and many of their ideas were promoted in the *New York Times* as part of debates about multiculturalism in universities (Rosaldo 1997; Flores and Benmayor 1997a; Rodriguez and Gonzales 1995; *New York Times* 1990). Rosaldo sees cultural citizenship as a "deliberate oxymoron" that bridges difference and sameness in calling for economic and political equality, on the joint grounds of maintaining identity and exercising "full membership" in the wider community (1994, 402). He claims that the difficulty with encouraging minority groups in the United States to vote, and the low levels of naturalization for non-Asian minority immigrants* can be addressed by promoting multiple affinities, to "former" languages, places, or norms, *and* to adopted countries. This kind of thinking is enshrined in the Indian Constitution which enforces a common criminal code, but regulates civil law through minority cultures—a legacy from thousands of years during which the Dharmashastra governed via collective identities rather than individual entitlements (Parekh 2000, 191; Das 2002, 85; Beteille 1999). It also informs UNESCO's Institute for Education, which emphasizes collective as much as individual human rights, and regards cultural citizenship as a development from, and antidote to, assimilationist ideals (1999).

Third, Canadian-based political theorist Will Kymlicka and a number of slightly heterodox Anglo-American colleagues seek a rapprochement between majority white settlement, "immigrant multiculturalism"—newer voluntary migrants, who deserve few cultural rights,—and "minority nationalism,"—First Peoples, the dispossessed, and the enslaved, who deserve many. The notion of culture as an aid to individual autonomy through engagement with collective as well as individual histories is the means of attaining this commingling. The position is in keeping with Canada's backdrop as the first commonwealth country to establish its own citizenship system, and as an official practitioner of multiculturalism since 1971. Kymlicka's admirers include the *Wall Street Journal*; the United Nations Development Programme, where he served as principal consultant for its 2004 venture into culture; and the UN's chief expert on indigenous peoples, Rodolfo Stavenhagen, whose keynote address at the 2003 Congreso Internacional de Americanistas, on moving from the status of indigeneity to cultural citizenship, indexed Kymlicka's influence (Kymlicka 1995 and 2000; Jenson and Papillon 2001; Zachary 2000; United Nations Development Programme 2004; *Spanish Newswire Services* 2003).

Other interlocutors include states dealing with ethnic minorities. When the Soviet Union broke up into nearly twenty countries, Moscow was content to see twenty-five million ethnic Russians remain in what it refers to as "the near abroad" (Rich 2003). The newly formed republics had two choices in dealing with these sizeable and often wealthy minorities: propound a retributive cultural nationalism that marginalized the Russian language and set reli-

---

*In the 1990s, 57.6% of Asian immigrants became U.S. citizens, versus 32.2% of Latino/as (Aleinikoff 2000, 130).

gious, racial, and linguistic criteria for citizenship,* or adopt a pragmatic civic policy that offered entitlements based on territory, fealty, and labor.† Those republics that chose the former option are now trying to defuse the resultant conflicts via Russian-language schools and cultural groups—courtesy of a Kymlicka consultancy. At the same time, they are changing their cultural image, abjuring the nomenclature "Baltic" and "post-Soviet" in favor of "Scandinavian" and "pre-European Union." Needless to say, they are "encouraged" to incorporate Russian minorities by the prospect of E.U. membership and money via adherence to the European Convention on Nationality (Tiryakian 2003, 22; Laitin 1999, 314–17; Zachary 2000; van Ham 2001, 4; Bauböck 2005, 2–3, 5; but see also Feldman 2005).

Where Rosaldo *et al.* seek to transform citizenship in the interests of those marginalized by the majority, Bennett *et al.* and Kymlicka *et al.* utilize it for a general purpose that takes account of minorities. For Rosaldo, U.S. culture is distinguished by Latino/a disenfranchisement. Cultural difference substantively trumps formal universalism, and it is not good enough to follow the standard arms-length approach of liberal philosophy, whereby state institutions adopt a neutral stance on cultural maintenance. Rosaldo is critical of neoliberalism and liberal philosophy for their myths of the acultural sovereign individual; both in fact assume a shared language and culture as the basis of government. Liberal philosophy's brand of "civic nationalism" involves an allegiance not merely to the state, but to images of nationhood that stretch across public and private realms (Runnymede Trust Commission 2000, 19, 36). Kymlicka thinks along similar lines, but endorses liberalism as a matter of justice and self-interest, provided that states protect minorities. For Bennett, culture is a set of tools for living. Each tool derives its value from the achievement of a specific purpose, rather than being an expressive end unto itself. He understands government to be a project of constituting, not drawing upon, the liberal individual, and is agnostic about its sovereign individual claims. Bennett and Kymlicka's cosmopolitan approaches remain rooted pragmatically in the nation, because it is assumed to provide a boundary of fealty that can appeal to the better sentiments of its inhabitants.

The fourth theoretical formation, vocalized by the philosopher Amélie Oksenberg Rorty, is a neoliberal capture of the first three positions. In her view, cultural maintenance and development should be by-products of the universal access to education, a "primary condition of free and equal citizen participation in public life" (Rorty 1995). Rorty opposes public funding to sustain

---

*Estonia and Latvia did do this, relegating Russians from "setting the cultural agenda of the public sphere" to "the private/communal" one.
†Such was done in Ukraine and Kazakhstan.

familial or religious cultural norms, instead calling for a curriculum that will generate flexible cosmopolitans who learn about their country and its "global neighbors" (1995, 162, 164; also see Stevenson 2003). Rorty's argument is a culturalist restatement of human capital *nostra* about individuals maximizing their utility through investment in skills. This recalls Bennett's mandate for citizens to learn a set of cultural competences. Rorty rejects cross-cultural awareness as a necessary component of good citizenship and justice, but endorses it as good business sense (Runnymede Trust Commission 2000, 234). This is in line with the United Nations Development Programme, which argues that "culturally diverse societies" are necessary preliminaries to the eradication of poverty, rather than a nice afterglow (2004, v). Clearly, Rorty's instrumental approach may lead to cultural erasure, for all its cosmopolitanism.

All of these ideologies are engaged by the fifth key formation of cultural citizenship—the U.K. Runnymede Trust Commission's report on *The Future of a Multi-Ethnic Britain* (2000). The commission's chair was the political theorist and future member of the House of Lords, Bhikhu Parekh. Its secondary public face in the U.K. media was his fellow commissioner, Stuart Hall. The commission examined racism within national institutions of culture, education, policing, and welfare. Reactions to their work reveal how deep cultural conflicts run within citizenship. It was called "'Sub-Marxist gibberish'; 'out-of-touch nonsense'; [and] 'an insult to our history and intelligence'" (*Independent* 2000). The authors were accused of having "a lack of loyalty and affection for Britain" (Parekh 2001). The *Daily Mail* reacted by producing a "list of ten dead white heroes of the last millennium" (Seaford 2001, 108). William Hague, the then leader of the Conservative Party, derided the *Report* as an index of the Left's "tyranny of political correctness and . . . assault on British culture and history" (2000, 28), while *The Scotsman* referred to it as "a grotesque libel against the people of this land and a venomous blueprint for the destruction of our country" (Warner 2000). Jack Straw, the then Home Secretary and later a notorious warmonger in Afghanistan and Iraq, rejected the linkage of Britishness to white racism (Back et al. 2002, 447). This indicates how much can be at stake in these debates, beyond Bennett's technical specifications of cultural-policy interventions, Rosaldo's feel-good vernacular multiculturalism, Kymlicka's attempt to "get along" in newly free, newly chauvinistic postsocialist environments, or Rorty's faith in an inclusive curriculum animated by enlightened self-interest.

That becomes clearer still in the sixth formation, which addresses the limits of neoliberalism. Amy Chua, a lawyer operating from a comparative ethnic-studies perspective—and publishing with an U.S. trade house, rather than an academic press—investigates in a global frame, the intersection of neoliberalism, ethnic-minority economic oligarchies, and democracy. She probes what happens when wealthy minorities confront popular backlashes against their economic power via majoritarian rejection of cultural difference. While the economy enriches "the market-dominant minority, democratization increases the political voice and power of the frustrated majority" (2003, 124). As Chua puts it, provocatively and with the clear regret of a fan of both capitalism and democracy, this is about the conundrum "that turns free market democracy into an engine of ethnic conflagration" (2003, 6). Her work details the way indigenous majorities protest their weakness. Class, corruption, and race jumble together, as "market-dominant minorities, along with their foreign-investor partners, invariably come to control the crown jewels of the economy . . . oil in Russia and Venezuela, diamonds in South Africa, silver and tin in Bolivia, jade, teak, and rubies in Burma" (2003, 10). Free markets concentrate *wealth dis*proportionately, while democracies concentrate *politics pro*portionately. Political enfranchisement and its economic opposite are mediated through cultural difference, with the outcome revolutionary. The horrors of Rwanda and the former Yugoslavia in the 1990s illustrate what happens when ethnonationalist populism draws on majority resentment to quash minority economic power, based on cultural difference (2003, 11–13, 16–17).

The seventh, and most powerful, formation derives from the work of Middle Eastern historian and professional anti-Palestinian, Bernard Lewis and Cold War political scientist, Vietnam War architect, and English-only advocate, Samuel Huntington. In the post-Soviet 1990s, these two men turned to culture for geopolitical explanations. Lewis coined the expression "clash of civilizations" to capture the difference, as he saw it, between the separation of church and state which had generated the successes of the United States, versus their interrelated position in Islamic nations, which had produced those countries' subordinate status (1990). Forget Yanqui support of authoritarian antidemocrats and coups that furthered oil exploitation—Islamic ressentiment is all about the United States insisting that Caesar get *his* due, and god *his*. Huntington appropriated the "clash of civilizations" to argue that future world historical conflicts would not be "primarily ideological or primarily economic" but "cultural" (1993, 22). This dematerializes politics—and most specifically, excuses the policies and programs of the United States government and corporations as only broadly relevant to its internationally loathed position.

The "clash twins" grotesque generalizations have gained immense attention over the past decade, notably since September 11, 2001. In the United States, Huntington's Olympian grandiosity was lapped up by the bourgeois media, ever-ready to embrace "a cartoon-like world where Popeye and Bluto bash each other" (Said 2001). Journalists promote the notion of an apocalyptic struggle between good and evil as the bifurcation of the United States and Islam, plundering Lewis and Huntington on the differences between Western and Islamic culture. Across the daily press and the weekly and monthly magazines of ruling opinion, extrastate violence is attributed to Islam's opposition to freedom and technology, but never as the act of subordinated groups against dominant ones. The *New York Times* and *Newsweek* gave Huntington room to account for what had happened in terms of his "thesis," while others took up the logic as a call for empire, from the supposed New Left (*Dissent* magazine and other progressives who share this common Yanqui blind spot on the region) to leading communitarians and the neoliberal *Economist*. After the attacks, Arab leaders met to discuss the impact of the Lewis-Huntington conceit, and Italian Prime Minister Silvio Berlusconi invoked it. As the U.S. occupation of Iraq entered its third year, military commanders and senior noncommissioned officers were required to read the book, along with V. S. Naipaul and *Islam for Dummies* (Rusciano 2003; Said 2001; Schmitt 2005).

Not everyone was so taken with these ideas. UNESCO's Director General prefaced the organization's worthy Declaration on Cultural Diversity with a specific rebuttal (Matsuura 2001). *El País'* cartoonist Máximo traumatically constructed the dialog alongside the tumbling Towers: "Choque de ideas, de culturas, de civilizaciones' [Clash of ideas, of cultures, of civilizations] with the reply "choques de desesperados contra instalados" [the clash of the desperate against the establishment] (quoted in García Canclini 2002, 16). Israel's *Ha-aretz* regarded the Lewis-Huntington thesis' "hegemonic hold" as "a major triumph" for Al Qaeda, and the *Arab News* aptly typified it as "Armageddon dressed up as social science" (quoted in Rusciano 2003, 175). Study after study has disproven Lewis and Huntington's wild assertions about growing ethnic tension since the Cold War, and a unitary Islamic culture opposed to a unitary "West." Such claims fatally neglect conflicts over money, property, and politics (Fox 2002; Norris and Inglehart 2003, 203; United Nations Development Programme 2004). The clash-of-civilizations thesis does not work if you apply it to Iran supporting Russia against Chechen rebels, or India against Pakistan, or the U.S. attitude to the Iran-Iraq War. But why bother with world-historical details when you are offered "international relations with politics taken out" (Abrahamian 2003 535)?

Huntington's later critiques of *hispano hablantes* in the United States (2004) led to support from the Center for Immigration Studies and the battery of influential pop-policy intellectuals whose scholarship lay long behind them, if it ever amounted to much. The chorus includes: Cold Warrior Zbigniew Brzezinski, old-school area studies founder Lucian Pye, Nixon and Reagan servant and advocate of severe punishments James Q. Wilson, reactionary *Newsweek* journalist Fareed Zakaria, and the agile cultural citizens of vdare.com, self-appointed keepers of the flame for a lost tribe of Yanqui whiteness (Krikorian 2004; Ajami et al. 2004; Brimelow 2005).

The awkward fact that just 21 percent of third-generation Latino/as identify with their countries of origin, that most U.S.-born Latino/as have much more conservative views on immigration than recent arrivals, and that third-generation Latino/as are predominantly monolingual English speakers must be left out for this nonsense to flourish. Furthermore, Huntington's beloved early settlers, whose ethos is supposedly central to the United States, were wrapped up in burning witches, haranguing adulteresses, and wearing foppish clothing and wigs (*Hispanic Fact Pack* 2005, 50; Alba 2004; Lomnitz 2005). The argument is morally, pragmatically, and empirically wrong, but it *is* cultural.

CONCLUSION

> Los derechos culturales incluyen la libertad de participar en la actividad cultural, hablar el idioma de elección, enseñar a sus hijos la lengua y la cultura propias, identificarse con las comunidades culturales elegidas, descubrir toda la gama de culturas que componen la herencia mundial, conocer los derechos humanos, tener acceso a la educación, estar exento de ser representado sin consentimiento o de tolerar que el propio espacio cultural sea usado para publicidad, y obtener ayuda pública para salvaguardar estos derechos.
>
> [Cultural rights include the freedom to participate in cultural activity, speak in the language of one's choice, school one's children in their own language and culture, identify with cultural communities as desired, discover the entire gamut of cultures that comprise our world heritage, resist accepting or tolerating one's culture being commodified, and obtain help from the state to safeguard these rights.]
> —George Yúdice (2002, 36)

Liberal ideals still expect minorities to throw off prior loyalties in order to become citizens. In order to join with nationals of their new countries, immigrants and their descendants are to put aside social divisions in favor of the common interest. Liberal philosophy, conservatism, and neoliberalism assume that people emerge into citizenship as fully formed, sovereign individuals with personal preferences. Multiculturalism, by contrast, anticipates that group loyalties override nationalism and individualism. Yet, it assumes, like liberal philosophy and neoliberalism, that this subjectivity is ordained *prior* to politics

(Shafir 1998, 10–11). In one formation, the individual emerges into the bright light of liberal rationality. In another, she emerges into the bright light of cultural belonging. Both sides also anticipate and require a protean subject—consumers must stand ready to adapt and change in their flexible identities as workers, and multiculturalists in their flexible identities as citizens.* One disaffected former staffer of the Runnymede Trust Commission said of its recommendations that "two-thirds concern the interests of middle-class professionals . . . If we tackle racism then the whole community could, like members of the Commission itself, become part of the bourgeoisie" (Seaford 2001, 112). In other words, the national narrative—who speaks for whom—was on the table for debate, but the economy was not. Difference trumped production as the axis of thought and entitlement (Delanty 2002).

The seven formations of cultural citizenship listed above have all proven influential, but all of them neglect the political economy of cultural citizenship in favor of its political technology. We need to combine the two. The economy must be problematized in discussions of cultural citizenship so that motors of injustice and inequality can be exposed through struggles enacted over the bodies of venerable citizens and pesky consumers. Secondly, the dominant formations do not address the media, particularly television, with sufficient precision or emphasis. The media are present, seemingly, to generate or retard political participation as defined through knowledge of parliamentary democracy, policy processes, and the judiciary, but not in ways that acknowledge the media's place at the heart of neoliberalism, nationalism, and social movements. The cultural Left pays a price when its dreams of governmental and commercial recognition come true, but are materialized with Samuel Huntington carried aloft rather than Stuart Hall—culturalism triumphant. The freedom to participate in culture is contingent on both freedom from prohibition *and* freedom to act via political, economic, and media capacities. The studies that follow are animated by that insight.

*I owe this formulation to Dana Polan.

2

TELEVISION TERROR

Being Ignorant, Living in Manhattan

> George Bush is the President, he makes the decisions, and, you know,
> as just one American, [if] he wants me to line up, just tell me where.
> —Dan Rather, CBS News anchor September 17, 2001
> (quoted in Navasky 2002, xv)

> Television is equivalent to a campfire in the days . . . [when] the
> wagon trains were making their way westward and there was a
> catastrophe on the trail. Some people pulled the wagons around, and
> sat down and discussed what was going on and tried to understand it.
> —Peter Jennings, ABC News anchor regarding domestic
> coverage of September 11, 2001
> (quoted in Zelizer and Allan 2002b, 3–4)

> Here's the rub: America is at war against people it doesn't know,
> because they don't appear much on TV.
> —Indian novelist Arundhati Roy regarding the invasion of
> Afghanistan (2001)

I N THE QUOTATIONS ABOVE, Dan Rather's jingoism is matched only by Peter Jennings' twee reference to dispossession. Roy tragically contextualizes their ignorance. Together, these remarks indicate the bizarre blend of hyperemotionalism and mythic folksiness that substitute for critical analysis in mainstream U.S. television. Ironically, some U.S. media professionals acclaimed Rather's words as signs of a renewal of journalism. His bellicose calls for retributive violence, just moments after the attacks on the Northeastern United States, were quickly echoed by NBC's Tom Brokaw (Zelizer and Allan 2002b, 5; Eisman 2003, 57–58). This chapter explains Rather's and Jennings' banal but dangerous comments in the context of U.S. media coverage of the terrorist actions and subsequent

---

*Victor Navasky, Forward to *Journalism after September 11*, ed. Barbie Zelizer and Stuart Allan (London: Routledge, 2002).

Yanqui invasions of Afghanistan and Iraq. It explores what happens when explanations such as the clash of civilizations, triumph, and changes to the political economy of television deracinate the medium itself. The U.S. populace and media are far from being shocked into chauvinism, and the period since the fall of 2001 has been just a blip in the tendencies outlined in the introduction to this book. For a moment after September 11, foreign news mattered. But Fox News' Roger Ailes, who doubled as an adviser to Bush Minor on foreign policy, described the cable network's new method of covering global stories in this helpful way: "We basically sent hit teams overseas" (*New Yorker* 2001). The resultant ignorance reached its apogee when talk-TV host Bill O'Reilly chillingly referred to Islamic fundamentalism as "the enemy of the US" (June 15, 2002) without defining his terms via either the adjective or the noun or engaging Hindu and Christian fundamentalism and the reigns of terror they have perpetrated. O'Reilly described required collegiate reading of the Koran as equivalent to assigning *Mein Kampf* during World War II (Alterman 2003, 37), and called on the government to "bomb the Afghan infrastructure to rubble—the airport, the power plants, their water facilities and the roads. . . . We should not target civilians, but if they don't rise up against this criminal government, they starve, period" (September 17, 2001). Fox News described the Taliban as "rats," "terror goons," and "psycho Arabs," (quoted in Thussu 2003, 127) and during the invasion of Iraq, O'Reilly identified UN Secretary-General Kofi Annan as "a villain" (April 24, 2003). Clearly, this was not about in-depth reportage—or reportage at all—but position taking as a form of entertainment. Leslie Moonves of CBS explained that entertainment dominates news. "As you get further away from September 11th, that will revert back to normal" (quoted in *New Yorker* 2001). Sure enough, the Project for Excellence in Journalism revealed that TV news coverage of national and international issues fell by 33 percent from October 2001 to March 2002, as celebrity and lifestyle issues took precedence over discussion of the various parts of the world that the United States directly and indirectly rules and controls (2002).

Part of what follows was written for an International Association for Media and Communication Research conference in Barcelona. Our panel looked at three events of world-historical significance that occurred on September 11:

- In 1714, the loss of an independent Barcelona, when invasion brought an end to the War of Succession.
- In 1973, the loss of a democratic Chile, when a *golpe* unseated Salvador Allende's government and killed three thousand people.
- In 2001, the loss of the World Trade Center in New York City, when terrorism also killed three thousand people.

The history of September 11 has other significance. On that day in 1978 at Camp David, Maryland, Egypt became a client state of the United States and gave up any sense of looking out for Palestinian interests. In 1990, George H. W. Bush announced the attack on Iraq, which led to the deaths of two hundred thousand people (Ahmad 2003, 15). The United States is a dangerous country, associated with deadly events on this ghastly, ghostly date.

We restricted ourselves at the conference to what was manageable. The three events we investigated had more in common than chronological coincidence. They all shared a violent loss of life and the introduction or solidification of regimes of domination, but had different historical and methodological frames. My colleagues on the panel, Jaume Guillamet and Patricio Bernedo, addressed the two earlier moments, respectively, through a combination of political history and content analysis. In the case of 1714, we know enough about the consequences of the event to assign it a full historical significance, even as we see its effects on everyday life in Catalunya, Spain. But primary documents, sources of memory and testimony, are not as readily available. For its part, 1973 still has many surreptitious aspects—understanding what it meant for Latin American politics, identifying the role of the United States, and deciphering truth from falsehood in the actions of the perpetrators who are still alive. The documents and the memory are there, but so is the guilt, and hence the obstructionism. By contrast, 2001 is very close to our own time. There is almost too much information available—a vast array of testimony, and an unparalleled media archive of a highly specific event. But the *significance* of that event is unclear; hence the need for interpretation, and hence this chapter's title. Many of us who were in Manhattan in 2001 seem to understand very little. We are cultural citizens adrift. In search of reliable navigation, this chapter looks at the history of U.S. state violence, the experience of September 11, coverage of the invasions of Afghanistan and Iraq and their casualties, the role of intellectuals, and alternatives to mainstream media.

CHILE?

Americans are leading busy lives, and sometimes they don't have the opportunity to read a story or listen to an entire broadcast. But if they can have an instant understanding of what the president is talking about by seeing 60 seconds of television, you accomplish your goals.
    —Dan Bartlett, White House communications director (quoted in Bumiller 2003)

"I like taxis. I was never good at geography and I learn things by asking the drivers where they come from."

"They come from horror and despair."

"Yes, exactly. One learns about the countries where unrest is occurring by riding the taxis here."

—Don DeLillo (2003, 16)

I remember September 11, 1973. I was in my parents' rented London studio, just after returning from a couple of months in the United States. I turned on the radio and learned of the brutal golpe that, we came to realize, Washington had engineered in order to remove the elected government of the Chilean people. By that time, everyone knew about government venality in Vietnam and Watergate. A combination of the *New York Times* and the *Washington Post* had revealed as much. But the clear and present involvement of the United States in the Chilean coup seemed unlikely to many people who were far removed from the South American nation. It took revelations about the astonishing acts of brutality funded, supported, and undertaken by Washington across Central America throughout the 1970s and 1980s to convince ordinary folks in the United States of something that most of the world had long held as an article of faith—that the Yanqui government and Yanqui corporations take as a self-ascribed divine right that they may intervene in the political economy of the Global South in any way and at any time the United States deems fit.

Those extraordinary revelations made it clear that the United States, as a country that advertised itself as the world's greatest promise of modernity, was dedicated to translating its own national legacy. A nineteenth-century regime of clearance, genocide, and enslavement as much as democracy, the United States built its modernity on brutality, and developed a foreign economic policy with similar effects and methods. The effect on Chile was thousands murdered and tortured, and a so-called economic miracle that was nothing of the kind. Under the democratically elected Allende, the unemployment rate was 4.3 percent. Under the dictator Augusto Pinochet, it reached 22 percent. Real wages decreased by 40 percent and poverty doubled—thanks to the intellectual allies and corporate chiefs affiliated with U.S. foreign and economic policy, freshly minted at University of Chicago graduate seminars in neoliberalism. Their mentor, Milton Friedman, attended the court of Pinochet in the same period as he was being wheeled around Australia and other U.S. client states to preach about deregulation (Palast 2003a, 201; Maira 2002: 83–84).

How could the United States, with its million warriors across four continents, 702 military facilities in 132 sovereign states, battleships in each key ocean, much vaunted desire to mount wars on two international fronts at the same time as ensuring domestic security, and "defense" budget greater than the next twelve biggest budgets put together, claim to have lost its "innocence" on September 11? How many destabilized governments and rigged elections will it take, from Lebanon, Indonesia, Iran, and Vietnam in the 1950s, through Japan, Laos, Brazil, the Dominican Republic, Guatemala, Bolivia, and Chile in the 1960s, Portugal, Australia, and Jamaica in the 1970s, and Central America in the 1980s, before people in the United States realize that they signify as antidemocrats (Carreño 2001; Mann 2003, 20; Eisman 2003, 63; Pinter 2005a; *Economist* 2003a; Sardar and Davies 2002, 110)?

In 2002, the Prime Minister of the Netherlands resigned because it was revealed that the Dutch army had failed to protect residents of Srebrenica seven years earlier. That same year, the United States attempted another golpe in Latin America, this time a failure in Venezuela, with no political impact whatsoever on Washington. Why did Bush Minor not resign after his administration's endorsement of a doomed coup against a democratically elected government? Why was there no congressional investigation of this malfeasance? Foreign-media professionals accustomed to functioning, responsible democracies questioned the lack of media appeals for sanctions against Bush's cabinet and advisors, and why a mere 6 percent of Yanquis even knew that there had been a coup. The reason why the U.S. population was so apathetic and uninformed is because all the major U.S. papers had reported, based on the lies they were told by the State Department, that Venezuelan President Hugo Chávez had resigned. Really, he had been kidnapped by groups funded by Washington DC's front organization, the National Endowment for Democracy, which had some practice at destabilization, from its attempt to destroy the Sandinistas (Osborn and Brown 2002; Kurlantzick 2004; Youngers 2003; Kaitatzi-Whitlock with Kehagia 2004, 143; Pew Charitable Trusts 2002b; Palast 2003b and 2003a, 192–96; Quaccia 2004; Schell 2005). The incident had become one more moment in the United States' convenient ongoing amnesia of its own duplicity and brutality as "a nation that seeks war" (Velvel 2004, 3). It is as if there is a "national Alzheimer's disease," (Turkel 2003) a disorder that nevertheless allows for a powerful embrace of military aggression. Anosognosia reigns, and beyond a neurological term, it is a public condition. When surveys address popular knowledge of U.S. foreign policy, again and again they reveal the incorrect assumption people hold that the state's primary overseas role has been, and continues to be, helping others, either in a selfless way, or one that relates to national security (Lewis 2001, 135, 165). Instead of producing sites where "the invisible can be made culturally discernible" (Beck 1999, 69), media owners and professionals have generated a geopolitically amnesiac readership whose opinions are mined much more than their understanding is developed. Links to the horrendous violence that founded and sustains the United States are lost on the public. Chileans ironically refer to their subjugation as the "little September 11" (quoted in Harvey 2003, 8), because it has been submerged by what happened in New York.

WAKING UP?

A recent poll tells us that one in two Americans now believe Saddam [Hussein] was responsible for the attack on the World Trade Center. But the American public is not merely being misled. It is being browbeaten and kept in a state of ignorance.
—John Le Carré (2003)

Twenty-eight years after the Chilean golpe, I was living in Manhattan. I worked late the night of September 10, 2001, and was awoken the next morning by a plane overhead. This happens sometimes and I have long expected a crash when I've heard the roar of jet engines so close—but I didn't this time. Often when that sound hit me, I would get up and go for a run down by the water, just near Wall Street. Something kept me back that day, and instead of heading for the river, I headed for my laptop. I cannot rely on the local media to tell me very much about cricket, real football, or the role of the United States in world affairs, so I was reading the *Guardian* online when a report about the planes flashed on the screen. I looked up at the calendar above my desk to see whether it was April 1st—April Fool's Day. I was one of the 0.8 percent of U.S. residents who learned of the incident online; 56.3 percent found out from TV. Then, so many people tried to use the Internet to learn what was happening, that major news services saw their servers shut down, and Google was obliged to direct people away from the Web and toward radio and television (UCLA Center for Communication Policy 2002; Pew Internet & American Life Project 2002).

Despite my concerns about the local press, after first reading the story on September 11, I gave myself over to television coverage of the event. I wanted to hear official word and see official action, but the news reports left me unsatisfied. Bush Minor was busy learning to read in Florida, then lead the country through the disaster from Louisiana and Nebraska, not New York. Finally, I went out to meet my friend Ana Dopico. We watched as people leapt from buildings that then collapsed to rubble. I tried to call my daughter in London and my father in Canberra, but to no avail, since the event disabled the phones. Visiting another friend, Jenine Abboushi, I got through to Illinois, and asked an ex-novia there to telephone England and Australia to report on me. Jenine managed to ring her relatives on the West Bank. Israeli tanks had commenced a bombardment there, within the hour that the planes had struck New York. Family members spoke to her from under the kitchen table, where they were taking refuge from the shells falling on their house. Then, I took to the streets again. Everywhere I went I met people with stories. One man had been on the subway when smoke filled the car. He said that no one could breathe properly and people were screaming. His only thought was for his dog DeNiro back in Brooklyn. From the panic of the train, he managed to call his mother on a cell phone and ask her to feed DeNiro that night because it looked like he wouldn't get home. A pregnant woman told me she had feared for her unborn as she fled the blasts while pushing the pram with her baby in it. Apart from these heart-rending tales of strangers, I was filled with dread. I pondered the horrible price would the U.S. government exact for this, and the overt and covert agents and targets of that suffering. What blood lust, what pattern of retaliation and counterretaliation, would this generate? What would become of domestic civil rights and cultural inclusiveness? Where was cultural citizenship now?

In the few days after the airplanes crashed into the World Trade Center, the Pentagon, and the Pennsylvania earth, certainties that had been carelessly assumed were just as carelessly disturbed. The sounds of lower Manhattan, which used to serve as white noise for residents—sirens, screeches, screams—were no longer signs without a referent. Instead, they made folks stare and stop, hurry and hustle, wondering whether the familiar noises were coefficients of a new reality rather than "one of those unexplained events in the sonic backdrop" (Gibson 2003, 135). "Everyone agrees, airliners look different in the sky these days, predatory or doomed" (McEwan 2005, 15). In terms of daily life, this represented a massive shift. Vice President Dick Cheney immediately and repeatedly spoke of the need for war against "40 or 50 countries" (quoted in Ahmad 2003, 16). There was a shift, in the words of the philosopher Leopoldo Zea, from "la Guerra fría a la sucia," from the Cold War to the Dirty War (2001).

In the first days after September 11, 68 percent of the U.S. population understood that the attack was linked to their country's ties to Israel. Within a month, that number had fallen to 22 percent (Abrahamian 2003, 538), as the culturalist ideologues went to work, trotting out the usual shibboleths. U.S. press coverage of terrorism has historically explained terror events as membershipping devices, to the virtual exclusion of social inequality or state-based practices. Terrorism is regarded as a struggle over ideas or feelings, never as political violence against civilians that derives from material causes. The *New York Times*, for example, was intellectually unprepared to report on the phenomenon. Because most terrorism occurred outside the United States prior to 2001, it was not rated as newsworthy. Throughout the 1970s and 1980s, reportage of overseas terror took up less than 0.5 percent of the paper. Additionally, the stereotyping of Arabs and Muslims occasioned by the media's lust for oil and Zion also plays a part in the systematic distortion of terrorism. Leading pundits for CBS News, the *New York Times*, and the *Washington Post*, inter alia, disgraced themselves in 1995 by immediately assuming that Islamists were responsible for bombing the federal building in Oklahoma City (Gerges 2003, 79, 87n9; Love 2003, 248; Schlesinger et al. 1983, 2, 5).

The causes of these failings were profound. In a post-2000 election, on-air conversation with Bush Minor's chief of staff Andy Card, CNN's Judy Woodruff said "we look forward to working with you" (quoted in Solomon 2001b). Such a remark would be unspeakable by a journalist in a functioning democracy, where official sources are starting points for work, not results, and the idea of "working with" a government is seen as "Soviet style" (Massing 2001). But inside the United States, there is a long heritage, dating from the evolution of journalistic codes and norms, of reliance on official sources as tools for monopolistic owners to distract attention from their market domination by proclaiming a nonpartisan professionalism (Clark and McChesney 2001; McChesney 2003; Herman 1999, 83, 87, 158). The White House, the State Department, and the Pentagon are referred to as "the Golden Triangle" by today's journalists (Love 2003, 246). Most U.S. news gathering produces a feedback loop of staggeringly self-interested proportions. Reporters do "research" based on leaks and leads provided by the administration, which in turn quotes the resulting stories as objective correlatives of its own position. Dissident writer and BBC and *Guardian* regular, Greg Palast, puts it this way, "I can't tell you how many reporters I've said, 'Where do you get this stuff?' And they say, 'Well, it was in a State Department press release,' as if that's an acceptable source" (Bosse and Palast 2003). Elsewhere, "It's not the job of a journalist to snap to the attention of generals" (Fisk in Fisk et al. 2003), but journalistic obedience appears to be a qualification in the United States. These quick-fix idées fixes are functions of both a lengthy history and more recent pressures from deregulation and concentration. Keen recruiting by the CIA also plays a role. The organization has paid and encouraged hundreds of U.S. journalists to work for it; approved by their seniors, but hidden from their readers (Boyd-Barrett 2004, 38–39).

Despite the claim that 2001 was a watershed, extensive content analysis discloses that September 11 saw coverage of terrorism differ very minimally from news norms—there was no depth of commentary or significant documentary investigation. A study of articles carried in *US News and World Report* indicates that in the seven months after September 11, explanations for the attacks focused entirely on Al Qaeda and domestic security failings. From September 2001 to December 2002, network-news coverage of the attacks and their aftermath ignored a stream of relevant topics: Zionism, Afghanistan after the invasion, and U.S. foreign policy and business interests in the Middle East (McDonald and Lawrence 2004, 336–37; Traugott and Brader 2003, 183–84, 186–87; *Tyndall Report* 2003).* The Pew Charitable Trusts report that opinion rather than fact dominated reporting in the months after September 11 (2002a). Official discourse dominated photojournalism in *US News and World Report*, *Newsweek*, and *Time* from September 11 to the Iraq invasion, with the usual banalities of nationalism, militarism, and exclusion of the other (Griffin 2004).

New York Times lead reporter Richard Bernstein edited an embarrassing volume about September 11 that eschewed anything even approximating a serious discussion of U.S. foreign policy, while his executive editor Howell Raines referred to Hiroshima's decimation by the United States as having arisen "from dictatorial passions run amok" in Japan (2002, xi) in his preface to the volume. The growing tendency of brash and faulty reportage reached its awful apogee in the weapons-of-mass-destruction falsehoods perpetrated by Bush Minor's apparatchiks and the *New York Times* in 2003. These falsehoods were of a cosmic magnitude, and drew zero public self-criticism for an entire year, even as the paper was purging staff for inventing human-interest stories (MacArthur 2003). In the aftermath of the invasion of Iraq, the *Washington Post*'s Karen Young said, "We are inevitably the mouthpiece for whatever administration is in power," while the paper's Pentagon correspondent, Thomas Ricks, acknowledged that his editors' position could be summarized as: "Look, we're going to war, why do we even worry about the contrary stuff." The *Post* ran one hundred and forty front-page articles promoting war in the months prior to the assault (quoted in Mitchell 2004).

Media martinet Rupert Murdoch, the ever-Oedipal son of an embedded journalist from the Somme, promised "We'll do whatever is our patriotic duty." Later he intoned that removing Saddam Hussein would reduce the price of oil: "The greatest thing to come out of this for the world economy" (quoted

*For further discussions of media coverage, see *Television & New Media*, 2002; Berrington, 2002; Silberstein, 2002; and Zelizer and Allan, 2002a; for an account of this renewed imperial project and its warm welcome by the *bourgeois* media, see Foster, 2002.

in Solomon 2001b and Greenslade 2003). Each of the 175 newspapers he owned across the world endorsed invasion (Harvey 2003, 12). British viewers were so taken aback by the partisanship of Fox News, which was rebroadcast in the U.K. via satellite, that they protested against it through the local regulator, the Independent Television Commission. In India, where Murdoch's Star TV had long been dominant in ratings, the invasion brought viewers flooding back to the hitherto moribund public broadcaster Doordarshan. The *Manila Standard* explained to its readers that Fox was the contemporary version of the Bible for extremist Christians, and Malaysia's *Berita Harian* editorialized that the threat of terrorism was being deployed "by Bush's accomplices to influence the media not to question any government actions" (Wells 2003; Sehgal 2003; Abayah 2004; *BBC Monitoring International Reports* 2001a).

Clear Channel Worldwide, the dominant force in U.S. radio and concert promotion with over twelve hundred stations, banned one hundred and fifty songs after September 11, including "Bridge over Troubled Water." In 2003, it refused permission for protest groups to disseminate literature at an Ani DiFranco concert, and organized pro-war rallies and boycotts of antiwar performers while it was lobbying for new ownership regulations from FCC Chair Michael Powell, son of the Secretary of State. Clear Channel's board included an R-Word activist who had paid Bush vast sums for his failed baseball team, and handed over public money to Bush and his apparatchiks during the presidency. Another media concentration beneficiary, Cumulus Media, rented a tractor that weighed thirty-three thousand pounds to destroy Dixie Chicks music and memorabilia and purged the band from 262 playlists for daring to question Bush, while Viacom chief Sumner Redstone announced that a second term for Bush would be "good for Viacom" (Grieve 2003; Krugman 2003b; Kellner 2003, 68; Jones 2003; Aufderheide 2004, 335; D'Entremont 2003; Redstone quoted in Nichols and McChesney 2005, 9). In this context, the distinguished media studies professor Oliver Boyd-Barrett, no fan of conspiracy theories, felt obliged to

> ask whether, in 2002–3, media giants bartered their support for Bush's "total spectrum dominance" policy in return for regulatory changes that would facilitate business acquisitions in lucrative media markets (2005, 342).

Susan D. Moeller's study of mainstream media coverage between the 1998 nuclear tests in South Asia and the occupation of Iraq indicates that a wild array of *matériel*, policies, and practices was essentialized under the emotive sign "Weapons of Mass Destruction." It became a "monolithic menace," with no distinctions drawn between radiological, nuclear, chemical, or biological weapons. There was also no recognition that most of these weapons were made, held, and sold by those countries that were most moralistic about their manufacture, possession, and sale—the United States and Britain (2004a). In 2005, when the White House suddenly discovered that it had invaded Iraq in the name of democracy rather than national security, local correspondents quickly fell into line, saliently and silently forgetting about Weapons of Mass Destruction. Meanwhile, the rest of the world's media was dedicating itself to the appalling duplicity exposed by the leaked memo from Downing Street of July 2002 that revealed the entire weapons claim had been a fiction from the beginning, a paltry alibi for the planned invasion. It took five weeks from when Britain's *Sunday Times* revealed the memo's contents for the sluggish Yanqui media to pay it any real heed (P. Hart 2005d; FAIR 2005e; K. Hart 2005).

A study conducted at the beginning of 2002 disclosed that in the months after September 11, CNN had covered 157 events featuring Bush operatives, and just seven with Democrats (Alterman 2003, 206). More than half of U.S. TV-studio guests talking about the impending action in Iraq in 2003 were superannuated white males (FAIR 2003c), "ex-military men, terrorism experts, and Middle Eastern policy analysts who know none of the relevant languages, may never have seen any part of the Middle East, and are too poorly educated to be expert at anything" (Said 2003a). During the war, news effectively diminished the dominant discourse to technical efficiency and state propaganda. Of 319 mavens giving "analysis" on ABC, CBS, and NBC in October 2003, 76 percent were current or previous officials. Of the civilians, 79 percent were R-Worders. In all, 81 percent of the sources were Yanquis. A sample of National Public Radio's guest list on all topics over one month shows that 64 percent were officials or corporate leeches. Local news coverage was similarly craven (Whiten 2004; Rendall and Butterworth 2004; Grand Rapids Institute for Information Democracy 2005).

The *New York Times* refers to these interviewees as "part experts and part reporters, they're marketing tools, as well" (Jensen 2003). Their links to arms trading are rarely divulged, and never discussed as relevant. Retired Lieutenant General Barry McCaffrey, employed in this capacity by NBC News, points to the cadre's "lifetime of experience and objectivity." In his case, this involves membership in the Committee for the Liberation of Iraq, a lobby group dedicated to influencing the media, and the boards of three munitions companies that make ordnance he has praised on MSNBC. Even among the thoroughly ideologized U.S. public, 36 percent believed the media overemphasized the opinions of these retirees (Roy 2004; Benaim et al. 2003; Pew Research Center for the People & the Press 2004d, 15). This figure is no surprise, given the retirees' laughable predictions about the Shi'a rising against the Ba'th, resistance from the Special Republican Guard and security agencies, and the deployment of gas and other mass destruction weaponry by the Iraqi military. The list of failed assessments is unremitting, and has a heritage in errors pundits made in the 1980s, when they welcomed the Iraqi regime as an ally. It is a constant, choreographed dance, oscillating between glorying and denying death.

KILLING

In the late 1980s . . . the United States Congress was about to decide whether to give money to the Contras in their campaign against the state of Nicaragua. I was a member of a delegation speaking on behalf of Nicaragua but the most important member of the delegation was a Father John Metcalf. The leader of the US body was Raymond Seitz (then number two to the ambassador, later ambassador himself). Father Metcalf said: "Sir, I am in charge of a parish in the north of Nicaragua. My parishioners built a school, a health centre, a cultural centre. We have lived in peace. A few months ago a Contra force attacked the parish. They destroyed everything . . . raped nurses and teachers, slaughtered doctors" . . .

Seitz . . . listened, paused and then spoke with some gravity. "Father," he said, "let me tell you something. In war, innocent people always suffer." There was a frozen silence. We stared at him. He did not flinch.
—Harold Pinter, speech accepting the Nobel Prize for
    Literature (2005b)

One of the things that we don't want to do is to destroy the infrastructure of Iraq, because in a few days we're going to own that country.
—Tom Brokaw, during the 2003 invasion
    (quoted in *EXTRA!Update* 2004b).

Brokaw's statement revealed more than he meant. "Infrastructure" was inanimate. As in Pinter's chilling account, people could move and bleed and die, but they were not worth owning in quite the same way. So the U.S. networks' censorship of footage of Afghan civilian casualties in October 2001 was as predictable as it was appalling (Hudson et al. 2002). The BBC filmed desperate Afghan refugees in camps, and then sold the footage to ABC. But the two broadcasts had two different soundtracks that gave them incompatible meanings.

British media presented the camps as consisting of refugees from U.S. bombing who said that fear of the daily bombing attacks had driven them out of the city, whereas U.S. media presented the camps as containing refugees from Taliban oppression and the dangers of civil war (Kellner 2003, 125).

To hide the carnage of its 2001 invasion, Bush's Pentagon bought exclusive rights to satellite photos of Afghanistan, shutting out scrutiny (Solomon, 2001b; Magder 2003: 38). Another kind of scrutiny took its place—a carnival of exaltation over matériel. Thirty-eight percent of CNN's coverage of the bombardment emphasized technology, and the other 62 percent focused on military activity as a matter of technical specifications, of instrumental rationality; there was no mention of history or politics. Yet only U.S. CNN viewers were exposed to this perversion of the news. While Arabic, German, and French stations devoted ample coverage to civilians, ABC offered *Tales from the Front Lines*, an entertainment series produced by noted Hollywood action-adventure maven Jerry Bruckheimer that depicted the invasion of Afghanistan as "an MTV-paced joy ride." Military maneuvers took second place to civilian suffering in the rest of the world's media coverage of the crises, invasions, and occupations occurring in Afghan and Iraqi crises. Thousands of civilian Afghan deaths reported by South Asian, SouthEast Asian, Western European, and Middle Eastern news services went essentially unrecorded in the United States because they could not be "verified" by U.S. journalists and officials. Several Yanqui newspapers instructed journalists to minimize coverage of Afghan civilian casualties during the invasion. Unlike CNN, the Qatar-based satellite news service Al Jazeera dedicated only a third of its stories to war footage, emphasizing human distress over electronic effectiveness—vernacular reportage rather than patriotic euphemism (Williams 2003, 177; Lewis et al. 2004a, 14; Rich 2003; Eller and Bates 2003; Jasperson and El-Kikhia 2003, 119, 126–27; Herold 2001; Flanders 2001; Kellner 2004, 334; della Cava 2003; Greenberg 2003).

Any discussion of victims of this violence that went beyond the technocratic form was bloodcurdling. Consider the commentary of Lawrence Eagleburger, a former Secretary of State, on CNN after the attacks on the United States. He said, "There is only one way to begin to deal with people like this, and that is you have to kill some of them even if they are not immediately directly involved." R-Word house intellectual Anne Coulter called on the government to identify the nations where terrorists lived, "invade their countries, kill their leaders and convert them to Christianity" (*National Review* Online, October 13, 2001). She then caricatured NBC's apolitical headliner Katie Couric as "Eva Braun" and "Joseph Goebbels." Coulter was also the voice of the notorious televised rebuke to a disabled Vietnam veteran that "People like you caused us to lose that war." She continued by proposing that the Right should "physically intimidate liberals, by making them realize that they can be killed too" and informing Fox News watchers and magazine readers that liberals desire "lots of 9/11s" and that "Arabs lie" (quoted in Alterman 2003, 3–5). Despite her hyperbolic ignorance, Coulter made frequent appearances on NBC, CNN, MSNBC, ABC, HBO, and a raft of other cable TV and talk-radio programs, in addition to receiving admiring profiles in the *New York Times*, *Newsday*, the *Wall Street Journal*, and the *New York Observer*, and a cover story in *Time* (Alterman 2003, 5; FAIR 2005d).

There were dissenters to counter the above. Robert N. Bellah, a member of the supposedly blameless generation born in the 1920s, and a fellow civil religionist with Putnam, drew on far more sinister histories than the latter's elegy to volunteerism and sacrifice, or Huntington's national self exculpation. Bellah stretched back three-quarters of a century to locate the trauma of September 11 in the Second World War, asking, "is it so entirely clear that we won?" Bellah was not referencing the military struggle, but "the extent that we became like the enemy we opposed." He concentrated on how early condemnations of the Germans for targeting civilians were displaced by comparable Allied atrocities, from bombing Dresden and Tokyo to the holocausts of Hiroshima and Nagasaki. Bellah traced this wanton regard for life as it spread to conflicts in Vietnam and elsewhere (2002, 255). The genealogy is apt. In 1991, Colin Powell responded to the question of how many Iraqis had died as a result of the Gulf War conflict, with "It's really not a number I'm terribly interested in" (quoted in Zinn 2003, x). The Pentagon declined to account for civilian deaths in Panama in 1989, or Yugoslavia ten years later (Herman 2004, 6–7), and, in 1996, Secretary of State Madeleine Albright said on national TV that although the death of half a million Iraqi children because of economic sanctions "was a very hard choice . . . we think the price is worth it" (quoted in Roy 2001).

An empirical approach to reportage on and inquiry into the human cost of the war were beyond the ken of the U.S. media. As the invasion loomed, Murdoch said "there is going to be collateral damage . . . if you really want to be brutal about it, better we get it done now" (quoted in Pilger 2003). Public Broadcasting Service (PBS) *News Hour* Executive Producer Lester Crystal dismissed coverage of the impact of the invasion as not "central at the moment" (quoted in Sharkey 2003). Fox News Managing Editor Brit Hume said that civilian casualties do not belong on television, since they are "historically, by definition, a part of war."* CNN instructed presenters to mention September

---

*When U.S. deaths in Iraq reached 2000, the highest number in three decades, Hume offered that 'by historic standards, these casualties are negligible'—one of many occasions when he spoke in such ways (FAIR, 2005h).

11 each time they discussed Afghani suffering, and Walter Isaacson, the network's president, worried aloud that it was "perverse to focus too much on the casualties or hardship" (quoted in Kellner 2003, 66, 107). In the fortnight prior to the 2003 invasion of Iraq, none of the three major U.S. networks provided any examination of the humanitarian impact of such an action. Human Rights Watch's briefing paper, and a UN Undersecretary General's warning on the topic, lay uncovered (FAIR 2003b). How could the U.S. commanding officer of the invasion, Tommy Franks' insistence that "we don't do body counts," be anything but a contravention of the Geneva Conventions' requirements to care for occupied populations? After all, the caregiver needs to survey the population to know its needs. This seemed too difficult for the U.S. media to fathom or report (Roberts et al. 2004). These slavish tendencies intensified with embedment.

During World War I, British newspaper correspondents wore army uniforms and obeyed official guides. Their dispatches reflected their interdependence, and became markers of inappropriate links to official interests. Embedding was subject to First Amendment challenges during the first Gulf War, because of the oppressive nature of pooling journalists under military charge (Thussu and Freedman 2003, 5–6; Magder 2003, 39). In keeping with the mendacious spirit of empire, the military co-opted journalists for the 2003 Iraq invasion through the embarrassing quasi-homonym of "embedding" them with the military. The military required reporters to sign a contract agreeing with Pentagon instructions on coverage, including no off-the-record interviews, which had been crucial to discovering battlefield brutalities in the Vietnam War. When magazine writer Michael Wolff questioned embedding, Fox accused him of being unpatriotic, and talk radio's Rush Limbaugh publicized Wolff's email address, leading to thousands of hate messages. This successful control of the media was in line with a longstanding Pentagon doctrine, exemplified by fifteen "information dominance centers" in the United States, Iraq, and Kuwait. Within a month of invasion, embedded journalists had given the networks free U.S. programming to be shown as propaganda (Taiara 2003; Thussu and Freedman 2003, 6; Payne 2005, 86–87; Keeble 2004, 50; Miller 2004, 9, 12).

Embedding was widely condemned in the international media as a deathblow to independent war reporting. It also had an impact on gender balance in 2003–2004. The limited opportunities for women to appear on Sunday-morning current-affairs TV were reduced still further after September 11. When combined with the sped-up routines of twenty-four hour news channels, embedding led to disgraces like the day when nine separate, inaccurate announcements were made that Umm Qasr had fallen to the invaders

(Jones 2003; Huff 2003b; White House Project 2005; Parameswaran 2006; Tryhorn 2003), and a Fox producer saying that "Even if we never get a story out of an embed, you need someone there to watch the missiles fly and the planes taking off. It's great television." NBC correspondent David Bloom said that the media were so keen to become adjuncts of the military that they were "doing anything and everything that they can ask of us" (quoted in Carr 2003). WABC radio's N. J. Burkett compared the Yanqui soldiers preparing their weapons to "an orchestra on an opening night" (quoted in Rutenberg 2003). Marcy McGinnis, senior vice president of news at CBS, claimed that the networks brought "this war into the living rooms of Americans . . . [It's] the first time you can actually see what's happening" (quoted in Sharkey 2003). Paul Steiger, Managing Editor of the *Wall Street Journal*, remarked that U.S. media coverage of the invasion "was pretty darned good" (quoted in Friedman 2003). What was distinguished as "what's happening" and "darned good" was extraordinarily misshaped and unbalanced—really, systematically distorted. Britain's Ministry of Defence noted approvingly that "90 percent of embedded correspondents' reporting was either positive or neutral" (2003). No wonder Bernard Shaw, the former CNN anchor, saw these journalists as "hostages of the military" (quoted in Bushell and Cunningham 2003). But, for the dominant side of the debate, all is justified because the events of September 11 meant "the rules have now changed" (Kalb 2003).

The Project for Excellence in Journalism's analysis of ABC, CBS, NBC, CNN, and Fox found that early in the Iraq invasion, 50 percent of reports from the thousand embedded journalists depicted combat—zero percent depicted injuries. As the war progressed, reporters kept with the fifty contractual terms required of them in return for their "beds" and only disclosed deeply sanitized images of the wounded from afar. The mainstream media ignored wounded U.S. soldiers, too, and conducted no bedside interviews from hospitals. Fallen men and women were the "disappeared." News photography only commemorated them with highly misleading, romantic imagery, in stark relief to battleground pictures from World War II and Vietnam (Arnow 2005; Berkowitz 2003; Boyd-Barrett 2004, 30–31; Pfau et al. 2005).

The mendacity and neglect of U.S. journalists reached their metacritical nadir in April 2004 when CNN's Daryn Kagan interviewed Al Jazeera's editor-in-chief, Ahmed Al-Sheik. The opportunity to learn about the horrendous casualties in the Fallujah uprisings, or to share professional perspectives on methods and angles of coverage, turned into an unreflective indictment of Al Jazeera for bothering to report the deaths of Iraqi noncombatants at the hands of the invaders. Kagan complained that "the story" was "bigger than just the numbers of people who have been killed or the fact that they might have been killed by the US military" (quoted in FAIR 2004a). When late in 2004 *The Lancet*, one of the major medical journals in the world, published an epidemiological paper suggesting that one hundred thousand people may have died from violence since the invasion, the U.S. media barely noted the fact, despite the story's prominence elsewhere. Three months later, the networks began to discuss the number of Iraqi dead, with their "estimates" ranging from sixteen thousand and five hundred to twenty thousand. Reporters discredited the *Lancet* study, despite support for it amongst mortality and biostatistical experts (Roberts et al. 2004; FAIR 2005b; Guterman 2005).

The politics and policies of the U.S. state and media in their self-righteous denunciations were so unitary, that much—though not all—of this censorship was self-inflicted. Monty Python film director Terry Jones suggested limits to this idiotic news management. He said,

> it's fiendishly difficult to get people to accept the label "rebels" for those Iraqis killed by American snipers when—as in Fallujah—they turn out to be pregnant women, 13-year-old boys and old men standing by their front gates (2004).

Perhaps it is not so difficult in the US though, where General Motors—the country's biggest advertiser—and other major corporations avowed that they "would not advertise on a TV program about atrocities in Iraq" (quoted in M. McCarthy 2004, 2B). It's no wonder Defense Secretary Donald Rumsfeld's thought-disordered remark about Baghdad—"It looks like it's a bombing of a city, but it isn't"—received much uncritical U.S. coverage. And, it's no wonder Lindsey Hilsum, of Britain's Channel 4, was moved to say, "Only the Americans could not see what was happening in Baghdad" as the U.S. media retreated from the shock and awe (quoted in Lewis et al. 2004a, 12). Statements by the International Red Cross and many other notable non-Pentagon sources detailing Iraqi civilian casualties from the bombing of Baghdad received virtually no coverage, nor did memorable Congressional speeches by Senators Robert Byrd and Ted Kennedy against bloodthirsty militarism. Firsthand accounts of an unarmed family in a car being shot by Yanqui soldiers were overridden by the Pentagon's strenuous insistence that the protocols for shooting an unarmed family in a car were followed. No networks mentioned the U.S. military's use of depleted uranium, or considered the impact of cluster bombs, even though they were both major stories everywhere else, and subjects of serious complaint by Amnesty International and Human Rights Watch. The thousands of cluster bombs that had to be "cleaned up" belied the U.S. claim to have dropped just twenty-six of them. This information was barely available through domestic media outlets—the Australian and European media referred to cluster bombs ten times as often as their U.S. counterparts. When it was reported that the United States had used white phosphorous as munitions in the attack on Fallujah, the Pentagon and the U.S. ambassador to Britain immediately claimed this was incorrect. It was not until three proud fighters published an academic article based on their experiences, boasting the effectiveness of the substance's use in Iraq as "a potent psychological weapon" that it was embarrassingly disclosed. Use of munitions in this way—as opposed to camouflage—is clearly prohibited under the Chemical Weapons Convention, to which the United States is a signatory. Then, when the United States moved toward an air war in late 2005, with dozens of sorties flown each day, the local media largely ignored it (Wilkinson 2003; FAIR 2003e, f, and h; Schlesinger 2003; Rampton and Strauber 2003, 197, 194; Nixon 2005; Cobb et al. 2005, 26; Reynolds 2005; Jamail 2005).

At Friday prayers in Tehran, Hashemi-Rafsanjani discussed the coverage. He was misleading in his implication of state censorship, but telling in his metaphorical understanding.

> The American newspapers are banned from printing the pictures of those killed or injured in Iraq. Aren't you really surprised? Those who exert pressure on countries like ours, as they claim, for the sake of freedom, do not allow their own newspapers, TVs, including private TV, to print or show these photos or films (quoted in *BBC Monitoring International Reports* 2004b).

Malaysian Prime Minister Datuk Seri Dr Mahathir Mohamad accused the United States of hypocrisy in its calls for a separation of media and state, saying that "when it suits them, there is no freedom of the Press." Similar critiques came from official Iranian sources and the *Turkish Daily News*, which pointed to the slow, begrudging reactions of the U.S. media and political class to revelations about torture at Abu Ghraib prison (*New Straits Times* 2003b, 2; *BBC Monitoring International Reports* 2004b; Aktan, 2004).

The impact of obfuscation on the U.S. citizenry was profound, causing U.S. citizens to show infinitely greater credulity regarding the war than any other country, including those with participant forces. After the invasion of Iraq, 82 percent of U.S. citizens believed that the military had made serious efforts to spare civilians. How could this proportion of the population have failed to remember the awful history of atomic attack in Japan and carpet bombing in North Korea, Laos, Cambodia, and North Vietnam? How could repeated revelations about the bloodthirsty war crimes of the U.S. military attract almost no media attention (Pew Research Center for the People & the Press 2003c; Sardar and Davies 2002, 113; Davis 2003)? Because U.S. atrocities had become technical issues of impression management, not violations of human rights, and part of the quest for freedom, not infractions of international law. So William Burns, the Assistant Secretary of State for the Middle East, praised the Algerian government for "controlling terror"—which it had done by killing one hundred and twenty thousand Islamists over eight years (quoted in Harvey 2003, 10). In Bush Minor's truly imperial words on September 20, 2001, "this country will define our times, not be defined by them."

Meanwhile, prisoners captured by the United States during its Afghanistan adventure and imprisoned in Guantánamo Bay remained uncharged years after their capture, with minimal legal, NGO, or media access. The U.S. Supreme Court finally queried this in mid-2004. The government argued that they were not entitled to legal counsel because they were *not* subject to the Geneva Convention, and that they could not be interviewed because they *were* subject to the Convention. The international media are appalled by this infraction of basic human rights. In the United States, it was left up to JAG, a CBS drama written by ex–military officers, to address—and sanitize—the issue. When the United States captured dictator Saddam Hussein, the hypocrisy defied description. One "journalist" after another lined up in mendacity and ignorance to celebrate his humiliation by the United States. In 2005, when *Newsweek* reported that military personnel may have flushed a copy of the *Koran* down a toilet, the administration, *Newsweek* itself, and the entire Yanqui media attributed the subsequent violence in Afghanistan to the sacrilegious act, despite disavowals of such a connection by everybody from the president of Afghanistan to the chair of the chiefs of general staff. Any allegation of improper conduct by the state came to be regarded as treason. Conversely, the tens of thousands killed as a consequence of inaccurate reportage about wars prior to the invasion of Iraq drew no such calumny (*Independent* 2003; *Mother Jones* 2003; *Center for Constitutional Rights* 2003; Shafer 2003; Human Rights Watch 2003; Burston 2003, 168; Naureckas 2004, 1; Naureckas 2005; Alterman 2005, 11).

INTELLECTUALS?

> I do not advocate that we turn television into a 27-inch wailing wall, where longhairs constantly moan about the state of culture and our defense.
> —Edward R. Murrow (1958)

> It is all in the grand tradition of American anti-intellectualism: the suspicion of thought, of words. And it very much serves the purposes of the present administration. Hiding behind the humbug that the attack of last 11 September was too horrible, too devastating, too painful, too tragic for words—that words could not possibly do justice to our grief and indignation—our leaders have a perfect excuse to drape themselves in borrowed words of contempt.
> —Susan Sontag (2002)

Outside their pedagogical tasks, intellectuals have two roles in U.S. public life. The first is to be technocrats and provide solutions to problems that will make money or allow governments to achieve policy targets. The second is to offer cultural critique and political intelligence to the élite, both inside and outside the state. Sometimes it appears as though critical public intellectuals in the United States are, in the words of the *Economist*, "a tiny, struggling species, whose habitat is confined to a few uptown apartments in New York and the faculties of certain universities" (*Economist* 2005p).

Neoliberals and conservatives utilize the media spectacularly. Policy proposals are left to their corporate masters, because right-wing media discourse does not undertake rational analyses aimed at technocratic outcomes. Instead, the latter works via a blend of grass-roots religious superstition and public outreach that stresses column inches and screaming punditry, not professional expertise (Kallick 2002). Funded by some of the wealthiest U.S. foundations and families, such as Olin, Scaife, Koch, Castle Rock, and Smith Richardson, there are over three hundred right-wing "coin-operated" think tanks in Washington, dealing with topics from sexuality to foreign policy. They hire ghostwriters to make their resident intellectuals' prose attractive—a project to market opinion, rather than to conduct research. Each "study" they fund is essentially the alibi for an op-ed piece. The corollary numbers for media coverage are striking. Progressive think tanks had a sixth share of media quotation compared to reactionary institutions during the 1990s. From 1995 to 2005, reactionaries averaged 51 percent of citations and progressives, 14 percent. Journalists even call the supposedly independent Heritage Foundation when the White House has no one available. If we believe in market-based rhetoric, then the people who appear on the major three TV networks' newscasts as experts should be indices of consumer desire. In which case, the public "wants" 92 percent of these mavens to be white, 90 percent born between 1945 and 1960, 85 percent male, and 75 percent Republican. That might expose us to the cohort that is responsible for our troubles, but not to disinterested critique (Karr 2005; Alterman 2003, 85; Dolny 2003; Dolny 2005; P. Hart 2005a, 52; Claussen 2004, 56; Love 2003, 246; Cohen 2005).

Media attention does not correlate with scholarly esteem or achievement, and most academics interviewed have worked in government. These public intellectuals are general rather than specific in their remarks, and disdainful of both theory and fact—an unusual combination. They have displaced expertise and journalism with position taking. It can be no accident that Fox News Channel, which employs few journalists and foreign bureaus, has the most pundits on its payroll of any U.S. network—over fifty in 2003 (Tugend 2003). Margaret Carlson, a correspondent for *Time* and one of CNN's vocalists, explained the key qualifications for her television work as "the less you know about something, the better off you are[;] . . . sound learned without confusing the matter with too much knowledge" (quoted in Alterman 2003, 32).

The system bespeaks the Right's success at tapping into a rich vein of anti-intellectualism that derives from far-right Christian fundamentalism, populism, and instrumentalism. It dates back to newspaper assaults on John Quincy Adams for being "book learn[ed]" and Adlai Stevenson as effeminate (Claussen 2004, 18–21, 40–41). There is minimal room for intellection on network television since the still-extant mass audience is the latter's target. So few if any professional academics appear on air to explain the history of U.S. foreign policy, in spite of the country's relationships with oil interests, arms manufacturers, and despots to keep oil prices low; its complex twists and turns supporting and undermining various brands of Islam and Arab rule; and its bizarre insistence on an ethical reputation, while essentially rejecting international law other than over copyright. Nor does the media ever competently contextualize the hypocrisies and horrors of opponents to the U.S. Instead, television facilitates a jingoistic and spiritual message, juxtaposing freedom and decency with repression and fanaticism in a way that breaks down the binary rather disturbingly, and heightens a sense of risk without explaining it other than in the manner of the clash twins. E pluribus unum is part of the networks' discourse, applied as a loyalty test. The networks thus equate talking in a way that is counter to the administration with lack of professional objectivity, and military action embodies the unity of the nation, seemingly the last legitimate government arena.

Ibrahim Al-Marashi was unusual—a critical Arab intellectual able to enter the lists of such discussions. He was ushered in because his work had been plagiarized in a British intelligence dossier which Colin Powell formally presented to the Security Council in 2003. Al-Marashi hoped to use his reputation as a platform to differentiate himself from on-air Iraqi-Americans who were calling for invasion and destruction (2004). But of the hundreds of interviews he gave, virtually none presented the opportunity for commentary on the war. He was restricted to the discourse on secreted weaponry. Similarly and not surprisingly, my search through Lexis-Nexis, a legal, news, and public records database, found cultural critic Edward Said's by-line did not appear in any US newspaper in the 18 months after September 11, finally reemerging in July 2003 (Said 2003b). By contrast, readers of the *Independent, El País,* the *Guardian,* the *Observer, Rebelión.org,* and the *Weekend Australian* had access to his thoughts during this period.

Academics are sometimes excluded by direct political action rather than deregulatory pressures, popular-cultural obsessions, ignorance, or jingoism. For example, the right-wing think tanks that dominate Washington policy on the Middle East have sought to discredit area studies across U.S. universities, especially Middle Eastern programs. The Washington Institute for Near East Studies is the key front organization for the Republican Party, while institutions like the American Jewish Congress, Campus Watch, and the American Council of Trustees and Alumni, run by the vice president's wife, warn against "Middle Eastern Arabs" in universities, and place conservatives in vital opinion-making forums that feed into TV current affairs, such as the op-ed pages of the *Wall Street Journal,* the *Jerusalem Post,* the *Los Angeles Times,* the *Washington Post,* and the *New York Times* (Beinin 2003, 135; Whitaker 2002; Brynen 2002; Davidson 2002; Abrahamian 2003; Merriman 2004).

Away from the live media, the Arab world has been chided for being closed to ideas from the outside, as measured by the fact that only three hundred and thirty books are translated from foreign languages annually. Yet the United States, with an almost equal population and a vastly bigger book trade, translates the same number! The comparison of these two regions with the rest of the world is highly unflattering for them, because books can be conduits to knowledge. Attorney General John Ashcroft recognized the importance of books when he interpreted the Uniting and Strengthening America by Providing Appropriate Tools Required to Intercept and Obstruct Terrorism Act (USA PATRIOT Act) to permit FBI scrutiny of book buying and borrowing, but not firearm purchase (Dilday 2003; Grieve 2003).

Meanwhile, the government establishes front organizations to select, train, and promote apparently independent figures. The State Department financed the Iraq Public Diplomacy Group, which coached Iraqis to appear on U.S.

television in support of positions prepared for them, with the idea that they would be more effective than Yanquis. The Iraqi National Congress was the creation and creature of the CIA, via the agency's public relations consultant, the Rendon Group, whose motto is "information as an element of power." Its advertised services run the gamut from generating "a favorable environment before privatization begins" to providing alibis for state violence. It coordinated propaganda for the 1989 invasion of Panama and the 1991 Gulf War, and has received more than US$100 million from the CIA (Alterman 2003, 82–83; Rampton and Stauber 2003, 55, 43; Downing and Husband 2005, 73; Chatterjee 2004).

The press should be interviewing intellectuals trained in area studies, military strategy, international law, business ethics, and battlefield medicine. However, that would allocate power to cosmopolitan working journalists rather than hack finance executives, and require serious action to provide multiperspectival media coverage rather than biased rhetoric. Instead, the paranoid form of reporting favored by U.S. networks militates against journalistic autonomy, other than when the information comes directly from battlefields and is a "soldier's story," or derives from the Pentagon or the Israeli government (Fisk 2003a). The prevailing doctrines of regulation favor ownership of television by a small number of large entities which appeal to anti-intellectualism, regardless of their niches. Scott Adams's comic strip *Dilbert* parodies this beautifully in the fictitious "Dogbert Easy News Channel." Easy News provides "all the news that's easy to gather" and features "a debate between two middle-aged white guys" about why "people in other countries want to kill us." One of the guests says it's because "we are so wonderful." The other warns, "Buy my book or you will all die" (Adams 2005).

I have limited personal experience of these tendencies. For many years I worked in Australian radio, then later as an academic commentator on popular culture. When I came to the United States, I was interviewed fairly regularly by several media sources, probably because I was at New York University and had a plausibly English accent. Just before September 11, I appeared on CNN International to talk about a crisis involving Afghan refugees in peril off the Australian coast. Contrary to CNN's parochial domestic stations, with their blinking, winking, walking dead presenters, dedicated to eastern-seaboard storms, missing white children, and entertainment news, the network has twenty-three satellites, forty-two bureaus, and one hundred and fifty foreign correspondents (Thussu 2003, 118). The day I was interviewed, most of the CNN employees in New York were watching CNN International, which covers more legitimate news stories than the network's domestic programs. During my interview, the anchorman looked at me disbelievingly as I listed the history of racialization by successive Australian administrations. He asked incredulously "So are you telling us that the Australian Government is racist?" He evinced another sign of the deluded faith in official sources that dogs contemporary Yanqui journalism's "stenographic reporting" (Moeller 2004b, 71).

When I appeared on New York 1, a local cable news channel, shortly after the attacks on the United States, I was asked to comment on the psychology of terrorists in a transhistorical way. I endeavored to direct the conversation toward U.S. foreign policy and its support of totalitarian regimes in the Middle East, which restricted access to politics, and thus turned religion into a zone of resistance. I spoke of U.S. TV journalists' sparse and prejudicial narrative frames and background knowledge. Later, the production staff told me how the board lit up with supportive reaction when the program accepted phone calls from the public. The callers-in I spoke with personally, thanked me for saying the *non dit*. The staff said I would be invited back, but I was not. Station management eventually acknowledged that most of its coverage at the height of the crisis had not been "analytical," because the attack was "an open, gaping wound" (quoted in Boehlert 2002). By contrast, when Radio Scotland came to town and interviewed a standup comedy venue owner, a media consultant, and myself about cultural reactions to these events, we were not dealing with overdetermined presuppositions from our questioners—there was time for me to draw on theory and history to complement their approaches. The same thing happened when I was interviewed on All-India Radio in Delhi. Yet, when CBS News contacted me in 2005 to discuss Bush's admission that he had instructed the National Security Agency (NSA) to spy on US citizens sans judicial review, contra the law, something quite different occurred. The producer first asked me if I could contextualize this in terms of the history of the media during wartime. I replied affirmatively. He then asked me about the limits to publicizing information, and I indicated that while most critics would agree that the precise timing and location of an event such as D-Day could legitimately be kept secret, extrajuridical contravention of civil liberties would generally be considered another matter. The producer thanked me for my time, and noted that he did not require my services. He already had a lawyer to support the revelation, and needed someone who would attack the *New York Times* for breaking the story and forcing Bush to tell the truth. He had wanted not the history of the media during wartime, but a nationalist opposed to civil liberties.

Most intellectuals who do obtain access to the U.S. media have adopted the logic of global manifest destiny. The neoconservative minority has taken the concept of imperialism, a term once used derisively by the Left, and made of it a badge of honor and identification (Wade 2003). For example, philosophical liberal Michael Ignatieff (2003) has called for a new and thoroughgoing imperialism in the *New York Times* magazine, echoing *Time*'s reference to Puerto Rico as an instance of the United States as a benign despot. Similar sentiments from think tankers are expressed in the *Weekly Standard*, *Foreign Affairs*, the *Harvard Review*, and *Atlantic Monthly*. Robert Kaplan hails the Monroe Doctrine, the justification for two centuries of aiding authoritarianism and mass poverty in Latin America, as a model for world hegemony by the United States, because it shows how to crush leftism (Schell 2003, 7). Drawing in part on the clash twins, Richard Brookhiser asserted in the *New York Observer* that the "world's losers hate us because we are powerful, rich and good"; the ever-simple Thomas Friedman divined that the motivation for September 11 was "pure envy"; Victor Davis Hanson claimed that Islamic "culture is backward and corrupt," as evidenced by its failed imperialism and stalled technologization; and journalism professor Lance Morrow's article "Case for Rage and Retribution" in *Time* called for "the nourishment of rage . . . purple American fury . . . focused brutality" (quoted in Sardar and Davies 2002, 19–20, 23; Eisman 2003, 60).

As for cultural critique, the *New York Times* quickly and tastelessly trumpeted September 11, 2001, as the end of postmodern cant, despite Al Qaeda being classified by its lack of relativism regarding truth (DerDerian 2002). Likewise, Karlheinz Stockhausen's work was banished, at least temporarily, from the canon of avant-garde electronic music when he described the attack on *las torres gemelas* as "the greatest work of art that is possible in the whole cosmos" (quoted in Lentricchia and McAuliffe 2002, 350–51). Then Baudrillard weighed in:

> The fascination with the terrorist act is first and foremost the fascination for an image. . . . Rather than the violence of the real being there first, and the shiver of the image being added, the image comes first and the shiver of the real is added to it. It is something like one more fiction, a fiction going beyond fiction. . . . After the fact, one tries to impose a meaning, any meaning on the event, to find any interpretation of it, but there is none. One finds instead the radicality of the spectacle, the brutality of the spectacle, which alone is original and irreducible (2002, 413).

For once, his stress on simulation as a referent rather than a signifier of the real did not cause offense. Nor did the lumbering Lacanian Slavoj Žižek's touchingly banal presumption of the "uncanny satisfaction" that "we got" from repeated footage of the Towers falling, as if in Hollywood cinema, or his inaccurate claim that the carnage itself was not broadcast, cause offense (2002, 12–13). The Retort group argued that the September 11 attackers were "brilliant exponents" of the notion that "control over the image is now the key to social control" (2004, 15). Newt Gingrich blamed Hollywood for the country's abject world status (Gingrich and Schweizer 2003), and novelist Don DeLillo told readers of *Harpers Magazine* that "the power of American culture to penetrate every wall, home, life and mind," via military and commercial action and iconography, too, was the problem (2001).

Arundhati Roy queried the claim that September 11 was an assault on the United States as a symbol of freedom by asking why the Statue of Liberty was left untouched, and military and economic power targeted (2001). Surely September 11 was what social theorist Aijaz Ahmad aptly named, a "privatized, retail violence" (2003, 19) that ties in to the spread of U.S. popular culture, finance, and militarism. On the score of changes to what was real and what was simulation, where truth and beauty met and parted, Harold Pinter's speech accepting the 2005 Nobel Prize for Literature makes the point. Forty-seven years earlier, he had written that he could find "no hard distinctions between what is real and what is unreal," noting that things could "be both true and false" (Pinter 2005b). Pinter was describing his artistic sensibility, his means of exploring the social world through drama and poetry. In 2005, those precepts remained constant: "as a writer I stand by them," he said; "but as a citizen I cannot." In that subject position, he needed to question things more frontally, to distinguish truth from falsehood. These latter explanations received very little mainstream media attention in the United States because they came from the wrong sort of intellectual.

ALTERNATIVES

> We Americans can and do keep track almost instantaneously of events the world over. Because we know and care about what is going on, we are perhaps better citizens.
> —Bob Siller et al. (1960, v)
> There are so many pictures of protestors out there. We want to show pictures of pro-Americans.
> —Steve Doocy, Fox & Friends (quoted in Folkenflik 2003)

So what alternative resources were available for understanding religious and state terrorism? In reviewing the post–September 11 period, the Newspaper-Guild-Communication Workers of America found that many of its members were expected by their employers to be "patriots first, and journalists second" and were victimized if they failed to comply (International Federation of Journalists 2001, 23–24). Adducing connections between the attack and U.S. foreign policy "somehow smacked of apologetics" (Navasky 2002, xiii). When Tom Gutting of the *Texas City Sun*, and Dan Guthrie of the *Daily Courier* in Oregon, wrote articles criticizing Minor, they were fired. After the president of ABC News, David Westin, told students at Columbia University's Graduate School of Journalism that he would refrain from taking a position on whether the attack on the Pentagon was legitimate, given that it could be regarded as a military target, the right-wing media reacted so intensely that he retracted his position and apologized (Ottosen 2004, 117; Alterman 2003, 203). TV news executives complied immediately when National Security Adviser, Condoleezza Rice, asked them to cease playing tapes of Osama Bin Laden. Meanwhile, Bush's Press Secretary, Ari Fleischer, had already said people should "watch what they say" about terrorism and U.S. foreign policy (quoted in Navasky 2002, xv–xvi), although this was excised from White House transcripts (Magder 2003, 36). Dan Rather acknowledged (on the BBC, where he was safe from the eyes of far-right Christian fundamentalists) that U.S. journalists "fear that you will be 'necklaced' here, you will have a flaming tire of lack of patriotism put around your neck . . . that keeps journalists from asking the toughest of tough questions" (quoted in Solomon and Erlich 2003, 23). He acknowledged that links between "Bush family business and [White House] policy" were weighing on him, but not enough to put them in front of the fragile domestic audience. He said, "I know the right question, but you know what, this is not exactly the right time to ask it" (quoted in Palast 2003a, 104–5). When he did finally report, albeit inadequately, the scandals of Bush's military career during the 2004 Presidential election campaign, it was the end of his *own* career.

It took until 2004 for the *Washington Post*'s Bob Woodward to confess "I think I was part of the groupthink" among officials (quoted in Kurtz, 2004). When the *New York Times* and the *Post* belatedly published quasi–mea culpa pieces about their preinvasion coverage, it was, in the words of the trade magazine *Editor & Publisher*, "a day late and a dollar short." At the end of his five years as ombudsman for the paper, Michael Getler said of the Iraq invasion "I cannot think of a story in the past forty years that offers more warning signs for journalism and for the role of the press in our democracy" (2005, B6). Not one of these people acknowledged that leftist journalists in the United States, and most journalists all over the world, did not need to learn this lesson, because they had looked for multiple perspectives beyond the DC line.

In the fortnight prior to the 2003 invasion, the major networks and PBS dedicated less than 1 percent of related airtime to opponents of the war—a startling indictment. CBS coverage featured state officials as three-quarters of its guests. Even reporting criticisms of the state led to floods of right-wing mail to media organizations—not just countering the position, but vilifying heterodox viewpoints. When the University of Missouri's TV station decided that presenters should not wear nationalistic symbols on air, the state legislature immediately threatened massive cuts to the school's budget (Rendall and Butterworth 2004; Rendall and Broughel 2003; P. Hart 2005c, 3; Kurtz 2004; Borden 2005, 31). Having repeatedly instructed him to feature more right-wing people on his program, MSNBC fired its liberal talk show host Phil Donahue immediately prior to the invasion, even though he hosted the network's top-rated program. MSNBC's reason was that his "anti-war agenda" would look bad when "our competitors are waving the flag . . . a difficult face for NBC in a time of war." Donahue's program already showcased more pro-war than anti-war guests—a two to one ratio—and the network told the show's producers that interviewing Michael Moore would necessitate three right-wingers on-screen to respond to him (quoted in FAIR 2003d and Nader 2003; also see Ellis 2003; P. Hart 2005a).

Efforts have long been made to restrain independent reporting of U.S. militarism. Consider the R-Word reaction to CNN's Peter Arnett and his Gulf War disclosure that Yanquis had bombed a factory that made baby formula, not a chemical-weapons facility as had been claimed. He was immediately described by the administration's news maven Marlin Fitzwater as a "conduit for Iraqi disinformation," and branded "the Joseph Goebbels of Saddam Hussein" by Representative Laurence Coughlin. Thirty-four Congresspeople petitioned CNN to protest the coverage, and Arnett was a target for Pentagon retribution for years afterword. In 1991, the contrast between CNN and the other networks like CBS, which notoriously offered to edit footage in order to conclude segments positively prior to commercials, was stark (Arnett 2003; Fitzwater quoted in Chris Jones 2003; Martin 2003; Hutton 2003b, 156). A decade on, CNN had learned its lesson. Its gleeful coverage of the invasion of Iraq was typified by one superannuated military officer, who rejoiced with "Slam, bam, bye-bye Saddam" as missiles struck Baghdad (quoted in Goldstein 2003b). Latino critics had already renamed the network "PNN," for "Pentagono News Network" (quoted in Leguineche 2002, 17).

Noted CNN foreign correspondent Christiane Amanpour told CNBC after the Iraq occupation began that:

I think the press was muzzled, and I think the press self-muzzled . . . I'm sorry to say, but certainly television and, perhaps, to a certain extent, my station was intimidated by the administration and its foot soldiers at Fox News. And it did, in fact, put a climate of fear and self-censorship, in my view, in terms of the kind of broadcast work we did (quoted in Zerbisias 2003).

She was immediately derided by Fox's Irena Briganti as "a spokeswoman for Al Quaeda" (quote in Allan and Zelizer 2004, 9). Conversely, Malaysia's *New Straits Times* editorialized that CNN's incompetence illustrated the need for an alternative global news network for Muslims (*New Straits Times* 2003a).

Because MSNBC's Ashleigh Banfield occasionally reported Arab perspectives during the 2003 conflict, Michael Savage, then a talkshow host on her network prior to being removed for telling a caller he hoped the person would contract HIV, called her a "slut," a "porn star," and an "accessory to the murder of Jewish children" on air. NBC executives rewarded this conduct by naming him their "showman" (quoted in Lieberman 2003). During the Iraq invasion, Banfield told a Kansas State University audience that "horrors were completely left out of this war. So was this journalism? . . . I was ostracized just for going on television and saying, 'Here's what the leaders of Hezbollah, a radical Moslem group, are telling me about what is needed to bring peace to Israel'" (quoted in Schechter 2003a). She was immediately demoted and disciplined by NBC for criticizing journalistic standards. Erik Sorenson, President of MSNBC, chortled that "one can be unabashedly patriotic and be a good journalist at the same time" (quoted in Allan and Zelizer 2004, 7).

CNN anchor Aaron Brown complained that "there was no center to cover" in opposition to the administration, because D-Worders had not opposed invasion even though most Democratic members of the House voted against authorizing Bush's plan for the invasion of Iraq. Fox News accompanied antiwar protests in Manhattan with a ticker-news crawl taunting the demonstrators. When its own program, *The Simpsons*, mocked this via a ticker that read "Do Democrats cause cancer? Find out at foxnews.com," the network immediately threatened the creator with legal action (Goodman et al. 2003; Folkenlik 2003; Byrne 2003b). Bush Minor dismissed the antiwar movement as "focus groups" (quoted in Grieve 2003) and R-Word intellectuals referred to these "few protestors in the streets" as akin to "mob rule" and other trite epithets (Boot in Goodman et al. 2003). Meanwhile, Viacom, CNN, Fox, and Comedy Central were refusing to feature paid billboards and commercials against the invasion, and UN activities in the region, including weapons inspections, became the least covered items on network news! Thus shall we know them. Despite months of demonstrations across the country that drew millions of protestors, and long-established international law that compromised the popular and legal justifications for belligerence, the U.S. media were utterly irresponsible. The same applied years later. When hundreds of thousands protested the occupation in September 2005, they attracted eighty-seven words on NBC news and none on CBS or Fox. NBC and *USA Today* gave equal coverage to pro-war protestors, who numbered a few hundred (Hastings 2003; Huff 2003a; FAIR 2005g).

State and corporate interests also interfered in media alternatives from elsewhere. Al Jazeera may assiduously expose Arab audiences to official Israeli points of view, and focus on U.S. suffering and reactions to September 11, but the Pentagon's Arabic Media and Programs Unit modestly promulgates a "truth matrix" to evaluate its broadcasts—quickly forgetting the White House's earlier description of the network as "a beacon of light" (Marquis 2004; *Economist* 2005u; Maluf 2005). Al Jazeera was subject to Rumsfeld's extraordinary remark that it was "Iraqi propaganda," and regular slander by the Bush Administration as "All Osama All the Time." U.S. politicians have nevertheless expected to obtain airtime on the network, with Rumsfeld, Colin Powell, and Rice all appearing to propagandize (International Federation of Journalists 2001, 20; Hafez 2001; Figenschou, 2006; el-Nawawy and Gher 2003; Miladi 2003, 159; Rumsfeld quoted in Getlin and Jensen 2003 and Rampton and Strauber 2003, 186).

Following U.S. governmental criticisms of Al Jazeera for televising prisoners of war and Arab criticisms of the attack, the New York Stock Exchange expelled Al Jazeera during the invasion of Iraq. The official explanation was that for "security reasons," the broadcasters allowed at the Exchange had to be limited to those offering "responsible business coverage." The NASDAQ exchange refused to grant Al Jazeera press credentials at the same time, for the same reason. It was then denied access by its U.S.-based Internet provider, and had to switch servers to France. The U.S. media derided Al Jazeera throughout the war and occupation, with CNN refusing to appear on a Nordic TV panel with its representatives (Agovino 2003; *Reuters* 2003a; FAIR 2003d; Association for Progressive Communications 2003; Fine 2003; Eide 2004, 280). The *New York Post* proposed that the Marines had been held back in Fallujah not "by the terrorists and insurgents," but "by Al-Jazeera" (quoted in Payne 2005, 81–82). The State Department systematically disrupted the network via pressure on Qatar's Emir Sheikh Hamid bin Khalifa al-Thaniof. Colin Powell complained to the emirate's foreign ministry about the channel (imagine the outrage if the opposite were done!) and the Qatar government was subject to so many threats from the United States that it elected to sell the network. This antidemocratic violence matched similarly tyrannical outbursts against it by the authoritarian governments of Bahrain, Libya, Saudi Arabia, Jordan, and Kuwait (Weisman 2005; Jasperson and El-Kikhia 2003, 130).

The channel's Washington correspondent was "detained" en route to a U.S.-Russia summit meeting in November 2001, and U.S. munitions shelled its offices in Iraq and Afghanistan, where it was the sole broadcast news outlet in Kabul. Rear Admiral Craig Quigley, U.S. Deputy Assistant Defence Secretary for Public Affairs, justified the attack on the network's Kabul operations by claiming that Al Qaeda interests were being aided by activities going on there. Al Jazeera denied the charge. Quigley's proof was that Al Jazeera had a satellite uplink and was in contact with Taliban officials—normal activities for a news service of any competence, but enough of a lead for the *New York Times* to denounce Al Jazeera as anti–United States and anti-Israel, and Rather to discern that it was funded by Osama bin Laden. The Committee to Protect Journalists and Amnesty International condemned U.S. assaults on Al Jazeera as violations of international humanitarian law. When Britain's *Daily Mirror* printed a portion of a 2004 Downing Street memo purporting to show that Bush had wished to blow up Al Jazeera's Qatar headquarters, this hardly seemed surprising, albeit difficult to verify once the British government invoked the Official Secrets Act to silence its media (Parenti 2004; Eide 2004, 280; Lobe 2003b; FAIR 2003g; Gowing 2003, 234; Calabrese 2005a, 162; Maguire and Lines 2005).

This type of violence was not only directed at Al Jazeera. The Committee to Protect Journalists, Reporters sans Frontières, the International Federation of Journalists, and the International Press Institute all condemned U.S. bombing of Iraqi state television. A BBC study indicates that journalists believed independent reporters in Iraq who were not embedded were exposed to Yanqui violence because of the U.S. military's lack of concern for their welfare and the Pentagon's distaste for "unilateral reporting." Noted correspondent Kate Adie revealed that the Pentagon had told her they would fire at journalists using satellite uplinks without their authorization. For nearly thirty years, the United States has refused to ratify the 1977 Geneva Conventions that regard journalists in war zones as civilians who should be guaranteed the safe passage of all noncombatants. In fact, the Pentagon's Office of General Counsel justifies such attacks quite brazenly. Associated Press Managing Editors sent an open letter of protest to the Pentagon, noting that "journalists have been harassed, have had their lives endangered and have had digital camera disks, videotape and other equipment confiscated" by the U.S. military. By early 2005, Yanquis had killed seventy-three reporters in Iraq. When CNN executive Eason Jordan publicly discussed this, the network forced him to resign (Lewis et al. 2004a, 5, 16; Schechter 2005a; Associated Press 2003; Zerbisias 2005; Paterson 2005; Payne 2005, 82–84).

There *are* resources of hope. ITN's *World News for Public Television* saw a U.S. ratings increase on September 11 of more than 50 percent, and BBC

News drew a large number of first-time viewers right across the United States. Amongst U.S. networks, C-SPAN offered international news feeds. Spanish-language media were the only local outlets that depicted the reality of the violence, like images of people leaping from the Towers. Alternative news Web sites in the United States reported a 300 percent increase in readers after the bombing of Afghanistan, while CNN's site visitors declined. In the weeks leading up to the invasion of Iraq, 49 percent of people reading the *Guardian*'s Web site, and 25 percent of visitors to the Australian Broadcasting Corporation's service, were from the Americas. The *Independent*'s site visits increased by 15 percent between September 11 and the invasion of Iraq, a third of which was from the United States. The Pacifica Radio Network, the only cosmopolitan English-language news outlet in the United States, had a record fund drive in early 2003 as war loomed. BBC World News audiences in the United States rose by 28 percent during the invasion of Iraq. Even the *Wall Street Journal* heralded this new cosmopolitanism as "Good News for the U.S."—dimly aware as it was that continued ignorance and small mindedness could spell disaster. Google's popular news page at the time drew on the *Hindustan Times*, the *People's Daily*, the *Toronto Star*, the *Sydney Morning Herald*, *Chosun Ilbo*, the BBC, and Deutsche Welle, inter alia. Its methods of selection are not made public, but readers' interests animate them and the war on terrorism had clearly driven this constituency away from amateur-hour local coverage. In the first week of the 2003 invasion, the top three terms searched for were "CNN," "Iraq," and "Al Jazeera"; the latter had only launched an Anglo site in late March. On the Lycos engine, Al Jazeera outranked "Pamela Anderson," "POWs," and "Dixie Chicks" (Zelizer and Allan 2002b, 12; Borden 2005, 41; Kahney 2003; Sousa 2002; Nichols 2003a; A. W. Matthews 2003; Goldberg 2003; Cox 2003; Gomes 2002; Suellentrop 2003; Brook 2005).

Al Jazeera doubled its European subscribers during the invasion—four million new viewers in one week—and was said to command 70 percent of Arab cable-news viewers worldwide. It appeals to cosmopolitan audiences, with a homepage read by people in 137 countries, most of whom are college graduates, nearly 20 percent with advanced degrees. The United States is its second largest audience base. Two thousand and five advertising figures gave Al Jazeera the world's fifth largest name recognition, and 40–50 million regular viewers. This is no surprise given its recruitment of secular, Muslim, Christian, feminist, Marxist, Ba'athist, and liberal workers—some distance from racialized U.S. notions of diversity. The *Index on Censorship* honored Al Jazeera with its free-expression prize, and analysis indicated that the framing devices it used—which so exercised the Pentagon and other antidemocrats—were identical to media norms everywhere, everywhere but one country, the United States (Cozens

2003; Fine 2003; Miladi 2003, 152; Jasperson and Al-Kikhia 2003, 120, 125; Timms 2005; Byrne 2003a; Lobe 2003b; Khouri 2003; Fisk 2003b; Auter et al. 2004; Cassara and Lengel 2004; *Economist* 2005u).

As the U.S. media and political establishment dithered over the centrality of the alleged weapons of mass destruction as alibis for the invasion of Iraq, and in the wake of revelation after revelation of White House duplicity through exaggeration and perhaps worse, the most effective 2003 search team proved to be Google, which offered a surprising first hit to those who typed in "Weapons of Mass Destruction."

Designed to resemble an error message, it ran for months, sometimes logging a million visits a week. Clicking on the "Bomb" button took viewers to an advertisement for the DVD of Stanley Kubrick's 1964 tragicomedy *Doctor Strangelove: Or, How I Learned to Stop Worrying and Love the Bomb* (*Reuters* 2003b). Military veteran Micah Ian Wright began a similarly deconstructive counterstrategy, taking right-wing posters and redisposing them at www.anti-warposters.com. Wright's inspiration had been his discovery that the NSA was borrowing from SS recruiting tactics (2003, 22).

Web logs created by individuals as clearing houses of information from reliable media systems grew strikingly in popularity. At the same time, Internet and non-Internet Yanquis were similarly dependent on television for news, with 70 percent of the U.S. public following the invasion on television. All news media increased audiences during the crisis, but the largest growth was achieved by cable TV.* Public affairs rates as the lowest area of news interest for heavy U.S. Internet users, whose habits are also determinedly provincial, while just 2 percent of Yanquis relied on the Internet for news reports in 2004. If anything, the Internet denizen was the most rabidly militaristic viewer (Pew Internet & American Life Project 2003a ; Fitzgerald 2003; Sharkey 2003; Lavine and Readership Institute 2003; Tewksbury 2003; Project for Excellence in Journalism 2005).

CONCLUSION

> I got a call on 9/11. I was on CNN, and I got a call at my home [from the White House] saying "You got to say this is connected. This is state-sponsored terrorism. This has to be connected to Saddam Hussein." I said, ". . . I'm willing to say it, but what's your evidence?" And I never got any evidence.
> —General Wesley Clark, NBC, June 15, 2003

*Despite the rhetoric of divinity surrounding the event, just 10% of US residents relied on churches to learn about the war (Pew Research Center for the People & the Press, 2003b).

> In the American media . . . coverage has tended to be very emotional . . .
> It's become extremely patriotic to the point of being jingoistic . . . the
> patriotism, the flag-waving that has been done in the context of what is
> supposed to be news reporting I think has been very problematic. The
> American media I find has been engaged in a lot of sloganeering, easy,
> simple phrases. It has followed the lead of the president.
> —Rami Khouri, Jordanian journalist (Hudson et al. 2002)

What the novelist GK Chesterton (1932) called the "flints and tiles" of urban
existence were rent asunder on September 11 2001, like so many victims of
high-altitude US bombing raids. As a First World disaster, it attained a high
profile because of the premium set on the lives of Manhattan residents. A few
weeks later, an American Airlines plane crashed on take off from Queens. That
borough was left open to all comers, but Manhattan was immediately locked
down and flown over by "friendly" bombers. In stark contrast to the open if
desperate faces on the street a month earlier, people went about their business
with heads bowed even lower than is customary.

The contradictory deconstructions and valuations of Manhattan lives mean
that September 11 will live in infamy and hyperknowability. The vengeful
United States government continues on its way. Local residents must ponder
insurance claims, real-estate values, children's terrors, and their own role in
something beyond their ken. New York has been forced beyond the center of
the financial, legal, media, diplomatic, and art worlds, beyond even its status
as the ur-city of modernity. It is a risk city, a military target, a place that is receiv
ing— as well as funding—the slings and arrows of global fortune. In one sense,
attrition-at-a-distance, as per Chile in 1973, has ended. The violence is suddenly
local. In another sense, as we have come to see since the fall of 2001, attrition-
at-a-distance is undergoing a frightening renewal. The blasé attitude toward
Venezuelan democracy adopted by the United States and its plutocratic media
provides yet further evidence, if any were needed. When Congress installed an
independent commission to inquire into what went wrong on September 11—
what successive administrations had known about Al Qaeda's intentions, how
the attacks were funded, how commercial airlines calculate profit versus safety,
why it took so long for fighter jets to scramble when four planes had been
hijacked, and so on—the bourgeois media showed virtually no interest in the
proceedings until lapsed terror bureaucrat Richard Clarke's revelations about
the Bush Administration's lack of concern about terrorism, and the commission's subsequent findings. When it provided an additional report four years after
the attacks, evaluating the Federal Government for its manifold failings, the
media subordinated coverage of these findings to cosmetic surgery, Saddam
Hussein's trial, and Tom DeLay (Corn 2003; Mitchell 2005).

Today, all people living outside the United States are *not* Americans, despite statements from the Israeli and French Governments and NATO that fateful September, because they are not all ignorant of what the United States does. As the noted economist and *New York Times* columnist Paul Krugman puts it, "the rest of the world simply doesn't trust Mr. Bush either to honor his promises or to tell the truth," but U.S. citizens have no idea because of an "ever-deferential, protective media" (2003a). Mexico City's *La Jornada* brilliantly mocked the devout earnestness with which Yanqui media reported the ludicrous efforts of the Administration to ascertain whether the "real" Saddam Hussein was standing up during the 2003 invasion. Noting Cheney's routine absence from public view, *Jornada* followed the CIA's example of trying to verify Hussein's photographs through the testimony of an ex-girlfriend. The newspaper sent reporters boldly into the field to undertake a similar audit of Cheney's lapsed lovers, but could not locate any. The rest of the world saw Bush Minor prissily primping prior to his address to the nation as he ordered the destruction of Iraq, but U.S. TV viewers were deemed too sensitive to witness this awkward, hilarious moment (Cason and Brooks 2003; Goldstein 2003b; Pew Research Center for the People & the Press 2004b).

In terms of knowledge of the events of September 11 and subsequent invasions, the population knew less about the world and its own government than seems possible. This empirically challenged group held firm to the fantasy that the invasion of Iraq had demonstrated that the United States was "trustworthy and supportive of democracy" (Pew Research Center for the People & the Press 2004b, 2). Comprehensive studies by the Program on International Policy Attitudes and Knowledge Networks found that a minority of the U.S. population knew that clear majorities all over the world opposed the 2003 invasion; and a significant minority thought the war was supported globally (2003 and 2004d; Kull et al. 2003–04). These people also believed weapons of mass destruction had been found in Iraq, and that there were indisputable ties between Iraq and September 11. The credulity held firm a year after the invasion, and it correlated with viewers' support for the R-Worders and their consumption of commercial TV news.

Time magazine asked two hundred and fifty thousand people across Europe, "Which country poses the greatest danger to world peace in 2003?" offering them a choice between Iraq, North Korea, and the United States. Eight percent selected Iraq, 9 percent chose North Korea, and . . . but you have already done the calculation about the most feared country of all (Pilger 2003). A BBC poll in eleven countries in mid-2003 confirmed this. It found sizeable majorities everywhere disapproving of Bush Minor and the invasion of Iraq, especially regarding civilian casualties (*BBC News Online* 2003).

Novelist Kurt Vonnegut quipped that "in case you haven't noticed, we are now almost as feared and hated all over the world as the Nazis were" (2004). After Bush's reelection, a poll across twenty-one sovereign states found 47 percent of people opposed to the United States in general—not just its government, now, but its population, too, while 58 percent thought Bush's mandate made life riskier. Longitudinal studies indicated that the big change between the contemporary moment and the last time the United States was led by an ideologically similar R-Worder, Reagan, was that while the whole world correctly loathed the United States government for its imperialism during the Reagan administration, they exempted the United States population from responsibility. Now, the rest of the world does not excuse the violence undertaken in the United States' name (BBC News Online 2005o; Pew Research Center for the People & the Press 2005a).

In 2003, after Cheney encouraged the unsubstantiated belief among the U.S. public that Iraq was behind the World Trade Center's destruction, even Bush Minor felt obliged to correct him. Yet, there was no attempt by the mainstream media to publicize this to the 70 percent of the population that had believed the original canard—the media did not deem Bush's admission as newsworthy. Of the country's twelve largest-circulation daily papers, only the *Los Angeles Times*, the *Chicago Tribune*, and the *Dallas Morning News* mentioned it on their front pages. The *New York Times* ran it on page twenty-two, *USA Today* on page sixteen, the *Houston Chronicle* on page three, the *San Francisco Chronicle* and the *New York Daily News* on page fourteen, the *Washington Post* on page eighteen, and *Newsday* on page forty-one. R-Word house organs—the *New York Post* and the *Wall Street Journal*—did not mention the revelation at all. Then when the Iraq Survey Group's final report to Congress, just prior to the 2004 elections, confirmed what the Left, the International Atomic Energy Agency, and the UN had painstakingly explained a year and a half earlier—that there were no significant weapons of mass destruction in Iraq until the United States arrived—the report attracted such minimal Yanqui press attention that the R-Word half of the population continued to believe the lies it had been told. When the final word came from U.S. authorities in January 2005 that no such weapons had been found, the reportage was so hard to find that it itself might have justified an invasion. Only ABC made it a lead story, Fox News barely touched on the topic, and CBS and NBC relegated it to a minor item—fewer than sixty words on the nightly news. The *New York Times* editorialized that the acknowledgment was "little noted" around the world. Furthermore, in 2005, 44 percent of Yanquis thought Iraqis had attacked their country on September 11, 2001 (Porges 2003; Program on International Policy Attitudes and Knowledge Networks 2004c;

Whiten 2005, 7; Harris Poll 2005). The truth was only known to Yanquis who watched or listened to public broadcasting. Goodbye discourse and the active audience, hullo ideology and the passive recipient.

The U.S. media system's mindless bluster is matched only by its awesome force. The extent and power of this bulwark of ignorance and violence has led the noted foreign correspondent Robert Fisk (2002) to the brink of despair at the hysteria his reports engender here. Ex-U.S. diplomat George Dempsey identified Fisk as partly to blame for the events of September 11 (International Federation of Journalists 2001, 13), and Yanqui actor John Malkovich told the Cambridge Union that he "would like to shoot" Fisk. The reporter's reaction was to say: "If we want a quiet life, we will just have to toe the line, stop criticizing Israel or America. Or just stop writing altogether." Three years on, he believed that the "lie-on-its-back frightened Labrador of the American media" had become "a vicious Rottweiler" because of the repeated failures in Iraq (Fisk, 2005). But, how long could that remain the case, given the political-economic pressures already outlined?

Meanwhile, the U.S. Government selected Grace Digital Media to run an Arabic-language, satellite television news service for postinvasion Iraq. Grace is a fundamentalist Christian company which describes itself as "dedicated to transmitting the evidence of God's presence in the world today" via "secular news, along with aggressive proclamations that will 'change the news' to reflect the Kingdom of God." It is dedicated to Zionism. The U.S. government gave responsibility of running Al Iraqiya, an Iraqi media network, to the Harris Corporation, a defense contractor with no news experience, but a history of contributing money to the R-Word (quoted in Mokhiber and Weissman 2003b; Lynch 2005). And the military clandestinely paid Iraqi newspapers to print pro-Yanqui stories written by "information operations" troops and placed by a private contractor, but appearing as the work of independent local journalists, many of whom were also on the payroll. Also, the Pentagon secretly purchased a paper and a radio station, all while Rumsfeld was boasting about the free Iraqi media as a means of legitimizing the invasion. The International Federation of Journalists condemned this as "a cynical campaign of double standards." Domestically, Michael Powell took the invasion as evidence that additional consolidation of media ownership was essential, because only gigantic firms could offer adequate coverage of such major events (Mazzetti and Daraghi 2005; E&P Staff 2005a; International Federation of Journalists 2005; Chester 2003).

U.S. citizens can only hope that Fisk's quiescence is as unlikely as his words are ironic. We must rely on such outside truth telling and political pressure. The places that provide the United States with bases, matériel, personnel, and ideological support, must change their tune. There must be pressure from the UN, the North Atlantic Treaty Organization (NATO), the Organization of American States/Organización de los Estados Americanos, the African Union, ASEAN, the Arab League, and the E.U., against the U.S. and Israel's position on territory claimed by the latter since 1967. There must be pressure on totalitarian U.S. allies, such as Egypt, Jordan, Algeria, Saudi Arabia, Morocco, and Pakistan, to become genuinely democratic. There must be pressure to open the U.S. media system to effective foreign ownership, and to retrain journalists in democratic practice.

High violent crime, profoundly politicized and widespread religious observance, routine state execution, and an unquestioning media are all identifiers of Global South despotism, not First World democracy. Yet, they are all characteristics of the First World democracy with the most powerful military and corporate forces in world history, and a blindly chauvinistic news media that can finance and feel, but cannot research or explain other than through the culturalist frame of antimaterialist history. Close to three thousand people died on September 11, 2001. The same year in the United States, one hundred and fifty thousand died of lung cancer, thirty-eight thousand in cars, and thirty thousand by gunshot, while two hundred and fifty were raped (Mann 2003, 103). This country is very, very unsafe because of the immense risks generated by local commerce and masculinity, and the failure to create citizenship codes that protect against that violence. U.S. residents who know what is going on must make a plea—help the country lose its ignorance. Make television more than a wasteland. Let U.S. citizens swim with the minnows, rather than hunt with the fowlers of media regulation. "A lie moves around the world at the speed of light" (Rumsfeld quoted in E&P Staff 2005b). "Either you are with us, or you are with the terrorists" (Bush 2001) and "the enemies of civilization" (The White House 2002). Help keep Manhattan alive.

3

TELEVISION FOOD

From Brahmin Julia to Working-Class Emeril

There seem to be but three ways for a nation to acquire wealth. The
first is by war, as the Romans did, in plundering their neighbors. This
is robbery. The second by commerce, which is generally cheating.
The third is by agriculture, the only honest way, wherein man receives
a real increase of the seed thrown into the ground, in a kind of
continual miracle, wrought by the hand of God in his favor, as reward
for his innocent life and his virtuous industry.
  —Benjamin Franklin (quoted in Doiron, 2003)

Food is the absolute beginning.
  —Dwayne Andreas, former Chair, Archer Daniels Midland
  (quoted in Cook 2004, 4)

Far too many cookery and gardening programmes. Dumb, dumb,
dumb.
  —Alasdair Milne, BBC Director General 1982–87, speaking of the
  twenty-first century BBC (quoted in *BBC News Online* 2004)

FOOD IS MATERIALLY and symbolically crucial to life and its
government. A key site of subjectivity in every society, food is
an index of power. It was the basis of the earliest class systems,
symbolized by consumption, and religions, organized around
harvesting. The three types of citizenship can be mapped by food: the
political by food policy; the economic by food resources; and the cultural
by food symbolism. Although food is often produced in rural settings, it is
increasingly an urban problem and pleasure—literally a moving feast, trav-
eling great distances, accreting and attenuating power and meaning
through cultural contact (Fernández-Armesto 2002, 19; European Food
Project 2005; Foucault 2003b, 103; Westheimer and Kahne 2004a, 242;
Bell 2002).

Put simply, food offers distinctions in social life that "shampoo and software do not." Hence the French farmer José Bové's capacity to attack

"McMerde" [McShit] for its neoliberal, Yanqui symbolism (*Economist* 2003d, 4). Hence General Mills' mid-1990s decision to remove the white, suburban Betty Crocker from its cereal and syrup marketing in favor of a digital composite of seventy-five U.S. women from various racial and ethnic backgrounds. The new goal was diversity at the point of decoding, and hence purchase. The continuity was women being held responsible for creating hearty meals. In Britain and the United States, studies have suggested an explanatory link between the high proportion of women in the labor force and convenience food in homes, along with growing numbers of people living alone, and children with purchasing capacity and authority. The President's Council of Economic Advisors reported in 2000 that sex and violence could be lessened, and scholarship enhanced, through children supping in the company of their parents (Minow 2003, 72; Holden et al. 2002, 7; *Life* 2005; *Economist* 2003f, 10). Women are increasingly held responsible for children's health—the gruesomely named "McDonald's Balanced, Active Lifestyles Team" repeatedly implores "moms" to be its partners in youth welfare (2005, 6).

At another extreme, hunger strikes thematize the hyperdrama of the state's responsibility to secure the relative heath—or at least survival—of its population, especially the incarcerated. Of the five hundred men held without charge or trial in Guantánamo from 2001, many refused food to protest their detention and conditions in 2005. This action was the latest in a long line of dietary resistance by prisoners against liberal hypocrisy through civil disobedience: British and U.S. feminists in the early twentieth century; Mohandas K. Gandhi between 1922 and 1942; the Berrigan brothers Daniel and Philip in 1969; Soledad inmates and César Chávez in the 1970s; 1981 Irish Republican Army members; and 1996 and 2004 Kurdish death-fasters (*BBC News Online* 2005d; *Columbia Electronic Encyclopedia* 2005; Larkspirit.com, 2005). Put simply, food's "you are what you eat" tag is a facile, if fallible, classificatory system.

Food signifies historically as well as anthropologically. European food riots were common between the seventeenth and early nineteenth centuries. They were spontaneous, local collective actions in protest at shortages. With the rise of a centralized sovereign state and a free press, both national and nongovernmental forms of information and control made for a different politics, with access to formalized chains of propaganda, critique, and policy formation. No functioning democracy or state with a free press has *ever* had a famine, because information about shortages can move around the country, outwitting corporations and states that try to deny problems. For example, there have been no famines in postindependence Australia, Botswana, or India. But with corporate trade in agriculture, a new international division of food labor, and the displacement of national by global forms of regulation that match business mobility, local control of food issues in general is becoming less feasible (L. Taylor 1996; Sen 1996; Atkins and Bowler 2001 38–39, 43).

A similarly global process applies to retailing meals. What we now know as restaurants began as open kitchens in medieval villages that fed passing travelers, as abbeys and convents along the Northern European coastline, and dens in Chinese cities. The modern form is commonly thought to have emerged in late eighteenth-century France, when cooks left aristocratic house-holds, and tables d'hôte were replaced by quasi-public sites and flexible meal-times. Restaurants were first named as such in France in 1825. They rapidly became sites for democratizing knowledge of different foodstuffs and prepa-rations, and spreading notions of correct conduct across societies beyond the ruling élite. In the United States, restaurants started as bars that offered food gratis to finesse the alcohol they sold. The tea tables and coffee houses of sev-enteenth and eighteenth-century London, Leipzig, Milan, and Paris provided spaces for discussions of science, insurance, religion, and art—the much-trum-peted Öffentlichkeit or public sphere of civil society (Spang 2002, 52; Finkel-stein 1989, 34–36, 46; Briggs and Burke 2003, 30–31, 71). In keeping with modernity's ethos of mobility, three decades ago, gourmet chef and author Ray-mond Oliver celebrated modern transportation and technology as articulators of cuisine across classes (1969, 7). Mobility enabled fast food; not the lan-guorous counterpublic sphere of the coffee house, but the quick-moving line at Starbucks. A leisurely yet vigorous place of democratic deliberation has given way to a hyperpaced site of postindustrial consumerism.

Fast food encapsulates structural adjustments in search of efficiencies, as per the time discipline of capitalism. Paragons of dietetic madness and worker exploitation, fast-food franchises began in the United States in the 1950s in response to rising labor costs. The industry reduced the workforce to a strict roster of required hours, transferred labor to the customer, introduced plastic and paper products, and dismissed supermarket purchasing in favor of insti-tutionalized prepreparation such as processed, sliced cheese and individually packaged condiments. Casual labor and environmental degradation sustain fast food. It is a service-industry model of exploited workers and despoiled space.

In the U.K., people spend two and a half more hours pursuing and eating food outside the household than forty years ago. The average time taken to prepare a meal in 1980 was two hours. By 2002, it was twenty minutes, with more and more people buying meals and bringing them home. The trend—less time making food and more time acquiring it—is spreading rapidly across Italy, Spain, and Germany. Three quarters of all Yanquis live within three miles of a McDonald's, and 30 percent of eating in the United States is now done in cars, with the 7-11 chain introducing "Dashboard Dining." In the first five years of the twenty-first century, these "restaurants" averaged 5.6 percent growth in annual sales. At the other end of the class spectrum lies a gentrified variety of fast food— the high-quality, made-to-order dining delivered to homes at a phone call (Reiter 1996, 43; Lang and Caraher 2001, 3, 5–6; Morgan and Morley 2002, 6; British Council 2005; Bedell 2002, 32–33; *Economist* 2005q; Bell 2002, 15).

Fast food's international popularity is often said to result from its symbolic connection to the United States, modernity, and efficiency. For those used to state socialism, McDonald's offered a game, with players given a multiple-choice test about the composition and size of the Berlin Wall! Sensational expectations were engendered amongst Russian and Chinese shoppers in the 1990s when the first McDonald's opened there. Moscow teenagers offered to break through the lines to buy hamburgers, and in Beijing, 40,000 customers were served the first day. In the People's Republic of China, McDonald's is opening a hundred outlets a year, and KFC, two hundred. Burger King, too, is expanding there (*Economist* 2003h; *Economist* 2005q). This exportation from the United States is ironic considering that the hamburger was invented in the Baltic, discovered by German sailors, repatriated to Hamburg, then popularized in the United States by Midwestern migrants as a European delicacy. And, it's misleading that fast food's exportation is constructed as the triumph of ordinary people over authoritarianism. In the northern summer of 1989, coverage of miners on strike in the Soviet Union elevated them as paragons of virtue against an authoritarian regime swamped U.S. TV news. A few years later, when McDonald's violated post-Soviet Russian law by refusing to recognize the relevant union, restive workers were granted no such coverage of their struggle, let alone a focus on democratic rights (Martin 2004, 16–17).

Comprising about 5 percent of the restaurant business in France, fast food has been growing rapidly there since the late 1980s. In the 1970s, eating at a chain was considered chic: the intelligentsia frequented the few outlets, and fashion shows associated themselves with hamburger stands. By 1989, this otherness had become ordinary fare. France opened its own fast-food chains with the names France-Quick, FreeTime, Magic Burger, B'burger, Manhattan Burger, Katy's Burger, Love Burger, and Kiss Burger. But, there is a dialectical movement here. Morrissey taunts in "America is not the World," "You know where you can shove your hamburger," and a globalizing food culture sounds Yanqui, such that national languages seem under threat. The French Government responded by creating a National Council of Culinary Art within the Ministry of Culture, dedicated to "protecting the culinary patrimony" from fast food and other stresses. The state provides assistance to keep specialist retailers thriving, and designates a special week each year in which children are taught about cooking and eating (Rogers 2002; Ritzer 1993, 2–3; Fantasia 1995, 202–3, 205–7, 213, 224, 230; Rensi 1995, xii; Stephenson 1989, 230; Fort 2003).

The impact of the United States on food around the world is always political. The U.S. Commerce Department prepared a report in 1961, arguing for the development of new restaurants in the Asia Pacific region as a means of attracting Yanqui tourists and discouraging Maoism and Marxism-Leninism. The quasi-religious fervor with which U.S. culture engages and subsidizes its huge, uncompetitive agricultural sector is matched only by the quasi-religious fervor with which it proselytizes for agriculture elsewhere to be regarded as beyond cultural significance or basic subsistence. So the WTO's Trade-Related Intellectual Property Rights, an ugly creature of neoliberalism, disavows the sacerdotal rituals and intellectual exchange associated with cultivating rice in South Asia. Its panels on food trade consistently rule in the interest of multinationals corporatizing seeds and evading safety rules. The World Bank and the IMF push Third World farmers away from providing food to local people. Instead, they must farm cotton for export, leading to mass suicides after crop failures, and huge increases in the costs of staple goods that were once abundant. While proponents of the WTO's Agreement on Agriculture celebrated its tenth anniversary in 2005 for its impact on increased trade, critics recognized a disaster for actual farmers, because MNCs were dumping food at subsidized rates, especially from the United States (Spang 2002, 54; Shiva 2000, 8–9, 10–11, 13; Wallach and Woodall/Public Citizen 2004, 68; Murphy et al. 2005). Partly as a consequence of U.S. and E.U. patterns of assistance/domination, the world uses less than 1 percent of available crop types for food. Other potentially cultivable flora have been dismissed as inappropriate, which increases the risk of crop failure in the Global South. These new restrictions demolish traditional knowledge, and deride other nutritional systems. Instead of seeking self-sufficiency and preserving farming land, the search for the EOI chimera of comparative advantage sees Third World nations growing luxury vegetables and cut flowers for export, and importing basic foods they once grew for themselves. This leads to energy-intensive packaging, and goods moving across agri-food chains in ways that are convenient and cheap for the Global North, but potentially destructive for the Global South. So, India is required to create industrial shrimp farms to feed the First World, destroying hundreds of acres of productive ecosystems as aquaculture displaces fisheries, traditional jobs, ground water, and local foodstuffs (Almås and Lawrence 2003, 11; Shiva 2000, 15).

Despite half a century of nutritional advice as to the benefits of grains, fruit, and vegetables, Yanquis persist with an animal-based diet, furthered by a clever food industry, a duplicitous state, and an enabling media, all of which disavow research findings and predictions about industrialized meat manufacture and consumption. With 90 percent of the world's managed water used to grow food, meat eaters utilizing five thousand liters of water a day to feed their habit versus the one to two thousand required by vegetarians, and eight hundred and forty million people suffering from undernourishment, the implications for continued industrial carnivorism should be apparent. A structure of dominance characterizes the global political economy of food. Large multinational corporations increasingly control agricultural industries, and health issues and specialist consumer niches in public niches subordinate farm incomes and working conditions. Indeed, it is a risk society, or perhaps a risk world, when agricultural corporations sell fungicides, herbicides, and pesticides that facilitate corporate agriculture but pollute waterways and soil, and where bovine spongiform encephalopathy appears to have resulted from corporations feeding offal to herbivores who were later consumed by people (Nestle 2002; Vidal 2004; Almås and Lawrence 2003, 11–12; Friedmann 1995, 512; Cook 2004).

At the same time as foodstuffs are massively standardized at the level of development and manufacture, their presentation is increasingly differentiated and deregulated. More and more countries over the late 1980s and 1990s imported cuisine from around the globe. Consumption of food became radically disaffiliated from its conditions of production and circulation. Consumers are not told of the complex economics and politics behind their purchase. Instead, they are given a spice of difference to do with the geographic origin of items on the menu, an enchanting quality to what is on offer. This is tourism in a bowl, as per the Beefeater chain adding South Asian, Mexican, Cajun, and Thai food to its traditional fare, under the slogan "Discover the world and eat it" (Fine and Leopold 1993, 151–52; Bowler and Atkins 2001, 115, 174–75; Cook and Crang 1996, 132, 144). This chapter looks at the places where such marketing circulates. It investigates the history of food and the media, the shift from early TV cooking to cable and satellite niches, and potential alternatives to a purely consumerist address of viewers that would engage progressive cultural politics.

MEDIA FOOD

> By offering the ideas of the marketplace rather than a marketplace of ideas, we are, in effect, rotting our seed corn.
> —Former FCC Commissioner Nicholas Johnson (2003, 527)

European advice books from the mid-1600s detailed table settings, measured distances between diners, and explained the need for a tablecloth to hide the lower body whilst eating. The earliest cookbooks date from this time, and communicate the way the élite comported itself as a model for the slightly lower orders. By the mid-nineteenth century, Mrs. Beeton's thousand-page *Book of Household Management* had thoroughly textualized food custom, blending the political economy of daily life with manners and recipes. U.S. newspapers first started publishing articles about food in the 1840s. By the 1880s, these columns had become social advice guides, with instructions on the behavioral correlatives of class mobility. Key links between food and the audiovisual media date from the telegraph and the radio providing data on commodity prices and weather, and overproduction leading to mass advertising. In the United States, automated grain milling began in the late 1890s. Oats had been popularly regarded as fodder, so the production of oatmeal en masse necessitated new marketing and markets—the formation of taste. This led to the institutionalization of breakfast as a daily repast through media promotions, and feedback from customers in order to improve the image of breakfast cereal. The innovation involved scientistic testimonials, boxtop premia, and railway-tour sampling (Beniger 1992).

In the post–World War II period, U.S. publishers discerned a variety of markets for food media, notably single working women. In 1961, forty-nine cookbooks were published; in 2001, over one thousand and seven hundred, and with cross-media links. By 2004, half of the twenty-five top sellers were "written" by Food Network presenters. All in all, five hundred and thirty million books on food and alcohol were sold in the United States in 2000. Where fifty years ago, the United States had about twenty food magazines, in 2002, it had 145. Approximately 25 percent of U.S. newspapers added "Style" pages between 1979 and 1983, of which 38 percent had circulations of more than one hundred thousand. Such sections now draw fairly rigorous distinctions between *dining* out—costly, occasioned, planned, and dressed for—and *eating* out—easy, standardized, and requiring minimal presentational effort. Both are styles of life as much as practices of food consumption, and they are truly big business—grocery purchase and restaurant dining in the United States amount to US$709 billion a year. Consider the shifting discourse on cuisine in the *Philadelphia Inquirer* and *Philadelphia Magazine*. In the early 1960s, the *Inquirer* ran recipe columns and advertisements related to home dining, with women as the target audience. Functional aesthetics articulated with home economics. All was simplicity and thrift, other than on special occasions. In the 1970s, a section appeared in the Sunday *Magazine* on places to go, dramatically displacing "Food and Family." The restaurant was described as a public, commercial, and cultural site of urban sophistication, even attracting the ultimate fetish of the 1970s—investigative reporting. By the 1980s, the Sunday food section included a wine guide, and food writers assumed the title "critics." They offered instruction on enjoyment rather than production—knowledge about, not knowledge of how to. Aesthetics had displaced functionality. Taste was not taken for granted as something that one simply had or did not. It was schooled. Gossip networks emerged, along with guides on obtaining the best service in restaurants (O'Neill 2003; Richard Jones 2003; Barnes 2004; Danford 2005; Harris 2003, 55; Harp 2006; Makala 2005; Martin 2004, 56; Hanke 1989, 221–33; Finkelstein 1989, 38; Fine and Leopold 1993, 167; Comcast 2000).

As the number of news pages dedicated to food increased, their style and generic placement changed. In 1940, the *New York Times* published 675 food stories, of which just 1 percent were light background fare, or what is now known as "foodie" news, such as profiles of chefs or recipes. The remainder reported on food poisoning, nutrition, or famine. Twenty years on, the corollary proportion of "foodie" news had doubled to 9 percent. But twenty years after that, in 1980, 36 percent of food stories in the *New York Times* were lifestyle related, and by 2000, 80 percent of the 1,927 food stories were on chefs and recipes (O'Neill 2003). The "foodie" trend in reportage and interest is celebrated as a response to affluent consumers, a skilled working class, efficient and effective transportation, and cosmopolitanism. Yet, in the words of the noted cookbook author and columnist Molly O'Neill, "some of the most significant stories today are about food. But you won't find them in the food section, where journalism has been supplanted by fantasy" (2003). Whitedot.org, an anti-television group that provides propaganda tools such as "Today's Special is TURN OFF THE DAMN TV" and "Conversation welcome here. This establishment is *not* RUINED BY TELEVISION," for distribution in restaurants, enables "foodie" snobbery.

This trivialization comes at a time of serious public health crises: thirty years ago, food-borne disease was rare in the United States, and generally attributable to community events like church picnics. Now, infected food makes seventy-six million people ill each year. Five thousand die, and three hundred and twenty-five thousand are hospitalized, at a public health cost of US$10 billion. But the federal government makes a quarter of the food-safety inspections that it did two decades ago, with the percentage of imported food examined dropping from 8 percent in 1993 to 2 percent in 2003. At the same time, it provides links between fast-food outlets and the President's Council on Physical Fitness, and attacks the World Health Organization's findings that fruit and vegetables help ward off obesity and diabetes. As rewards, R-Worders get 80 percent of campaign contributions from the livestock and meat-processing industries, and the National Cattlemen's Beef Association endorsed

Bush in 2004—its first decision of this kind in a century of promoting death and despoliation (Hutton 2003b, 154; Wallach and Woodall/Public Citizen 2004, 52–53; Post 2005, 169; Allan 2002, 147; Cook 2004, 6; Farsetta 2004; Jones 2003; *Los Angeles Times* 2004b; Ruskin and Schor 2005).

Front organizations for the food and pesticide sectors, such as the Harvard Center for Risk Analysis and the Center for Consumer Freedom, arm themselves with slogans like "Promoting Personal Responsibility and Protecting Consumer Choice," and TV commercials that depict a lawyer promising "a mega-sized lawsuit to go with those fries" (Grossman 2004, 22; Lawrence 2004, 64, 71). The delightful new domain of "litigation public relations" quashes attempts by investigative journalists to reveal corporate malfeasance in the food sector. Corporations seeking to discredit revelations of their venality by focusing on clandestine newsgathering, target potential jurors, attorneys, judges, and journalism faculty. At the same time, serious conflicts of interest are generated by interlocking directorates between media and food corporations. General Electric and the *Washington Post* share company directors with Coca-Cola, and Pepsi's board has people from the boards of directors of the *New York Times*, Gannett, and the Tribune Company. Tribune also has directors in common with McDonald's and Quaker Oats, while Anheuser-Busch and Kellogg represent General Electric (Raphael et al. 2004; Phillips 2005).

Despite clear correlations between youth obesity and local prices of fresh fruit and vegetables—nothing to do with consumer choice—the high moralism so prevalent in the U.S. media has led to a doctrine of personal responsibility, militating against both collective identification and action. Average caloric intake in the United States increased from 2,080 to 2,347 between 1980 and 2000, and adult obesity grew by 80 percent, leading the surgeon general to place overeating alongside smoking as the principal lifestyle killer in the country. But only a third of the public holds MNCs responsible for obesity (RAND Corporation 2005; Saad 2003b; also see Lee and Oliver, 2002; *Economist* 2003d, 4; Lee and Oliver 2002). Meanwhile, groups lobby the Vatican to remove gluttony from the seven deadly sins (Harris 2003, 57), the National Association for the Advancement of Fat Americans increases in size, and the North American Association for the Study of Obesity's obesityonline.org forms as a one-stop shop for related scientific knowledge. The cost of overweight people to public health touches US$70 billion a year, and discussion of obesity in the national media has increased fivefold since 1992. They cover the topic as a matter of individual choice and medical definition, measurement, and treatment (Lawrence 2004). Can one really attribute these facts to a conscious, wise choice by consumers? According to the Center for Consumer Freedom, a diligent servant of food corporations that masquerades as an independent, individualist lobby group, defending "food liberty," as "fought for by the original American patriots." Its bizarre *Declaration of Food Independence* denounces "aspiring Big Brothers" (such as the National Resources Defense Council and Physicians for Responsible Medicine) and accuses animal-rights activists of killing dogs (Krugman 2005; Center for Consumer Freedom 2005).

Food TV is a key site of risk and moral panic, a space that physically forms and maintains citizens, gives them pleasure, and makes them vulnerable to medical hazards. In India, for instance, the claim that the amount of TV advertising for "junk" food doubled between 2002 and 2004 is a political topic (*News Today* 2005). A long running but rapidly intensifying discourse blames television for obesity; it tropes Minow in announcing that TV "creates a vast wasteline" (Nicholas Johnson 2003, 522). Children's eating habits worry nutritionists, regulators, teachers, and parents, with advertising a particular site of anxiety, research, and critique. The research on media effects and food is inconclusive, and focused on commercials to the exclusion of programming and the everyday lives of the young, where overall food representation is as important as specific promotional techniques. The sparse investigations of food portrayals across genres disclose a pattern of sugary, fatty foods appearing again and again during fictional television as well as advertising, with a stark contrast between the somatotypes of actors and the diets they appear to favor. Ninety percent of women in primetime U.S. TV drama are below normal weight, and overweight women are twice as likely as others to be laughed at. The Centers for Disease Control and Prevention argue that genre is irrelevant—the mere fact of watching TV makes children fat—and the Institute of Medicine of the National Academies avows that the stress on marketing low-nutrient, high-calorie foodstuffs to children is dangerous. Then again, perhaps the positive correlation between low food regulation and high obesity is the real culprit, given the inverse correlation in the E.U. versus the United States (Dickinson 2005; Lee and Oliver 2002; Teinowitz and Thompson 2005; McGinnis et al. 2005; *Economist* 2003e, 7).

Almost 70 percent of the US$30 billion spent on food advertising annually (US$2.1 billion to TV commercials) promotes "convenience" foods, rather than fresh grains, vegetables, and fruit, which garner about 2 percent of such funds. Persistent critiques from Senators, Governors, the Kaiser Family Foundation, and the Federal Trade Commission pushed the Children's Advertising Review Unit, a laughable self-regulatory body, into action in 2005 after decades of rubber-stamping. The response was little more than brief embarrassment and a minor shake-up. The methods of targeting children used by, for example, soft-drink firms are so extensive and varied that cutting them back would take serious regulation. Within schools, they place logos on vending machines, sporting facilities, and uniforms; advertise in hallways, textbooks, and buses; and set up agreements guaranteeing "pouring rights." Elsewhere, they use TV, magazine, and Internet commercials, phone cards, prizes, and product placement. Licensing agreements have transmogrifed sweetmeats into characters in children's literature, and annual expenditure on confectionary is close to thirty times the total budget of the UN (Pearce and Hansson 2000; Power 2004, 18; Ketchum 2005, 219; Halweil and Scowcroft 2002; *Economist* 2003g, 12; Cook 2004, 45; Nestle 2002, 187; McChesney and Foster 2003, 6; Holden et al. 2002, 6)

The FCC tried to regulate children's television on cable for the first time in 2006, but Disney, Viacom, and Time Warner were strenuously lobbying and engaging in CSR to prevent this. Viacom's Nick at Night has decreed each September 26 "family-dinner night," encouraging parents and children to eat healthily and collectively. Its preschooler programming and network, Nick Jr. and Noggin, have a cynical partnership with the Clinton Foundation and the American Heart Association to promote diet and exercise. Meanwhile, Time Warner's Cartoon Network has discovered the benefits of health discourse in a "Get Animated" initiative. These MNCs pursue such "enlightened" policies even as they mount court challenges against regulation of programming for the young. "Cheeseburger" legislation wended its way through the U.S. Federal system in 2004, along with dozens of "Baby McBills" in state legislatures, seeking to prevent customers who grow fat from suing the "restaurants" they eat in. All were created at the bidding of the food industry and all mobilized rhetorics of neoliberal self-governance (Downey 2005b; *Life* 2005; Ruskin and Schor 2005; Zernike 2004).

Meanwhile, McDonald's has joined the Global Obesity Task Force, an Orwellian outlet for creators of the world's iatrogenic problems to explain them away. The company claims to sell more salad more than anybody else, and has hired Oprah Winfrey's personal trainer to encourage customers to work out. It unleashed a 2005 campaign to encourage youthful eaters to remain "active," utilizing celebrities, athletes, commercials, Web sites, NGO links, and other promotions. The campaign urged viewers to replicate Ronald McDonald climbing up a building and playing basketball with Yao Ming; all part of a corporate attempt to move from "being a fat purveyor to a phat icon." They even made the clown look thinner to match the promotion (Sanders 2005a; MacArthur 2005a, 2005b; Teinowitz 2005a, 2005b, and 2005c; *BBC News Online* 2005a; Hawken 2003; *Economist* 2003c; *Economist* 2004b, 63). In 2005, Kraft Foods responded to intense criticism regarding obesity by shifting its food advertising away from sugar cookies and drinks and toward a new "Sensible Solution" line of products oriented to child consumers. As the trade magazine *Advertising Age* put it:

food industry observers fear that Kraft's strategy bolsters the position of the consumer advocates and government officials who favor an over-all ban on the big business of marketing "junk" food to children (*Economist* 2005s, 39).

Communications scholar Eileen Meehan has demonstrated that any engagement with food media must look at the political economy of owner-ship and control, product placement, and intertextuality with U.S. consumer life (2001). Consider the NBC-produced *Restaurant*, a 2003–04 reality show about life in a restaurant run by celebrity Food Network chef Rocco DiSpir-ito. Produced by the advertising agency Interpublic Sports and Entertain-ment Group, it guaranteed "top clients access to integration deals" (quoted in McChesney and Foster 2003, 3). This amounted to covert advertising through product placement by such companies as Mitsubishi, Coors, and American Express, which were also the principal noncovert advertisers. For preternaturally anxious cultural critics, the program and its ilk had "a hidden or perverse side . . . analogous to pornographic films," as evident from sur-real colors and improbably symmetrical chickens ready for visual capture — the food equivalent of the proverbial money shot (B. Morris 2003; Chan 2003; also see Kaufman 2005). Getting to that level of concern is some dis-tance from Julia Child's world of public broadcasting, but a difference of his-tory as much as degree, as we shall see.

BEGINNINGS

In her voice — "to-mah-toe," "herbs" with a hard "h" — you hear the patrician New England ancestry, the Smith education, the dozen years spent living abroad. In her manner, you see at heart a California girl, raised in Pasadena, supremely un-self-conscious. Drop a fish in your kitchen, and "Whoooo is going to know?"
    —Diane Cyr (2000, 40)

The towering Mrs. Child was a maniac with blades, never meeting a knife she didn't like. . . . An offending loaf was tossed over her shoulder among the potted plants; a misflipped potato was scraped off the range and back into the pan; her false teeth were firmly readjusted in front of the camera. She began her demonstration of coq au vin by dropping a whole chicken on the floor, dusting it off and remarking: "It's OK. No one's looking."
    —*The Economist* (2004d)

Television and food have had a loving and a functional relationship, with viewers addressed variously as fans of drama, students learning science and dietetics, consumer-workers purchasing pleasurable subsistence, and cooks. *TV Dinner Date* on WOR in New York promised a nice 1952 night's entertainment without moving from the lounge room, while the *Continental* on CBS offered women an imaginary male companion, as per the lonely homemaker fruitlessly setting a table for two at dinnertime in *Rear Window* (Alfred Hitchcock 1954). Food can be a plot device, like the episode of *Alfred Hitchcock Presents* that features Barbara Bel Geddes killing her husband with a leg of frozen lamb then serving the evidence to police officers as they rest from seeking the murder weapon, or poisons used in *Murder She Wrote*. The kitchen is a cheap, credible place for family issues to be discussed in situation comedies from *The Goldbergs* and *I Love Lucy* in the 1940s and 1950s, all the way to *Seinfeld* and *Friends* from the 1990s. *The Mary Tyler Moore Show* of the 1970s even had a fictional program-within-a-program, *The Happy Homemaker*—which found "host" Betty White avowing that "a woman who does a good job in the kitchen is sure to reap her rewards in other parts of the house." Latter-day Indonesian television features a bizarre hybrid of variety, commercial, and reality genres, including a program presented by McDonald's in which the hosts dress in company uniforms and telephone a local franchise to arrange home delivery (Crist 2003; Spigel 2001, 47, 196; Barkin 2002).

On the other hand, television as entertainment was quickly part of dinner *itself*, with frozen meals first marketed in the United States in 1953; meals to be had in front of the TV or because of an emergency, and to aid companies with a poultry surplus. Popular culture references to happy young homemakers' frustration at their inability to attract children away from the set to the excitement of a meal en famille abound. Conversely, television dinner's inventor, Gerry Thomas, was honored by having his handprints cemented into "Hollywood Boulevard" to recognize his contribution to U.S. culture (Smith-Spark 2005; *BBC News Online* 1999).

As for preparing food, from 1946 through the 1950s, chefs on screen included James Beard and Dionne Lucas. They had an haute-couture style, which was distinctive alongside supposedly desultory cooking programs that featured "white dresses and sensible shoes" (Food Network 2004) and diegetic inserts into other shows that provided product-placement devices for new kitchen appliances and brands. Beard and Lucas stood in contrast to programs like NBC's *Mystery Chef*, which urged women to walk briefly away from soap operas so that they could "be an artist at the stove, not just someone who cooks" (Crist 2003; Kackman 2004, 585; Adema 2000).

Food television changed a decade later with Julia Child. She made regional public television into a "platform for international fame and fortune"

(Ledbetter 1998, 89). The A&E cable network's video biography of her, *An Appetite for Life*, describes Child as "a national icon," and her *French Chef* series as "a new French Revolution . . . televised." When she died in 2004, the Food Network stated that she had "brought Americans out of the culinary dark ages," and the *New York Times* called her "French Chef for a Jell-O Nation" (Food Network 2004; Schrambling 2004). Before the start of national public TV, Boston's WGBH syndicated her show through National Educational Television, at almost the same moment as Raymond Oliver's recipe program began in France. Child's avowed intent on television was to illustrate that "cooking was not a chore but an art." She was also central to public television's commodification. Her first appearance in 1962 was an attempt to promote sales of her book *Mastering the Art of French Cooking*. Then producers decided she was the person to build a program around. The noted San Francisco station KQED sold her cooking knives as its first membership gifts, and Polaroid underwrote the series. She made 119 episodes of *The French Chef*. By the mid-1960s, KQED was receiving twenty thousand letters a week about the show. With national distribution in 1964, the coming of putatively noncommercial TV to the United States was signaled by Julia Child as much as anyone else. The program was produced in color from the 1970s, when she was a columnist for *Parade* and *McCall's* magazines. Other series followed in the following three decades: *Julia Child and Company*, *Julia Child and More Company*, *Dinner at Julia's*, *Cooking with Master Chefs*, *In Julia's Kitchen with Master Chefs*, *Baking with Julia*, *Cooking in Concert* pledge-drive specials, and *Julia Child & Jacques Pepin: Cooking at Home*. She won a Peabody Award, six Emmys, the National Book Award, and the Légion d'Honneur, and made the cover of *Time*, while *Newsweek* said she was "helping to turn Boston, the home of the bean and the cod, into the home of the brie and the coq." Child remained part of PBS branding over four decades, a key signifier of the network and its alleged superiority to, and separateness from, commercial TV. When the Clintons were preparing to move into White House, Child successfully urged them to privilege U.S. food over the French cuisine that had dominated there since John F. Kennedy was president (Stewart 1999, 42, 61, 130–31, 133, 138–39; Barnes 2004; Dolce 2003a, 88; Schrambling 2004; Baker and Dessart 1998, 243; Clinton 2003, 139). Secure in her legacy of transplantation, she could now endorse a derivative culture.

The ontology of immediacy that live TV can offer was evident in her early shows. At that time, programs were rehearsed, then shot in a single take onto kinescopes. Editing was virtually impossible. Child's manifold errors and eccentricities on camera, such as flipping an omelet or pancake onto the stove then putting it back in the pan, or slapping her hip to identify the loin for Steak

Diane aficionados, made a virtue of low production values, adding a dollop of authenticity and approachability. Just as the wine bottles on display testified to her jolly attitude, but were generally filled with nonalcoholic beverages by her husband, so "mistakes" and quirks hid the fact that she spent nineteen hours preparing for each program, and relied on a large team of unpaid workers behind the scenes (Stewart 1999, 131; Schrambling 2004; Cooper 2000). Her casual air mystified the Tayloristic managerial devices underpinning her performances.

Child offered tips on hosting a party as well as preparing food, so her audience could become accomplished hostesses; an image that stood in some contrast to the Puritanism of much U.S. society. The context was a widespread U.S. suspicion of supposed Gallic indolence, blended with a paradoxical admiration for that lifestyle; and a mistrust of big government, mixed with a sense of inferiority next to national cultural institutions. This duality was apparent in the fetishization of French food. Something odd, foreign, but somehow better, needed introduction by a Child-like figure, ensconced in an allegedly Anglo-Celtic Boston, to be acceptable; brokered into ordinariness by the white ruling class. The PBS archives hold her recipes from those days, plainly typed lists and instructions that were mailed out on demand. Her braised salmon from program number 302 promises it is "not nearly the tour de force that it sounds." The sentence includes French-language bravura, a high note of achievement, but it begins with a careful Anglo adverbial qualifier, a sensible prefix to Gallic style. In the famous program number 261—"The Omelet Show"—she avows that viewers require "a devil-may-care attitude for those that may fall on the stove or onto the floor." Such was her stature and folksiness that she qualified for parody on both NBC's *Saturday Night Live*, where Dan Aykroyd played her drunkenly bleeding to death and crying "Save the liver," and in the 1974 feminist countertext by Martha Rosler, *The Art of Cooking: A Mock Dialogue Between Julia Child and Craig Claibourne*.

Across the Atlantic, food TV had similarly complex origins. In Britain, the improbably named Fanny Craddock birthed the cookery genre in 1955 and dominated early food TV. Adorned in ball gowns, she dispensed instruction to viewers and her cowed husband-assistant Johnny. But in the late 1970s, she condescended to the winner of an amateur-cook-of-the-year contest and was exiled from television. Stunning revelations ensued, notably that she was a polygamist who lived on cornflakes and sardines. Transcending this heritage, the next key British TV chef was Delia Smith. She began preparing food for advertisements and the cover of The Rolling Stones' *Let it Bleed* (1969), then went on to write books and make television, turning her company into a major publishing venture, and collecting honorary doctorates en route. She customized French dishes, re-nationing them for her public by substituting ingredients to make the food more accessible to Anglo audiences. The impact was immense. When she promoted cranberries in 1995, sales rose by 30 percent. Three years later, on-air praise for a specialty item—a frying pan that usually sold at a rate of two hundred a year—propelled orders toward one hundred thousand. Her books were released in France in 2002, minus her last name, because "Smith" was seen as too British. Somewhat more compellingly, Madhur Jaffrey, a renowned film actress, introduced Indian cuisine to British television in the 1980s, but never became an equivalent public figure. Internationally, the person who took kitchen food directly back to the commodity form—and did the same for products across the home—was Martha Stewart, who articulated U.S. culinary preparation to everything from growing fruit to polishing chairs (Foster 2004; Barkham 2005; MacColl 2005; Jones 2003; Adema 2000). Like Smith, she became known not just for her "perfect domesticity" (Brunsdon 2005, 110) but as a "knowledge entrepreneur," blending celebrity, skill, and cultural industrialization (Hartley 2003, 62–63). Gordon Ramsay, a celebrity British figure from fancy London restaurants, turned himself into a quality-management guru (*Economist* 2005c, 57).

Graham Kerr was a queer-acting but avowedly straight ex-New Zealand air-force officer, originally from the U.K., whose fey and seemingly drunken rushes around the set of *The Galloping Gourmet* were famous in the United States, Australia, and Britain from 1969. Kerr practiced what he called "hedonism in a hurry" (quoted in Negra 2002, 74n32). I interviewed dozens of food TV watchers for this chapter, many of whom recalled him as the first "flamboyant" man they saw live on TV, a sort of culinary Paul Lynde, even though he became more sober in every way in a later incarnation on the health conscious, quasi-spiritual Food Network program *Gathering Place*. However, a queer component to the genre *was* highlighted when Montréal's main celebrity television chef, Daniel Pinard, came out as gay on New Year's Eve 2000. Many regarded his announcement as a critical moment in queer mainstreaming because of his cultural stature between convention and innovation (Brooke 2000). By 2005, NBC's *The Apprentice: Martha Stewart* included openly gay contestants, Fox's *Kitchen Confidential*, a drama series, featured a queer waiter, and the Food Network screened *Entertaining with the Hearty Boys*, a follow-up based around queer lovers who had won *The Next Food Network Star* program.

Jamie Oliver's *Naked Chef* series gave a cross-class metrosexual appeal to the genre, and made cooking seem like a legitimate pastime for the man who is equally at home in front of the football or the foie gras. He came to be known as "Lord Oliver of Crouton," at the culmination of a decade in which U.K.

and U.S. journalists were declaring that "cooking was the new rock 'n' roll." The BBC specialized in this genre, accounting for 89 percent of such shows in 2004 versus 47 percent in 1999 (Hollows 2003; de Solier 2005; Behr 2005; David Graham & Associates 2004). The proliferation of cooking on British TV prompted Michel Roux, a London chef with the requisite *Michelin Guide* stars, to suggest that "we have become the laughing stock of the world" (quoted in Richard Jones 2003). Universities and colleges offering classes in the culinary arts across Britain were reporting record enrollments because of the popularity of TV food (British Council 2005)—and deindustrialization, of course. Elsewhere, Malaysian cultural critics welcomed Oliver, while suggesting his program had been marginalized to late nights because of its provocative title (Teh 2005), and the Hong Kong Trade Development Council noted the correlation between his popularity and cookware sales as a result of product placement (2003). His female equivalent in sex appeal was Nigella Lawson, whose high-Tory background as the daughter of a leading Thatcherite was leavened by being a single mother following the death of her husband, and the image of *How to Be a Domestic Goddess*. Paul Bocuse was a key European figure. His French cuisine went onto Australia's multicultural station SBS in the 1980s and the Federal Republic of Germany alongside Max Enzinger's *Trimm Dich* [*Get Fit*], which introduced nouvelle cuisine there. In Spain, José Andrés and *Vamos a cocinar* [*We'll Eat*] (2005) were crucial. PBS's *Frugal Gourmet* series with Jeff Smith was immensely successful, and spin-off books were bestsellers, until its pastor-host was implicated in the sexual abuse of children (*Los Angeles Times* 2004a).

Child's male equivalent and collaborator since the 1990s is Jacques Pépin. Pépin, a Frenchman, uses his daughter, a Franco-Yanqui, as a naïve inquirer, a viewer brought onto the set for participant observation. Their book for PBS explains that "Claudine sees her role as that of the voice of the people." Her asking "Can I freeze it?" domesticates Pépin's terpsichories and flights. The book concludes with a paean to the "generous corporate citizens" who underwrite the show. Or rather, it doesn't quite end there. On the reverse page are color advertisements for the products vended by these CSR "citizens" (Pépin 1996, xviii, 267–68). Pépin also became a United Airlines "Celebrity Chef," complete with the corporation's ringing endorsement of him as a "classically trained native of France" (Porterfield 1999, 149). United colored its front-of-house flight menus with quotations from Virginia Woolf, and claimed that its food came from "a lifetime of discipline," as per "the collected works of say, O'Keeffe, Bach or Dickinson." For its part, Air Canada informs passengers that there is a trichotomy to television cookery, from the modernity of Pépin (food as quality), through the postmodernity of Child (food as self-referential fun), and on to the twenty-first century's "loony, arrogant, gorgeous" stars. These corporations avow that élite customers change carriers based on food, because they have a special interest in "breads of good character" (*enRoute* 2002; Davenport 2005). Certainly true of me.

The culture of preparing food as a pleasure has two antecedents. The first is a sexual division of labor that has required women to undertake unpaid domestic tasks on behalf of others. The second is the unattainability of perfectly prepared fine food—the sense that one can never get it right, but that the search is an asymptotic, autotelic pleasure of its own. This blend of the high and low meet, of course, at a place called midcult. The neoliberal conditions of possibility and operation of the new media technologies and deregulatory policies of the last two decades both draw on the existence of midcult and problematize it. Their niche audiences are cross-class and cross-racial. Food TV normalizes the exotic for suburbanites, and exoticizes the normal for the hip. It caters to both middle-class home-workers and late-night revelers, in what amounts to bread-and-circus recipes for incorporating difference into everyday life. As food writer Joe George puts it, "the Food Network never stops" (2001).

CABLE AND SATELLITE

> Gone are the days when all a cookery show needed was a pretty host, a chef, a recording studio laid out with 15 bowls of measured-out ingredients and cooking utensils. The host's job then was to look pretty, stack up empty dishes and make remarks like "masukkan marjerin ke dalam adunan, ya, puan-puan," (add the margarine into the mixture, ladies).
> —Lydia Teh (2005)

> People lined up at 6 a.m. to get seats—on a Saturday morning, no less. Inside, the 2,000-person crowd jumped to its feet, cheering and clapping in unison as the music keyed up and an announcer shouted, Let's get ready to rumble. . . . Whooping fans were assembled for the taping of a show by Emeril Lagasse, a gourmet master chef with blue-collar appeal who has turned the Food Network into Must See TV. Once a 24-hour outlet for Julia Child reruns, the cable channel has become eye-candy for food voyeurs who watch more for entertainment than cooking advice.
> —Jennifer Brown (1999)

The 1992 Cable Act required cable firms to pay or offer a quid pro quo to local broadcasters for use of their signals. Then, in 1993 the Television Food Network, later the Food Network, began broadcasting on U.S. cable. Partly owned by the Chicago Tribune company, which had equity in many local stations and therefore gained access to cable networks, it was the idea of CNN's creator and Providence Journal, drawn to the fact that half the country's biggest advertisers were in food. Early programs were made with a standard set, an immobile single camera, an emphasis on information over style, and a narrowly targeted audience (Mullen 2004; *Time International* 1993, 15; Haley 2003; Ketchum 2005, 219; *Multichannel News* 2003). This drew criticism for low production values—too many "talking-heads-behind-the-stove" and mundane mise en scènes. The *New York Times* called the network "no-frill, low-cost television" and the *New Yorker* asked "has there ever been anything to eat worth watching?" (quoted in Adema 2000). By 1996, three firms had owned the business, and three people had run it, presumably all seeking an answer to this provocation.

In the late 1990s, British television featured Carlton's satellite food, followed by UKTV Food. Carlton stressed that presentational norms apply equally to professional chefs, amateur hosts, and the solitary but discriminating home cook (2001 and 2002). The common theme was that food could be fun, and the common *requirement* for programs to be included on the channel was that food companies pay for the fun. Thanks to an annual programming budget of over US$40 million, this premium on fun saw the U.S. Food Network feature Al Roker and other mainstream TV personalities. In 1997, EW Scripps, which had helped found the network, traded a San Antonio TV station for a 56 percent share, which it has subsequently turned into 69 percent. The network lost US$13 million in 1997, but was profitable by 2000. A 25 to 30 percent growth in advertising revenue in 2003 was twice the average for cable, with profit of US$52.6 million up from the previous year's US$16.2 million (*Chicago Sun-Times* 1999; *Electronic Media* 1999, 4; Beard 2003, 14; *Broadcasting & Cable* 2003; Haley 2003; Grotticelli 2004).

The Food Network's U.S. audience has grown steadily. From the 1997–98 to 1998–99 season, occasional viewers increased from one hundred and seventy thousand to two hundred and thirty thousand among people aged eighteen to thirty-four, and from four hundred and fifty thousand to six hundred and seventy thousand among people aged eighteen to forty-nine. Most of the network's spectators were working women, with an average age of forty-four and household income of US$53,900, the third largest for audiences to basic cable. As of late 2001, the network was available in sixty-six million U.S. households, up from thirty million in 1998, as well as being on-air in Japan, Canada, France, South Korea, the Philippines, and Australia. After adding nine hundred and fifty new hours of programming that year, network ratings went up 25 percent. By 2003, with ratings up 43 percent over 2001 and 20 percent from 2002, the audience was 60 percent female, with both sexes predominantly aged between twenty-five and fifty-four—a key demographic group for advertisers. It stood seventh amongst women viewers of that age group earning more than US$75,000 a year. In 2004, prime-time numbers improved by 7 percent, to six hundred and eighty-one thousand viewers, and an overall average of four hundred and sixty-nine thousand (*Business Wire* 1999a; *PR Newswire* 1999; Food Network 2001; Abdel-Shehid 2002; *Electronic Media* 1999; Comcast 2000; *Media Daily* 1997; Food Network 2002; Haley 2003; *Broadcasting & Cable* 2003; Danford 2005; Downey 2005a; Ketchum 2005, 220; *Times Union Albany* 2000; Brech 2000; Summerfield 2003).

In 2002, the network moved its studios to the top of the Chelsea Market's international food area in New York City, blending the latest digital technology with a location central to U.S. culinary trends. Far from the studio-based, instructional format of the early years, the station has evolved into an entertainment format, with shows from around the world. The network now features a bifurcation between daytime shows, which are still fairly didactic, and prime-time ones, which stress glamour and expense. It also hires talent from the History Channel, A&E, and Discovery Channel. Six solo minutes of TV necessitate the labor of six invisible sous-chefs, working for over forty minutes. Sixty full-time workers comprise the kitchen staff, preparing food that appears to come from the star of each show. Confronted with a 2004 study that revealed an appalling level of hygiene on camera, the network replied that "the need for programs to be educational and entertaining made it difficult for chefs to follow safe food preparation practices" (*Multichannel News* 2003; Romano 2004; Grotticelli 2004).

Pépin's rough-and-ready Fall River, Massachusetts equivalent on the Food Network is Emeril Lagasse, complete with his doctorate from the Johnson and Wales University culinary program—the largest cooking school in the world, it had suggested the creation of a Food Network in 1991 (Dolce 2003b). Lagasse can be heard on TV recommending what he calls "Hallapeenose [jalapeños]," doing network promos at the Super Bowl (*Emeril's Tailgating Jam*), and featuring celebrities *manqués* or *jamais* keen on remaking themselves as food and liquor entrepreneurs, like Sammy Hagar. The Emerilware line of cooking technology includes one hundred and fifty products, *Time* has listed his show as one of the best on television, and he has been named a *GQ* magazine man of the year (Stanley 2004; *Multichannel News* 1999, 66; Food Network 1999; Romano 2004; Adema 2000; Cooper 2000). Lagasse commands the Food Network's top ratings, and is paid US$25,000 per episode. When the station offered free tickets to a taping of his show in 1997, fifty thousand people telephoned in twenty-two minutes to form the "boisterous audience" that matches his unprecedented blend of populist address, fast food, and haute cuisine. Four years later, Food Network Canada had one hundred thousand people enter the network's lottery for two thousand spots to watch him (Romano 2004; Brown 1999; Brooker 1998, 34; Mullen 2002, 73; Demontis 2001, 22).

In addition to *Emeril Live!* and *Essence of Emeril* on the network, NBC tried him in a situation comedy, *Emeril*, in 2001 (scheduled against *Emeril Live!*) and he became ABC's *Good Morning America* food correspondent (Critchell 2001). Most of his programs begin modestly with "In case you just landed from another planet, I'm Emeril Lagasse." Only the disaster of September 2001 could cut short this exuberance, as tapings of the show were temporarily deemed inappropriate, "in deference to the tragic events in New York City," as the channel put it. The Food Network suspended all its programming at that time, but was petitioned by large numbers of viewers to resume broadcasts (*Multichannel News* 2003). In any event, it was soon "right" to move on. The National Restaurant Association self-seekingly stage-managed the transition, avowing that "dining out is an important way to resume our daily lives, demonstrate our resolve and help keep America's economy strong" (quoted in Kinnick 2004, 34). How very CSR. This image of strength is equally part of what Lagasse signifies. Dozens of food TV watchers admiringly told me he is a "manly man," and indeed his audience is split by gender almost down the middle, unlike other programs on the network. Blue-collar masculinity can broker cordon bleu as Lagasse delivers a "fraternity brother vibe" (Adema 2000; McCarthy 2005).

Crass working-class credentialism has displaced Child-ish blue-blood shamateur excellence. A popularization is underway at a level far beyond the cryptocommodified, quasi-bake-sale-funded, kindness-of-strangers-like-you ghetto of PBS. The Food Network has constructed sophisticated links to retail chains and the Internet, and transcended gender and class divisions in the audience by making gourmet food available beyond the sphere of conventional cultural capital, via both Lagasse and such programs as *Wine 101*. While the network sometimes shows viewers how to prepare cheap, unlabeled food, it also offers such programs as *Unwrapped*, which shill for mass-produced, identified brand items. This is what the Cable TV AdBureau delightfully refers to as "converged experience." (Oh, to be paid to invent such wondrous pabulum.) There is a similar synergy in *Epicurus*, a Web and TV format on the Discovery Channel that blends cookware sales, culinary instruction, and recipes from *Bon Appetit* and *Gourmet* magazines (Mullen 2002, 72–73, 76–77; McAllister 2005, 228; quoted in Ketchum 2005, 220).

In addition to crass nativist populism and training in embourgeoisement, food television has taken a globalizing, commercial turn, which mines the past even as it invents the present. Examples include the Australian Broadcasting

Corporation's multicultural but very French-influenced *Kylie Kwong: Cooking with Heart and Soul* and *Simple Chinese Cooking*, and two U.S. Food Network shows, *East Meets West with Ming Tsai* and *Ming's Quest*. Looking "like a self-improvement infomercial, or maybe a Visa ad," Ming Tsai quickly won a daytime Emmy and selection by *People* magazine as one of its fifty most beautiful. This Asian American image also worked for Padma Lashmi, whose fusion included revealing outfits to match Ming's squash gear. They favor a carefully anti-essentialist fusion fashion, with culturally respectful combinations to match a dollop of authenticity (Schillinger 1999, 60; Mannur 2005).

The network's high-rating Japanese import, *The Iron Chef* [*Ryori no Tetsujin*, literally *Cooking Iron Man*], featured one of Robert De Niro's Nobu restaurant employees in regular contests with other celebrities. The pastiche-like program was as likely to offer deep-fried sushi with a Gorgonzola sauce, or a mix of Mexican, French, and Japanese recipes, as more traditional fare (Ervolino 2001). Shot "as if it were a sporting event [with] chefs as gladiators, doing battle before a rich and demonic lord," in the words of production executives at Fuji Television, it screened in Japan for six years from 1993 and has been syndicated since 1999 in the United States. The show features a mix of subtitles, dubbing, and the original language — the protagonist refused to be dubbed into English — not to mention theme music from *Hunt for the Red October* (1990) or *Backdraft* (1991), depending on your source, and has been massively popular from Malaysia to Australia (Gallagher 2004, 180; Struck 1999; executives quoted in *Iron Chef Compendium* 2000; Tch 2005; Warncke 2003).

Cultural theorist Dana Polan calls the *Iron Chef*, with a wry but critical fondness, "a quintessential spectacle of machismo" (2001, 1), while the Food Network promotes the show as "*Ultimate Fighting Champion* meets Julia Child" (quoted in Gallagher 2004, 176). Audiences of displaced hipsters, lost in nameless Midwestern graduate schools, lay down their Jacques Lacan or Bruno Latour long enough to hold cook-offs in emulation of this feral television show. In Jennifer Weiner's novel *Good in Bed*, the difference between weight- and relationship-obsessed Cannie Shapiro, daughter of a newly lesbian mother and a venerably delinquent plastic-surgeon father, and film star Maxie Ryder is encapsulated when Cannie describes the *Iron Chef* as "fun . . . free . . . cheaper than renting a movie." Maxie, by contrast, is "never home on Fridays or Saturdays" to watch it (2001, 142). *Iron Chef*'s popularity soared to the point where the network scheduled an "Iron Chef Weekend" in 2001. It even attracted the ultimate U.S. accolade — format purchase. That same year, the "exhaustively self-parodying" William Shatner became the Iron Chef, thanks to the mininetwork UPN's mimicry, and 2004 saw the Food Network itself offering a domesticated remake (Gallagher 2004, 180).

Not all multiculturalism works the same way. White presenters Keith Floyd and Robert Carrier fronted the British travelogue series *Floyd on Africa* and *Carrier's Caribbean*, which touched on Francophone and Anglophone colonial "traditions." *Far Flung Floyd* took him to the "Far East," where he offered the following to reporters: "We'll have wonderful fun, you know. There are wonderful curries and rice dishes. We can go fishing, we can go into the jungle, we can even eat coconut milk" (Beattie et al. 1999, 153; Floyd quoted in Strange 1998, 305). No wonder the British Tourist Board opportunistically declares curry "authentic British fare" and London's 3,000 South Asian restaurants claim Chicken Tikka Masala as their own (Board quoted in United Nations Development Programme 2004, 15; Richard Jones 2003). Golly gee, what fun—the "Great Game" administered on a platter. Similarly, on the Food Network's *Tamales on Tour*, Mary Sue Milliken and Susan Feniger visit the Global South in merry search of exotica they can bring back to market. This show is in line with studies that show that, since the Cold War, most "coverage" of the Global South on U.S. TV networks is via entertainment programming. These "plausibly live"* instantiations of fusion cooking appear to reference the ability of the United States to incorporate difference into a very literal, delicious, melting pot. Instead of a threatening index of difference, ethnic cuisine has become a commodity sign, a safely self-governing domain of assimilation, a sanitized quarantine of bread and circuses (Meister 2001, 176; Thussu 2003, 129; Downing and Husband 2005, 12; Mannur 2005).

The spread of TV cooking around the world invites many spectators in the southern hemisphere to prepare meals with ingredients that are out of season (Warneke 2003)—one more way they must read imported television against the grain. Of course, discounts often apply to such cultural exchanges. Two TV anecdotes explified the ambiguous British reaction to French food. On a 1990 episode of the talk show *That's Life*, the studio audience was fed some snails, unaware of what they were eating. Once they were told, their faces distorted into English versions of barnyard animals, and they sought to vomit up the remains. Consider also a 1989 commercial for precooked sausages ready for microwave preparation. A white yuppie male is taking advantage of his health conscious wife's temporary absence to eat some "bangers." His conspiratorial gaze at the viewer concludes with a satisfied "Now that's what I call *nouvelle cuisine*" (quoted in Fiddes 1991, 33, 97).

Meanwhile, vintner Robert Mondavi's Copia American Center for Wine, Food and the Arts in the Napa Valley has "Julia's Kitchen" as a cornerstone.

*NBC uses the expression "plausibly live" to describe its deceitful practice of delaying coverage of major Olympic sporting events to coincide with prime time, making them look as though they are unfurling live.

Opening in 2001, its lowbrow-food corporate sponsorship, mixed with a desire to emulate European taste cultures, drew cynical responses from Napa residents, most of whom are working-class servants to the wealthy. They regarded "Julia's Kitchen" as a property-value device, likely to make their homes too costly for them to remain in. The Smithsonian Institution has custody of her actual kitchen. When she moved to a West Coast retirement community, her *cocina* was lovingly transplanted with all its thousand objects from Boston to Washington, relocated in the Institution, near the original metal trays for frozen television dinners (which are also available as a fetish room-service item in ritzy LA and New York hotels). The event was accompanied by a performance of Lee Hoiby and Child's opera *Gâteau au Chocolat: l'Éminence Brune* [*Chocolate Cake: The Brown Eminence*], taken from an episode of *The French Chef* (*Smithsonian National Museum of American History* 2002; Kalins 2004, 71).

When Child died, PBS, the Food Network, CNN, and all major U.S. papers and magazines offered tributes. Each one interpreted her as opening a *lumpen* land up to sophistication in a way that it could stomach (Kessler 2004). Multicultural, commodified hosts had displaced Child and her corporate underwriters onto off-peak reruns and "Prime Video Cuts" from PBS online. Julia Child, farewell. She provided a model Anglo citizen, brokering a surreptitiously commercial importation of difference, via what *Newsweek*'s obituary fetchingly referred to as a "WASP merry prankster" convinced that "you must have the courage of your convictions" (Kalins 2004, 71; Kellinger 1999).

Now, we rely on openly capitalistic multiculturalism to provide the new. Nature is once and for all associated with pleasure through purchase, but the means of commercializing it, and any hidden costs, are fetishized away in a world of "excessive consumption, technological dependence, and the commodification of nature" (Meister 2001, 168, 173):

> In order to cheat spectators on an entrepreneurial scale, the entrepreneurs have to designate the spectators themselves as entrepreneurs. The spectator must sit in the movie house or in front of the TV set like a commodity owner: like a miser grasping every detail and collecting surplus on everything (Kluge 1981–82, 210–11).

The Food Network viewer is addressed as a potentially knowledgeable consumer of neoclassical fables. This consumption is as *con*spicuous as its enabling labor and underlying environmental and equity impacts are *in*conspicuous. The overall package represents niche cultural citizenship under the sign of commodity capital. The consumer is sovereign. The fetishization of the consumer's work through an active-audience media address renders the work invisible and makes the consumer easily oppressed. But this commodified discourse is not inevitable. In 2001, Carlton scrapped its Taste Network interactive joint venture with Sainsbury's supermarket and the Food Network, a blow to retailer-broadcaster links (Milmo 2001)—which suggests alternative futures.

THINKING OTHERWISE

> Besides providing the energy needed to maintain our bodies, food is associated with several environmental factors that also implicate science. Environmental components such as geography, climate, growth yields, soil conditions, depleting ozone levels, and chemical overusage (pesticides, insecticides, fertilizers) impact the quality and availability of the food we eat.
> —Mark Meister (2001, 169)

> *When I wear a pair of Armani pants they do not become a part of Carlo Petrini. But when I eat a slice of ham, it becomes a part of Carlo Petrini.*
> —Carlo Petrini, President of Slow Food (quoted in Fort 2003)

Not surprisingly, the principal television outlets in the United States provide minimal engagement with food issues, other than moralistic shibboleths about Third World famine, or insulting assaults on the alternative-food sector. The Food Network used to have a *Food, News and Views* show (Halweil and Scowcroft 2002; *Economist* 2003g; Schonfeld 2002, 10), but it appears to have gone the way of all flesh, in keeping with the view of on-air talent Sara Moulton that food is "the only thing in our lives right now" that is "not controversial" (Danford 2005). In 2005, the network announced that it was "moving out of the kitchen" to court younger, male viewers, but that meant weight-loss reality TV (Downey 2005a). Is this the only option for change?

There are many signs of increased public interest in consumer movements, concerns regarding new technology, struggles over state regulation, criticisms of multinational takeovers of the family farm and its mythology, the search for "natural" brands, the emergence of agricultural cooperatives, animal-rights discourse, nontraditional medicine, the sexual politics of eating disorders, and Third World poverty. These issues offer abundant evidence of a potential audience for a more responsible, politicized approach, especially as the middle-class cohort desired by television dominates many such movements, and a new approach could add to the Food Network's CSR ethos. The Vegan Research Panel was established in 2000 to promote its profile to advertisers and other commercial interests (2005), and KTYM-AM in Los Angeles and KCEO-AM in San Diego have found an audience on commercial radio for vegan programming.

Perhaps television can learn from "Go Vegan with Bob Linden" (www.GoVeganRadio.com). Also, Christian Gomez's *Green Eats* began on NBC in 2005, with a focus on organic foods *and* growers. And the grisly side to Yanqui capital punishment can be highlighted by Weblogs such as deadmaneating.com, which details last suppers on death row.

The fast-food complex described earlier is both promoted on, and designed for, a television world, a society based around pace. But a countertendency has emerged, via the "slow food" movement, dedicated to pointing out problems with the corporatization of food. The Italian Slow Food Association began in 1986 because leftist chefs and food writers in the small Piedmont town of Bra were exercised by the likely impact of McDonald's on local food cultures and small businesses that sold to a cross class clientele, and in recognition that food "is the main factor of interaction between human beings and nature" (Petrini 2002, 25). This "movement for the protection of the right to taste" went international three years later. Over sixty-five thousand members from five continents—many of them artists, gastronomists, politicians, and journalists—form a decentralized network that organizes activism and symposia to record and preserve disappearing foodstuffs and practices in the name of cultural memory and biodiversity. The notion is that pleasure should be sustained and recognized for its interdependence on the pleasure of others, focusing on home, hospitality, and deliberateness rather than work, distance, and haste (Slow Food 2003; European Food Project 2005; Miele and Murdoch 2003; Petrini 2001).

Petrini proselytizes against "de-contextualised foods" produced from "a global industrial culture" that is "the identity of a brand, not of a people." He is critical of progressives who do not consider the economics of where their food comes from, favors a focus on "material culture," and supports cooperative Third World ventures via the Slow Food Foundation for Biodiversity. Subsequent ecotourism possibilities have, ironically, seen struggles over intellectual property rights, with cheese and tequila inserted into global legal and economic conflicts (Petrini 2002, 28 and 2001, 10, 12, 62; Coombe 2005). The challenge is to make such counterdiscourses available on food TV, in a deregulated era of consumer targeting.

Clearly, for consumers to comprehend their place in the commodity chain that brings food to them, they need to understand the global processes of the eating industries, as per social-movement activism. For example, it can be argued that the much-trumpeted clamp on First World inflation through the 1990s resulted from political-economic pressure on the Global South to suppress commodity prices. Other cases abound that are more local. For instance, the overt rather than covert advertising of foodstuffs has seen major consumer activism. The diet industry's overblown claims in commercials came under attack during the 1980s in the United States, as criticisms of fad dieting pointed out how unhealthy and counterproductive it was. This led to revised campaigns the following decade. As a consequence of consumer activism, from 2005, Unilever purchased seafood from corporations engaged in sustainable fishing, while Heineken withdrew from Burma/Myanmar in the mid-1990s because of public pressure over the nation's totalitarian government (McMichael 1996, 1; Sardar and Davies 2002, 78–79; Bishop 2001; Giddens and Hutton 2000b, 22).

That same decade, Monsanto Chemicals briefly went from being a leader in biotechnology and genetically-modified (GM) crops to a poorly valued and disorganized company in the face of protest action, notably in Europe where risk society and moral panic merged over nutrition. The company revived, however, because of the leaps forward being made, often stealthily, by GM food, with the United States, Brazil, Argentina, and Canada using the WTO to undermine the E.U.'s anti-GM regulations, and the United States threatening trading partners that do not support the complaint. Now Monsanto produces over 90 percent of such crops worldwide. The rest comes from Syngenta, Bayer Cropscience, Du Pont, and Dow. So, five multinationals will potentially soon run global food production, pressuring states to buy from them, and excluding other forms of farming from the market. The tendency is clear—in 2003, worldwide seeding of GM crops increased by 20 percent, almost two-thirds of it in the United States. Although most of the headlines about GM feature Europe versus the United States, Asia may hold the key to future developments. China is a large producer but not consumer and other nations are potentially big customers, albeit cautious, notably Japan, a vast food importer. GM mavens and the U.S. government must deal with a complex contradiction of their own making: the simultaneous claim that GM is so new that it requires patents, but not so new that it needs special scrutiny and regulation! A 2005 Monsanto study disclosed that rats fed GM corn developed abnormalities in their blood and internal organs. But these results were only disclosed because they were "obtained" by a newspaper clandestinely and released to the public, causing an immediate outcry and subsequent action in German courts to force the MNC to reveal its findings. Meanwhile, CorpWatch noted that the firm was selling a pesticide that in fact harms soil and necessitates GM seeds that are resistant to it, and was also kindly offering employment to thousands of children in India (Giddens and Hutton 2000a, viii; Pearce and Hansson 2000; *Guardian* 2003b; Wallach and Woodall/Public Citizen 2004, 68; Feffer 2004; Brack et al. 2003; *Economist* 2005r, 59; Lean 2005; P. Brown 2005; CorpWatch 2005).

The Left can capitalize on this issue. A 2003 poll taken for ABC News shows major concern even amongst the U.S. public about GM food (D. Morris 2003). Despite their typically technophilic opinions, most Yanquis have inchoate worries that articulate to other wealthy populations' concerns, as the Pew Research Center for the People & the Press (2003e) found. The next frontier is nanofoods. Already worth several billion dollars annually, this emergent sector can be applied to packaging, rice, cheese, and surveillance, as tiny additives, fertilizers, and sensors are developed, with huge investments by Nestlé, Campbell, and Kraft—what some are calling "round two in the 'frankenfood' debate." Once again, there are some disturbing results from these substances when trialed on animals; and once again, there are some exciting activists to engage, notably Topless Humans Organized for Natural Genetics, aka THONG (Feffer 2005a).

A responsible broadcasting system would require food programming to engage these issues, both in a domestic and an international context. This is especially important in the United States, where biotechnology has been favored over its critics in media coverage, despite the subjective blathering of its proponents that they receive less attention than leftist critics. As per the slavish devotion to official sources outlined in Chapter Two, it seems as though the media are wedded to such banal, self-interested shibboleths as the Department of Agriculture's insistence that Third World hunger can be ended by upping productivity and crop quality via biotechnology. The main causes of hunger—wars, dictatorships (most of which are legacies of the Cold War) and First World protectionism—are irrelevant. Video and audio news releases, produced by the Department at an annual cost in the millions, aid state propaganda. They are sent to the bourgeois media and played as if they were the outcome of independent reporting (AgBiotech in the News 2003; Farsetta 2005; Giese 2002).

What might a different kind of food television look like? How would it contextualize food through history, politics, economics, and culture, transferring a consumer address to a citizen's one? Here are some stories. Each would take five to ten minutes to tell and some excellent footage is available to do so.

In 1988, the U.S. National Heart Savers Association criticized McDonald's for serving food with dangerously high levels of cholesterol and fat. McDonald's attacked this as "reckless, misleading, the worst kind of sensationalism." In 1990, the Association took out full-page advertisements in twenty-two major newspapers, entitled "The Poisoning of America" and "McDonald's, Your Hamburgers Still Have Too Much Fat! And Your French Fries Still are Cooked with Beef Tallow." At the same time, the Citizens Clearinghouse on Hazardous Waste organized a national campaign against the company's use of plastic foam containers. In 1990–91, fast-food sales figures went down in the United States for the first time. In July 1991, McDonald's, Wendy's, and Burger King announced that they would cook fries in vegetable oil. Following legal proceedings about their deceptive cooking practices, McDonald's paid US$12 million, mostly to charity. Then it retained a public relations firm laughably called the Environmental Defense Fund, promised to recycle, and funded the "Keep America Beautiful" campaign to support the notion that pollution is a matter of individual responsibility. Footage is plentiful of the advertisements, the fries, the activists, the spin group's texts, and claims regarding the source of pollution. Julia Child went on record supporting McDonald's use of animal fat, not to mention irradiation, and ranted against "nutritional zealots." No doubt this had nothing to do with Bush Minor bestowing the Presidential Medal of Freedom on her (Zernike 2004; Dolce 2003a, 88; Kessler 2004; Barnes 2004).

Archival footage also abounds from documentaries and news and current affairs of the lengthy McLibel trial from the mid-1990s, when the company was publicly shamed. It had sued two working-class Greenpeace activists, Helen Steel and Dave Morris, for publishing a pamphlet in 1986 that accused the corporation of depleting rainforests to raise cattle, forcing farmers in the Global South to vacate their farms in the interests of exportable livestock, mistreating animals, causing pollution, increasing health risks, busting unions, and targeting children as consumers. The trial revealed the ugly side of corporate tactics—hiring spies to infiltrate Greenpeace, denying workers legitimate overtime pay, fallaciously claiming to be a recycler, and arguing that Coca-Cola was nutritious because it was partially comprised of water. Although the activists were found guilty and called to pay thousands to the corporation, it was a public relations trauma for fast food, and in 2004, the Court of Human Rights overturned the decision. The events are memorialized in *McLibel* (2005), which features chickens being gassed at a company plant (Klein 1999, 387–93; MacArthur 2005a; Thrupkaew 2005).

The Food Network could also feature performances by People for the Ethical Treatment of Animals (PETA), who have protested McDonald's by standing in front of the chain's "restaurants" and handing out "Unhappy Meal" boxes sporting Ronald McDonald wielding an ax. The corporation eventually complied with PETA's recommendations, all the while claiming that it was not doing so because of these actions.

The network could cover protests in Mexico against establishing McDonald's outlets in town squares, which are seen as bearers of cultural history, and a reply from the company as part of its newly adopted CSR strategy (Keilman 2002; *La Jornada* 2002; Rogers 2002, 1). It might also examine the edgy Web critiques of mcspotlight.org, which advertises itself as the "biggest, loudest, most red, most read Anti-McDonald's extravaganza the world has ever seen," with twenty-one thousand files on its Web site, a million hits a month, and volunteer contributors from sixteen nations (2005).

There's always Coke. There is a famous photograph depicting a large billboard in the center of Chennai, India. It is the work of Sharad Haksar, a distinguished photographer and winner of the 2005 Cannes Silver Lion. The dry water pump and empty jars symbolize the dire impact of Coca-Cola's water policies on local life. Coca-Cola's CSR response? A suit seeking two million rupees and an unconditional written apology. The network might also investigate protestors outside Coke's local bottling plant in Kerala, India, demonstrating against the company and in favor of their local council's decision to deny the MNC an operating license. Coke knows what such plants have done to shrink water tables elsewhere, thanks to its own pipelines, which distort the flow of water and pollute the soil—not to mention selling drinks with toxicity far above levels permitted in the United States (*India Resource Center* 2005; IndiaResource.org 2005).

Or consider the company's "H2NO" consultancy service, designed to drive U.S. customers away from ordering free water, which Olive Garden restaurants appropriated for their "Just Say No to H2O" policy, and its sorry history of global employment abuses (*Harper's Magazine* 2002, 14; CorpWatch 2005). Engagements with the privatization of public space could derive from debates over school textbooks underwritten by advertisements for soda and sweetmeats, and teachers who take money for their schools from corporations in return for encouraging pupils to "test" food and drink products in class—a tasty tactic, common in both the United States and Britain (Giroux 2000, 96–97, 101; Watson 2004, 9). And the American Academy of Pediatric Dentistry might wish to explain why it takes money from Coca-Cola to do research (2003) even as local school districts ponder contracts with Pepsi that ban local beverage businesses from serving their districts (Leavy 2002).

Similar stories abound. Tyson Food Inc., the largest poultry processor in the world, feeds low-cost Midwestern grain to chicken in Arkansas. Breast meat is then removed for use by the U.S. fast-food market, with the remainder of the carcass shipped to Mexico and deboned by low-paid female laborers. The resulting "yakatori stick," marinated chicken impaled on bamboo, is exported to Japan (Bonanno and Constance 1996, 5–6).* Footage of the transformations of these animals could include maps and interviews with workers

*For more on labor relations and poultry in the United States, see Striffler (2002); for meat, see Olsson (2002); for tomato pickers, who make the same wage as a quarter of a century ago, see Coalition of Immokalee Workers (2002).

and consumers, along with the firm's lengthy and deep past of illegal political gifts and labor violations. It might also look at Tyson's delightful CSR decision to "position themselves as faith friendly to connect with spiritual Americans"—free downloads of prayers (*Giving Thanks at Mealtime*) from its web
site (Thompson 2005). Tyson customers presumably do not care about people or animals, provided that their downloaded paeans to magic come gratis.

R-Worders' sudden turn in favor of guest worker programs after the 2004
election was in large part about the desire of many major financial contributors to utilize labor without incurring on-costs via health insurance, collective-
bargaining rights, and so on. As regards the key industry sectors, consider the
major entities involved: the American Meat Institute, the American Hotel and
Lodging Association, the National Council of Chain Restaurants, and the
National Restaurant Association, along with building and retail areas. Their
intellectual fellow traveler was the right-wing libertarian think tank, the Cato
Institute. Undocumented workers recognized what this newfound openness
was really about, and opposed it. Of all the major political configurations, only
the Black Congressional Caucus endorsed proper legalization of workers, an
expansion in the availability of permanent residency, and avoidance of temporary worker programs that deny basic rights (Bacon 2004). This issue would
make for cutting-edge coverage, in concert with consideration of working conditions in meat and poultry areas, disclosed by Human Rights Watch (2004).

At one remove from the immediate eating habits of U.S. denizens, there
could be discussions of land reform. For example, the story of *o Movimiento
dos Trabalhadores Rurais Sem-Terra* [*The Movement of Landless Rural Workers*] in Brazil is an inspiring tale of three decades of struggle by a million people to force the government to live by its own laws and redistribute arable
land, despite the brutal opposition of gangs, police, the military, and the bourgeoisie. The idea of subsistence for hundreds of thousands of poor families not
only encourages a focus on the social function of economic policy. It also
problematizes the environmental consequences of development, since use of
existing land challenges the claim that expansion of the frontier into the for-
est is an answer to national poverty (Wright and Wolford 2003). Depictions of
these struggles, interviews with workers and negotiators, images of the spaces
under dispute, and so on could make for dynamic programming.

The famous Cabbages & Condoms restaurant-and-resort chain in Thailand thematizes and engages the sex industry by profiting the Population and
Community Development Association and promoting safe sex and family planning (circleofasia.com). Could this be part of food tourism on screen? It is asking little of the Food Network to reach beyond corporate sponsors and
enlighten citizens' knowledge of that meal. Is it? After all, those bizarre

homonyms the "Too Hot Tamales" have been cochairs of National Food Safety Education Month. Changing in that direction would necessitate a true citizen's address, something beyond the parochialism characteristic of the national media. It would require addressing controversial issues. It would mean looking at working conditions, consumer issues, and Third World catastrophe.

Child targeted her first book to "the servantless American cook" (quoted in Schrambling 2004). And on PBS, five decades later, the *News Hour*, long a beneficiary of financial aid from the grain corporation Archer Daniels Midland, continued on its merry way of minimizing reportage when the company was convicted of breaking the law. The network's new cooking show for 2005 was *Copia*, a reality series pitting young chefs across the country against one another for a post in New York City. PBS also stood ready to air *America's Heartland*, agribusiness propaganda produced by front organizations and Monsanto. But across the Atlantic, Jamie Oliver was speaking out in *Jamie's School Dinners* against the very supermarket chain that he endorsed in advertisements, for selling unhealthy products to children. He then generated a petition calling for improved school meals, which obtained a quarter of a million signatures (Barsamian 2001 30; Woodward 2005; Hartley 2005).

In the era of "open" TV, food television's address of the consumer has displaced any meaningful address of the citizen, thanks to deregulatory policies that facilitate media businesses targeting specific cultures. The dominant interpellation is about learning to govern the self through orderly preparation, style, and pleasure—the transformation of potential drudgery into a special event, and the incorporation of difference into a treat rather than a threat. Sometimes this kind of cultural practice is derided as "recreational," and juxtaposed to "real" issues like housing or employment (Waters 2003, 119). If properly engaged, the cultural politics of food could be central to everyday citizenship.

No wonder the British Potato Council organized its constituents to protest outside the offices of Oxford University Press because the latter's venerable dictionary included "couch potato" as a term criticizing TV viewing, thereby demeaning the vegetable (*BBC News Online* 2005b). You are what you watch, so watch well. The chore of cooking has become a joy—but others are laboring away off camera to make it so. For all that the new cosmopolitanism of Northern menus and cable bills allows for intense individuation, it must also emphasize the fundamentally sociocultural sharing of resources—that "adequate food intake is the most basic right of every citizen" (Holden et al. 2002, 5, 13).

4

TELEVISION WEATHER

Tomorrow Will Be . . . Risky and Disciplined

> 24-hour programming on the Weather Channel has a wonderful
> narcotic effect. Not only is its focus so narrow as to exclude 98 percent
> of all human excitements, but we've spent an entire evolution trying
> to insure our safety from the elements. So what could be more
> soothing than the contemplation of huge climatic events reduced to a
> pixeled 19-inch image, rendered in cartoon symbols and schematic
> maps and narrated by preoccupied "weather hosts."
> —Daniel Menaker (1998)

> Fortune returns when the weatherman's voice calms the airwaves.
> —Tom Conley (1987, 218)

> For me, the weather has always been the most reliable witness that the
> world would soon change.
> —Andrew Ross (1991, 13)

WHEN THE WEATHER wreaks havoc, it turns the world
upside down. Objects and processes once considered
straightforward and benign (sparkplugs, drainage, com-
muting, or sitting by the window) are transformed into
sites of peril. An "other" side to domestic and professional life emerges as
monstrous under altered conditions of existence, with the very weather
itself anthropomorphized as willful. So the flooding Mississippi is "angry,"
and Midwesterners and Southerners struggling against it are industrious
folk who deserve divine deliverance as a reward for their labors. The folly
of their interventions to bend the river to the will of capital is deemed
heroic, and the reality that flash floods are on the increase because of
urban development that has eroded natural drainage is off the agenda. No
wonder meteorology performs the same structural task as religion: explaining forms of life seen as outside the control of those experiencing them.
This is crucial to the mythology of the Torah/Old Testament. In Genesis, God manifests omniscience with a flood to punish the world for its

wickedness. A narrowcast to Noah predicts the torrent, and enables redemption and continuation of life. In the New Testament, Jesus Christ foretells weather from the previous night's sky. There are counterparts in Babylonia's *Epic of Gilgamesh*, and stories from ancient Rome, India, Myanmar, and Papua New Guinea. The Kaguru people explain the existence of baboons as an unworthy evolution from humans—when newly circumcised boys and novice girls consorted after the rains had come, they turned into beasts. This serves as a taboo. The historical and contemporary field of weather is sodden with demographic knowledges and governmentalizing and commodifying practices. Meteorology is supplemented by economics, to assess the value of a public good; by psychology, to evaluate individual and collective conduct; by statistics, to plot trends and probabilities; and by management studies, to run organizations (Langer 1998, 115, 117; Fry 2003, 6–7, 133; Gelber 2002, 172; Genesis 6: 17–18; Brewer 1970, 310–11; Beidelman 1997, 121, 124; Jarvie 1983, 317; Katz and Murphy 1997, ix).

The cultural politics of weather are pervasive. Consider the gendered way that from 1953, natural disasters were given female names, thus signifying their capriciousness. It was not until second-wave feminism lobbied for a more even-handed nomenclature that the rules changed a quarter of a century later. This captures the duality of nature, coded as female in its nurturance and its irrationality, male in its strength and serenity—the beautiful and the awesome in aesthetic terms. The duality continues at the weather's edgy encounter with psychological complexes and Wall Street. Today, not only are people who feel unhappy subject to diagnoses of Seasonal Affective Disorder due to lack of natural light, but neoclassical economists postulate a relationship between market returns on Mondays and the amount of weekend cloud cover. Demoralized by miserable holiday skies, traders are said to make decisions about stocks that correlate darkness and light with business success. These findings, and their subsequent reinterpretation and rebuttal, have drawn narcissistic coverage from the business press (Seabrook 2000; Department of Commerce 2005; Sturken 1998, 3; Saunders 1993; Dare et al. 2005; Trombley 1997; Kamstra et al. 2003; Hirshleifer and Shumway 2003; Goetzmann and Ning 2002; also see Parker 1995).

So weather is in a state of culture, which in turn is in a state of weather. Of course, it is tempting to get metaphysical about the weather by stressing the elemental humanness that supposedly emerges as people battle it. And its spiritual significance has been marked by almost a century of fights between physicists and theologians over whether heaven or hell is hotter, given the Bible's ambivalent calculation of these matters (Morrow 1996, 72; Shandler 1999). At once transterritorial and highly specific, weather knowledge shuttles between macrocosmic and microcosmic settings with great ease, thanks to its *toujours déjà* dependence on technology and a vast network of governmental and amateur workers who provide information that can be sold on by companies.* Our mediated ways of knowing the weather derive not from a disinterested search after truth, but the informational needs of rural producers, airlines, electricity companies, and the military, and the commodity needs of advertisers. Their readiness to pay large sums to satisfy those desires grants the weather exchange value, while the nearly universal need to make our way through it, and organize our days around it, renders the weather part of consumption and citizenship. Knowing the weather is a central practice of a calculating population.

Gigantic development projects alter the weather's impact, such as the dams that the World Bank is funding in Laos. These endeavors are predicated not just on infrastructural development to change geography and industry, but inculcation into the population of doctrines of personal responsibility for self and others. The people of the Mekong are expected to abandon their traditional forms of life on the environmentalist argument that they are incompetent conservationists who must be reeducated by such bodies as the Wildlife Conservation Society, the Swedish International Development Agency, and the World Conservation Union. At the other end of liberal governance, pension fund and money market custodians of US$1 trillion debate the likely impact of global warming on financial markets, and conclude that the results could be catastrophic. Swiss Reinsurance, one of the largest insurance firms in the world, asks its clients to reveal their dependence on fossil fuels, and adjusts premia accordingly. It has sponsored a report on climate change, and its "Gherkin," a giant glass office tower in central London, embodies environmentalism through green architecture. Britain's Aviva funds a research prize on the topic (Goldman 2001; Magdoff et al. 2004; Hertsgaard 2004; Gelbspan 2004, 9–10; *Foreign Policy* 2004, 18).

In a fractured world of television, where ratings are so critical, the drive toward sensationalism that impels weather today causes unnecessary hysteria. So the *Miami New Times* foregrounds the institutionalized anxiety of WFOR-TV's Bryan Norcross, referring to him as "South Florida's favorite weatherman-in-catastrophe," and deriding his "breathless, panic-mongering hyperbole" (*Miami New Times* 1998). I well recall my first week as a cabled subject. I had been in New York a fortnight, and at last TV was mine. I turned it on, planning to take myself out shortly to a movie and dinner. But I was confronted by local news, specifically the forecast: "Whatever you do, don't go out. No

*Such groups as Hurricanecity and WABN provide amateur services.

matter what happens, do not go out. Stay home, stay tuned to . . ."; and so it went. I stayed home, I stayed tuned, and the city below stayed dry. The same thing happened the weekend before I drafted the first version of this chapter. Five years on, and The Weather Channel announced dire storms for the New York area. Same result—no storms, lots of TV watching, and much anxiety about turning on the word processor to write, given the risk of a lightning strike. This time I knew what was up. The station was trying to secure viewers, which was confirmed when I later read Al Roker's confession that "to boost ratings, local news management wants us weather people to play up the storm" (2002). By the mid-1990s, TV weather forecasts were the most popular news segment in most U.S. markets, and the mantra at the 2004 convention of the National Association of Broadcasters was. "If you win the weather game, local news will win the ratings game." Hucksters gush at the prospect of "street-by-street, and backyard forecast[s]" as part of local stations' ongoing rivalry with The Weather Channel. Competitors are so focused on developing product differentiation from one another via technology that they have even become key resources for experimentation into the proxemics of computing, speech, images, and gestures (Wind 2004, 43; Miles 2004; Reynolds 2003, 8; Randle and Mordock 2002, 248; Kettebekov and Sharma 2001).

The time discipline inscribed by weather organizes key social institutions and their personnel around risk, in keeping with cultural citizenship. The message reads:

- Get to work on time by allowing for nature, so that the sale of your labor power is not interrupted.
- Dress your children appropriately, so that they can turn up and obey the dictates of school as preparation for work.
- Plan your renovation to allow for climatic variations and safety costs.

As Deborah Wilson, who became President of the Weather Channel in 2004, puts it: "Weather helps us make certain decisions: where to go, what to do, what to wear" (quoted in Miles 2004, 22). Like schools across the United States teaching their pupils songs that prepare them for the seasons, TV weather manifests liberal government at a distance. It is part of what criminologist Thomas Mathiesen (1997) calls "the synopticon"—training viewers to emulate a small number of iconic figures (presenters) who symbolize self-discipline and achievement. This is the *recto-verso* of the panopticon, where a few oversee the many. Technological knowledge of a natural phenomenon, the stretching and calibration of a key component of everyday life, is more than it appears. Televisual representations of the weather derive from and inform an economy of work and control, of time disciplined and described by institutions of capital and education which operate from the workplace and the department store to the school and college. Here, discipline is instilled through simultaneous scrutiny of performers by audiences. Their achievement in getting to work each day is ordinary, like that of their viewers, and both do so through weather conditions. Forecasters encapsulate the midpoint between technology and nature. As handservants to contradictory masters, they perform the parable of the dutiful worker.

For all this functionalism, weather is about something more than norms and routines. The dogged time-discipline of working life under capitalism must equally deal with difference, because the diverse U.S. population parallels our climatic variations, occasioned by the absence of horizontal mountain ranges and proximity to both polar and equatorial climes. This is matched in turn by regional identifications that buttress states' rights with the fabric of climatic specificity—a crucial part of anticentralism (Ross 1991, 197, 215). And blue-collar workers may broker inclement climatic norms into improved wages and conditions. Unlike the news' psychology and victimology of crime and illness, the weather's capacity to destroy can engulf an entire news program, permitting the closing calm of the forecast to stand in for crisis management of suburbs, cities, regions, and nations. At this point, the forecast becomes a local, national, or international technique for binding communities together. More than information, it is an article of faith in empathy and sympathy, a demographic interpellation (Langer 1998, 111). In a system of highly centralized, networked television, the forecast looks local at the same time as it engages national identification and emblematizes incompetence. Consider the response to Hurricane Katrina and its revelations about race and poverty in the South, juxtaposed with Bush singing in California then flying over debris when his attention wandered eastwards.

TV weather embodies the desire of modernity to know and control— that quirky combination of respect, struggle, and destruction that characterizes industrial approaches to climate. This allegory of domination pits applied science against forces of nature. It establishes cause-and-effect relations between people and climate, via models that set naturally occurring norms and breach conditions *against* human activity. So, when we are given average temperatures for July, these are just "up" on the norm. TV weather draws no conclusion about global warming as a consequence of pollution from the fact that the 1990s were the hottest decade on record. The seeming reality, acknowledged again and again by the Intergovernmental Panel on Climate Change (IPCC)—that carbon dioxide from gaseous emissions permits the sun to penetrate the atmosphere and stay there, rending the ozone layer asunder (Anderson 1997: 2; Depledge, 2002)—is not tied to television weather's daily policing of life, as might be the case if the latter were seriously concerned with explaining climatic relations of cause and effect. New results from distributed-computing studies under the auspices of climate *prediction*.net suggest that the IPCC's assumptions about global warming are less than half the likely increase (National Environment Research Council, 2005). Even the ever-careful National Academies of Science (2005) came to this conclusion, albeit in an overly euphemistic manner. The bourgeois media barely note these findings, because in place of a macro-political-economic-scientific analysis, they ready citizens for daily normality. The fundamental linkage between fossil fuels and First World economies is as mystified as their relation to everyday life (Egan and Levy 2001, 68).

In the strange climate of 2003, when the weather made so many in the Global North ponder climate change, activist Jane Holtz Kay drew attention to a familiar acronym in need of redesignation. She troped "WMD" to refer to *Weather* of Mass Destruction—soaring temperatures and rising sea levels induced by carbon dioxide. That year the White House cut antipollution standards, deleted references to global warming from the Clean Air Act, dismissed carbon-dioxide limits, and rejected global environmental protocols. Bush Minor described the revised Clean Air Act as "Clear Skies," but the Sierra Club preferred "Clear Lies" (Clarren 2005). Across the Atlantic, John Houghton avowed in the *Guardian* that:

> As a climate scientist who has worked on this issue for several decades, first as head of the Met Office, and then as cochair of scientific assessment for the UN intergovernmental panel on climate change, the impacts of global warming are such that I have no hesitation in describing it as a "weapon of mass destruction" (2003).

Houghton explains that the 1990s were probably the hottest decade in a thousand years, as the extraordinary monsoon heats in South Asia, massively higher than ever before, killed half the numbers who died in the World Trade Center. Houghton, and the vast majority of academic scientists, link these events to polluting practices of the First World, most notably the United States. The proof is in the weather. "Extreme weather," "strange weather," and other terms that market weather programs describe events that derive from global warming generated in the Global North (Dobson 2003, 31). But the generic distinction that puts the Rio de Janeiro or Kyoto conventions on climate control into the main body of the news (when such matters are reported on at all) hermetically seals them in politics, separate from their indexical corollary at the end of the same program. This defines the risky living engendered by economic modernity as natural, thus permitting a radical break between green politics and how to dress the children that morning.

When weather proves ungovernable, it has a special place in the public sphere that can both illuminate and conceal social relations. When news editors select "natural" disasters for coverage, it is critical to public policy and civil society. For the Global South, First World largess depends on Western media organizations defining a disaster as newsworthy, and supposedly beyond human agency—the *"sudden, elemental"* kind occasioned by weather and geology. It is ludicrous to understand these events as apolitical. For example, the very notion of there *being* a sovereign state of the Republic of the Maldives relies on its not being consumed by the sea, while Bangladesh necessarily experiences floods and tidal waves (Benthall 1995, 11–13). There is much debate in the aid community over "compassion fatigue" in the West. Supposedly, "the unacknowledged cause of much of the failure of international reporting today" is because of "the public's short attention span, the media's peripatetic journalism, the public's boredom with international news, [and] the media's preoccupation with crisis coverage." Countering this fatigue leads to a focus on simple formulas, images of childlike innocence disrupted and imperiled, and a ratcheting up of capricious horror as a qualification for attention (Moeller 1999, 2).

Nevertheless, in discussing the 2004–05 tsunami across the Indian Ocean, the *Economist* noted that foreign aid for disasters "is generally thought to be different: everyone is for it" (*Economist* 2005l). "Everyone" also seems to acknowledge that natural disasters "are not socially neutral in their impact" (Bidwai 2005). They differ from the supposed corruption and dependency endemic to conventional development aid. But the magazine went on to blur the distinction, quoting the outgoing U.S. Secretary of State, Colin Powell, on Yanqui assistance to sufferers of the tsunami. Powell avowed that the disaster would "give the Muslim world . . . an opportunity to see American generosity, American values in action" (quoted in *Economist*. 2005l). This was clearly a response to media pressure, which criticized the White House's tightfisted reaction to the tragedy. At the same time, the media themselves became obsessed with the story. It received more press coverage in over two hundred English-language newspapers globally in the first month and a half afterwards than the world's ten largest emergencies of the past year *combined*, and has crowded out ongoing reporting of them since. Needless to say, tsunami coverage saw the United States lagging far behind all other Anglo nations. When it comes to natural disasters, other countries only figure in U.S. national news if they are culturally proximate to the United States and geographically to New York City (Collins 2005; Jones 2005; Fry 2003, 145).

Since 1997, a series of shocks, such as a massive economic crisis, followed by burning forests in Indonesia, had devastated much of the region affected by that tsunami. The Bali bombings in 2002 and the outbreak of Severe Acute Respiratory Syndrome in 2003 were disastrous for tourism, while December 26, 2004 reinforced what is being called "constant shock syndrome" (*Economist* 2005b, 55). These traumas and reactions involve both purposive and accidental human action and inaction, some to a greater extent than others do. Clearly, the insistence on structural adjustment by the World Bank, the IMF, the WTO, and the sovereign states that dominate them, has been crucial in creating the conditions of existence for all these tragedies. By preaching the liturgy of comparative advantage, the neoliberal clerisy has encouraged many parts of the world to turn away from subsistence agriculture and toward tradable goods, beyond manufacturing capacity and in the direction of service exchange. In much of Southeast Asia, structural adjustment has animated a movement of people to littoral regions in search of work. Since the 1980s, crayfish-farming corporations have created a new aquaculture that has displaced the natural environment of mangroves and coral reefs protecting people and land—effectively by order of the World Bank. Areas not directed to remove natural barriers suffered dramatically fewer casualties in the tsunami. The push for the Global South to constitute itself as a diverting heritage site and decadent playground for the West caused Thailand, Indonesia, and Malaysia to undertake the massive construction of resorts located at the point where high tides lap, simultaneously attracting workers and decimating natural protection such as mangroves. Ironically, there was an eerie connection to an earlier, overt era of colonialism. In 1854, the British meteorologist Henry Piddington warned Imperial authorities that plans to build a port in Kolkata, India were ill advised, because clearing mangroves would expose the city to climatic danger. Five years after his advice was rejected, a tsunami destroyed the port. Meanwhile, the NGOs that garnered US$12 billion in donations after 2004–05, failed spectacularly in relief efforts due to the pitiful level of coordination we should expect of amateur-hour welfare (Bidwai 2005; Sharma 2005; Shiva 2005; Freudenberger 2005; McGirk 2005). Over at the Asian Development Bank, twenty-first-century econocrats advise that good will come from the disaster. The economic impact will be "somewhat positive" because despite "a deep sentiment of sadness" created by such disasters, "a quick recovery process follows in a V-shape" with "a large multiplier effect" (2005). So that's all right then.

The Chicago and London Mercantile Exchanges' first innovation of the twenty-first century was to sell weather derivatives for the United States and Europe, with a utility-industry benchmark of 18.3 degrees centigrade. The Exchanges offer a hedge service against unwelcome weather, and keeps book over whether the temperature will go above or below 65° F (*Economist* 2000a; Seabrook 2000). Giant polluters with CSR pretensions like BP America, DuPont, and Ford developed the grotesque Chicago Climate Exchange as a means of voluntarily cutting emissions, then selling this "virtue" to companies obliged to reduce pollution by government. The Chicago Mercantile Exchange's (CME) Web site advises that:

> CME®'s Industrial Commodity products (Weather, NYMEX e-miNY, Chemicals) offer a range of new risk management tools designed to serve markets and industries that have not traditionally had access to futures. Some of these products—weather, for example—are based on new definitions of tradeable commodities. Others, such as the petrochemical and e-miNY energy products, stem from innovative partnerships. All of these products demonstrate CME's commitment to recognizing market needs and developing products to meet them.

Business.com (2001) offers a Web page chillingly entitled "Market Research on Weather and Catastrophe," while brokers involved in agricultural futures can be seen clustering around televisions at the stock market to see what the Weather Channel has to say. After September 11, 2001, weather-risk models were modified to predict probabilities and counters to terrorism (Zorach 2003). This is what the Weather Channel calls "value-added weather" (Batten with Cruikshank 2002, 242).

Do these people have no shame? Or a limit to how risk can be calculated for profit? *New Yorker* cartoonist Michael Crawford playfully tropes this commodification with his notion of hurricanes sponsored by corporations, such as the "Verizon Wireless Hurricane Kandee" and "Bristol-Myers Squibb Hurricane Midge" (2003). Where such phenomena were once known by women's names, emphasizing their quixotry and capacity to elude masculine domination, today they could just as easily be named for the business activities that swirl around them. How about "Hurricane Arbitrage," "Cyclone Hedge Fund," "Tropical Storm Day-Trader," and "Typhoon 401(k)?" That kind of spectacular cultural politics is investigated here via the seemingly most mundane of TV topics, weather forecasting, through the history of weather media, coverage of environmentalism, cable and satellite niches, and alternatives.

WEATHER MEDIA

Very quickly, the TV weather forecast turned out to be a very saleable commodity. There were always sponsors for it. It always made money.
—Frank Field (1981, 12)

Australia has a magnificent TV weather service. In the US, weather is showbiz.
—John Zillman, Australian Director of Meteorology (quoted in Henry, 1989)

Others may scoff at the idea of heading directly toward a CAT 5 hurricane or twister, but we understand. There has always been and will continue to be an uncanny fascination with the forces of nature and it is our intention to cater to that desire.
—wildweather.com

Media weather exemplifies vicarious living. You could look outside, consult a temperature gauge, or open a window to examine the sky, heat, or wind. But instead, you turn to TV. So it's tempting to say that television weather makes for passive spectatorship and defers us from the direct experience of life, distracting viewers from collective and autotelic pleasures and the great tasks of history. Data from the Chiat/Day advertising agency's evaluations of TV weather aficionados indicate that they "had to have control. They couldn't just look out the window" (quoted in Seabrook 2000). Only television could satisfy. The response is to engage in reactive management of the situation at an individual level, rather than to inquire about collective responsibility for the environment.

The weather is located in traditional news formats after politics and sports, and hence on the cusp of entertainment. It brackets commercials and politics, neither one nor the other: "a kind of bridge from news of a very serious nature to something at least a little lighter" (Field 1981, 23). The weather simply happens, and is reported well or ill. There seems to be no politics to its "immobilizing power" (Conley 1987, 218). Critics point to the gimmicky absurdity of TV weather reports, for example from cookouts. When presenters become celebrities, as per the Weather Channel's Cheryl Lempke featuring in a 1999 *Mirabella* fashion shoot, it exacerbates this almost jocular banality (Flick 2000; Fabrikant 1999). PBS maven Susan Murphy refers to the weather as "extraneous" and "fluffy" in explaining to viewers why they should support *The News Hour* and *BBC World News* rather than commercial bulletins. As she put it during a 1999 pledge drive on New York's WLIW: "Only special people watch *BBC News*. . . . I know you're a responsible citizen."

There is a clear history to the making of media weather into a matter of consumption rather than citizenship. In the nineteenth century, weather observers posted forecasts at railways stations, and soon migrated to newspapers, which printed weather warnings to shipping from 1861. The weather was a key feature on college radio in the early twentieth century, with Morse code transmitting forecasts before the first news breaks. Amongst audiences, there was competition to pick up the most distant signals in the face of both geography and climate. As one of these self-styled "radio maniacs" put it, the search for perfect reception pitted self-reliance against "the endless perversity of the elements" (quoted in Douglas 1987, 308). The new medium was both a carrier of weather information, and a sign of humanity's capacity to succeed in spite of it. By 1921, the University of Wisconsin's 9XM aired full forecasts. Soon, the U.S. Department of Agriculture embraced radio and supplied stations with market and weather information for farmers, while that same decade, the U.S. Navy used radio to transmit weather maps to its ships. This use of radio grew into part of rural-extension distance education. The early days of broadcast weather in the United States had a direct link to the Weather Bureau, where stolid bureaucrats offered brief synopses. The first full-time weather presenter was hired by Cincinnati's WLW in 1940, and forecasting was one of the few media-presentation jobs open to women. In Britain, the BBC, which commenced broadcasting in 1922, was providing weather forecasts within its first year, and eight of them a day by 1955. The BBC produced the first weather telecast in 1936, with the service ending in 1939 and restarting ten years later (*BBC Weather* 2005b). From the 1920s, Canadian government stations broadcast forecasts for ships plowing the Great Lakes and the Atlantic, while in Switzerland, broadcast meteorology was a key selling point in marketing radio sets. During the Second World War, radio weather was militarized. In Australia, for example, synoptic amalgams were assembled from a wide variety of weather centers and synchronized with information from allies, while bases were established offshore to go beyond the limits of landlines—and the weather itself was subject to censorship. After the War and the simultaneous suburbanization and televisualization of the United States, the weather report was positioned as an entertaining forum for stations to "help" audiences plan their work and leisure via a blend of accreditation and presentation, scholarship and fun, risk and pleasure, citizenship and consumption, science and chance (*BBC Weather* 2005a; Veder and Fleming 2001; Smulyan 1994, 21–22; Bliss 1991, 14, 458; Davis 1945; Briggs and Burke 2003, 226; Thomas 1971a; Haldane 1997; Australian Broadcasting Corporation 2001).

On the one hand we can see the power of technology in forecasts. In the 1950s, the DuMont network had a repeated morning feature called C-W-T (for clock-weather-temperature) and pointed a camera onto Madison Avenue as a real-world climatic referent. The first televised radar images of a hurricane appeared in 1955, and a decade later, Ameco's "Weather-Matic" provided time and weather from a digital display. By 1959, community-antenna TV automated weathercasts commenced in New Mexico, with a camera panning weather gauges. Britain's first TV forecast that actually showed the presenter came in 1954. Prior to that point, synoptic charts were very busy and comparatively nonpictorial, with basic topographic features added to by numbers, letters, etcetera, to depict microregional variations of temperature, air pressure, wind direction, and so on. This cluttered format soon gave way to much broader categories and zones in order to simplify viewing. In the 1960s, interest in space and science, plus the advent of satellite photography, encouraged the networks to expand their coverage. By the 1970s, many TV stations owned radar. They upgraded to Doppler technology the following decade, which also saw the first computer graphics. A few local weather stations appeared on small cable systems, with details given in text across the screen, and images from a single camera aimed at wind-speed and temperature gauges. The advent of personal computers and satellite images in the early 1980s offered professionals a blend of local calculation and global vision. By the 1990s, weather was once again intensely localized. New maps offered prognostications on whether the heaviest rainfall would come on the corner of Broadway and either Great Jones or Fourth St (Mullen 2003:,43; J. Brown 2005; *The Meteorological Magazine* 1954; Weinstein 2004, 53; Field 1981, 12–14, 25; Hughes 1995, 68; Ravo 1999; *BBC Weather* 2005b; Batten with Cruikshank 2002, 22; *TVyVideo.com* 2003 2003).

Weather television was also an entertaining and awesome matter, a place where the sublime and the beautiful meet at the popular. Stations looked for presenters who could offer fun (either through beauty or gimmickry) as well as qualifications (via study in college or the military) (Monmonier 1999). There were many personality-driven segments, the first being NBC's "Wooly Lamb," an animated sheep that pronounced the weather in the 1940s. "Wooly" quickly ran into competition from women in bikinis, and Jan Crockett playing the ukulele—CBS held that "women sell more." NBC countered with a singing weather presenter and puppeteers, though there were also spots for returning GIs who had worked in meteorology during World War II. The Midwest held out against comedy routines—its storms were deemed too dangerous to permit such levity—and instead featured the redoubtable Clint Youle, inventor of a cattle gate that permitted vehicles and people free passage, but smacked cows in the head should they try to pass through. He resigned in a huff when his time for reading the weather was cut to a little over two minutes to accommodate more commercials. The first professionally qualified and nationally prominent U.S. weather forecaster was NBC's Frank Field (father of the wonderfully named Storm Field, who *had* to follow Frank's lead into TV). In addition to the diet book *Take it off with Frank!* he wrote *Dr. Frank Field's Weather Book*. The latter catches the dynamic of science as prophecy and fun that characterizes the profession. Dr. Frank records moments when he would be aided by a pet dog, or greeted by anchors with a hail of snowballs and accusations that he personally devastated the weather (1981, 11).

In the 1960s, orchestra leader Guy Lombardo complained to the FCC that New York TV forecasts were diminishing crowds for his outdoor summer shows at Jones Beach, while the Car Wash Institute lobbied the commission to require that meteorologists displace the expression "partly cloudy" with "partly sunny," in order to assist summer business (Field 1981, 34). This combination of jollity and expertise continues to be deemed crucial to ratings, especially in the morning. Willard Scott's former occupation was as Bozo the Clown before he graduated to being the first Ronald McDonald, and he once read the weather passing as Carmen Miranda; John Coleman told Chicago viewers in the 1970s that he'd deliver the next evening's forecast standing on his head unless the rain stopped; David Letterman's humor derives from his forecasting style of the past; and the Weather Channel was sued for age discrimination in 2005 by a forty-one-year-old woman meteorologist who noted the network's desire for "top button open in the blouse" (quoted in *UPI NewsTrack* 2005). In Britain, years after the noted BBC presenter Bert Foord had retired, radio personality Terry Wogan began a spirited "Bring Back Bert Foord" campaign, arguing that the weather had deteriorated since his departure (*BBC Weather* 2005c). Cultural critic Svetlana Boym notes that watching TV in the Soviet Union during the attempted 1991 coup was only possible via CNN. Muscovites saw footage of the revolt interspersed with Hurricane Bob's progress across New England. The flow between these stories produced an intertextual slippage, with some viewers believing the hurricane was headed for Siberia and would wreak inordinate havoc. Of the three events, one mythic and two real, Radio Beijing found space to cover only the major storm season in the United States (Boym 1993, 118, 120–21). In China, it took until 1999 for the news media to be granted freedom to report temperatures in excess of the human body's own norm (Johnson, 1999).

In the late 1970s, I read forecasts on Australian Broadcasting Commission radio for four years, to an audience that was taken with the ideology of rurality in much the same way the United States is. Most of the time this simply involved giving local information, but once a week I had to read on a regional network for twelve to fifteen minutes without a break, detailing country town after country town's rainfall readings. This was usually followed by a summary of district agronomists' views, then stock prices—old-fashioned instrumentalism. In

Australia, most TV weather presenters came from the Weather Bureau on a rostered basis until one of their number, Alan Wilkie, appeared umbrella-in-hand to signify rain. This indexically inclined official became the country's first star performer, subsequently leaving the bureau and public television for a career on the networks. In Aotearoa/New Zealand, Yanqui import Augie Auer offended locals in 2001 when he opposed seeding clouds to counter a drought, and had to be gently led away from the studio (Davies 1981, 54; *Wildweather.com* 2002).

Alongside this hyperconsumerism lay an equally assiduous form of governance, expertise, and technology. By Youle's retirement in 1959, the American Meteorological Society (which had begun in 1919) felt moved to start a Seal of Approval program to license weathercasters. U.S. TV forecasters are neatly divided between those with college degrees in meteorology versus communications. Half boast seals of approval from the American Meteorological Society and a quarter from the National Weather Association (NWA). The NWA grew from 644 members in 1976 to 2,690 in 2000 (Wilson 2002, 253; National Weather Association 2005). In 2005, Texas legislators became so exercised by credentials that they considered a bill outlawing use of the term "meteorologist" for anyone without formal qualifications. Many weather people do not resemble *Vogue* models, athletes, or clouds. They could be from next door, admittedly spruced up. But whereas the early days of the Weather Channel were dominated by "anchors . . . who look like carpet salesmen from the local mall," (Browne 1991, 50) they now vary between the elderly gentleman, the technocrat, and the halfway young and beautiful. The absence of environmental deduction or induction in their presentations illustrates the genre's decontextualized, apolitical blend of theory, empiricism, and prediction (Morrow 1996, 72). In 2000, the Weather Channel's Web site featured some on-camera meteorologists' "Top Ten List[s] of favorite weather events." Rather than spectacular summer swimming or mild autumnal walks, these are frequently dominated by violence: "The Blizzard of '79" and "Hurricane Agnes in 1972" (preferred by Rich Johnson), "Hurricane Andrew of 1992" (Marny Stanier), Georgia's "Governor's Tornado" (Terri Smith), Cincinnati's 1974 F5 "tornado event" (Kim Perez), and East Coast snowstorms in general (Mike Bono). Mike shares with us that his "favorite weather event is a 'good snowstorm'. He also enjoys severe thunderstorms, when they're not threatening property." Ah ha. Good to know the latter. Must keep that property secure.

During the 1998 storm season, as Hurricane Georges swept along the Caribbean and Floridian coasts, New Orleans' WWL-TV took a call from Nash Charles Roberts, Jr., an 80-year-old ex-weathercaster at the station known for deriding National Weather Service (NWS) forecasts as "house thinking."

Roberts alerted the news director that "it's time for me to go on." His televised message, conveyed via ink markers on a white board in place of the usual presenter's Doppler computer technology, was that the National Hurricane Center had got it wrong. New Orleans would *not* be the next landfall. He was proven correct. Roberts based this counterprediction on a combination of NWS data and information from oil rigs in the Gulf Coast, for whom he was doing private work (Kilgannon 1998, 26). This story references three interconnected tendencies: residual media Luddism (Laskin 1999); the use of corporate resources to supplement governmental ones (or alternatively, the fact that meteorology is part of corporate welfare); and a sense of the weather presenter as a magician, descended from the "specialist of the occult arts" who divined daily conduct for absolutist European monarchs and Nancy Reagan (Conley 1987, 220). Britain, too, features eccentrics, especially in long-range forecasting, but these are definitely batty amateurs rather than nonnormative businessmen. Bill Foggitt, an old-age pensioner who appeared in media interviews for decades until his death at ninety-one in 2004, argued that closed pine cones portended a rainy summer, while rooks nesting high-up suggested warmth. In 1985, he famously, and correctly, predicted a cold period would end after seeing a mole's nose emerge from snow (Michael McCarthy 2005).

As deregulation and technology transformed Western Europe in the 1990s, from a sphere of highly controlled media systems dedicated to a comprehensive service into wild TV markets, the weather came to loom large. After the devolution of self-government to Wales and Scotland in the late 1990s, the BBC instructed its announcers not to refer to "national weather" any more. The now-defunct mid-1990s British satellite station L!ve TV marked out its early days with darts played topless, trampolining dwarves, the News Bunny (a person dressed as a rabbit who would give thumbs up and down while standing behind newsreaders) (Bagehot 1999, 58; Duffy 1999) and a woman in a bikini reading late-night forecasts of U.K. weather in Norwegian, with English subtitles, and Norwegian weather in English, with Norwegian subtitles. Similarly, Canada's nakednews.com, "borrowed" from a Russian original called *Naked Truth*, features nude weather reporters. The service recently upgraded to offer male as well as female stars in order to diversify its hitherto 80 percent male audience. *Time* magazine describes it as "the best international coverage this side of the BBC," while weather presenter Dianne Foster is confident that "people are watching it for the news not the nakedness" (*Time* and Foster quoted in Kay 2001). Certainly true of me. At the same moment, the BBC, all of whose forecasters are employees of the governmental Met Office, is finally adding (clothed) young women weather presenters to what has been a very male-dominated position, in order to attract younger audiences. Metrosexual weather boys are being recruited for Norway's TV Norge to draw in women viewers, and Lebanese networks feature young women pantomiming mountain rain. Use of the weather to make a cultural point was clear in a noted episode of *Will & Grace*, an NBC situation comedy of the late 1990s about a straight woman and gay man living as roommates. In the episode, a network censors a sequence featuring two men kissing from a series; this enrages two gay characters. In protest, they passionately and lengthily embrace in front of Roker as he delivers the weather forecast from Rockefeller Center on *The Today Show* (BBC News 2000; Lyall 2002; *Economist* 2004f, 27; Buxton 2004, 2070).

The requirement to give pleasure in delivering the weather has connections to narrative form. In 1963, NBC nightly news executive producer Reuven Frank instructed his staff that with the expansion of their program from fifteen minutes to half an hour, each story must "display the attributes of fiction, of drama. It should have structure and conflict, problem and denouement, rising action and falling action. . . . These are not only the essentials of drama; they are the essentials of narrative" (quoted in Graber 1994, 483). And they remorselessly emphasize risk. Television studies analyst John Langer (1998, 104–33) deploys narratology to understand disasters on TV, arguing that coverage mimics fiction. A state of equilibrium is assumed, where life is ordinary and manageable; a problem occurs, which sets disequilibrium in play; then normalcy is restored.

This structuring narratology is eerily reminiscent of sociological functionalism: An organic condition of consensual harmony may occasionally suffer disruption, but the consensus deals with the disturbance, and renews its time-discipline. Examples of such disruptions and responses would be hurricane devastation followed by weather forecasts, and related stories about overseas aid, emergency services, martial law, insurance, and so on. A particular instance would be Oklahoma City residents who survived tornadoes in 1999 attributing their escape to information from television that pinpointed the path of the hazard (Lyman 1999).

But cultural studies scholar Justin Lewis doubts the relevance of narrative analyses to understanding news on television. He argues that narrative codes do not organize the genre—no equilibrium is established, disrupted, and restored. Rather, viewers are greeted in medias res (1994). A wild and wooly program provides only restricted information about the backdrop to stories, and the structure is fundamentally disjointed, albeit hinged to other programs by sport and weather. Lewis notes that empirical audience research suggests recollection of the news is minimal, compared to genres driven by etiological narrative. The news lacks an historical element, which reduces spectatorial recall by contrast with soap opera or situation comedy. The absence of historical context, and the chaotic interpretations it induces, are not celebrated by Lewis as forms of resistance. He identifies a repetition of various orientations that sustain the status quo of politics. In this sense, TV weather is a nation-binding technique. It acknowledges difference, but contained within averaged norms, reassurances of predictable change, and consumer utility. In its specialized form, as the news segment that became a genre and then a network, the weather's lack of a full narrative arc—the storm begins and ends, but the climate never does—addresses viewers as perfectly knowledgeable and empowered consumers, able to switch on and off once their immediate needs are met. They are like the reader of the classic realist text, addressed as competent customers.

As Lewis notes, while the weather can form the basis of headline stories about chaos, it equally demarcates the news from the next program or break, reassuring viewers through the rhythms of climate and the materiality of geography. In this sense, it redresses the impact of the potentially inchoate news genre—there's always the weather to bring things to a conclusion and describe tomorrow. The forecast also represents a crucial part of TV's star system—the weather presenters' scientific aura matches their humanizing one. Unlike experts who are interviewed on air, forecasters can represent themselves by opening and closing their segments and directly addressing the camera. The combination makes meteorology accessible, for an essential stability in TV weather's order and reach characterizes it. The same population centers are mentioned each night, located in the same spatial relation to one another. This helps to fix the otherwise asymptotic quandary of the weather as a component of time and space—infinitely knowable, via the expansive reach and measurement of technology; but infinitely willful, frustrating all efforts to control it, and sucking up the detritus of industrialization, generating unintended tomorrows.

ENVIRONMENTALISM

> What standing we still have in the environmental world now comes not
> from our cleverness, our resolve, our initiative, but the opposite—from the
> sheer size of our unrestrained appetite.
> —Bill McKibben (2004)

So what happens when the climate *itself* changes? Although the *Saturday Evening Post* introduced U.S. readers to the concept of global warming in 1950, and "environmental surveillance" was listed at the time as a journalistic duty (Wilson 2002, 249), there was little uptake of such topics for decades.

When *Time* magazine introduced an environmental section in 1969, it was responding to fears about recent spectacular oil-tanker disasters. There was an immediate corporate search for the right vocabulary to describe environmental questions. Over time, public-relations officers offered a counter-discourse to horror, fear, or anticapitalism, by focusing on care, pleasure, and progress (Allan 2002, 104–5), while environmentalism ceased to claim imminent catastrophe as its route to headlines.

Special occasions still demand renewed focus from across the newsroom, such as the moment in 1988 when NASA scientist James Hansen testified to Congress that it was "time to stop waffling so much. We should say that the evidence is pretty strong that the greenhouse effect is here." The nation's lengthy drought and heat wave had drawn all the major networks to cover his testimony (Mazur 1998, 462), a high-water mark in news and current affairs' uptake of ecological issues. But, for all the flurry of intergovenmental scientific congresses that followed, Hansen's remarks did not turn the weather report into an environmental watch, because of an ideological counteroffensive. *Forbes* magazine offered a conspiracy theory, that "just as Marxism is giving way to markets, the political 'greens' seem determined to put the world economy back into the red, using the greenhouse effect" (quoted in Paterson 1996, 1). The R-Word Wise Use Coalition protested that environmentalists were "putting rats ahead of family wage jobs" (quoted in von Moltke and Rahman 1996, 336).

This was part of a bizarre intellectual offensive conducted by right-wing think tanks such as the Cato Institute, the Hoover Institution, the Foundation for Research on Economics and the Environment, the Heritage Foundation, the American Enterprise Institute, and the Citizens for a Sound Economy Foundation. Like their work on politics, media, and food, the offensive was suffused with a weighty conspiracy theory about intellectuals falsifying evidence and quelling dissent. The think tanks' bottom-feeding scientists justified their failure to secure academic publication as a consequence of this conspiracy. With the R-Word victory in the 1994 congressional elections, vanity-published scholars took center stage at formal hearings on climate change, which became public fora deploring universally accepted scientific fact, arguing there was no global warming, and if there were, it would be beneficial. These outliers dominated political discourse and decisions; they attained an even share of media attention with "normal science" in the ensuing decade, despite the fact that their work was academically discredited. In 2005, Joe Barton, a former employee of the mineral extraction sector, a major beneficiary of political contributions from it, and Chair of the House of Representatives Committee on Energy and Commerce, commenced formal investigations into scholars whose work explained global warming as the product of greenhouse gases. It comes as no surprise that amongst U.S. intellectuals (academic, press, diplomatic, security, religious, and military) the group with the lowest estimation of Bush by the end of 2005 was engineers and scientists—only 6 percent approved of his performance (Monastersky 2005; McCright and Dunlap 2003; Engelhardt 2004b; Gelbspan 2004, 37–61).

Once the political class and coin-operated think tanks had done their bidding, large U.S. corporations moved in to appear like worthy self-regulators by proposing "flexible emissions trading mechanisms"—that is, transmogrifying regulation of pollutants into a market in poisonous externalities. This charade even goes by its own oleaginous nomenclature—Global Business Citizenship. It simultaneously admits responsibility beyond national regulation, even as it embodies the rootless nature of decision making, or perhaps its rooted*ness* in market value. In addition, the American Chemistry Council, the U.S. Chamber of Commerce, and the National Association of Manufacturers formed an obfuscatory and oxymoronic CSR-style Global Climate Coalition, and funded dummy civil-society groups, vaguely verdant front organizations ostensibly comprised of Putnam-like U.S. volunteer citizens that together amount to a "Carbon Club." They lobbied against the Kyoto international global-warming treaty protocols on greenhouse-gas emissions (as per McDonald's "environmental" and obesity efforts from Chapter Three). British Petroleum and Shell left the coalition in 1999 following shareholder and public pressure and soon after it folded. The coalition's failure mattered little given what was happening in U.S. politics. When the Environmental Protection Agency (EPA) (2002) admitted the truth about global warming, the R-Worders rebutted with disavowals and the head of the EPA stepped down (Engel 2002). Whenever pockets of government endowed with technocratic independence dare to publish or endorse internationally recognized science on the subject, front organizations such as the Competitive Enterprise Institute stand ready to oppose the findings, acting with clandestine encouragement from the White House itself, and unquestioned by Yanqui reporters. Any attempt to expose the front organizations draws immediate, banally predictable, but effective opposition—even scholarly articles that debunk these entities ritualistically draw critiques. The few references to climate change in the U.S. bourgeois media's coverage of 2004 storms were dominated by right-wing activists (Rondinelli 2002, 400; Egan and Levy 2001, 69–70; *Economist* 2002, 60; Maxwell T. Boykoff and Jules M. Boykoff 2004, 130; Logsdon,2004; Gelbspan 2004, 40–41, 57; Mooney 2005; Jules Boykoff and Maxwell Boykoff 2004, 24; Mooney 2004).

This is reminiscent of the situation described by the 1987 Nobel Laureate in Economics, Robert Solow. Responding to criticism for parodying neoliberal economics rather than debating it on "technical" grounds, he said:

Suppose someone sits down where you are sitting right now and announces that he is Napoleon Bonaparte. The last thing I want to do with him is to get involved in a discussion of cavalry tactics at the battle of Austerlitz . . . Now . . . [the neoclassicists] like nothing better than to get drawn into technical discussions because you have tacitly gone along with their fundamental assumptions (quoted in Marshall 1988, 8–9).

Together with anti-environmentalists, these cultural citizens have shielded extreme weather from political life, or have linked a discourse of conservation to reactionary identity politics. When southern California sustained record-breaking floods in 2004–05, Cato's "resident meteorologist" was ready (and bizarrely credible/relevant) to tell NPR listeners that the event reminded him of conditions seventy years earlier—a perfect way to turn discussion toward caprice over climate change. And the extraordinary hurricanes that affected the Caribbean and the Gulf of Mexico were newsworthy in the United States because they were First World disasters, but were equally deemed to be acts of God or "Mother Nature." Elsewhere, they were understood as related to pollution, whether viewers were listening to Fidel Castro or Tony Blair (Engelhardt 2004a and 2004b). Blair avows that just because certain scientists contest the causes of global warming, opinion is far from evenly divided, and the vast majority's view must be fundamental to policy. Even he criticizes the United States for failing to ratify Kyoto (2005, 45, 46)!

Of course, "real" environmentalism itself has many problems. Domestically, the environmental movement in the United States has adopted CSR-style reformism, reducing all questions to the tactical-technical, not the strategic-structural. So discussion of hybrid cars is welcome, but debate over capitalism and R-Word finance is not. Away from reformism and toward more overtly reactionary forms of talk, environmentalism has been deployed to support a "blood-and-soil" essentialism steeped in racism and xenophobia (Teague 2004; Shellenberger and Nordhaus 2004; Haste 2004, 419). Anti–Mexican immigrant groups fund radio commercials that offer the likes of the following:

Congratulations Ventura County. You're known for some of California's most polluted beaches. Ventura isn't coping with the waste products from its ongoing population explosion and associated development.

Such advertisements, and others that utilize environmental discourse to push an antidiversity agenda, are the work of groups such as Californians for Population Stabilization (Lovato 2004). In England and France, environmental arguments have been appropriated increasingly by the Right. The British National Party and the Groupement de Recherche et d'Études pour la Civilisation Européene [Research and Study Group on European Civilization] argue against development and on behalf of wildlife and national tradition as a means of humanizing themselves to voters, and Migration Watch opposes immigration on environmental grounds (Sexton et al. 2005). Some Global Southists regard U.S. media and governmental concerns about the environment as crypto-colonialist, with anxiety about climate change an alibi for shutting down development in the Global South. And segments of the domestic left fear that eco-panic might be a last, desperate, post–Cold War lunge for money by the remnants of "big science." It was indeed a remarkable, symbolic coincidence that 1989 saw the Berlin Wall demolished at the same moment that the first major congresses on planetary ecological survival were being convened in France, England, and the Netherlands, and the Slow Food people were forming themselves in Italy. The dominance of liberalism was problematized at the very moment of its victory, as side effects of industrialization were recognized to be both more and less than progress (Paterson 1996, 2; Latour 1993, 8; Petrini 2001, 12).

The "conspiracy," whether it was the creature of big business, big leftism, big neocolonialism, or big science, did not retain governmental or media interest beyond the early 1990s. Greenish Al Gore left the Senate for veepish pastures, overseeing a 15 percent increase in carbon emissions across the country during his tenure, and a series of key journalists resigned. Content analysis of the *New York Times* and the *Washington Post* between 1980 and 1995 reveals a movement from coverage of global warming as a potential disaster to a topic of intramural scientific controversy. In the period between 1999–2000, German and British quality papers dedicated three times the coverage to the topic as their Yanqui equivalents. These papers, plus the *Los Angeles Times* and the *Wall Street Journal*, give unprecedented access to right-wing fringe doubters of the consensus on global warming in the name of "balance," with the *Journal* offering just 5 percent of all the articles appearing in these papers that addressed the topic between 1988 and 2002 (McComas and Shanahan 1999; Gelbspan 2004, 70; Wilson 2002, 251; Boykoff and Boykoff, 2004a).

Gore invited a hundred TV weathercasters to the White House in 1997 to discuss climate change, but many were offended by what they saw as a politicization of their work (Mazur 1998, 467–69; McKibben 2005, 35). When a major network TV news editor was asked a few years back why his programs never led with the links between weather calamities and industry, he replied: "We did that. Once. But it triggered a barrage of complaints from the Global Climate Coalition to our top executives" (quoted in Gelbspan 2004, 80). The upshot is that the three major network-news programs devoted fifteen minutes to global warming in 2003, and 4,047 minutes to Iraq. Their environmental coverage since September 11 is down from 617 minutes in 2001 to 236 minutes in 2002. The U.S. bourgeois media have used the term "junk science" to discredit environmentalists again and again over this period. And there is evidence that some TV corporations forbid use of the syntagm "global warming," while less than one in ten hires environment reporters. As for PBS, it has screened three infamous documentaries: *Living Against the Odds* (1991), a special funded by Chevron, which avowed "We have to stop pointing the finger at industry for every environmental hazard"; *The Prize: The Epic Quest for Oil, Money and Power* (1993), which was paid for by oil industry financier PaineWebber and consultant Daniel Yergin; and *Commanding Heights: The Battle for the World Economy* (2003), courtesy of BP, Enron, and FedEx. BP distinguished itself two years later by adopting an "ad-pull" policy, in which it threatened to withdraw advertising from magazines and newspapers that dared to publish *anything* about the firm, its competitors, or its grisly industry without asking permission first (Lobe 2003b and 2004; Wilson 2002, 251, 254; Herman 1999, 235; *Advertising Age* 2005; Barsamian 2001, 40). At the same time, it pretended that its acronym, which stands for "British Petroleum," signified "Beyond Petroleum."

Gallup Polls from 2002 and 2003 indicate that while most Yanquis acknowledge global warming and human responsibility for its impact, only a third are "gravely concerned," and another third moderately so. Public worry about the environment in general declined over the first two years of Bush Minor in office. But there is hope. A University of Oregon study reveals that over 80 percent of Yanquis favor reduction of greenhouse gas emissions. The Program on International Policy Attitudes and Knowledge Networks' 2004 poll confirms this, and discloses massive support for tax incentives to encourage corporate cleanliness and ratification of Kyoto. The following year, similarly positive responses emerged to the rest of the G-8's challenge to limit greenhouse gas emissions, and in support of tax incentives for alternative energy. In addition, there is a powerful endorsement of protecting rainforests amongst the youngest school pupils, while many corporations now see great opportunities from the postpollutant technologies promised by Kyoto, and oppose Bush over it. The population tends to favor positions espoused by environmental groups over the policies of the Bush administration, and prefers conservation to production as a focus of energy policy by 60 percent to 29 percent. A majority opposes opening the Arctic National Wildlife Refuge in Alaska for oil exploration, and rejects expanded use of nuclear energy. Three quarters say the state "should do whatever it takes" to conserve the environment.

Yet the Bush administration continues to use and create policies that ensure increased greenhouse gas emissions, and makes dubious allocations of research funds into the problem that delayed action by unnecessarily investigating what is considered normal science (Hertsgaard 2002; Kay 2003; Program on International Policy Attitudes 2005; Haste 2004, 420; Westcott 2005; Saad 2003a; Pew Center for Global Climate Change 2002; Revkin 2003).

The R-Worders are no doubt emboldened by the fact that far-right Christian fundamentalists, their core demotic alibi against charges of being corporate servants, are the most skeptical people in the Yanqui population about the necessity for environmental protection. Apparently there is no future for the planet. God's design is to destroy it and deliver true believers to safety in a kinky theological draft of wind. These Christians have half the Senate and much more of the House voting their way, even as the U.S. population believes that Bush and his lackeys concur with the Kyoto Treaty. Meanwhile, the decade-long advantage that the United States had enjoyed over Japan in high technology is threatened, as the latter may pull ahead with computers designed to explain climatic change while the United States continues to sponsor technology that simulates and stimulates weaponry (Pew Forum on Religion & Public Life 2004b; Pew Research Center 2005, 17; Scherer 2004; Lewis et al. 2005, 38; Wallerstein 2003, 26). Imagine the part that TV meteorology could play if it cared to describe the impact of corporations, governments, technologies, and techniques on the weather.

THE WEATHER CHANNEL

> Doctor, help me, I'm hooked on The Weather Channel.
> —Russell Baker (quoted in Gunther 1999, 46)

> Fuck: The Weather Channel
> —Postfarm discussion string (2004)

Working within Fowler's brave new world of deregulated television, the weather got its own national network in 1982. Landmark Communication's Weather Channel began broadcasting to a potential cable audience of 2.5 million sets, from a Georgia location chosen for its temperate climate and unions. At a press conference to announce the new project, the media response was "silence. Then a collective groan" (Batten with Cruikshank 2002, 3, 77). In attempts to obtain enough audiences to gain attention from cable companies, the Weather Channel offered "Beach Party Barbecue" travel contests, cruises, and flights on the Concorde. But it had lost US$20 million by 1986, with rumors spreading of its demise. As late as 1994, the oleaginous *Sports Illustrated* implied that the channel was a perfect match to sponsor the U.S. Olympic handball team, because both parties lacked a significant audience. Then the network started advertising itself by showing people sitting in a bar and cheering for warm versus cold fronts—a trope of the breakthrough in forecasting that occurred when the Norwegian School developed frontal theory during the Great War. It followed a successful revenue formula of commercials from car manufacturers, the grail of the national advertiser, localized through satellite downloading and articulated with regional dealerships. In 1998, a "Look Up! Challenge Sky Contest," invited school pupils and teachers to express themselves on the topic of the sky via poems, pictures, or photographs, with the winning schools receiving television sets. This tactic combined an address of future adults with an insertion of the channel into their daily lives, and associated it with more than the mundane. As the only national station offering local information, it gave cable companies the ability to segment advertising geographically and climatically (Beschloss 1989; *Sports Illustrated* 1994, 11; J. Brown 2005; Batten with Cruikshank 2002, 52; *Technological Horizons in Education Journal* 1998, 49; Miles 2004). Or so we are told. This does not preclude my being treated to snow-oriented commercials even though I live in Venice Beach. We don't really *have* a great deal of weather in southern California. We have fault lines and freeways.

Today, the Channel's audience extends to over 90 percent of cabled households. This rate of growth easily outstrips the average, and delivers numbers to advertisers that are far beyond MTV's performance. Cable operators themselves prefer it to all other stations apart from CNN (Miles 2004; Reynolds 1999; McConville 2000, 6; Reynolds 2003; Kevin Johnson 2000). The average rating in 1999 was 0.4 percent of cable viewers, up 33 percent on the previous year. The network boasted that, "If hell freezes over, you'll hear it first," a claim taken up by two million viewers who tuned in over fifteen minutes during Hurricane Fran in 1996 (quoted in Lowry 1998). Hurricane Floyd (1999) averaged 1.7 million spectators each hour, and on one occasion 2.5 million, in addition to making it into sports bars (McConville, 2000; Associated Press, 2000; Revkin, 1999). The Weather Channel rushed to circulate a press release entitled "Powerful Hurricane Floyd Blew out all the Ratings at the Weather Channel" (quoted in Gunther 1999). Bill Clinton cut short a peace mission in East Timor because of the hurricane, and both Al Gore and Bush Minor issued statements about it; Gore was interviewed on the Weather Channel. A 2005 blizzard was covered through Intellistar technology, which enables alternate messages across the network, producing an average viewership of a million homes across the twenty-two markets affected by the storm. That year, Hurricane Katrina saw four and a half million dwellings tuning in. The 2.2 rating was greater than Fox News, CNN, or MSNBC (Seabrook 2000; *Multichannel News* 2005, 10; Little 2005b; Smith 2005).

The Weather Channel generates anxiety over the potential for "audiences addicted to information pertaining only to their own special interests" (Bliss 1991, 459), with weather-watchers identified as addictive personalities. Presenters privately refer to their employer as "The Map Channel." The station's early research divided audiences between the "deeply serious" and the "weather-involved" (who watched anything and numbered 20 percent), "busy planners" and "instant users" (pragmatists in search of immediate information), the "weather-concerned" (cosmopolitans who followed where they used to live or had relatives and friends), and "weather enjoyers" (who liked the network's apolitical style of "television wallpaper") (Randle and Mordock 2002, 248; Associated Press 2000; Kevin Johnson 2000; National Public Radio 1995). It named the profoundly committed viewer as a "weather weenie" (quoted in Fabrikant 1999), addicted to the "weatherporn" habit of voyeurism—enjoying the sorrow of others. Now the channel distinguishes between the "weather-engaged" (41 percent), "weather planners" (28 percent), and "commodity users" (31 percent) among its spectators. Some fanatics follow presenters around during crises. Their number includes five naked teens with bags over their heads who once charged toward a camera on location (Seabrook 2000; Kloer 2001).

The network has developed MétéoMédia/The Weather Network in Canada, and El Canal del Tiempo (8.2 million viewers and services to networks with forty-three million viewers) and O Canal do Tempo (one million viewers) for Latin America and the Caribbean, with locations in Miami, the new entrepôt for Latin/U.S. cultural production. Spanish and Portuguese speakers receive "lifestyle information" on *fútbol/futebol*. Needless to say, José Rubiera, the charismatic Cuban TV expert on cyclones who held audiences spellbound at the 2004 World Conference of Media Meteorologists, does not feature. The Weather Channel's one TV failure was a 1995 move into Europe. Merrill Lynch dubbed the network "a cash machine" after its 1998 revenue of US$200 million, operating profit of US$100 million, and reported 1999 revenues of US$235 million. The new century brought cable competition through the Discovery Channel's "Tornado Week" and "Hurricane Week" documentary festivals, plus a direct rival in NBC Weather Plus. The Weather Channel responded with a 10 percent increase in expenditure on training, clothing, and new programs (Stamler 2001; *Business Wire* 2001b; Kempner 2001; Sólociencia 2004; Fabrikant 1999; Johnson 2000; McConville 2000; Johnson 2000; Donohue 2004).

Weather is by far the major reason Yanquis read the news online; this was true for 76 percent of readers in 2004, compared to 48 percent in 1998. Competition for the online audience has led to bizarre contests with AccuWeather over business subscriptions. The latter now claims to be able to forecast fifteen days in advance. AccuWeather, which boasts ten thousand clients in the forty years since it began at Pennsylvania State University, also assists the fossil fuel industry in spreading misinformation, and offered the first U.S. high-definition weather on the short-lived VOOM satellite system. Weatherplanner.com gives advice on weddings, parties, anything a year in advance for an annual fee of US$39.95. It is the consumer-oriented subsidiary of a corporate servant, Strategic Weather Services, that advises retailers and the U.S. military of garden equipment and outdoor furniture (Project for Excellence in Journalism 2005; Egan and Levy 2001, 72; Wind 2004; Revkin 2001, F1; AccuWeather 2005; Seabrook 2000).

The Weather Channel's principal site has over three hundred and fifty million page views, three million hits, and fourteen million unique users each day (twenty-three million during Hurricane Floyd). It routinely ranks first in surveys of content-based addresses and was the twenty-first most-visited site in January 1999. In addition, the company has a phone card call-in service; email lists with personalized forecasts, a direct presence in two hundred and fifty U.S. radio markets; sale of weather information to sixty-four U.S. newspapers and many corporate Web sites; and customized wireless content covering forty-four thousand locations through pagers, cellular phones, and personal digital assistants (The Weather Channel 1998, 2001; Fabrikant 1999; *Business Wire* 1998, 1999b, 2000, 2001a). When a number of storms lashed the eastern U.S. seaboard in January 2000, Weather.com received 63,976 email messages over the month, including 4,331 on one day—evidence that confirms the Web service's boast that the it gives "designer weather,"—a fine oxymoron standing for total commodification (Laughlin 2000). There are dedicated chat rooms, archives, and such special events as *Severe Tuesday, Killer Quake, Lightning,* and *Hurricane*. The channel also sells a *Nature's Fury* video package and CD-ROM. In 2005, it announced plans to send video forecasts and recordings to cell phones (The Weather Channel 2000; Fry 2003, 132; *RCR Wireless News* 2005).

NEW WEATHER

> [Freshmen at meteorology school] already sound like minions of the
> Weather Channel. Same language, same descriptions, same body
> movements. It's almost Orwellian. Though I have to say the Weather
> Channel has increased enrollment.
> — Lee Grenci, Pennsylvania State University instructor in meteorology
>   (quoted in Seabrook 2000)

> Weather forecasting has become a fast-food science.
> — Lee Grenci (quoted in Weed 2004)

Some critics of the Weather Channel have said it encapsulates "'detextualized'
television" (Allen 1992, 12). Communications professor Marita Sturken describes
it as "a story . . . without politics" (2001). But forecasts have the potential to be
"a classroom-of-the-commons" (Hughes 1995) — giving viewers technical information about industrial and political aspects of climatic change — if the extraordinarily unscientific conservative biases of on-camera staff (Wilson 2002, 266) are
countered. HBO's dyspeptic situation comedy *Curb Your Enthusiasm* was the
only twenty-first-century program on a major network that routinely addressed
environmental issues, albeit to color marital politics and misanthropy (Siegel
2005). We need "*social meteorology*," a form of knowledge that makes sense of
the weather at the intersection of "social life, natural life, and economic life" (Ross
1991, 13). That can happen, as when Washington DC forecaster Bob Ryan stood
on Capitol Hill at the 1990 Earth Day rally and shouted in the direction of the
White House: "This is what clean air looks like. This is the kind of sky we want"
(quoted in Ross 1991, 196). Such a mixture of passion about nature with the "scientific" endorsement of media personalities is dangerous for capital, because it
portends a populist critique of social relations (Anderson 1997, 55).

Just as I suggested that the Food Network restructure its hyperconsumerist
programming to address cultural citizenship, so the Weather Channel could
engage the impact of global warming on agricultural production, as climatic
change meets flooded coastal planes, and the agrochemical and transportation
industries pollute the environment. The channel could be an excellent platform to stage the "jobs vs. the environment" debates, which have so often
divided progressive forces. The Weather Channel's 2001 promotional campaign was entitled "Live By It" — a means of linking viewers' daily lives to their
product (Atkins and Bowler 2001, 109; Klein 1999, 266–67; Stamler 2001).
The next step is connecting those lives to environmental despoliation.

This new direction could derive from "green citizenship." According to
political theorist Hartley Dean (2001), environmentalism has affected citizenship in three ways:

- Claims to rights have expanded to include clean air and water.
- National boundaries and interests have been brought into question by the border-crossing impact of despoliation.
- Corporate economic citizenship has been rearticulated beyond gleeful receipt of welfare.

More than an addition to the rights and responsibilities of territorially based citizenship, this new direction amounts to a critique of them, a corrective that looks to saving infrastructure and heritage from capitalist growth. By surpassing contemporary needs to enter the sphere of historic and future obligations, it transcends conventional political-economic space, extending rights beyond today, in search of a sustainable ecology. There is an additional corollary of this threat to economic citizenship, corporate style. So elemental are the risks created by industry that for now, rather than looking to the next generation to carry on, forecasts must look centuries ahead in order to guide policy today. There is a good side to governing at a distance through an ethos of personal responsibility, provided that it does not lose itself in the sands of individualism. Those with the greatest responsibility are First World industries and the mutual funds and financial institutions that invest in them, not the lone camper or solitary sweet-eater. Such stories do not have to be distant from the everyday—quite the opposite, as when the *Miami Herald* correlated housing destruction wrought by hurricane conditions with corrupt enforcement of building regulations, not just bad luck (Dobson 2003, 87, 89, 99, 110, 167; Marvin and Meyer 2005, 402).

As regards CSR, when finances interfere, it becomes a luxury, and the resultant reneging on corporate citizenship needs to be explained to the public by outlets such as the Weather Channel. Take the Ford Motor Company for example. Its corporate citizenship reports marking the twenty-first century were greeted favorably by environmental activists because of their serious address of sport-utility vehicles' impact on pollution and global warming. With the economic downturn under Bush Minor, the corporation's response was to neglect these issues, and make more and more vehicles with dangerous implications for future generations. In addition to exposing such decisions, there are positive stories to tell, such as Ford shareholders calling for a nexus between executive salaries and reduction of greenhouse emissions (Hakim 2002; Frel 2005). Or consider the stunning success of Greenpeace's 1995 action against Shell Oil for seeking to dump a discarded rig in the sea, undertaken by the nonprofit organization's global "televised indictments" of the company, consumer boycotts, and political pressure (Beck 1999, 40). The corporation gave in. The indictments themselves, footage of rigs, interviews with workers and consumers, and coverage of Greenpeace would make for terrific environmental TV.

The *Guardian* newspaper and Best Foot Forward offer a Carbon Calculator service for readers to work out their own role in environmental despoliation. Imagine what a service this could be on the Weather Channel's Web site, with results subject to weekly (humorous) discussion on a current-affairs show! A visit to the virtual march for the environment at www.stopglobalwarming.org could feature politicians, NGOs, religious leaders, academics, and media people.

These issues have not been central to the Weather Channel's brand of citizenship, despite all their visibility and importance to the population. But in 2000, the Channel altered its programming to include more features and background pieces (Zbar 2001), offering room for the new programming I am proposing. Some of it could look at weather metatexts, from novels, films, and music to emergent genres in electronic gaming. Science fiction would be a key genre for debating utopic and dystopic visions of the future. And since the channel claims that it is interested in the weather from the perspective of its viewers—as parents, workers, and vacationers—it might consider the poll data I listed earlier on risk perception and rejection of the R-Word environmental agenda. If truly interested in vernacular perspectives on the weather, the channel could feature the everyday health risks posed by global warming, as set up for U.S. journalists by Environmental Media Services in 2001:

INFECTIOUS DISEASE
- A reduced range of temperatures—both day-to-day and seasonally—makes it easier for disease-carrying insects to survive.
- Warmer and wetter weather may increase rodents and insects and hence malaria, yellow fever, dengue, Hantavirus, and Lyme disease, according to the Centers for Disease Control and Prevention.
- Approximately 45 percent of people live where mosquitoes transmit malaria; models predict will increase to about 60 percent in the next fifty to one hundred years.
- Warming sea surface temperatures promote harmful algal blooms, which can cause massive fish kills and human memory loss.
- Evidence suggests heavy precipitation and runoff will increase, significantly contributing to water- and seafood-borne diseases. In urban watersheds, more than 60 percent of contaminants (i.e., Escherichia coli) are transported during storms.

AIR POLLUTION
- Ground-level ozone forms more readily when temperatures are higher because of a chemical reaction between volatile organic compounds and nitrogen oxides in the presence of heat and sunlight.
- Higher levels of ozone, air pollutants, and pollen could compromise air quality, exacerbating respiratory diseases.
- Volatile organic compounds include toxins emitted from power plants, waste combustion units, dry cleaners, and automobiles. They are associated with negative reproductive, neurological, and developmental effects. Higher temperatures cause these volatile organic compounds to evaporate and disperse more rapidly into the atmosphere.
- Global warming affects temperatures and humidity, exacerbating allergies and respiratory diseases through pollen-producing plants.

FLOODS
- Flooding due to storm surges affects forty-six million people in an average year, mostly in developing countries. Studies suggest this figure could rise along with sea level increases caused by climate change.
- Severe rainstorms and floods wash raw sewage, pesticides, and agricultural waste into water supplies, spreading giardiasis and Cryptosporidiosis.

HEAT
- Heat waves will intensify with climate change.
- Studies show an increase of three degrees Fahrenheit could increase heat-related deaths by 50–100 percent in cities such as Boston.
- Examples of heat-related disease are heat cramps, heat exhaustion, and heat stroke.
- The elderly are at great risk for heat-related ailments, as are infants, those with cardiovascular disease, and people on certain medications.

The network's neglect of these issues presumably derived from its apolitical self-image. In 2000, senior meteorologist Stu Ostro advised that "once you say global warming is caused by human means, you have to say whose fault it is, and what do you do about it, and then you're in a very difficult situation" (quoted in Seabrook 2000). But the Weather Channel and its corresponding sites have delivered what they were pleased to call "War forecasts" for Kosovo, Afghanistan, and Iraq (*PR Newswire* 2001). In 2002, the network engaged in a cross-promotion with A&E's imperialist miniseries *Shackleton*, and ran a *Weather and War* feature that rated excellently (Fass 2002; Thomas 2002). In 2005, the channel profiled military meteorologists, sandstorm scouts, wandering around Iraq during the invasion to give the air force information on coming weather. And between 2002 and 2004, it was paid by the EPA to make programs about ozone depletion and other environmental questions and broadcast them in prime time. Although the EPA's participation was mentioned in teletext, the videos did not say that they were financed by the state. The contradictions came out when the network's executive suite told the *Washington Post* that the idea was to offer the EPA an opportunity "to toot their horns" without the channel being "a puppet or a mouthpiece." The agency was also busy hiring nonscientists to ghostwrite putatively scholarly articles for publication in academic journals (executive quoted in C. Lee 2005; Barringer 2005).

Since the Weather Channel wishes to politicize weather, let it begin. About thirty nations suffer from water scarcity, and this number is expected to double by 2025. Many brutal struggles over natural resources, especially water, are masked as ethnic strife, such as the contest for the Punjab region (Shiva 2002, xi, 1). So if World Bank Vice President Ismail Serageldin was correct in 1995 when he said "the wars of the next century will be fought over water" (quoted in Shiva 2002, x) then the channel may be obliged to make more programs like *Weather and War*, but in a self-reflexive way. The World Bank might have to be similarly self-reflexive and allocate some funds to renewable energy, as opposed to the 94 percent of loan money that currently goes to fossil-fuel projects. At the same time, the localism of U.S. weather does not have to translate into the usual dangerous banalities of nativism. Below the level of the appalling U.S. federal government, state and regional officials have somewhat enlightened attitudes, and the desire and capacity to link local and global. Consider the mayoral summit meeting at Sundance in 2005, when Robert Redford convened a bipartisan group that noted how many U.S. cities have gone far beyond Kyoto precepts, saved hundreds of millions of dollars, and attracted new investment (Hertsgaard 2004; Little 2005a).

Help is on the way. In 2003, the Weather Channel released a policy document on global warming that acknowledged "human activities" as a problem (Weather Channel 2003), and it was happy to be given a product placement in *The Day After Tomorrow* (2004) as the network featuring belated R-Word recognition of environmentalism. When the film was released, as part of a series of promotional tie-ins, the Weather Channel admitted that fossil fuels play a part in global warming. Later in 2004, it ran programs about the impact of global warming on Alaska, and appointed a climate expert, Heidi Cullen, to its staff to explain "weather theories" about the human impact on the environment. Euphemized as "climate stories," these programs made the Weather Channel the only major U.S.-weather media outlet to consider these questions—all based on Cullen's working toward "the development of new products," of course. Cullen acknowledges the role of lost wetlands in the devastation of Hurricane Katrina, and notes diminishing skepticism amongst on-air colleagues. In addition, the Weather Channel hired the leftist comedian Lewis Black to appear in 2005 (About.com 2004; *Greenwire* 2004; The Weather Channel 2000; Little 2005b ; Keegan 2005).

At the same time, the trend in TV weather is toward "now-casting," with the emphasis on a technological account of the present, and network weather's engagement with public opinion on the environment is basically zero (Veder and Fleming 2001; Lewis et al. 2005, 62). The chances are that tomorrow will be . . . risky and disciplined. "Good" cultural citizens will make the right moves based on that reality, and not bother with the causes of risks and disciplines, beyond their apparent origins in the sky and on the land. These citizens are safe in the arms of the Weather Channel's owner, who basks in his forecast that "weather is not necessarily a perishable commodity" (Batten with Cruikshank 2002, 224).

On the far Right, science-fiction author Michael Crichton's best seller *State of Fear* (2004), about environmental graduate-student zealots, assures everyone that a "guess is just a guess" about global warming. Promoted by the American Enterprise Institute, his lecture "Science Policy in the 21st Century" likened environmental scientists to the controllers of Auschwitz. Yet we know that Bush Minor recognizes the power of the environment, as evidenced in his retreat to a bunker when a cloud moved unusually quickly over the White House in the spring of 2005 (Horton 2005; Mooney 2005, 36; Borger 2005).

With the terrorist attacks on London that year, the R-Word media were quick to applaud renewed press attention to "real" politics. Bill Sammon of the *Washington Times* welcomed the fact that "We're not talking about global warming . . . We're back to the basics," and Joe Scarborough criticized the G-8 for their "focus on global warming and the causes of the moment, instead of fighting the war of our lifetime" (quoted in FAIR 2005f). Just a few weeks prior to the London bombings, the FBI's Deputy Assistant Director for Counterterrorism told Congress that environmental activists posed the major terrorist threat to the United States, and the Department of Homeland Security focused on them to the exclusion of the radical Right (Kavanagh 2005).

No doubt they were correct. After all, authentic environmental concerns were being taken care of by General Electric in the shape of "ecoimagination," a word that emerged from US$90 million of product development, and led to advertisements in which trees grow from smokestacks to show that the company was "addressing the problems of tomorrow, today." In reality, it was a response to sane regulations imposed by the E.U. (quoted in Anderson 2005; Fisher 2005). So, it really *is* ok, then. Let's just watch the weather while the world warms.

CONCLUSION

Our leaders are sick of all the solid information that has been dumped
on humanity by research and scholarship and investigative reporting.
    They think the whole country is sick of it, and they want
standards, and it isn't the gold standard. They want to put us back on
the snake-oil standard.
    —Kurt Vonnegut (2005, 39)

L ET US RETURN to where we began, and the seven formations
that have theorized cultural citizenship (see Figure 2).
    Both the arid lands of Bennett and the humidispheres of
Rosaldo, Kymlicka, Parekh, and Chua illustrate the improba-
bility of wiping from history the differences between indigenes, dominant
settlers, and minority migrants. Yet, Rorty contrives a human-capital merger
of all the above, and Lewis and Huntington offer an ideological justification for hollowing out material history and accounting for Western hegemony in cultural terms. A neoliberal worldview, whose limits are set via
the hyperculturalism and closet nationalism of the "clash" theorists, can
seemingly accomodate Bennett's competences, Rosaldo's resistances, and
Kymlicka, Parekh, and Chua's relativisms, albeit with their rhetorics soft-
ened at some points and hardened at others. This is all for the "cultural"
in the most "cultural" of all possible worlds, the capstone being an efficient and effective workforce, whose cosmopolitanism is brokered on a
respect for difference that guarantees individual advantage in a globally
competitive labor market.

Each of these approaches deals with heavily practical yet highly emotional, profoundly populist yet avowedly technical forms of thought. As
such, they inevitably rub up against contradictions. Bennett must deal
with the incommensurability of neoliberal and statist prescriptions.

AUTHOR	DISCIPLINE	FIELD OF INFLUENCE	LIBERAL SUBJECTIVITY	CULTURAL POLICY
Tony Bennett	Sociology/ cultural studies	Australian/E.U. cultural policy	Created via cultural competences	Social engineering
Renato Rosaldo	Cultural studies/ anthropology	U.S. Chicano/a studies, *Fresno Bee, New York Times*	Undermined via awareness of dispossession	Vernacularity and tactics
Will Kymlicka	Political theory	Baltic States, Canada, *Wall Street Journal*	Enriched by migration and dispossession	Language equality
Bhikhu Parekh	Political theory	British Commission, Indian debates	Undermined by immigration	Deinstitutional-ization of racism
Amélie Oksenberg Rorty	Philosophy	Neoliberalism	Created as human capital	Training for global competition
Bernard Lewis and Samuel Huntington	History and international relations	U.S. media and foreign policy	Forged via the western tradition	Judaeo-Christian ethos
Amy Chua	Law	U.S. public culture	Undermined by ethnic inequality	Antinationalism, philanthropy

FIGURE 2.

Rosaldo must make peace with the fact that government is frequently the court of appeal for vernacular protest. Kymlicka and Parekh must come to terms with the economic limits to liberal philosophy. Rorty must engage the obstinate collectivism and hybridity of culture, and the fact that neoliberalism is no more metacultural than any other form of thought. Chua must acknowledge the constitutive inequality and brutality of capitalism. Lewis and Huntington must explain the reality of U.S. Middle Eastern policy, and more precise histories than their grandiosities will allow. And all must do so in a context that Clinton has correctly identified as an environment of global interdependence without global integration, where the media, especially television, are much more than epiphenomena or indices (2002). Instead, the media both incarnate social change as aspects of neoliberal policy and commodification *and* report on it. As such, they perform simultaneous functions of exemplification and metacommentary. They are test cases and rhetorical platforms all at once.

For reactionaries, cultural citizenship signifies a loss of national and spiritual unity, as sectarianism and secularism overwhelm patriotism and superstition. For the Left and for cultural studies, cultural citizenship concerns the maintenance, development, and exchange of cultural lineage—a celebration of difference, which is also a critique of the status quo. For the neoliberal Right, of course, it offers a new set of market and ecclesiastical niches and sites of self governance. My concern is that the cultural Left got what we wanted—culture at the center of politics and sociopolitical analysis. But it wasn't Queer Nation and Stuart Hall. It was fundamentalist Christianity and Samuel Huntington. We need to rearticulate culture to the economy and capitalize the "p" in politics, not a misleading, antimaterialist sphere of ideation. We need to start with television, because that is where Yanquis learn about war, subsistence, and the environment—this nation's major influences on the globe.

In addition to taking adequate account of popular culture, doctrines of cultural citizenship can work toward a more equitable world if they reject the technicism, utopianism, liberalism, nationalism, and neoliberalism of business-as-usual cultural citizenship, and recognize their reliance on deregulatory consumerist projects as much as leftist social-movement populism. In answer to the theoreticism and technocracy of neoliberalism, we can point to participatory/popular budgeting systems undertaken by leftist regional and urban governments in Kerala, Mexico City, and Porto Alegre over the past fifteen years, and Brazil's *sindicato cidadão* [citizens' trade union] (Chathukulam and John 2002; Heller 2001; Dagnino 2003, 7; Ziccardi 2003). We can also form strategic alliances with opponents of neoliberalism from within, such as George Soros, who made his fortune on the financial markets, but now sees that "the untrammeled intensification of laissez-faire capitalism and the spread of market values into all areas of life is endangering our open and democratic society" (1997).

In his "Ten Dispatches About Place" from 2005, the noted cultural critic John Berger responds to the query "Are you still a Marxist?" After tracking through the unparalleled "devastation caused by the pursuit of profit," he concludes that "Yes, I'm still among other things a Marxist." Those "other things" are terribly important; they register crucial forms of life that operate with varying degrees of autonomy from the economy. But they can only be engaged alongside the equally crucial aspects addressed here. So I have a related query: Are you still a culturalist?

REFERENCES

Abayah, Antonio C. 2004. "Aimez-Vous Bush?" *Manila Standard*, September 16.

Abdel-Shehid, Gamal. 2002. "Cultural Globalization and the Soul Food Memoir: Austin Clarke, Ntozake Shange and Marlon Riggs." *Journal of Historical Sociology* 15 (4): 451–63.

Abizadeh, Arash. 2002. "Does Liberal Democracy Presuppose a Cultural Nation? Four Arguments." *American Political Science Review* 96 (3):495–509.

About.com. 2004. "The Weather Channel(R) Announces Position on Global Warming." May 6. http://environment.about.com.

Abrahamian, Ervand. 2003. "The US Media, Huntington and September 11." *Third World Quarterly* 24 (3): 529–44.

Abu-Laban, Yasmeen. 2000. "Reconstructing an Inclusive Citizenship for a New Millennium: Globalization, Migration and Difference." *International Politics* 37 (4): 509–26.

Accuweather.com. 2005. "The AccuWeather Story." http://www.accuweather.com.

Active Citizenship Centre. 2005. "About Active Citizenship." http://www.Active-citizen.org.uk.

L'Actualité. 2004. "Juan Valdez Affronte Starbucks." February: 17.

Adams, Scott. 2005. "Dilbert." *Los Angeles Times*, August 21.

AdCouncil. 2002. "I am an American." www.adcouncil.org.

Adelstein, Jonathan S. 2003. "A Dark Storm Cloud is Looming over the Future of the American Media." Common Dreams News Center, June 2. http://www.*common dreams.org*.

Adema, Pauline. 2000. "Vicarious Consumption: Food, Television and the Ambiguity of Modernity." *Journal of American & Comparative Cultures* 23 (3): 113–24.

Adorno, Theodor W. 1996. *The Culture Industry: Selected Essays on Mass Culture*, trans. Gordon Finlayson, Nicholas Walker, Anson G. Rabinach, Wes Blomster, and Thomas Y. Levin. Ed. J. M. Bernstein. London: Routledge.

Advertising Age. 2005. "Debating the 'Ad-Pull' Policy Controversy." May 31.

Advertising Age with Association of Hispanic Advertising Agencies. 2005. *Hispanic Fact Pack.*

AgBiotech in the News. 2003. "The Odd Couple: Biotechnology and the Media." 2, no. 11.

Agovino, Teresa. 2003. "NYSE Revokes Credentials for Al-Jazeera." *Editor & Publisher,* March 25.

Ahmad, Aijaz. 2003. "Contextualizing Conflict: The US 'War on Terrorism.'" In *War and the Media: Reporting Conflict 24/7,* ed. Daya Kishan Thussu and Des Freedman, 15–27. London: Sage Publications.

Ahmed, Rashmee Z. 2005. "Days of Raj: Let's Get Over It?" *Times of India,* January 16.

Airey, Dawn. 2004. "Golden Age—Myth or Reality?" RTS Huw Wheldon Memorial Lecture of the Royal Television Society. Cambridge, March 17.

Ajami, Fouad, Richard Betts, Gerge Borjas, Stephen Bosworth, Zbigniew Brzezinski, Eliot Cohen, Francis Fukuyama et al. 2004. "In Defense of Huntington." *Foreign Policy* (November/December): 4.

Aktan, Gunduz. 2004. "Denigration and Democratization." *Turkish Daily News,* May 15.

Alba, Richard. 2004. Language Assimilation Today: Bilingualism Persists More Than in the Past, but English Still Dominates. Working Paper 111, Center for Comparative Immigration Studies, University of California, San Diego.

Aleinikoff, T. Alexander. 2000. "Between Principles and Politics: U.S. Citizenship Policy." In *From Migrants to Citizens: Membership in a Changing World,* ed. T. Alexander Aleinikoff and Douglas Klusmeyer, 119–72. Washington: Carnegie Endowment for International Peace.

Alexander, Jeffrey C. 2001. "Theorizing the 'Modes of Incorporation': Assimilation, Hyphenation, and Multiculturalism as Varieties of Civil Participation." *Sociological Theory* 193: 237–49.

Alibhai-Brown, Yasmin. 2005. "The Dishonesty of the Immigration Card." *Independent,* April 11: 33.

Allan, Stuart. 2002. *Media, Risk and Science.* Buckingham: Open University Press.

Allan, Stuart, and Barbie Zelizer. 2004. "Rules of Engagement." In *Reporting War: Journalism in Wartime,* ed. Stuart Allan and Barbie Zelizer, 3–21. London: Routledge.

Allen, Brooke. 2005. "Our Godless Constitution." *The Nation* 280 (February 21): 14–20.

Allen, David S. 2001. "The First Amendment and the Doctrine of Corporate Personhood: Collapsing the Press-Corporation Distinction." *Journalism: Theory, Practice and Criticism* 2 (3): 255–78.

Allen, Robert C. 1992. "Introduction to the Second Edition: More Talk about TV." In *Channels of Discourse, Reassembled: Television and Contemporary Criticism,* ed. Robert C. Allen, 1–30. Chapel Hill: University of North Carolina Press.

Al-Marashi, Ibrahim. 2004. "An Insider's Assessment of Media Punditry and 'Operation Iraqi Freedom'." *Transnational Broadcasting Studies* 12.

Almås, Reidar, and Geoffrey Lawrence. 2003. "Introduction: The Global/Local Problematic." In *Globalization, Localization, and Sustainable Livelihoods,* ed. Reidar Almås and Geoffrey Lawrence, 3–24. Aldershot: Ashgate.

Alperovitz, Gar. 2005. "The New Ownership Society." *The Nation* 280 (June 27): 30–32.

Alterman, Eric. 2003. *What Liberal Media? The Truth about Bias and the News.* New York: Basic Books.

Alterman, Eric. 2005. "In Re *Newsweek*: Which Side are You on?" *The Nation* 280 (June 20): 11.

American Academy of Pediatric Dentistry. 2003. "Partnership to Promote Pediatric Dental Health." March 3. http://www.aapd.org/hottopics/news.asp?NEWS_ID=212.

American Meterological Society. 1993. *Challenges of Our Changing Atmosphere: Careers in Atmospheric Research and Applied Meterology.*

American Political Science Association Task Force on Inequality and American Democracy. 2004. *American Democracy in an Age of Rising Inequality.*

Amin, Samir. 1997. *Capitalism in the Age of Globalization.* London: Zed.

Amin, Samir. 2003. "World Poverty, Pauperization & Capital Accumulation." *Monthly Review* 55 (5): 1–9.

Andersen, Kenneth E. 2005. *Recovering the Civic Culture: The Imperative of Ethical Communication.* Boston: Pearson.

Anderson, Alison. 1997. *Media, Culture and the Environment.* New Brunswick: Rutgers University Press.

Anderson, Chris. 2005. "Little Green Men." *Flow: A Critical Forum on Television and Media Culture* 2, no. 8. http://jot.communication.utexas.edu/flow/?jot=view&id=850.

Anderson, Sarah, John Cavanagh, Scott Klinger, and Liz Stanton. 2005. *Executive Excess 2005: Defense Contractors Get More Bucks for the Bang—12th Annual CEO Compensation Survey.* Washington and Boston: Institute for Policy Studies/United for a Fair Economy.

Annan, Kofi. 2003. "Emma Lazarus Lecture on International Flows of Humanity." Lecture presented November 21, 2003 to the Columbia Law School, New York.

Aristotle. 1963. "Politics," trans. Benjamin Jowett. In *Social and Political Philosophy: Readings from Plato to Gandhi,* ed. John Somerville and Ronald E. Santoni, 59–100. New York: Doubleday.

Aristotle. 2005. *Meteorology,* trans. E. W. Webster. Internet Classics Archive.

Arnett, Peter. 2003. "You are the Goebbels of Saddam's Regime." *Guardian,* February 14.

Arnow, Pat. 2005. "Where Have all the Bodies Gone?" EXTRA! July/August: 18–20.

Asad, Talal. 2005. "Reflections on Laïcité & the Public Sphere." *Items and Issues* 5 (3): 1–11.

Asian Development Bank. 2005. *An Initial Assessment of the Impact of the Earthquake and Tsunami of December 26, 2004 on South and Southeast Asia.*

Associated Press. 2000. "Channel Weathers High Pressure Role." *Florida Times-Union,* February 14.

Associated Press. 2003. "APME Requests Pentagon Halt Harassment of Media in Iraq." November 12.

Association for Progressive Communications. 2003. "Statement Opposing Actions Against the Online Presence of Middle East News Agency, Al-Jazeera." April 4.

Atkins, Peter, and Ian Bowler. 2001. *Food in Society: Economy, Culture, Geography.* London: Arnold.

Atkinson, Claire, and Abbey Klaassen. 2005. "Roger Ailes Defends Fox News Practices." *Advertising Age,* March 31.

Atlanta Journal and Constitution. 2001. "Weather Channel Cuts 18 Jobs." October 12: 4F.

Aufderheide, Pat. 2004. "Big Media and Little Media: The Journalistic Informal Sector During the Invasion of Iraq." In *Reporting War: Journalism in Wartime,* ed. Stuart Allan and Barbie Zelizer, 333–46. London: Routledge.

Auletta, Ken, and Ted Turner. 2003. "Journalists and Generals." *New Yorker,* March 24. http://www.newyorker.com.

Australian Broadcasting Corporation. 2001. "History of ABC Radio." December 12. http://abc.net.au.

Auter, Philip, Mohamed M. Arafa, and Khaled Al-Jaber. 2004. "Who is Al Jazeera's Audience? Deconstructing the Demographics and Psychographics of an Arab Satellite News Network." *Transnational Broadcasting Studies* 12.

Aysha, Emad El-Din. 2003. "Samuel Huntington and the Geopolitics of American Identity: The Function of Foreign Policy in America's Domestic Clash of Civilizations." *International Studies Perspectives* 4:113–32.

Babb, Florence E. 2004. "Recycled *Sandalistas*: From Revolution to Resorts in the New Nicaragua." *American Anthropologist* 106 (3): 541–55.

Bacon, David. 2004. "The Political Economy of Immigration Reform." *Multinational Monitor* 25, no. 11.

Back, Les, Michael Keith, Azra Khan, Kalbir Shukra, and John Solomos. 2002. "New Labour's White Heart: Politics, Multiculturalism and the Return of Assimilation." *Political Quarterly* 73, no. 4: 445–54.

Bagehot. 1999. "Sunshine and Showers." *Economist*, April 10: 58.

Baker, William F., and George Dessart. 1998. *Down the Tube: An Inside Account of the Failure of American Television*. New York: Basic Books.

Barbrook, Richard, and Andy Cameron. 1996. "The Californian Ideology." *Science as Culture* 6:44–72.

Barkham, Patrick. 2005. "*The Guardian* Profile: Delia Smith." March 4.

Barkin, Gareth. 2002. "Oldest Trick in the Book: Interactivity and Market Interests in Indonesian Television." *M/C Reviews*.

Barkin, Steve M. 2003. *American Television News: The Media Marketplace and the Public Interest*. Armonk: M. E. Sharpe.

Barlow, Rich. 2004. "Weighing Teachings on Gluttony." *Boston Globe*, October 16: B2.

Barnes, Bart. 2004. "Giving Americans Entrée to Cuisine." *Washington Post*, August 14: A1.

Barringer, Felicity. 2005. "Public Relations Campaign for Research Office at E.P.A. Includes Ghostwriting Articles." *New York Times*, July 18.

Barry, Brian. 2001. *Culture and Equality: An Egalitarian Critique of Multiculturalism*. Cambridge: Polity Press.

Barsamian, David. 2001. *The Decline and Fall of Public Broadcasting*. Cambridge, MA: South End Press.

Basel Action Network. 2004. *CRT Glass Recycling Survey Results*.

Basel Action Network and Silicon Valley Toxics Coalition. 2002. *Exporting Harm: The High-Tech Trashing of Asia*.

Batten, Frank, with Jeffrey L. Cruyikshank. 2002. *The Weather Channel*. Cambridge, MA: Harvard Business School.

Bauböck, Rainer. 2000. Introd. to *Migrants to Citizens: Membership in a Changing World*, ed. T. Alexander Aleinikoff and Douglas Klusmeyer. Washington: Carnegie Endowment for International Peace.

Bauböck, Rainer. 2005. "Citizenship Policies: International, State, Migrant and Democratic Perspectives." *Global Migration Perspectives* 19. Geneva: Global Commission on International Migration.

Baudrillard, Jean. 1988. *Selected Writings*, ed. Mark Poster. Stanford: Stanford University Press.

Baudrillard, Jean. 1999. "Consumer Society." In *Consumer Society in American History: A Reader*, ed. Lawrence B. Glickman, 33–56. Ithaca: Cornell University Press.

Baudrillard, Jean. 2002. "L'Esprit du Terrorisme," trans. Michel Valentin. *South Atlantic Quarterly* 101 (2): 403–15.

Baum, Matthew A. 2002. "Sex, Lies, and War: How Soft News Brings Foreign Policy to the Inattentive Public." *American Political Science Review* 96:91–110.

BBC Monitoring International Reports. 2004a. "BBC Monitoring Quotes from Malaysian Press." July 28.

BBC Monitoring International Reports. 2004b. "Rafsanjani Says 'Total Censorship' of Casualties in US Media." April 30.

BBC News Online. 1999. "Has Dinner had its Chips?" August 31.

BBC News Online. 2000. "BBC's Weather Girl Power." February 21.

BBC News Online. 2001. "New Burma TV Shows 'Myanmar Mosaic'." August 8.

BBC News Online. 2003. "Poll Suggests World Hostile to US." June 16.

BBC News Online. 2004. "Ex-BBC Boss Slates 'Dumb' Shows." August 10.

BBC News Online. 2005a. "Clownish Burger Icon Crosses Over." September 26.

BBC News Online. 2005b. "Farmers Stew Over 'Couch Potato'." June 20.

BBC News Online. 2005c. "Global Poll Slams Bush Leadership." January 18.

BBC News Online. 2005d. "Guantanamo Detainees Refuse Food." July 22.

BBC Weather. 2005a. "80 Years of Radio Weather Forecasting."

BBC Weather. 2005b. "A History of Weather Broadcasting."

BBC Weather. 2005c. "BBC Weather Broadcasters in History."

Beard, Alison. 2003. "Building Growth through Homes and Gardening." *Financial Times,* October 7: 14.

Beardsworth, Alan, and Teresa Keil. 1990. "Putting the Menu on the Agenda." *Sociology* 24 (1): 139–51.

Beattie, Liza, Furzana Khan, and Greg Philo. 1999. "Race, Advertising and the Public Face of Television." In *Message Received: Glasgow Media Group Research 1993–1998,* ed. Greg Philo, 149–70. Harlow: Longman.

Beck, Ulrich. 1999. *World Risk Society.* Cambridge: Polity Press.

Bedell, Geraldine. 2002. "Food Is not Fuel." *Domus Collection* 18·31–36

Begley, Louis. 1998. "Talk of the Town." *New Yorker,* October 5: 34.

Behr, Rafael. 2005. "Hob-Nobbing." *Observer,* April 6.

Beidelman, T. O. 1997. *The Cool Knife: Imagery of Gender, Sexuality, and Moral Education in Kaguru Initiation Ritual.* Washington: Smithsonian Institution Press.

Beinin, Joel. 2003. "The Israelization of American Middle East Policy Discourse." *Social Text* 75:125–39.

Belden, Paul. 2003. "Arab Media Outdoes U.S. Networks." *Japan Today,* March 26.

Belkin, Lisa. 2004. "Office Messes." *New York Times Magazine,* July 18.

Bell, David. 2002. "Fragments for a New Urban Culinary Geography." *Journal for the Study of Food and Society* 6 (1): 10–21.

Bell, David, and Gill Valentine. 1997. *Consuming Geographies: We Are What We Eat.* London: Routledge.

Bellah, Robert N. 2002. "Seventy-Five Years." *South Atlantic Quarterly* 101 (2): 253–65.

Benaim, Daniel, Visesh Kumar, and Priyanka Motaparthy. 2003. "TV's Conflicted Experts." *The Nation* 276 (April 21): 6–7.

Benhabib, Seyla. 2002. *The Claims of Culture: Equality and Diversity in the Global Era.* Princeton: Princeton University Press.

Beniger, James R. 1992. "Communication and the Control Revolution." *Organization of American Historians Magazine of History* 6.

Bennett, Tony. 1998. *Culture: A Reformer's Science.* London: Sage.

Bennett, Tony. 2001. *Differing Diversities: Transversal Study on the Theme of Cultural Policy and Cultural Diversity.* Strasbourg Cedex: Council of Europe Publishing.

Bennett, William J. 1992. *The Devaluing of America: The Fight for Our Culture and Our Children.* New York: Touchstone.

Benthall, Jonathan. 1995. *Disasters, Relief and the Media.* London: IB Tauris.

Benton, Charles. 2004. "Launch of Community-by-Community Campaign for Better Local Broadcasting." Lecture given at National Press Club, Washington DC, July 19.

Benton Foundation. 2005. *Citizen's Guide to the Public Interest Obligations of Digital Television Broadcasters.*

Berger, John. 2005. "Ten Dispatches About Place." *Le Monde Diplomatique,* August.

Berkowitz, Bill. 2003. "Wounded, Weary and Disappeared." *TomPaine.com,* August 28. http://www.tompaine.com.

Bernstein, Richard. 2003. "The Fetish of Difference." In *The Fractious Nation? Unity and Division in American Life,* ed. Jonathan Rieder, assoc. ed. Stephen Steinlight, 57–66. Berkeley: University of California Press.

Bernstein, Richard and the Staff of *The New York Times.* 2002. *Out of the Blue: The Story of September 11, 2001 from Jihad to Ground Zero.* New York: Times Books.

Berrington, Eileen. 2002. "Representations of Terror in the Legitimation of War." In *Beyond September 11: An Anthology of Dissent*, ed. Phil Scraton, 47–54. London: Pluto Press.

Beschloss, Steven. 1989. "Praying for Rain." *Channels of Communication* 9 (5): 16, 18.

Beteille, Andre. 1999. "Citizenship, State and Civil Society." *Economic and Political Weekly*, September 4.

Bidwai, Praful. 2005. "Prevent, Prepare & Protect." *Rediff: India Abroad*, January 4. http://www.*Rediff.com*.

Biltereyst, Daniel. 2001. "Global News Research and Complex Citizenship: Towards an Agenda for Research on Foreign/International News and Audiences." *News in a Globalized Society*, ed. Stig Hjarvard, 41–62. Göteborg: NORDICOM.

Birch, David. 1998a. "An 'Open' Environment: Asian Case Studies in the Regulation of Public Culture." *Continuum* 12 (3): 335–48.

Birch, David. 1998b. "Constructing Asian Values: National Identities and 'Responsible' Citizenship." *Social Semiotics* 8 (2–3): 177–201.

Bishop, Ronald. 2001. "Old Dogs, New Tricks? An Ideological Analysis of Thematic Shifts in Television Advertising for Diet Products, 1990–2000." *Journal of Communication Inquiry* 25 (4): 334–52.

Blair, Tony. 2005. "A Year of Huge Challenges." *Economist*, January 1: 44–46.

Bliss, Edward, Jr. 1991. *Now the News: The Story of Broadcast Journalism*. New York: Columbia University Press.

Boal, Iain, T. J. Clark, Joseph Mathews, and Michael Watts. 2004. "Afflicted Powers: The State, the Spectacle and September 11." *New Left Review* 27:5–21.

Boehlert, Eric. 2002. "Too Hot to Handle." *AlterNet*, August 26. http://www.alternet.org.

Bonanno, Alessandro, and Douglas Constance. 1996. *Caught in the Net: The Global Tuna Industry, Environmentalism, and the State*. Lawrence: University Press of Kansas.

Boot, Max. 2005. "Uncle Sam Wants Tu." *Los Angeles Times*, February 24.

Borden, Sandra L. 2005. "Communitarian Journalism and Flag Displays after September 11: An Ethical Critique." *Journal of Communication Inquiry* 29 (1): 30–46.

Borger, Julian. 2005. "Incoming Cloud Forces Bush into Safe Bunker." *Guardian*, April 29.

Borna, Shaheen, and James M. Stearns. 2002. "The Ethics and Efficacy of Selling National Citizenship." *Journal of Business Ethics* 37 (2): 193–207.

Bosniak, Linda. 2000. "Citizenship Denationalized." *Indiana Journal of Global Legal Studies* 7:447–509.

Bosse, Eric, and Greg Palast. 2003. "Anybody Using this First Amendment?" *AlterNet*, March 17. http://www.alternet.org.

Bourdieu, Pierre. 1994. *Distinction: A Social Critique of the Judgement of Taste*, trans. Richard Nice. Cambridge, MA: Harvard University Press.

Bourdieu, Pierre. 1998. On Television, trans. Priscilla Parkhurst Ferguson. New York: New Press.

Bourne, Randolph S. 1916. "Trans-National America." *Atlantic Monthly*, July: 86–97.

Boyce, James K. 2004. *A Future for Small Farms? Biodiversity and Sustainable Agriculture*. Working Paper Series 86. Amherst, MA: Political Economy Research Institute.

Boyd-Barrett, Oliver. 2004. "Understanding: The Second Casualty." In *Reporting War: Journalism in Wartime*, ed. Stuart Allan and Barbie Zelizer, 25–42. London: Routledge.

Boyd-Barrett, Oliver. 2005. "Journalism, Media Conglomerates and the Federal Communications Commission." In *Journalism: Critical Issues*, ed. Stuart Allan, 342–56. Maidenhead: Open University Press.

Boykoff, Jules, and Maxwell Boykoff. 2004. "Journalistic Bias as Global Warming Bias." *EXTRA!* November/December: 22–25.

Boykoff, Maxwell T., and Jules M. Boykoff. 2004. "Balance as Bias: Global Warming and the US Prestige Press." *Global Environmental Change* 14·125–36.

Boym, Svetlana. 1993. "Power Shortages: The Soviet Coup and Hurricane Bob." In *Media Spectacles*, ed. Marjorie Garber, Jann Matlock, and Rebecca L. Walkowitz, 117–34. New York: Routledge.

Bozza, Anthony 1999. "The TV Program Pressure Cooker on the Food Network." *Rolling Stone*, February 18: 67.

Brack, Duncan, Robert Falkner, and Judith Goll. 2003. *The Next Trade War? GM Products, the Cartagena Protocol and the WTO*. Royal Institute of International Affairs Sustainable Development Programme Briefing Paper 8.

Bratten, Frank with Jeffrey L. Cruikshank. 2002. *The Weather Channel: The Improbable Rise of a Media Phenomenon*. Boston: Harvard Business School Press.

Brech, Poppy. 2000. "P&G among the first to use Carlton Interactive Service." Brand Republic, May 10. http://www.marketing.haynet.com/news/n000511/P&G_amon.html.

Brewer, Ebenezer Cobham. 1970. *Brewer's Dictionary of Phrase and Fable*, Centenary Edtion, ed. Ivor H. Evans. London: Cassell.

Brewer, Paul R., Sean Aday, and Kimberly Gross. 2005. "Do Americans Trust Other Nations? A Panel Study." *Social Science Quarterly* 86 (1): 36–51.

Briggs, Asa, and Peter Burke. 2003. *A Social History of the Media: From Gutenberg to the Internet*. Cambridge: Polity.

Brimelow, Peter. 1996. *Alien Nation: Common Sense about America's Immigration Disaster*. New York: HarperPerennial.

Brimelow, Peter. 2005. "Why VDARE.COM/The White Doe?" *VDARE.COM*. http://www.vdare.com.

British Council. 2005. "UKInFocus: Trends and Television."

Broadcasting & Cable. 2003. "Sizzling Sales." November 24: 6A.

Brook, Stephen. 2005. "Al-Jazeera is World's Fifth Top Brand." *Guardian*, February 1.

Brooke, James 2000. "Peppery Plea for Tolerance from a Chef in Montreal." *New York Times*, August 6: K9.

Brooker, Katrina 1998. "On the Food Network: Lust, Weirdos, Saturated Fat." *Fortune*, July 6: 34.

Brooks, Renana. 2003. "A Nation of Victims." *The Nation* 276 (June 30): 20–22.

Brown, Chris. 2000. "Cultural Diversity and International Political Theory." *Review of International Studies* 26 (2): 199–213.

Brown, Jennifer 1999. "Food Network Audience Increases." *Associated Press Online*, March 26. http://www.ap.org.

Brown, Jonathan. 2005. "Weather Forecasters: What a Shower." *Independent*.

Brown, Michael E., and Šumit Ganguly. "Introduction." In *Fighting Words: Language Policy and Ethnic Relations in Asia*, ed. Brown, Michael E., and Šumit Ganguly, 1–18. Cambridge, MA: MIT Press.

Brown, Paul. 2005. "EU Votes to Continue Ban on GM Crops." *Guardian*, June 25.

Browne, David. 1991. "Watching the Weather Channel Hooked on High-Pressure Systems." *Entertainment Weekly*, December 6: 50.

Brunsdon, Charlotte. 2005. "Feminism, Postfeminism, Martha, Martha, and Nigella." *Cinema Journal* 44 (2): 110–16.

Brynen, Rex. 2002. "Cluster-Bombs and Sandcastles: Kramer on the Future of Middle East Studies in America." *Middle East Journal* 56 (2): 323–28.

Bumiller, Elisabeth. 2003. "Keepers of Bush Image Lift Stagecraft to New Heights." *New York Times*. May 16.

Burawoy, Michael, Joseph A. Blum, Sheba George, Zsuzsa Gille, Teresa Gowan, Lynne Haney, Maren Klawiter, Steven H. Lopez, Seán Ó Riain, and Millie Thayer. 2000. *Global Ethnography: Forces, Connections, and Imaginations in a Postmodern World*. Berkeley: University of California Press.

Burch, David, and Geoffrey Lawrence. 2004. "Supermarket Own Brands, Supply Chains and the Changing Agri-Food System: The UK Experience." Paper presented June 2003 to the Annual Meeting of the Agri-Food Research Network, Canberra, Austrailia.

Burchell, David. 2002. "What to do with the Civic Body?" *Continuum* 16 (1): 67–79.

Burroughs, William James. 1997. *Does the Weather Really Matter? The Social Implications of Climate Change.* Cambridge: Cambridge University Press.

Burston, Jonathan. 2003. "War and the Entertainment Industries: New Research Priorities in an Era of Cyber-Patriotism." In *War and the Media: Reporting Conflict 24/7*, ed. Daya Kishan Thussu and Des Freedman, 163–75. London: Sage Publications.

Busch, Lawrence. 1994. "The State of Agricultural Science and the Agricultural Science of the State." In *From Columbus to ConAgra: The Globalization of Agriculture and Food*, ed. Alessandro Bonanno, Lawrence Busch, William H. Friedland, Lourdes Gouveia, and Enzo Mingione, 69–84. Lawrence: University Press of Kansas.

Bush, George W. 2001. "Address to a Joint Session of Congress and the American People." *Harvard Journal of Law and Public Policy* 25 2:xiii–xx.

Bush, George W. 2005. "Second Inaugural Address." *Washington Post*, January 21.

Bushell, Andrew, and Brent Cunningham. 2003. "Being There." *Columbia Journalism Review*, March/April.

Business.com. 2001. "Market Research on Weather and Catastrophe as a Commodity."

Business for Social Responsibility. 2004. http://www.bsr.org.

Business Wire. 1998. "The Weather Channel Reigns; the All-Weather Network Reaches 98% of all U.S. Cable Households." March 30.

Business Wire. 1999a. "Scripps Networks Programming to Air in Philippines." July 21.

Business Wire. 1999b. "The Weather Channel Reaches Growing Spanish-Speaking Internet Community throughout Latin America with Weather.Com/Espanol." January 24.

Business Wire. 1999c. "Univision Announces Record 1998–1999 Season and May Sweeps." July 21.

Business Wire. 2000. "The Weather Channel Puts the Weather in your Pocket." August 14.

Business Wire. 2001a. "AOL Latin America Announces Regional Content Agreement with the Weather Channel." August 7.

Business Wire. 2001b. "The Weather Channel Embraces Latin American Market." October 30.

Butsch, Richard. 2000. *The Making of American Audiences: From Stage to Television, 1750–1990.* Cambridge: Cambridge University Press.

Buttel, Frederick, Olaf Larson, and Gilbert Gillespie, eds. 1990. *The Sociology of Agriculture.* Wesport: Greenwood Press.

Buxton, Rodney A. 2004. "Sexual Orientation and Television." *Museum of Broadcast Communications Encyclopedia of Television.* 2nd ed., ed. Horace Newcomb, 2066–72. New York: Fitzroy Dearborn.

BuyBlue.org. 2004. "Buy Blue's Mission." December 16. http://www.buyblue.org.

Byrne, Ciar. 2003a. "Al-Jazeera Returns to NY Stock Exchange." *Guardian*, May 1.

Byrne, Ciar. 2003b. "*Simpsons* Parody Upset Fox News, Says Groening." *Guardian*, October 29.

Calabrese, Andrew. 2005a. "Casus Belli: U.S. Media and the Justification for the Iraq War." *Television & New Media* 6 (2): 153–75.

Calabrese, Andrew. 2005b. "The Trade in Television News." In *A Companion to Television*, ed. Janet Wasko, 270–88. Malden: Blackwell.

Carens, Joseph H. 2000. *Culture, Citizenship, and Community: A Contextual Exploration of Justice as Evenhandedness.* Oxford: Oxford University Press.

Carlton Food Network. 2001. http://www.cfn.co.uk.

Carlton Food Network. 2002. "TV to Tempt Your Tastebuds." http://www.ntl.co.uk/adsales/channels/carltonfood.asp.

Carnegie Corporation of New York. 2005. *Improving the Education of Tomorrow's Journalists.* http://www.carnegie.org/sub/program/initiativedocs/Exec_Sum_Journalism.pdf.

Carnegie Corporation of New York and John S. and James L. Knight Foundaion. 2005. "A Vision for Journalism Education." May.

Carr, David. 2003. "Reporting Reflects Anxiety." *New York Times,* March 25.

Carreño, José. 2001. "El día en que los estadunidenses desperataron de un sueño." *11 de septiembre de 2001,* ed. Frida Modak, 20–23. Buenos Aires: Grupo Editorial Lumen.

Carter, Hill. 2005. "Alter CBS's Decision, Networks Face Many More." *New York Times,* October 27.

Cason, Jim, and David Brooks. 2003. "Inasistencia de Cheney a actos públicos desata especulaciones en medios de EU." *La Jornada,* April 6.

Casper, Monica J. and Lynn M. Morgan. 2004. *Anthropology News,* December. 17–18.

Cassara, Catherine, and Laura Lengel. 2004. "Move Over CNN: Al Jazeera's View of the World Takes on the West." *Transnational Broadcasting Studies* 12.

Castles, Stephen, and Alastair Davidson. 2000. *Citizenship and Migration: Globalization and the Politics of Belonging.* Basingstoke: Macmillan.

Castles, Stephen, and Mark J. Miller. 2003. *The Age of Migration,* Third edition. New York: Guilford Press.

Center for Constitutional Rights. 2003. "CCR Says US Government Hypocritical on Application of Geneva Conventions." March 24.

Center for Consumer Freedom. 2005. *Declaration of Food Independence.* http://www.consumerfreedom.com/article_detail.cfm?article=155.

Center for Media and Public Affairs. 2005. "What's the Matter with Kansas? Media Apathy." http://www.cmpa.com/WhatstheMatterWithKansasMediaApathy.htm.

Central Board of Film Certification. 2004. *Citizen's Charter.*

Chadha, Kalyani, and Anandam Kavoori. 2000. "Media Imperialism Revisited: Some Findings from the Asian Case." *Media, Culture & Society* 22 (4): 415–32.

Chan, Andrew. 2003. "'La grande bouffe': Cooking Shows as Pornography." *Gastronomica: The Journal of Food and Culture* 3 (4). 16–53.

Chaney, David. 2002. "Cosmopolitan Art and Cultural Citizenship." *Theory, Culture & Society* 19 1–2:157–74.

Chase-Dunn, Christopher, and Terry Boswell. 2004. "Global Democracy: A World-Systems Perspective." *Proto Sociology: An International Journal of Interdisciplinary Research* 20:15–29.

Chathukulam, Jos, and M. S. John. 2002. "Five Years of Participatory Planning in Kerala: Rhetoric and Reality." *Economic and Political Weekly,* December 7.

Chatterjee, Partha. 1993. *The Nation and its Fragments: Colonial and Postcolonial Histories.* Princeton: Princeton University Press.

Chatterjee, Pratap. 2004. "Information Warriors." *Corpwatch,* August 4. http://www.corpwatch.com.

Chester, Jeff. 2002. "Strict Scrutiny: Why Journalists should be Concerned about New Federal Industry Media Deregulation Proposals." *Harvard International Journal of Press/Politics* 7 (2): 105–15.

Chester, Jeff. 2003. "Time is now to Fight for Future of TV." *AlterNet,* April 1. http://www.alternet.org.

Chesterton, G. K. 1932. "A Defence of Detective Stories." *Essays of To-Day: An Anthology,* ed. F. H. Pritchard, 226–29. London: George G. Harrap.

Chicago Council on Foreign Relations/Program on International Policy Attitudes. 2005. "Large Bipartisan Majority of Americans Favors Referring Darfur War Crime Cases to International Criminal Court." March 1.

Chicago Sun-Times. 1999. "Food Network Switches Menu." March 31: Section 2 5XS.

Cho, Jaeho, Michael P. Boyle, Heejo Keum, Mark D. Shevy, Douglas M. McLeod, Dhavan V. Shah, and Zhongdang Pan. 2003. "Media, Terrorism, and Emotionality: Emotional

Differences in Media Content and Public Reactions to the September 11th Terrorist Attacks." *Journal of Broadcasting & Electronic Media* 47 (3): 309–27.

Chomsky, Noam. 2004. "Terror and Just Response." In *U.S. and the Others: Global Media Images on "The War on Terror,"* ed. Stig A. Nohrstedt and Rune Ottosen, 35–49. Göteborg: NORDICOM.

Christ, Judith. 2003. "TV Nation." *Gourmet* 53 (9): 82, 85.

Chua, Amy. 2003. *World on Fire: How Exporting Free Market Democracy Breeds Ethnic Hatred and Global Instability.* New York: Doubleday.

Citizenship Foundation. 2004. *Individuals Engaging in Society.*

City of Heroes: Prima's Official Strategy Guide. 2004. Prima.

Clark, Jessica, and Bob McChesney. 2001. "Nattering Networks: How Mass Media Fails Democracy." *LiP,* September 24.

Clark, Jessica, and Tracy Van Slyke. 2005. "Making Connections." *In These Times,* April 27.

Clarren, Rebecca. 2005. "Dirty Politics, Foul Air." *The Nation* 280 (March 14): 6–8.

Claussen, Dane S. 2004. *Anti-Intellectualism in American Media: Magazines & Higher Education.* New York: Peter Lang.

Clinton, Bill. 2002. "The Path to Peace." *Salon.com,* September 10.

Clinton, Hilary Rodham. 2003. *Living History.* New York: Simon & Schuster.

Coalition of Immokalee Workers. 2002. "Boycott the Bell."

Cobb, James T., Christopher A. LaCour, and William H. Hight. 2005. "TF 2-2 in FSE AAR: Indirect Fires in the Battle of Fallujah." *Field Artillery,* March–April: 23–28.

Cohen, Mark Francis. 2005. "The Quote Machines." *American Journalism Review,* April/May.

Cohen, Robin. 1991. *Contested Domains: Debates in International Labor Studies.* London: Zed.

Cohen, Robin. 1997. *Global Diasporas: An Introduction.* Seattle: University of Washington Press.

Cohen, Robin. 2003. "Crossing the Line." *Index on Censorship* 322:60–69.

Collins, Carole J. L. 2005. "World's Worst Disasters Overlooked." *EXTRA!* May/June: 15–16.

Collis, Roger. 2001. "Zeroing in on the Weather: New Sites and Services Offer Fine-Tuned Forecasts." *International Herald Tribune,* August 31.

Columbia Electronic Encyclopedia, Sixth ed. 2005. "Hunger Strike." Columbia University Press.

Columbia Journalism Review. 2001. Conference on September 11, 2001.

Comcast. 2000. http://www.comcastnow.com/networks/foodnetwork.htm.

Compton, James. 2004. "News as Spectacle: The Political Economy and Aesthetics of 24/7 News." *Democratic Communiqué* 19:49–74.

The Conference Board. 2002. *European Research Working Group on Corporate Citizenship.*

Conley, Tom. 1987. "Le quotidien météorologique." *Yale French Studies* 73:215–28.

Cook, Christopher D. 2004. *Diet for a Dead Planet: How the Food Industry is Killing Us.* New York: New Press.

Cook, Ian, and Philip Crang. 1996. "The World on a Plate: Culinary Culture, Displacement and Geographical Knowledge." *Journal of Material Culture* 1 (2): 131–53.

Cook, Timothy E. 2005. "Public Policy Towards the Press: What Government does *for* the News Media." In *The Press,* ed. Geneva Overholser and Kathleen Hall Jamieson, 248–62. Oxford: Oxford University Press.

Coombe, Rosemary J. 2005. "Legal Claims to Culture in and Against the Market: Neoliberalism and the Global Proliferation of Meaningful Difference." *Law, Culture and Humanities* 1 (1): 32–55.

Cooper, Gael Fashingbauer. 2000. "In the Beginning, There was Julia." *Minneapolis Star Tribune,* October 5: 1T.

Cooper-Chen, Anne. 2002. "Review." *Journalism & Mass Communication Quarterly* 79 (3): 768–69.

Copps, Michael J. 2003. "I Dissent Because Today the FCC Empowers America's New Media Elite with Unacceptable Levels of Influence." *Common Dreams News Center*, June 2. http://www.commondreams.org.

Cordasco, Paul. 2002. "ISS Swinging Shareholder Votes toward Social Issues." *PRWeek*, June 10: 9.

Corn, David. 2003. "Probing 9/11." *The Nation* 277 (July 7): 14–18.

CorpWatch. 2005. "The 14 Worst Corporate Evildoers." *Global Exchange*, December 12.

Costanza-Chock, Sasha. 2002. *White Paper #1: Background and Context for the Application of coyBOTt Software to Systematic Analysis of Branding, Boycott, and Cultural Sponsorship*.

Cotton, William R., and Roger A. Pielke. 1995. *Human Impacts on Weather and Climate*. Cambridge: Cambridge University Press.

Coutin, Susan Bibler. 2003. "Cultural Logics of Belonging and Movement: Transnationalism, Naturalization, and U.S. Immigration Politics." *American Ethnologist* 30 (4): 508–26.

Cowan, Jane K., Marie-Bénédicte Dembour, and Richard A. Wilson, eds. 2001. Introd. to *Culture and Rights: Anthropological Perspectives*. Cambridge: Cambridge University Press.

Cox, Ana Marie. 2003. "The Un-American Media." *In These Times*, March 28.

Cozens, Claire. 2001. "Viewers Greet September 11 Coverage with Cynicism." *Guardian*, October 26.

Cozens, Claire. 2003. "Europeans Flock to Al-Jazeera." *Guardian*, March 25.

Craft, Erik D. 1999. "Private Weather Organizations and the Founding of the United States Weather Bureau." *Journal of Economic History* 59 (4): 1063–71.

Crawford, Michael. 2003. "Corporate Sponsorship Comes to Hurricanes." *New Yorker*, September 29: 30.

Crichton, Michael. 2004. *State of Fear*. New York: HarperCollins.

Crick, Bernard. 2003. "How to be British." *The Spectator*, March 8: 22–23.

Crist, Judith. 2003. "Food and Television." *Gourmet*, September.

Critchell, Samantha. 2001. "NBC Puts Emeril on Prime-Time Menu." *Associated Press Online*, August 27.

Crook, Clive. 2005. "The Good Company." *Economist*, January 22: Survey 3–4.

Crossland, John. 1997. "MI5 Ordered to Spy on 'Subversive' Opinion Poll." *Independent*, July 21: 6.

Crouch, Colin. 2004. *Posdemocracia*, trans. Francisco Beltrán. Madrid: Taurus/Pensamiento.

Crumley, James. 2005. *The Right Madness*. New York: Penguin.

Curtis, P. 2002. "Creative Accounting." *Guardian*, January 22.

Cyr, Diane. 2000. "A Matter of Good Taste." *US Airways Attaché*, May: 40, 42, 45.

D'Entremont, Jim. 2003. "Clear and Present Danger." *Index on Censorship* 32 (3): 124–28.

Dagnino, Evelina. 2003. "Citizenship in Latin America: An Introduction." *Latin American Perspectives* 30 (2): 3–17.

Danford, Natalie. 2005. "Video Made the Cookbook Star." *Publishers Weekly*, March 21: 24–26.

Dare, William H., William B. Elliott, and Thomas F. Gosnell. 2005. *Forget About CNBC, Turn on the Weather Channel*. Working Paper.

Das, Veena. 2002. *Critical Events: An Anthropological Perspective on Contemporary India*. New Delhi: Oxford University Press.

Davenport, Philippa. 2005. "Down to Earth Fare in the Air." *Financial Times*, July 8.

David Graham & Associates. 2004. "UK Cookery Shows: Six-Year Analysis." July 8.

Davidson, Lawrence. 2002. "Ivory Towers on Sand: The Failure of Middle Eastern Studies in America." *Middle East Policy* 9 (3): 148–52.

Davies, Brian. 1981. *Those Fabulous TV Years*. Sydney: Cassell Australia.

Davis, Ian. 2005. "The Biggest Contract." *Economist*, May 28: 69–71.

Davis, Jesse. 1945. "Weather Broadcasting in Winston-Salem." *The Breeze*, March 10: 4–5.

Davis, Mike. 2003. "The Scalping Party." *Tomdispatch.com*, November 14. http://www.tomdispatch.com.

Davis, Mike. 2004. "Planet of Slums: Urban Innovation and the Informal Proletariat." *New Left Review* 26:5–34.

Day, Gary. 2002. "A Brief History of how Culture and Commerce Were Really Made for Each Other." *Critical Quarterly* 44 (3): 37–44.

De Albuquerque, Afonso. 2003. "Brazil." *openDemocracy*, April 16. http://www.opendemocracy.net.

de Pedro, Jesús Prieto. 1991. "Concepto y Otros Aspectos del Patrimonio Cultural en la Constitución." *Estudios sobre la Constitución Española: Homenaje al Profesor Eduardo Garcia de Enterria*, 1551–72. Madrid: Editorial Civitas, S. A.

de Pedro, Jesús Prieto. 1999. "Democracy and Cultural Difference in the Spanish Constitution of 1978." *Democracy and Ethnography: Constructing Identities in Multicultural Liberal States*, ed. Carol J. Greenhouse with Roshanak Kheshti, 61–80. Albany: State University of New York Press.

Dean, Hartley. 2001. "Green Citizenship." *Social Policy & Administration* 35 (5): 490–505.

Debord, Guy. 1995. *The Society of the Spectacle*, trans. Donald Nicolson-Smith. New York: Zone.

Delanty, Gerard. 2002. "Two Conceptions of Cultural Citizenship: A Review of Recent Literature on Culture and Citizenship." *Global Review of Ethnopolitics* 1 (3): 60–66.

DeLillo, Don. 2001. "In the Ruins of the Future." *Harper's Magazine*, December.

DeLillo, Don. 2003. *Cosmopolis*. New York: Scribner.

della Carva, Marco R. 2003. "Iraq gets Sympathetic Press around the World." *USA Today*, April 2: 1D.

Demontis, Rita. 2001. "Running on Emeril\Bam!" *Calgary Sun*, July 2: 22.

Department of Commerce. 2005. *Reason to Name Hurricanes*.

Depledge, Joanna. 2002. *Climate Change in Focus: The IPCC Third Assessment Report*. London: Royal Institute of International Affairs Briefing Paper New Series no. 29.

DerDerian, James. 2002. "The War of Networks." *Theory and Event* 5: 4.

Dickinson, Roger. 2005. "Food on British Television: Multiple Messages, Multiple Meanings." *Discussion Papers in Mass Communications* 2.

DiIulio, John J. Jr. 2003. "The Moral Compassion of True Conservatism." In *The Fractious Nation? Unity and Division in American Life*, ed. Jonathan Rieder, assoc. ed. Stephen Steinlight. Berkeley: University of California Press. 217–24.

Dilday, K. A. 2003. "Lost in Translation: The Narrowing of the American Mind." *openDemocracy*, May 1. http://www.opendemocracy.net.

DiMaggio, Paul. 1994. "Culture and Economy." *The Handbook of Economic Sociology*, ed. Neil J. Smelser and Richard Swedberg, 27–57. Princeton: Princeton University Press.

DiMaggio, Paul. 2003. "The Myth of Culture War: *The Disparity between Private Opinion and Public Politics*." In *The Fractious Nation? Unity and Division in American Life*, ed. Jonathan Rieder, assoc. ed. Stephen Steinlight, 79–97. Berkeley: University of California Press.

Dionne, E. J., Jr. 2003. "Shaking off the Past: *Third Ways, Fourth Ways, and the Urgency of Politics*." In *The Fractious Nation? Unity and Division in American Life*, ed. Jonathan Rieder, assoc. ed. Stephen Steinlight, 225–47. Berkeley: University of California Press.

Diven, Polly J. 2001. "The Domestic Determinants of US Food Aid Policy." *Food Policy* 26 (5): 455–74.

Dobson, Andrew. 2003. *Citizenship and the Environment*. Oxford: Oxford University Press.

Doiron, Roger. 2003. "Of Food, Farming, and Freedom." *Common Dreams News Center*, July 2. http://www.commondreams.org.

Dolce, Joe. 2003a. "The Accidental Purist." *Gourmet* 53 (9): 86–92.

Dolce, Joe. 2003b. "Stir it up." *Gourmet* 53 (9): 94–95.

Dolny, Michael. 2003. "Spectrum Narrows Further in 2002: Progressive, Domestic Think Tanks see Drop." *EXTRA!* July/August. http://www.fair.org/index.php?page=1149.

Dolny, Michael. 2005. "Right, Center Think Tanks Still Most Quoted." *EXTRA!* May/June: 28–29.

Domke, David, Mark D. Watts, Dhavan V. Shah, and David P. Fan. 1999. "The Politics of Conservative Elites and the 'Liberal Media' Argument." *Journal of Communication* 49 (1): 35–58.

Donohue, Steve. 2004. "Weather in NBC's Forecast: DTV-Distributed Net will Bow in New York." *Multichannel News,* November 8: 6.

Donzelot, Jacques. 1991. "The Mobilization of Society." In *The Foucault Effect,* ed. Graham Burchell, Colin Gordon, and Peter Miller. London: Harvester Wheatsheaf.

Douglas, Susan J. 1987. *Inventing American Broadcasting 1899–1922.* Baltimore: The Johns Hopkins University Press.

Douglas, Susan J. 2004. "We are What we Watch." *In These Times,* July 1,

Douglas, Susan J. 2005. "Fairness Now." *In These Times,* May 9: 12.

Downey, John, and Graham Murdock. 2003. "The Counter-Revolution in Military Affairs: The Globalization of Guerrilla Warfare." In *War and the Media: Reporting Conflict 24/7,* ed. Daya Kishan Thussu and Des Freedman, 70–86. London: Sage Publications.

Downey, Kevin. 2005a. "Food Network." *Media Life,* March 15.

Downey, Kevin. 2005b. "Kids TV, Now with More Vitamins." *Broadcasting & Cable,* November 14: 25–26.

Downing, John, and Charles Husband. 2005. *Representing "Race": Racisms, Ethnicities and Media.* London: Sage.

Dreher, C. 2002. "What Drives U.S. Cities." *Hamilton Spectator,* July 20.

Drutman, Lee, and Charlie Cray. 2005. "The People's Business: Controlling Corporations and Restoring Democracy." *In These Times,* March 14: 16–19, 28.

Duffy, Jonathan. 1999. "UK LIVE TV: Talking Topless Darts." *BBC News Online,* October 22.

Dummett, Kel. 2004. "Don't Write Off Corporate Social Responsibility—We Need It." *On Line Opinion,* December 16.

Economic Times New Delhi. 2002. "English Test for Immigrants." February 10: 13.

Economist. 1999. "Time for a Redesign?" January 30: 3–5 (Survey: Global Finance).

Economist. 2000a. "Cold Comfort Farm." January 22: 73–74.

Economist. 2000b. "Pupil Power." November 18: 40.

Economist. 2000c. "Sins of the Secular Missionaries." January 29: 25–27.

Economist. 2002. "Trading Hot Air." October 19: 60.

Economist. 2003a. "A Nation Apart." November 8. 3–4.

Economist. 2003b. "A World of Exiles." January 4: 41–43.

Economist. 2003c. "Big Business." September 27: 64, 67.

Economist. 2003d. "Filling the World's Belly." December 13: 3–6.

Economist. 2003e. "Make it Cheaper, and Cheaper." December 13: 6–8.

Economist. 2003f. "Make it Convenient." December 13: 10–11.

Economist. 2003g. "Organic? Don't Panic." December 13: 12.

Economist. 2003h. "Selling to the Developing World." December 13: 8.

Economist. 2004a. "An Amish Exception." February 7: 33.

Economist. 2004b. "Big Mac's Makeover." October 16: 63–65.

Economist. 2004c. "Forging a Nation." October 23: 44.

Economist. 2004d. "Julia Child." August 28: 78.

Economist. 2004e. "Living Dangerously." January 24: 3–5.

Economist. 2004f. "Out of the Shadows, into the World." June 19: 26–28.

Economist. 2004g. "Signing on for Uncle Sam." September 18: 38.

Economist. 2004h. "There's a Word for That." November 6: 14.

Economist. 2004i. "Tommy Foreigner." August 14: 51.

Economist. 2004j. "Trials and Tribulations." June 19: 62–63.

Economist. 2004k. "The War of the Headscarves." February 7: 24–26.

Economist. 2005a. "The Americano Dream." July 16: 8–9.

Economist. 2005b. "Back to the Beach?" January 8: 54–55.

Economist. 2005c. "Barnes' Storming." March 12: 57.

Economist. 2005d. "Breaking Records." February 12: 12–13.

Economist. 2005e. "Centrifugal Forces." July 16: 4–7.

Economist. 2005f. "Debating Islam." June 4: 39–40.

Economist. 2005g. "Electronics, Unleaded." March 12: 6–7.

Economist. 2005h. "Ever Higher Society, Ever Harder to Ascend." January 1: 22–24.

Economist. 2005i. "Give Us Your Tired Computers." January 29: 60.

Economist. 2005j. "Know Thine Enemy." May 7: 28.

Economist. 2005k. "Making a Meal of it." May 7: 57–58.

Economist. 2005l. "More Generous than Thou." January 8: 26–27.

Economist. 2005m. "A Plug for the Plains Drain?" May 7: 29.

Economist. 2005n. "Stressed Out and Traumatised." March 5: 30–31.

Economist. 2005o. "Subsidising Virtue." March 12: 57.

Economist. 2005p. "Susan Sontag." January 8: 77.

Economist. 2005q. "Thin Pickings." July 16: 60.

Economist. 2005r. "Trade Trouble Ahead." January 15: 59.

Economist. 2005s. "The Vote Next Time." March 5: 39.

Economist. 2005t. "Warfare in the Aisles." April 2: 6–8.

Economist. 2005u. "The World Through Their Eyes." February 26: 23–25.

E&P Staff. 2005a. "So Who is Behind Planting Stories in Iraqi Press?" *Editor & Publisher,* December 1.

E&P Staff. 2005b. "Gloves Off: Rumsfeld Attacks Press on Iraq Coverage." *Editor & Publisher,* December 5.

Editor & Publisher. 2005. "Garrett of 'Newsday' Rips Tribune Co. 'Greed' in Exit Memo." March 1.

Egan, Daniel, and David Levy. 2001. "International Environmental Politics and the Internationalization of the State: The Cases of Climate Change and the Multilateral Agreement on Investment." In *The International Political Economy of the Environment: Critical Perspectives,* ed. Dimitris Stevis and Valeire J. Assetto, 63–85. Boulder: Lynne Rienner.

Eide, Elisabeth. 2004. "Warfare and Dual Vision in Media Discourse." In *U.S. and the Others: Global Media Images on "The War on Terror,"* ed. Stig A. Nohrstedt and Rune Ottosen, 263–84. Göteborg: NORDICOM.

Eisman, April. 2003. "The Media of Manipulation: Patriotism and Propaganda—Mainstream News in the United States in the Weeks Following September 11." *Critical Quarterly* 45 1–2:55–72.

El Nasser, Haya, and Lorrie Grant. 2005a. "Diversity Tints New Kind of Generation Gap." *USA Today,* June 9: 4A.

El Nasser, Haya, and Lorrie Grant. 2005b. "Immigration Causes Age, Race Split." *USA Today,* June 9: 1A.

Electronic Media. 1999. "Food Network Gets Its Show on the Road." April 5: 4.

Elkin, Tobi. 2003. "CBS News Chief Bemoans Network 'Sameness'." *Advertising Age,* May 6.

Eller, Claudia, and James Bates. 2003. "Hollywood Top Gun Leads Charge onto Small Screen." *Los Angeles Times,* February 26.

Ellis, Rick. 2003. "The Surrender of MSNBC." *All Your TV*, February 25. http://www
.allyourtv.com.

Elster, Jon. 2003. "The Market and the Forum: Three Varieties of Political Theory." *Philosophy and Democracy: An Anthology*, ed. Thomas Christiano, 138–58. Oxford: Oxford University Press.

Engel, Matthew. 2002. "It's Official, Global Warming Does Exist, says Bush." *Guardian*, June 4.

Engelhardt, Tom. 2004a. "The Imperfect Media Storm or George Bush and the Temple of Doom." *TomDispatch.com*, August 18. http://www.tomdispatch.com.

Engelhardt, Tom. 2004b. "Xtreme Weather Meets Xtreme Media Bubble." *TomDispatch.com*, September 27. http://www.tomdispatch.com.

enRoute. 2002. "TV Cooks Through the Ages." February. http://www.enroutemag.com/e/
archives/february02/archives02.html.

Environmental Protection Agency. 2002. "Global Warming."

Erjavec, Karmen. 2004. "The *Newsweek* War on Terrorism: A Construction of Risk." In *U.S. and the Others: Global Media Images on "The War on Terror,"* ed. Stig A. Nohrstedt and Rune Ottosen, 93–106. Göteborg: NORDICOM.

Ervolino, Bill. 2001. "Kitchen Gladiators Turn Up the Heat." *Record*, May 31: F6.

European Food Project. 2005. http://www.ericarts.org/profood.html.

Eviatar, Daphne. 2003. "The Press and Private Lynch." *The Nation* 277 (July 7): 18–20.

EXTRA! 2005a. "The Consumer is Always Right." May/June: 5.

EXTRA! 2005b. "A Shining Standard." May/June: 5.

EXTRA!Update. 2004a. "No Desire to Argue." April: 2.

EXTRA!Update. 2004b. "Who are 'We'?" February: 2.

Fabrikant, Geraldine. 1999. "The Weather Channel's High-Profit Center: Low Costs and Loyal Viewers Create One of Cable TV's Success Stories." *New York Times*, March 15: C9.

FAIR. 2003a. "Bush Uranium is Tip of the Iceberg." July 18.

FAIR. 2003b. "Do Media Know that War Kills?" March 14.

FAIR. 2003c. "In Iraq Crisis, Networks are Megaphones for Official Views." March 18.

FAIR. 2003d. "Is Killing Part of Pentagon Press Policy?" April 10.

FAIR. 2003e. "Media Should Follow Up on Civilian Deaths." April 4.

FAIR. 2003f. "New York Times, Networks Shun U.N. Spying Story." March 11.

FAIR. 2003g. "Official Story vs. Eyewitness Accounts." April 4.

FAIR. 2003h. "Some Critical Media Voices Face Censorship." April 3.

FAIR. 2003i. "TV Not Concerned by Cluster Bombs, DU: 'That's Just the Way Life is in Iraq'."
May 6.

FAIR. 2004a. "CNN to Al Jazeera: Why Report Civilian Deaths?" April 15.

FAIR. 2004b. "Hard to Find Women's March on Television News." May 3.

FAIR. 2005a. "Are 2,000 U.S. Deaths 'Negligible'?" October 25.

FAIR. 2005b. "Counting the Iraqi Dead." March 21.

FAIR. 2005c. "Disappearing Antiwar Protests." September 27.

FAIR. 2005d. "Justifying the Silence on Downing Street Memos." June 17.

FAIR. 2005e. "Lessons from London." July 11.

FAIR. 2005f. "Rather's Retirement and 'Liberal Bias'." March 2.

FAIR. 2005g. "*Time* Covers Coulter." April 21.

FAIR. 2005h. "Women's Opinions Also Missing on Television." March 24.

Falk, Pasi. 1994. *The Consuming Body*. London: Sage.

Falk, Richard A. 2004. *The Declining World Order: America's Imperial Geopolitics*. New York: Routledge.

Fallon, Kathleen M. 2003. "Transforming Women's Citizenship Rights within an Emerging Democratic State: The Case of Ghana." *Gender & Society* 17 (4): 525–43.

Fantasia, Rick. 1995. "Fast Food in France." *Theory and Society* 242:201–43.

Farhi, Paul. 2003. "Everybody Wins." *American Journalism Review*, April 6.

Farsetta, Diane. 2004. "How Now, Mad Cow?" *AlterNet*, December 23. http://www.alternet.org.

Farsetta, Diane. 2005. "A Bumper Crop of Government-Produced 'News'." *PR Watch* 12 (2): 4–6.

Fass, Allison. 2002. "Advertising." *New York Times*, April 4: C5.

Feffer, John. 2004. "Asia Holds the Key to the Future of GM Food." *YaleGlobal*, December 2.

Feffer, John. 2005a. "The Evolution of Frankenfoods?" *AlterNet*, July 18. http://www.alternet.org.

Feffer, John. 2005b. "Food and Communism." *Z Net* (July 22). http://www.zmag.org/weluser.htm.

Feldblum, Miriam. 1997. "'Citizenship Matters': Contemporary Trends in Europe and the United States." *Stanford Humanities Review* 5 (2): 96–113.

Feldman, Allen. 2005. "On the Actuarial Gaze: From 9/11 to Abu Ghraib." *Cultural Studies* 19 (2): 203–26.

Fenix, James L. R. 2002. "A History in Communications Technology Evolution." National Oceanic and Atmospheric Administration's National Weather Service. http://www.weather.gov.

Ferguson, Iain, and Caspar Henderson. 2003. "Corporate Timeline." *openDemocracy*, March 12. http://www.opendemocracy.net.

Fernández-Armesto, Felipe. 2002. "Too Rich, Too Thin?" *Demos Collection* 18:19–24.

Fiddes, Nick. 1991. *Meat: A Natural Symbol*. London: Routledge.

Field, Frank. 1981. *Dr. Frank Field's Weather Book*. New York: G. P. Putnam's.

Fierlbeck, K. 1996. "The Ambivalent Potential of Cultural Identity." *Canadian Journal of Political Science/Revue canadienne de science politique* 29 (1): 3–22.

Fine, Ben, and Ellen Leopold. 1993. *The World of Consumption*. London: Routledge.

Fine, Janet. 2003. "Al Jazeera Winning TV Credibility War." *Transnational Broadcasting Studies* 10.

Finkelstein, Joanne. 1989. *Dining Out: A Sociology of Modern Manners*. New York: New York University Press.

Fisher, Daniel. 2005. "GE Turns Green." *Forbes*, August 15: 80–85.

Fisk, Robert. 2002. "Why Does John Malkovich Want to Kill Me?" *Independent*, May 14.

Fisk, Robert. 2003a. "How the News will be Censored in the War." *Independent*, February 25.

Fisk, Robert. 2003b. "Under US Control, Press Freedom Falls Short in Iraq." *Madison Capital Times*, November 20.

Fisk, Robert. 2005. "U.S. Coming Around to the Truth." *Seattle Post-Intelligencer*, December 7.

Fisk, Robert, Amy Goodman, and Jeremy Cahill. 2003. "Live from Iraq, an Un-Embedded Journalist." *Democracy Now!* March 25.

Fitzgerald, Mark. 2003. "Study Shows Readership at Crossroads." *Editor & Publisher*, May 6.

Flanders, Laura. 2001. "Media Criticism in Mono." *WorkingForChange*, November 9.

Flick, Bill. 2000. "Weather Channel: Now, it's Even Getting Competition?" *Pantagraph*, August 20.

Flores, William V., and Rina Benmayor, eds. 1997a. *Latino Cultural Citizenship: Claiming Identity, Space, and Politics*. Boston: Beacon Press.

Flores, William V., and Rina Benmayor. 1997b. "Constructing Cultural Citizenship." In *Latino Cultural Citizenship: Claiming Identity, Space, and Politics*, ed. William V. Flores and Rina Benmayor, 1–23. Boston: Beacon Press.

Folkenflik, David. 2003. "Fox News Defends its 'Patriotic' Coverage." *Baltimore Sun*, April 2.

Food Network. 1999. http://www.foodtv.com

Food Network. 2001. "About Food Network."

Food Network. 2002. "Food Network Fact Sheet."

Food Network. 2004. "Tribute to Julia Child." August 13.

Food Network. n.d. http://www.foodtv.com.

Ford Motor Company. 2002a. *Connecting with Society: Our Learning Journey.*

Ford Motor Company. 2002b. *Corporate Citizenship.* http://ford.com/en/ourCompany/ corporateCitizenship/default.htm.

Ford, Sabrina. 2005. "In a Green Mood." *AlterNet,* March 16. http://www.alternet.org.

Foreign Policy. 2004. "Covered for Climate Change." November/December: 18.

Formulatv.com. 2005. "'Vamos a cocinar' con José Andrés llega a TVE." April 30. http:// formulatv.com.

Fort, Matthew. 2003. "The Death of Cooking." *Guardian,* May 10.

Foster, John Bellamy. 2002. "The Rediscovery of Imperialism." *Monthly Review* 54 (6): 1–16.

Foster, Nicola. 2004. "Jaffrey, Madhur 1933– ; British Actor, Television Personality, Cookery Host." In *Museum of Broadcast Communications Encyclopedia of Television.* 2nd ed., ed. Horace Newcomb, 1204–6. New York: Fitzroy Dearborn.

Foucault, Michel. 1997. *Ethics: Subjectivity and Truth: The Essential Works of Foucault 1954–1984 Volume One,* ed. Paul Rabinow, trans. Robert Hurley et al. New York: Free Press.

Foucault, Michel. 2003a. *"Society Must be Defended": Lectures at the Collège de France 1975–1976,* ed. Mauro Bertani and Alessandro Fontana, trans. David Macey. New York: Picador.

Foucault, Michel. 2003b. *Abnormal: Lectures at the Collège de France 1974–1975,* ed. Valerio Marchetti and Antonella Salomoni, trans. Graham Buchell. New York: Picador.

Fowler, Mark. 1981. *"Reason* Interview: Mark S. Fowler." Reason Online. http://*Reason.com*/ 9812/interviews.shtml.

Fox, Jonathan. 2002. "Ethnic Minorities and the Clash of Civilizations: A Quantitative Analysis of Huntington's Thesis." *British Journal of Political Science* 32 (3): 415–35.

Frank, Dana. 2003. "Where are the Workers in Consumer-Worker Alliances? Class Dynamics and the History of Consumer-Labor Campaigns." *Politics & History* 31 (3): 363–79.

Frank, Thomas. 2000. *One Market Under God: Extreme Capitalism, Market Populism, and the End of Economic Democracy.* New York: Anchor Books/Random House.

Fredrickson, George M. 2003. *The Historical Construction of Race and Citizenship in the United States.* Conflict and Cohesion Programme Paper 1, United Nations Research Institute for Social Development Identities.

Freedom from Religion Foundation. 2004. "Health & Human Services Suspends Funds to Faith-Based Mentoring Group Being Sued by Watchdog Foundation." News Release, December 20. http://ffrf.org/news/2004/mentorsuspend.php.

Freeman, Carla. 2000. *High Tech and High Heels in the Global Economy: Women, Work, and Pink-Collar Identities in the Caribbean.* Durham: Duke University Press.

Freeman, Gary P., Luis F. B. Plascencia, Susan González Baker, and Manuel Orozco. 2002. "Explaining the Surge in Citizenship Applications in the 1990s: Lawful Permanent Residents in Texas." *Social Science Quarterly* 83 (4): 1013–25.

Freeman, Richard. 2004. "Fighting Turnout Burnout." *American Prospect,* June: A16.

Frel, Jan. 2005. "'Tis the Season for Shareholder Activism." *AlterNet,* May 10. http://www .alternet.com.

Freudenberger, Nell. 2005. "Words Apart." *The Nation* 280 (June 13): 24–28.

Friedman, Jon. 2003. "Editors See Success in Iraq Coverage." *CBS Market Watch,* May 8.

Friedmann, Harriet. 1995. "The International Political Economy of Food: A Global Crisis." *International Journal of Health Services* 25 (3): 511–38.

Fry, Katherine. 2003. *Constructing the Heartland: Television News and Natural Disaster.* Cresskill: Hampton Press.

Fuentes, Carlos. 2004. "Huntington and the Mask of Racism," trans. Thomas D. Morin. *New Perspectives Quarterly*, Spring: 77–81.

Gallagher, Mark. 2004. "What's so Funny About *Iron Chef?*" *Journal of Popular Film & Television* 31 (4): 176–84.

Gallup Polls. 2002–3. gallup.com.

García Canclini, Néstor. 1995. *Hybrid Cultures: Strategies for Entering and Leaving Modernity*, trans. Christopher L. Chiappari and Silvia L. López. Minneapolis: University of Minnesota Press.

García Canclini, Néstor. 1999. *Imaginarios Urbanos.* 2nd ed. Buenos Aires: Eudeba.

García Canclini, Néstor. 2001a. *Citizens and Consumers*, trans. George Yúdice. Minneapolis: University of Minnesota Press.

García Canclini, Néstor. 2001b. "Pensar en Medio de la Tormenta." In *Imaginarios de Nación: Pensar en Medio de la Tormenta*, ed. Jesús Martin-Barbero, 11–15. Bogotá: Ministerio de Cultura.

García Canclini, Néstor. 2002. *Latinoamericanos Buscando Lugar en este Siglo.* Buenos Aires: Paidós.

García Canclini, Néstor. 2004. *Differentes, Desiguales y Desconectados: Mapas de la Interculturalidad.* Barcelona: Editorial Gedisa.

Gelber, Ben. 2002. *The Pennsylvania Weather Book.* New Brunswick: Rutgers University Press.

Gelbspan, Ross. 2004. *Boiling Point: How Politicians, Big Oil and Coal, Journalists, and Activists are Fueling the Climate Crisis—and What We can do to Avert Disaster.* New York: Basic Books.

George, Joe. 2000. "Food for Thought: The Corporate Assault on Cooking." *Alter Net*, September 5. http://www.alternet.org.

Gerges, Fawaz A. 2003. "Islam and Muslims in the Mind of America." *The Annals of the American Academy of Political and Social Science* 588:73–89.

Getler, Michael. 2005. "A Parting Thought on Iraq, Again." *Washington Post*, October 9: B6.

Getlin, Josh, and Elizabeth Jensen. 2003. "Images of POWs and the Dead Pose a Dilemma for the Media." *Los Angeles Times*, March 24.

Gibson, William. 2003. *Pattern Recognition.* New York: GP Putnam's Sons.

Giddens, Anthony, and Will Hutton. 2000a. Preface to *Global Capitalism*, ed. Will Hutton and Anthony Giddens. New York: New Press.

Giddens, Anthony, and Will Hutton. 2000b. "In Conversation." In *Global Capitalism*, ed. Will Hutton and Anthony Giddens, 1–51. New York: New Press.

Giese, Rachel. 2002. "Few Scraps for Poor at Food Summit." *Toronto Star*, June 13.

Gingrich, Newt, and Peter Schweizer. 2003. "We Can Thank Hollywood for our Ugly-American Image." *Los Angles Times*, January 21.

Girardelli, Davide. 2004. "Commodified Identities: The Myth of Italian Food in the United States." *Journal of Communication Inquiry* 28 (4): 307–24.

Giroux, Henry A. 2000. *Stealing Innocence: Youth, Corporate Power, and the Politics of Culture.* New York: St. Martin's Press.

Glickman, Lawrence B. 1999. "Introduction: Born to Shop? Consumer History and American History." In *Consumer Society in American History: A Reader*, ed. Lawrence B. Glickman, 1–14. Ithaca: Cornell University Press.

Goetzmann, William N., and Ning Zhu. 2002. *Rain or Shine: Where is the Weather Effect?* Working Paper 02–27, Yale International Center for Finance.

Golan, Guy, and Wayne Wanta. 2003. "International Elections on US Network News." *Gazette: The International Journal for Communication Studies* 65 (1): 25–39.

Goldberg, Andy. 2003. "The Web at War." *Independent*, March 17.

Goldman, Michael. 2001. "Constructing an Environmental State: Eco-Governmentality and other Transnational Practices of a 'Green' World Bank." *Social Problems* 48 (4): 499–523.

Goldstein, Richard. 2003. "The Shock and Awe Show." *Village Voice*, March 26–April 1.

Gomes, Lee. 2002. "Boomtown: Globalization is now a Two-Way Street—Good News for the U.S." *Wall Street Journal*, December 9: B1.

Goodman, Amy, Aaron Brown, Steve Rendall, and Jeremy Scahill. 2003. *Democracy Now!* April 4.

Goodman, Amy, Arthel Neville, and Max Boot. 2003. *Talk Back Live*, March 4.

Gore, Al. 2004. "The Politics of Fear." *Social Research* 71 (4): 779–800.

Gould, Paul. 2005. "Vegetarianism Bites." *Financial Times*, June 18.

Gowing, Nik. 2003. "Journalists and War: The Troubling New Tensions Post 9/11." *War and the Media: Reporting Conflict 24/7*, ed. Daya Kishan Thussu and Des Freedman, 231–40. London: Sage Publications.

Graber, Doris A. 1994. "The Infotainment Quotient in Routine Television News: A Director's Perspective." *Discourse & Society* 5 (1). 483–508.

Grand Rapids Institute for Information Democracy. 2005. *Violence, Soldier Deaths and Omissions*.

Grantham, Bill. 1998. "America the Menace: France's Feud with Hollywood." *World Policy Journal* 15 (2): 58–66.

Graser, Marc. 2005a. "McDonald's Buying Way into Hip-Hop Song Lyrics." *Advertising Age*, March 28.

Graser, Mark. 2005b. "McDonald's Rap Song Product Placement Plan Stalls." *Advertising Age*, September 26.

Gray, John. 2003. *Al Qaeda and What it Means to be Modern*. London: Faber and Faber.

Greenberg, David. 2003. "We Don't Even Agree on What's Newsworthy." *Washington Post*, March 16: B1.

Greenslade, Roy. 2003. "Their Master's Voice." *Guardian*, February 17.

Greenwire. 2004. "Weather Channel Tunes to Changing Climate." January 18.

Greider, William. 2005. "The New Colossus." *The Nation* 280 (February 28): 13–18.

Grieve, Tim. 2003. "'Shut your Mouth'." *Salon.com*, March 25. http://www.salon.com.

Griffin, Michael. 2004. "Picturing America's 'War on Terrorism' in Afghanistan and Iraq: Photographic Motifs as News Frames." *Journalism: Theory, Practice and Criticism* 5 (4): 381–402.

Grimson, Alejandro. 2005. "Ethnic (In)Visibility in Neoliberal Argentina." *NACLA Report on the Americas*, January/February: 25–29.

Grossman, Karl. 2004. "Waiting Till the First Cow Dies: Herd Reporting on Mad Cow Disease." *EXTRA!* March/April: 19–22.

Grotticelli, Michael. 2004. "Food Network Serves up Digital Production." *Broadcast Engineering*, December 1.

Guardian. 2003a. "A Diet based on Worry?" May 10.

Guardian. 2003b. "GM Crops." June 3.

Guevara, Michelle. 2004. "Best Corporate Citizens 2004: Latin America Companies Set the Standard for Corporate Citizenship in the Region." *Latin Trade*, May.

Gumbel, Andrew. 2002. "Fast Food Nation: An Appetite for Litigation." *Independent*, June 4.

Gunther, Marc. 1999. "The Weather Channel: Hot Enough for Ya?" *Fortune*, October 25: 46.

Gunther, Marc. 2001. "How One Advertising Agency is Scrambling to Find Words and Images for the Moment." *Fortune*, October 15.

Guterman, Lila. 2005. "Dead Iraqis." *Columbia Journalism Review*, March/April.

Habermas, Jürgen. 1998. *The Inclusion of Others: Studies in Political Theory*, ed. C. Cronin and P. DeGrieff. Cambridge, MA: Massachusetts Institute of Technology Press.

Hafez, Kai. 2001. "Al Jazeera Meets CNN." *Message*.

Hague, William. 2000. "Why I am Sick of the Anti-British Disease." *Daily Telegraph*, October 13: 28.

Hakim, Danny. 2002. "Ford Stresses Business, but Disappoints Environmentalists." *New York Times*, August 20: C4.

Haldane, T. 1997. "War History of the Australian Meteorological Service in the Royal Australian Air Force April 1941 to July 1946." *Metarch Papers* 10.

Haley, Kathy. 2003. "Five Star TV." *Multichannel News*, November 24: 3A.

Hall, Stuart. 1991. "Old and New Identities, Old and New Ethnicities." In *Culture, Globalization and the World-System: Contemporary Conditions for the Representation of Identity*, ed. Anthony D. King, 41–68. Basingstoke: Macmillan.

Halliday, Fred. 2001. *The World at 2000: Perils and Promises*. Basingstoke: Palgrave.

Halliday, Fred. 2004. "The Crisis of Universalism: America and Radical Islam After 9/11." *openDemocracy*, September 16. http://www.opendemocracy.net.

Halweil, Brian, and Bob Scrowcroft. 2002. "Organic Foods' new Day." *Los Angeles Times*, October 21.

Hamilton, John Maxwell, and Eric Jenner. 2004. "Redefining Foreign Correspondence." *Journalism: Theory, Practice and Criticism* 5 (3): 301–21.

Hanke, Robert. 1989. "Mass Media and Lifestyle Differentiation: An Analysis of the Public Discourse about Food." *Communication* 113:221–38.

Hannah, Matthew G. 2001. "Sampling and the Politics of Representation in US Census 2000." *Environment and Planning D: Society and Space* 19 (5): 515–34.

Hans, Dennis. 2001. "Bush's Definition of Terrorism fits Northern Alliance like a Glove." *Common Dreams News Center*, November 23. http://www.commondreams.org.

Hargreaves, Ian, Justin Lewis, and Tammy Speers. 2003. *Towards a Better Map: Science, the Public and the Media*. Swindon: Economic & Social Research Council.

Harper's Magazine. 2002. "When You're Here, You're Thirsty." October, 14.

Harris, Lis. 2003. "The Seductions of Food." *Wilson Quarterly* 273:52–60.

Harris Poll. 2005. "Sizeable Minorities Still Believe Saddam Hussein had Strong Links to Al Qaeda, Helped Plan 9/11 and had Weapons of Mass Destruction." December 29.

Hart, Kim. 2005. "Web Special: A Story at Last." *American Journalism Review*, June/July.

Hart, Peter. 2005a. "Struggling MSNBC Attempts to Out-Fox Fox." *EXTRA!Update*, February 4.

Hart, Peter. 2005b. "Media Bias: How to Spot it—And How to Fight it." In *The Future of Media: Resistance and Reform in the 21st Century*, ed. Robert W. McChesney, Russell Newman, and Ben Scott, 51–61. New York: Seven Stories Press.

Hart, Peter. 2005c. "Rather's Real Bias." *EXTRA!* April: 3.

Hart, Peter. 2005d. "The Great Emancipator." *EXTRA!* May/June: 8–10.

Hart, Peter, and Steve Rendall. 2005. "A 'Right-Wing Coup'." *EXTRA!* June: 1.

Hartley, John. 1998. "'When Your Child Grows Up too Fast': Juvenation and the Boundaries of the Social in the News Media." *Continuum: Journal of Media & Cultural Studies* 12 (1): 9–30.

Hartley, John. 2003. *A Short History of Cultural Studies*. London: Sage.

Hartley, John. 2005. "Disappointment and Disgust, or Teaching?" *Flow: A Critical Forum on Television and Media Culture* 2, 2.

Harvey, David. 2003. *The New Imperialism*. Oxford: Oxford University Press.

Hassell, Greg. 2001. "Altruistic Ads Try to Unite Americans." *Houston Chronicle*, September 25.

Haste, Helen. 2004. "Constructing the Citizen." *Political Psychology* 253:413–39.

Hastings, Michael. 2003. "Billboard Ban." *Newsweek*, February 26.

Haug, W. F. 1986. *Critique of Commodity Aesthetics: Appearance, Sexuality and Advertising in Capitalist Society*, trans. Robert Bock. Cambridge: Polity Press.

Hawken, Paul. 2003. "McDonald's a 'Green Business?' I Resign." *Common Dreams News Center*, May 19. http://www.commondreams.org.

Hawken, Paul. 2004. "Green is Good." *AlterNet*, October 8. http://www.alternet.org.

Hawken, Paul. 2005. "The Truth about Ethical Investing." *AlterNet*, April 29. http://www.alternet.org.

Heller, Patrick. 2001. "Moving the State: The Politics of Democratic Decentralization in Kerala, South Africa, and Porto Alegre." *Politics & Society* 29 (1): 131–63.

Hemphill, Thomas. 2004. "Corporate Citizenship: The Case for a New Corporate Governance Model." *Business and Society Review* 109 (3): 339–61.

Henry, Scott. 1989. "Weathermen." *Australian Magazine*, November 25–26: 94.

Herman, Edward S. 1999. *The Myth of the Liberal Media: An Edward Herman Reader*. New York: Peter Lang.

Herman, Edward S. 2004. "'Selective Information is Misinformation'." *Democratic Communiqué* 19:1–12.

Herold, Marc W. 2001. "Who will Count the Dead?" *Media File* 211

Hertsgaard, Mark. 2002. "The Truth on Warming." *The Nation* 275 (July 8): 6–7.

Hertsgaard, Mark. 2004. "Weathering the Crisis." *AlterNet*, February 24. http://www.alternet.org.

Hickey, Neil. 2004. "TV: Hype Takes a Hit." *Columbia Journalism Review*, May/June: 6.

Higham, Nick. 2001. "Media Confronts a New World." *BBC News Online*, September 25.

Hill, Annette. 2005. *Reality TV: Audiences and Popular Factual Television*. London: Routledge.

Himmelstein, Jerome L., and Mayer Zald. 1984. "American Conservatism and Government Funding of the Social Sciences and Arts." *Sociological Inquiry* 54 (2): 171–87.

Hindess, Barry. 1993. "Marxism." In *A Companion to Contemporary Political Philosophy*, ed. Robert E. Goodin and Philip Pettit, 312–32. Oxford: Blackwell.

Hindess, Barry. 1998. "Divide and Rule: The International Character of Citizenship." *European Journal of Social Theory* 1 (1): 57–70.

Hirshleifer, David, and Tyler Shumway. 2003. "Good Day Sunshine: Stock Returns and the Weather." *Journal of Finance* 58 (3): 1009–32.

Hobbes, Thomas. 2002. *On the Citizen*, trans. and ed. Richard Tuck and Michael Silverthorne. Cambridge: Cambridge University Press.

Höijer, Birgitta, Stig A. Nohrstedt, and Rune Ottosen. 2004. "Introduction: Media and the 'War on Terror'." In *U.S. and the Others: Global Media Images on "The War on Terror,"* ed. Stig A. Nohrstedt and Rune Ottosen, 7–22. Göteborg: NORDICOM.

Holden, John, Lydia Howland, and Daniel Stedman Jones. 2002. "Closing the Loop." *Demos Collection* 18:5–15.

Holland, Joshua. 2005. "Disarming Trade." *AlterNet*, December 20. http://www.alternet.org.

Hollows, Joanne. 2003. "Oliver's Twist: Leisure, Labour and Domestic Masculinity in *The Naked Chef*." *International Journal of Cultural Studies* 6 (2): 229–48.

Hong Kong Trade Development Council. 2003. "Cookware Sector Gets Hot, Thanks to Canadian TV." November 27.

Honig, Bonnie. 1998. "Immigrant America? How Foreignness 'Solves' Democracy's Problems." *Social Text* 56:1–27.

Horton, Richard. 2005. "Threats to Human Survival: A WIRE to Warn the World." *Lancet* 365 9455.

Horton, Sarah. 2004. "Different Subjects: The Health Care System's Participation in the Differential Construction of the Cultural Citizenship of Cuban Refugees and Mexican Immigrants." *Medical Anthropology Quarterly* 18 (4): 472–89.

Houghton, John. 2003. "Global Warming is now a Weapon of Mass Destruction." *Guardian*, July 28.

House Appropriations Committee — Minority. 2003. http://www.house.gov/appropriations_democrats/caughtonfilm.htm.

Hudson, Michael, Marvin Kalb, Hafez Al-Mirazi, Rami G. Khouri, and Jacques Charmelot. 2002. "Covering the War on Terrorism." *Transnational Broadcasting Studies* 8.

Huff, Richard. 2003a. "Blitz of War Coverage on Nightly News." *Daily News*, March 24.

Huff, Richard. 2003b. "The Nets' Gender Gulf." *Daily News*, March 24.

Hughes, Patrick. 1995. "The Meteorologist in your Life." *Weatherwise*, June 16: 68.

Human Rights Watch. 2003. "Iraq Must Not Parade POWs." News Release, March 24. http://hrw.org/english/docs/2003/03/24/iraq5427.htm.

Human Rights Watch. 2004. *Blood, Sweat, and Fear: Workers' Rights in U.S. Meat and Poultry Plants.* http://www.hrw.org/reports/2005/usa0105/.

Huntington, Samuel P. 1993. "The Clash of Civilizations?" *Foreign Affairs* 72 (3): 22–28.

Huntington, Samuel P. 2004. ¿*Quiénes somos? Los desafíos a la identidad nacional estadounidense*, trans. Albino Santos Mosquera. México: Paidós.

Hutton, Will. 2003a. "Crunch Time for Uncle Sam." *Observer*, January 5.

Hutton, Will. 2003b. *A Declaration of Interdependence: Why America Should Join the World.* New York: W. W. Norton.

Ibrahim, Dina. 2003. "Individual Perceptions of International Correspondents in the Middle East." *Gazette: The International Journal for Communication Studies* 65 (1): 87–101.

Ignatieff, Michael. 2003. "The American Empire (get used to it)." *New York Times Magazine*, January 5.

Immigration and Naturalization Service. 2001. *General Naturalization Requirements.*

Independent. 2000. "'British' is Already Inclusive and Elastic." October 12: 3.

Independent. 2002. "An Avalanche of Unnecessary Vetting set off by Moral Panic." September 7: 18.

Independent. 2003. "President Bush is Right to Condemn Iraq's Treatment of Captured Soldiers—but his Outrage Rings Hollow."

IndiaResource.org. 2005. "*Coca-Cola: Destroying Lives, Livelihoods and Communities*." www.indiaresource.org.

India Resource Center. 2005. "Coca-Cola Threatens Top Indian Photographer with Lawsuit." July 12.

International Association of Broadcast Meterology. 2005. "The History of the IABM." 2005. http://iabm.org.

International Business Leaders Forum. 2004. Corporate Social Responsibility Forum. iblf.org.

International Federation of Journalists. 2001. *Les Journalists du Monde entier Produisent un Rapport sur les Médias, la Guerre et le Terrorisme*. October 23.

International Federation of Journalists. 2005. "World Journalists Condemn US Campaign of 'Stooge Journalism' in Iraq." December 5.

Ip, David, C. Inglis, and C. T. Wu. 1997. "Concepts of Citizenship and Identity among Recent Asian Immigrants to Australia." *Asian and Pacific Migration Journal* 6 3–4:363–84.

Iron Chef Compendium. http://www.ironchef.com/about_show.shtml.

Ives, Nat. 2005. "New Food Magazine Welcomes Product Placement." *Advertising Age*, July 21.

Jackson, Jesse, Jr. 2005. "Securing the Right to Vote as a Citizenship Right." *Common Dreams News Center*, March 9. http://www.commondreams.org.

Jaggi, Maya. 2000. "Bhikhu Parekh: First Among Equalisers." *Guardian*, October 21: 6.

Jamail, Dahr. 2005. "Ignoring the Air War." *Tomdispatch.com*, December 14. http://www.tomdispatch.com.

Jameson, Fredric. 1991. *Postmodernism, or, the Cultural Logic of Late Capitalism.* London: Verso.

Jarvie, I. C. 1983. "The Problem of the Ethnographic Real." *Current Anthropology* 24 (3): 313–19.

Jasperson, Amy E., and Mansour O. El-Kikhia. 2003. "CNN and al Jazeera's Media Coverage of America's War in Afghanistan." In *Framing Terrorism: The News Media, the Government, and the Public*, ed. Pippa Norris, Montague Kern, and Marion Just, 113–32. New York: Routledge.

Jeffrey, Clara. 2006. "Limited Ambitions." *Mother Jones*, January/February: 22–23.

Jencks, Christopher. 2004. "Our Unequal Democracy." *American Prospect*, June: A2–A4.

Jensen, Elizabeth. 2003. "Network's War Strategy: Enlist Armies of Experts." *Los Angeles Times*, March 18.

Jenson, Jane, and Martin Papillon. 2001. *The Changing Boundaries of Citizenship: A Review and a Research Agenda*. Canadian Policy Research Networks.

Johnson, Bradley. 2005. "How U.S. Consumers Spend their Time." *Advertising Age*, May 2.

Johnson, Ian. 1999. "Hot News: Chinese Media Stifled Reports of Stifling Heat for Years." *Wall Street Journal*, July 29: B1.

Johnson, James. 2000. "Why Respect Culture?" *American Journal of Political Science* 44 (3): 405–18.

Johnson, Kevin V. 2000. "Weather Channel." *Times Union Albany*, August 7.

Johnson, Nicholas. 2003. "Forty Years of Wandering in the Wasteland." *Federal Communications Law Journal* 55:521–33.

Johnson, Peter. 2003. "Media Question Authority Over War Protests." *USA Today*, February 24.

Johnson, Stanley R., and Matthew T. Holt. 1997. "The Value of Weather Information." In *Economic Value of Weather and Climate Forecasts*, ed. Richard W. Katz and Allan H. Murphy, 75–107. Cambridge: Cambridge University Press.

Jonas, Andrew E. G., and Gavin Bridge. 2003. "Governing Nature: The Re-Regulation of Resources, Land-Use Planning, and Nature Conservation." *Social Science Quarterly* 84 (4): 94–97.

Jones, Chris. 2003. "Peter Arnett: Under Fire." *BBC News Online*, April 4.

Jones, Mark. 2005. "Tsunami Coverage Dwarfs 'Forgotten' Crises—Research." *AlertNet*, March 10. http://www.alertnet.org.

Jones, Richard. 2003. "The New Look—and Taste—of British Cuisine." *Virginia Quarterly Review* 79 2.

Jones, Terry. 2004. "Iraq: Realities the Words Can't Hide." *Arab News*, May 1.

Jones, Tim. 2003. "Media Giant's Rally Sponsorship Raises Questions." *Chicago Tribune*, March 19.

La Jornada. 2002. "No al Maczócalo, consigna en la *tamaliza* de Francisco Toledo." August 19.

Kackman, Michael. 2004. "Cooking Shows." In *Museum of Broadcast Communications Encyclopedia of Television*, 2nd ed., ed. Horace Newcomb, 584–85. New York: Fitzroy Dearborn.

Kahney, Leander. 2003. "Media Watchdogs Caught Napping." *Wired News*, March 17.

Kaitatzi-Whitlock, Sophia, with Dimitra Kehagia. 2004. "'All that is Solid Melts into Air': How the September 11 Tragedy was Presented in the Greek Press." In *U.S. and the Others: Global Media Images on "The War on Terror,"* ed. Stig A. Nohrstedt and Rune Ottosen, 131–55. Göteborg: NORDICOM.

Kalb, Marvin. 2003. "Journalists Torn Between Purism and Patriotism." *Editor & Publisher*, March 24.

Kalins, Dorothy. 2004. "A Master of the Art of Living." *Newsweek*, August 23: 71.

Kallick, David Dyssegaard. 2002. *Progressive Think Tanks: What Exists, What's Missing?* Report for the Program on Governance and Public Policy, Open Society Institute.

Kamstra, Mark, Lisa Kramer, and Maurice Levi. 2003. *Winter Blues: A SAD Stock Market Cycle*. Working Paper 2002–13a, Federal Reserve Bank of Atlanta.

Kant, Immanuel. 1991. *Political Writings*, 2nd ed., trans. H. B. Nisbet, ed. Hans Reiss. Cambridge: Cambridge University Press.

Kaplan, Esther. 2004. "Follow the Money." *The Nation* 279 (November 1): 20–23.

Karr, Timothy. 2005. "Is Cheap Broadband Un-American?" *Media Citizen*, April 12.

Katz, Richard W., and Allan H. Murphy, eds. 1997. Preface to *Economic Value of Weather and Climate Forecasts*. Cambridge: Cambridge University Press.

Kaufman, Frederick. 2005. "Debbie Does Salad: The Food Network at the Frontiers of Pornography." *Harper's Magazine*, October: 55–61.

Kavanagh, Michael J. 2005. "Environmentalists on the Fringe." *Grist Magazine*, July 13.

Kay, Jane Holtz. 2003. "Hostile Climate." *TomPaine.com*, July 18. http://www.tompaine.com.

Kay, Katty. 2001. "Tuning in for Naked News." *BBC News Online*, April 26. http://news.bbc.co.uk.

Keeble, Richard. 2004. "Information Warfare in an Age of Hyper-Militarism." In *Reporting War: Journalism in Wartime*, ed. Stuart Allan and Barbie Zelizer, 43–58. London: Routledge.

Keegan, Rebecca Winters. 2005. "People." *Time*, November 14: 99.

Keeler, Dan. 2002. "Spread the Love and Make it Pay." *Global Finance*, May: 20–25.

Keeter, Scott, Cliff Zukin, Molly Andolina, and Krista Jenkins. 2002. *The Civic and Political Health of the Nation: A Generational Portrait*. Center for Information & Research on Civic Learning & Engagement.

Keilman, John. 2002. "Food Retailers Press for Humane Farming." *Chicago Tribune*, June 26.

Kellinger, Kathryn. 1999. "Julia Child: Still Cookin' After All These Years." *Salon.com*, August 20. http://www.salon.com.

Kellner, Douglas. 2003. *From 9/11 to Terror War: The Dangers of the Bush Legacy*. Lanham: Rowman & Littlefield.

Kellner, Douglas. 2004. "Media Propaganda and Spectacle in the War on Iraq: A Critique of U.S. Broadcasting Networks." *Cultural Studies ↔ Critical Methodologies* 4 (3): 329–38.

Kempner, Matt. 2001. "Weather Channel Expanding on Net." *Atlanta Constitution*, July 6: F3.

Kennard, William E. 2000. "'What does $70 Billion Buy You Anyway?' Rethinking Public Interest Requirements at the Dawn of the Digital Age." Speech to Museum of Television and Radio, Chicago, October 10.

Kern, Montague, Marion Just, and Pippa Norris. 2003. "The Lessons of Framing Terrorism." In *Framing Terrorism: The News Media, the Government, and the Public*, ed. Pippa Norris, Montague Kern, and Marion Just, 281–302. New York: Routledge.

Kessler, John. 2004. "America's French Chef: Julia Child: 1912–2004: Mastering the Art of Life." *Atlanta Journal-Constitution*, August 14: 1C.

Ketchum, Cheri. 2005. "The Essence of Cooking Shows: How the Food Network Constructs Consumer Fantasies." *Journal of Communication Inquiry* 29 (3): 217–34.

Kettebekov, Sanshzar, and Rajeev Sharma. 2001. "Toward Natural Gesture/Speech Control of a Large Display." *Lecture Notes in Computer Science* 2254.

Khouri, Rami G. 2003. "Shooting the Messenger." *Index on Censorship* 32 (4): 170–72.

Kiesling, B. C. 1937. *Talking Pictures: How They are Made How to Appreciate Them*. Richmond: Johnson Publishing.

Kilgannon, Corey. 1998. "Forecaster is Right on After Gulf Storms." *New York Times*, October 4: 26.

Kim, Nancy S. 1997. "The Cultural Defense and the Problem of Cultural Preemption: A Framework for Analysis." *New Mexico Law Review* 27:101–39.

King, Samantha. 2001. "An All-Consuming Cause: Breast Cancer, Corporate Philanthropy, and the Market for Generosity." *Social Text* 69:115–43.

Kinnick, Katherine N. 2004. "Advertising Responses to Crisis." *Society* 42 (1): 32–36.

Kitch, Carolyn. 2003a. "'Mourning in America': Ritual, Redemption, and Recovery in News Narrative after September 11." *Journalism Studies* 4 (2): 213–24.

Kitch, Carolyn. 2003b. "Generational Identity and Memory in American Newsmagazines." *Journalism: Theory, Practice and Criticism* 4 (2): 185–202.

Kitzinger, Jenny, and Jacquie Reilly. 1997. "The Rise and Fall of Risk Reporting: Media Coverage of Human Genetics Research, 'False Memory Syndrome' and 'Mad Cow Disease'." *European Journal of Communication* 12 (3): 319–50.

Klaasen, Abbey. 2005. "2005 Ad Spending to Increase 3.4%." *Advertising Age*, June 28.

Klein, Naomi. 1999. *No Logo*. New York: Picador USA.

Klein, Naomi. 2003. "Downsizing in Disguise." *The Nation* 276 (June 23): 10.

Kloer, Phil. 2001. "Neither Wind nor Rain, nor Hurricane . . ." *American Journalism Review* 23 (6): 16–17.

Kluge, Alexander. 1981–82. "On Film and the Public Sphere," trans. Thomas Y. Levin and Miriam B. Hansen. *New German Critique* 24–25:206–20.

Krikorian, Mark. 2004. "Post-Americans." *National Review Online*, June 22.

Kroll, Theo, and Edith Champagne. 2002. "13 Months after the 9/11 Attacks—Terrorism, Patriotism and Media Coverage." *Transnational Broadcasting Studies* 9.

Krugman, Paul. 2003a. "Threats, Promises and Lies." *New York Times*, February 25.

Krugman, Paul. 2003b. "Channels of Influence." *New York Times*, March 25.

Krugman, Paul. 2005. "Girth of a Nation." *New York Times*, July 4.

Kull, Steven, Clay Ramsay, and Evan Lewis. 2003–04. "Misperceptions, the Media, and the Iraq War." *Political Science Quarterly* 118 (4): 569–98.

Kumar, Deepa. 2004. "War Propaganda and the (Ab)uses of Women: Media Constructions of the Jessica Lynch Story." *Feminist Media Studies* 4 (3): 297–313.

Kurlantzick, Joshua. 2004. "Outfront." *Mother Jones*, November/December: 15–17.

Kurtz, Howard. 2004. "*The Post* on WMDs: An Inside Story." *Washington Post*, August 12.

Kymlicka, Will. 1995. *Multicultural Citizenship: A Liberal Theory of Minority Rights*. Oxford: Oxford University Press.

Kymlicka, Will. 2000. "A North American View." *Journal of Ethnic and Migration Studies* 26 (4): 723–31.

Laitin, David D. 1999. "The Cultural Elements of Ethnically Mixed States: Nationality Reformation in the Soviet Successor States." In *State/Culture: State-Formation after the Cultural Turn*, ed. George Steinmetz, 291–320. Ithaca: Cornell University Press.

Lakoff, George. 2003. "Metaphor and War, Again." *AlterNet*, March 18. http://www.alternet.org.

Lang, Tim, and Martin Caraher. 2001. "Is There a Culinary Skills Transition? Data and Debate from the UK About Changes in Cooking Culture." *Journal of the Home Economics Institute of Australia* 8 (2): 2–14.

Langer, John. 1998. *Tabloid Television: Popular Journalism and the "Other News."* London: Routledge.

Lappé, Anna. 2002. "Organic Diet for a Small Planet." *Toronto Globe & Mail*, July 25.

Larkspirit.com. 2005. *The Irish Hungerstrikes: A Commemorative Project*. http://larkspirit.com.

Laskin, David. 1999. "Stormy Weather—Live!" *Smithsonian* 30 (1): 142–53.

Latour, Bruno. 1993. *We Have Never Been Modern*, trans. Catherine Porter. Cambridge, MA: Harvard University Press.

Latour, Bruno. 2004. *Politics of Nature: How to Bring the Sciences into Democracy*, trans. Catherine Porter. Cambridge, MA: Harvard University Press.

Laughlin, Kirk. 2000. "Weathering the E-storm." *Teleprofessional* 13 (5): 51–53.

Lavine, John, and Readership Institute. 2003. *Beyond Impact: Engaging Younger, Lighter Readers: A Joint Venture of NAA, ASNE, & Media Management Center*.

Lawrence, Geoffrey, and Lynda Herbert-Cheshire. 2003. "Regional Restructuring, Neoliberalism, Individualisation and Community: The Recent Australian Experience." Paper presented to the European Society for Rural Sociology Congress, Sligo.

Lawrence, Regina G. 2004. "Framing Obesity: The Evolution of News Discourse on a Public Health Issue." *Harvard Journal of Press/Politics* 9 (3): 56–75.

Layman, Geoffrey C. 1999. "'Culture Wars' in the American Party System: Religious and Cultural Change Among Partisan Activists since 1972." *American Politics Quarterly* 27 (1): 89–121.

Le Carré, John. 2003. "The United States of America Has Gone Mad." *Times*, 15 January.

Leadbeater, Charles. 2004. *Personalisation Through Participation: A New Script for Public Services*. London: Demos.

Lean, Geoffrey. 2005. "Revealed: Health Fears Over Secret Study into GM Food." *Independent*, May 22.

Leavy, Pamela Griner. 2002. "Pepsi Sweetens Pot for Hillsborough Schools." *Tampa Bay Business Journal*, August 30.

Ledbetter, James. 1998. *Made Possible By . . .: The Death of Public Broadcasting in the United States*. London: Verso.

Lee, Christopher. 2005. "EPA Paid Weather Channel for Videos." *Washington Post*, July 18.

Lee, Taegu, and J. Eric Oliver. 2002. *Public Opinion and the Politics of America's Obesity Epidemic*. Faculty Research Working Papers Series 02–017, John F. Kennedy School of Government Harvard University.

Leguineche, Manu. 2002. "Cuidado con lo que dice, cuidado con lo que pregunta." In *La Télévisión en Tiempos de Guerra*, ed. Paco Lobatón, 13–21. Barcelona: Editorial Gedisa.

Lentricchia, Frank, and Jody McAuliffe. 2002. "Groundzeroland." *South Atlantic Quarterly* 101 (2): 349–59.

Leonard, Tom. 2001. "BBC Overrun by Women Clones, says Lord Taylor." *Daily Telegraph*, August 14.

Leong, Laurence Wei-Teng. 1992. "Cultural Resistance: The Cultural Terrorism of British Male Working-Class Youth." *Current Perspectives in Social Theory* 12:29–58.

Levitt, Peggy. 2001. "Transnational Migration: Taking Stock and Future Directions." *Global Networks* 1 (3): 195–216.

Lewis, Bernard. 1990. "The Roots of Muslim Rage: Why so Many Muslims Deeply Resent the West, and Why Their Bitterness will not be so Easily Mollified." *Atlantic Monthly*, September: 47–58.

Lewis, Justin. 1994. "The Absence of Narrative: Boredom and the Residual Power of Television News." *Journal of Narrative and Life History* 4 1–2:25–40.

Lewis, Justin. 1999. "The Opinion Poll as Cultural Form." *International Journal of Cultural Studies* 2 (2): 199–221.

Lewis, Justin. 2001. *Constructing Public Opinion: How Political Elites do What They Like and Why We Seem to Go Along with it*. New York: Columbia University Press.

Lewis, Justin, Sanna Inthorn, and Karin Wahl-Jorgensen. 2005. *Citizens or Consumers? What the Media Tell Us About Political Participation*. Maidenhead: Open University Press.

Lewis, Justin, Terry Threadgold, Rod Brookes, Nick Mosdell, Kirsten Brander, Sadie Clifford, Ehab Bessaiso, and Zahera Harb. 2004a. *Too Close for Comfort? The Role of Embedded Reporting During the 2003 Iraq War: Summary Report*. British Broadcasting Corporation.

Lewis, Justin, Karin Wahl-Jorgensen, and Sanna Inthorn. 2004b. "Images of Citizenship on Television News: Constructing a Passive Public." *Journalism Studies* 5 (2): 153–64.

Lexington. 2005. "Minding the Gap." *Economist*, June 11: 32.

Lieberman, David. 2003. "NBC Hopes Big Investment in News Coverage Pays Off." *USA Today*, March 24.

Life. 2005. "America Makes Room for Sunday Dinner." September 23: 13–14.

Lister, Ruth. 1997. *Citizenship: Feminist Perspectives*. New York: New York University Press.

Little, Amanda Griscom. 2005a. "The Revolution will be Localized." *Grist Magazine*, July 20.

Little, Amanda Griscom. 2005b. "If You Don't Like the Climate, Wait a Minute." *Grist Magazine*, September 24.

Lizárraga, Lizardo Seiner. 2004. "Los inicios de la meteorología en el Perú y la labor del Cosmografiato, 1753–1856." *Journal of the History of Meteorology* 1 1.

Lloyd, David, and Paul Thomas. 1998. *Culture and the State*. New York: Routledge.

Lloyd, John. 2002. "Wanted." *Financial Times*, January 12: Weekend FT1.

Lloyd, Mark. 2005. "Lessons for Realistic Radicals in the Information Age." In *The Future of Media: Resistance and Reform in the 21st Century*, ed. Robert W. McChesney, Russell Newman, and Ben Scott, 73–95. New York: Seven Stories Press.

Lobe, Jim. 2003a. "All the World's a TV Screen." *Asia Times*, January 4.

Lobe, Jim. 2003b. "Press Watchdogs Protest U.S. Killings of Journalists in Baghdad." *OneWorld.net*, April 9. http://oneworld.net.

Lobe, Jim. 2004. "Television's Myopic Global Eye." *Inter Press Service*, January 6.

Logsdon, Jeanne M. 2004. "Global Business Citizenship: Applications to Environmental Issues." *Business and Society Review* 109 (1): 67–87.

Lomnitz, Claudio. 2005. "American Soup." *Boston Review*, March 10.

Lopez, Tiffany Ana. 2003. "Emotional Contraband: Prison as Metaphor and Meaning in U.S. Latina Drama." In *Captive Audiences: Prison Issues on the American Stage*, ed. Thomas Fahy and Kimball King, 25–40. New York: Routledge.

Los Angeles Times. 2004a. "Jeff Smith, 65; Pastor, PBS' 'Frugal Gourmet'." July 10: B18.

Los Angeles Times. 2004b. "TV Chefs Who Don't get an A." July 7: E3.

Los Angeles Times. 2005. "Europe's Rules Forcing U.S. Firms to Clean Up." May 16: A1, A6.

Lovato, Roberto. 2004. "Fear of a Brown Planet." *The Nation* 278 (June 28): 17–21.

Love, Maryann Cusimano. 2003. "Global Media and Foreign Policy." In *Media Power, Media Politics*, ed. Mark J. Rozell, 235–64. Lanham: Rowman & Littlefield.

Lowry, Brian. 1998. "Stormy Weather Brings Bright Ratings to Network." *Los Angeles Times*, August 26: A-8.

Lowry, Brian. 2003. "Will the TV Factory Shape a New War?" *Calendar Live*, February 26.

Lowry, Dennis T., Tarn Ching Josephone Nio, and Dennis W. Leitner. 2003. "Setting the Public Fear Agenda: A Longitudinal Analysis of Network TV Crime Reporting, Public Perceptions of Crime, and FBI Crime Statistics." *Journal of Communication*, March: 61–73.

Luhrmann, Tanya M. 2004. "Metakinesis: How God Becomes Intimate in Contemporary U.S. Christianity." *American Anthropologist* 106 (3): 518–28.

Lule, Jack. 2004. "War and its Metaphors: News Language and the Prelude to War in Iraq, 2003." *Journalism Studies* 5 (2): 179–90.

Lyall, Sarah. 2002. "TV's New Climate: It's Raining Boys." *New York Times*, March 29: A4.

Lyman, Rick. 1999. "Residents Watched on TV as the Tornadoes Neared." *New York Times*, May 6: A31.

Lynch, Alexander. 2005. "The Media Lobby." *AlterNet.org*, March 14. http://www.alternet.org.

MacArthur, John. 2003. "All the News that's Fudged to Print." *Globe & Mail*, June 6.

MacArthur, Kate. 2005a. "New Documentary Reopens Old McDonald's Wounds." *Advertising Age*, June 13.

MacArthur, Kate. 2005b. "McDonald's Plans to Reinvent Employee Uniforms." *Advertising Age*, July 4.

MacColl, Katharine. 2005. "Who was the First TV Chef?" *The Answer Bank: Film & TV*.

MacFarquhar. 2003. "Arabic Stations Compete for Attention." *New York Times*, March 25.

Magder, Ted. 2003. "Watching What We Say: Global Communication in a Time of Fear." In *War and the Media: Reporting Conflict 24/7*, ed. Daya Kishan Thussu and Des Freedman, 28–44. London: Sage Publications.

Magdoff, Harry, John Bellamy Foster, and Robert W. McChesney. 2004. "The Pentagon and Climate Change." *Monthly Review* 56 (1): 1–13.

Maguire, Kevin, and Andy Lines. 2005. "Bush Plot to Bomb his Arab Ally." *Daily Mirror*, November 22.

Mahmud, Tayyab. 1997. "Migration, Identity, & the Colonial Encounter." *Oregon Law Review* 76 (3): 633–90.

Mahmud, Tayyab. 1999. "Colonialism and Modern Constructions of Race: A Preliminary Inquiry." *University of Miami Law Review* 53 (4): 1219–46.

Maira, Luis. 2002. "El Amarre Institucional del General Pinochet y las Restricciones de la Transición Chilena." In *Globalización, Identidad y Democracia: México y América Latina*, ed. Julio Labastida Martín del Campo and Antonio Camou, 82–110. Mexico: Siglo Veintiuno Editores.

Maitland, Alison. 2002. "How to Become Good in all Areas." *Financial Times*, September 11: 10.

Makala, Jeffrey. 2005. "The Joys of Cooking." *Chronicle of Higher Education*, February 18: B19.

Maluf, Ramez. 2005. "Al Jazeera: The Enfant Terrible of Arab Media." *European Journal of Communication* 20 (4): 531–37.

Maney, Kevin. 2003. "IBM Makes Play for 'Next-Generation Pixar'." *USA Today*, July 24.

Mann, Michael. 2003. *Incoherent Empire*. London: Verso.

Mannur, Anita. 2005. "Model Minorities Can Cook: Fusion Cuisine in Asian America." In *East Main Street: Asian American Popular Culture*, ed. Shilpa Davé, LeiLani Nishime, and Tasha G. Oren, 72–94. New York: New York University Press.

Markillie, Paul. 2005. "Crowned at Last." *Economist*, April 2: 3–6.

Marquis, Christopher. 2004. "U.S. Protests Broadcasts by Arab Channels." *New York Times*, April 29.

Marshall, Eliot. 1988. "Nobel Economist Robert Solow." *Dialogue* 82:8–9.

Marshall, P. David. 1997. *Celebrity and Power: Fame in Contemporary Culture*. Minneapolis: University of Minnesota Press.

Martin, Christopher R. 2004. *Framed! Labor and the Corporate Media*. Ithaca: ILR Press/Cornell University Press.

Martin, Patrick. 2003. "The Firing of Peter Arnett: Right-Wing Straitjacket Tightens on the US Media." *World Socialist Web Site*, April 1. http://www.wsws.org.

Martin, Randy. 2002. *Financialization of Daily Life*. Philadelphia: Temple University Press.

Martín-Barbero, Jesús. 2000. "Nuevos mapas culturales de la integración y el desarrollo." In *Capital Social y Cultura: Claves Estratégicas para el Desarrollo*, ed. Bernardo Kliksberg and Luciano Tomassini, 335–58. Washington: Banco Interamericano de Desarrollo/Fundación Felipe Herrera, Universidad de Maryland/Fondo de Cultura Económica.

Martín-Barbero, Jesús, ed. 2001a. Introd. to *Imaginarios de Nación: Pensar en Medio de la Tormenta*. Bogotá: Ministerio de Cultura.

Martín-Barbero, Jesús. 2001b. "Colombia: Ausencia de Relato y Desubicaciones de lo Nacional." In *Imaginarios de Nación: Pensar en Medio de la Tormenta*, ed. Jesús Martín-Barbero, 17–28. Bogotá: Ministerio de Cultura.

Martín-Barbero, Jesús. 2003. "Proyectos de Modernidad en América Latina." *Metapolítica* 29:35–51.

Marvin, Carolyn, and Philip Meyer. 2005. "What Kind of Journalism does the Public Need?" In *The Press*, ed. Geneva Overholser and Kathleen Hall Jamieson, 400–11. Oxford: Oxford University Press.

Marx, Karl. 1994. "Human Emancipation." In *Citizenship*, ed. Paul Barry Clarke, 137–40. London: Pluto Press.

Maryniak, Irena. 2003. "The New Slave Trade." *Index on Censorship* 32 (3): 87.

Mason, R. 1999. "The Gift of Clarification." *Jerusalem Post*, May 19.

Massey, Douglas S. 2003. "The United States in the World Community: The Limits of National Sovereignty." In *The Fractious Nation? Unity and Division in American Life*, ed. Jonathan Rieder, assoc. ed. Stephen Steinlight, 143–54. Berkeley: University of California Press.

Massing, Michael. 2001. "Press Watch." *The Nation* 273 (October 15): 6, 31.

Massing, Michael. 2005. "The End of News?" *New York Review of Books*, December 1.

Mass-Observation. 1939. *Britain*. London: Penguin.

Mathiesen, Thomas. 1997. "The Viewer Society: Michel Foucault's 'Panopticon' Revisited." *Theoretical Criminology* 1 (2): 215–34.

Matsuura, Koichiro. 2001. "La riqueza cultural del mundo reside en su diversidad dialogante." *Déclaración Universal de la UNESCO Sobre la Diversidad Cultural*. UNESCO.

Matsuyama, K. 2002. "The Rise of Mass Consumption Societies." *Journal of Political Economy* 110 (5): 1035–70.

Mattelart, Armand. 2003. *The Information Society*, trans. Susan G. Taponier and James A. Cohen. London: Sage Publications.

Matthews, Anna Wilde. 2003. "Pacifica Radio Network Becomes Antiwar Voice." *Wall Street Journal*, March 24.

Matthews, Virginia. 2003. "Trust in Community Schemes." *Independent*, February 25.

Maxwell, Richard. 2002. "Citizens, You Are What You Buy." *Times Higher Education Supplement*, December 20.

Mazur, Allan. 1998. "Global Environmental Change in the News: 1987–90 vs 1992–6." *International Sociology* 13 (4): 457–72.

Mazzetti, Mark, and Borzou Daragahi. 2005. "U.S. Military Covertly Pays to Run Stories in Iraqi Press." *Los Angeles Times*, November 30: A1, A12.

McAllister, Matthew P. 2005. "Television Advertising as Textual and Economic Systems." In *A Companion to Television*, ed. Janet Wasko, 217–37. Malden: Blackwell.

McCarthy, Anna. 2005. "An Open Letter to the Food Network." *Flow: A Critical Forum on Television and Media Culture* 1 9.

McCarthy, Michael. 2004. "Violence in Iraq Puts Advertisers on Edge." *USA Today*, May 18: 2B.

McCarthy, Michael. 2005. "Amateur Weather Sleuths Join the Met by Predicting a Long, Hot Summer (Probably)." *Independent*, March 26.

McChesney, Robert W. 2003. "The Problem of Journalism: A Political Economic Contribution to an Explanation of the Crisis in Contemporary US Journalism." *Journalism Studies* 4 (3): 299–329.

McChesney, Robert W. 2004. *The Problem of the Media: U.S. Communication Politics in the 21st Century*. New York: Monthly Review Press.

McChesney, Robert W., and John Bellamy Foster. 2003. "The Commercial Tidal Wave." *Monthly Review* 54 (10):1–16.

McComas, Katherine, and James Shanahan. 1999. "Telling Stories about Global Climate Change." *Communication Research* 26 (1): 30–57.

McConville, Jim. 2000. "A Revised Forecast." *Electronic Media* 19:6.

McCright, Aaron M., and Riley E. Dunlap. 2003. "Defeating Kyoto: The Conservative Movement's Impact on U.S. Climate Change Policy." *Social Problems* 50 (3): 348–73.

McDonald, Ian R., and Regina G. Lawrence. 2004. "Filling the 24 x 7 News Hole." *American Behavioral Scientist* 48 (3): 327–40.

McDonald's Balanced, Active Lifestyles Team. 2005. *McDonald's Policies, Plans and Strategies to Support Balanced, Active Lifestyles*. March.

McEwan, Ian. 2005. *Saturday*. New York: Doubleday.

McGinnis, J. Michael, Jennifer Appleton Gootman, and Vivica I. Kraak, eds. 2005. *Food Marketing to Children and Youth: Threat or Opportunity?* Washington: National Academies Press.

McGirk, Jan. 2005. "Western NGOs and the Tsunami Test." *openDemocracy*, December 21. http://www.opendemocracy.net.

McKibben, Bill. 2004. "One Nation, Underperforming." *Grist Magazine*, April 5.

McKibben, Bill. 2005. "Introduction." *Mother Jones*, May/June: 34–35.

McLemee, Scott. 2003. "Murder in Black and White." *Newsday*, August 31: D29.

McMichael, Philip. 1996. *Development and Social Change: A Global Perspective*. Thousand Oaks: Pine Forge Press.

McSpotlight. 2005. http://www.mcspotlight.org.

"Media Information." 2004. *Bitterwaitress.com*, June 16. http://www.bitterwaitress.com.

Media Daily. 1997. "Cable's Food Network to Launch Regional Web Sites." 4, no. 5.

Meehan, Eileen. 2001. "Culture: Text or Artifact or Action?" *Journal of Communication Inquiry* 25 (3): 208–17.

Meek, Nigel. 1998. "'Society' does not Exist (and if it did it Shouldn't)." *Political Notes* 144.

Meijer, Irene Costera. 2001. "The Public Quality of Popular Journalism: Developing a Normative Framework." *Journalism Studies* 2 (2): 189–205.

Meister, Mark. 2001. "Cultural Feeding, Good Life Science, and the TV Food Network." *Mass Communication & Society* 4 (2): 165–82.

Mellinger, Andrew D., Jeffrey D. Sachs, and John L. Gallup. 2000. "Climate, Coastal Proximity, and Development." In *The Oxford Handbook of Economic Geography*, ed. Gordon L. Clark, Maryann P. Feldman, and Meric S. Gertler with the assistance of Kate Williams, 169–94. Oxford: Oxford University Press.

Menaker, Daniel. 1998. "My Favorite Show." *New York Times Magazine*, September 20: 108.

Menezes, Francisco. 2001. "Food Sovereignty: A Vital Requirement for Food Security in the Context of Globalization." *Development* 44 (4): 29–33.

Meredyth, Denise, and Jeffrey Minson, eds. 2000. "Citizenship and Cultural Policy." Special issue, *American Behavioral Scientist* 43, no. 9.

Merriman, Rima. 2004. "Middle Eastern Studies Seen as Against American Interests." *Jordan Times*, March 11.

Met Éireann. 2005. "Our History." 2005. http://www.met.ie/about/our-history.asp.

Met Office. 2005. *History of the Met Office*.

The Meteorological Magazine. 1954. "Weather Forecasts by Television."

Miami New Times. 1998. "Hype that Hurricane." September 10–16: 16–18.

Micheletti, Michele. 2003. *Political Virtue and Shopping: Individuals, Consumerism, and Collective Action*. New York: Palgrave Macmillan.

Michels, Robert. 1915. *Political Parties: A Sociological Study of the Oligarchical Tendencies of Modern Democracy*, trans. Eden and Cedar Paul. London: Jarrold & Sons.

Miele, Mara, and Jonathan Murdoch. 2003. "Fast Food/Slow Food: Standardizing and Differentiating Cultures of Food." In *Globalization, Localization, and Sustainable Livelihoods*, ed. Reidar Almås and Geoffrey Lawrence, 25–40. Aldershot: Ashgate.

Miladi, Noureddine. 2003. "Mapping the Al-Jazeera Phenomenon." In *War and the Media: Reporting Conflict 24/7*, ed. Daya Kishan Thussu and Des Freedman, 149–60. London: Sage Publications.

Miles, Laureen. 2004. "Cable's Perfect Storm: A Confluence of Forces has put The Weather Channel at the Forefront of Forecast." *MediaWeek*, June 14: 22–23.

Miliband, David. 2004. Foreword to *Personalisation Through Participation: A New Script for Public Services*, by Charles Leadbeater, 11–14. London: Demos.

Mill, John Stuart. 1974. *On Liberty*. Harmondsworth: Penguin.

Miller, David. 2004. "Information Dominance: The Philosophy of Total Propaganda Control?" In *War, Media, and Propaganda: A Global Perspective*, ed. Yahya R. Kamalipour and Nancy Snow, 7–16. Lanham: Rowman & Litlefield.

Miller, Peter, and Ted O'Leary. 2002. "Rethinking the Factory: Caterpillar Inc." *Cultural Values* 6 1–2:91–117.

Miller, Toby. 1993. *The Well-Tempered Self: Citizenship, Culture, and the Postmodern Subject*. Baltimore: The Johns Hopkins University Press.

Miller, Toby, Geoffrey Lawrence, Jim McKay, and David Rowe. 2001. *Globalization and Sport: Playing the World*. London: Sage.

Miller, Toby, Nitin Govil, John McMurria, Richard Maxwell, and Ting Wang. 2005. *Global Hollywood 2*. London: British Film Institute.

Miller, Toby, and George Yúdice. 2004. *Política Cultural*, trans. Gabriela Ventureira. Barcelona: Editorial Gedisa.

Milmo, Dan. 2001. "Carlton Axes Taste Network." *Guardian*, August 10.

Ministry of Defence. 2003. *Operations in Iraq: Lessons for the Future*.

Minow, Martha. 2003. "Fragments or Ties? In *The Defense of Difference*." *The Fractious Nation? Unity and Division in American Life*, ed. Jonathan Rieder, assoc. ed. Stephen Steinlight, 67–78. Berkeley: University of California Press.

Minow, Newton N. 1971. "The Broadcasters are Public Trustees." In *Radio & Television: Readings in the Mass Media*, ed. Allen Kirschener and Linda Kirschener, 207–17. New York: Odyssey Press.

Minow, Newton N. 2001. "Television, More Vast than Ever, Turns Toxic." *USA Today*, May 9: 15A.

Minow, Newton N., and Fred H. Cate. 2003. "Revisiting the Vast Wasteland." *Federal Communications Law Journal* 55:407–40.

Mintz, Sidney W. 1993. "Feeding, Eating, and Grazing: Some Speculations on Modern Food Habits." *Journal of Gastronomy* 7 (1): 46–57.

Mitchell, Greg. 2004. "Why the "Washington Post" Inside Story on Iraq Pre-War Coverage Falls Short." *Editor & Publisher*, August 18.

Mitchell, Greg. 2005. "Media Fell Short in Covering 9/11 'Report Card'." *Editor & Publisher*, December 6.

Mitchell, Katharyne. 2003. "Educating the National Citizen in Neoliberal Times. From the Multicultural Self to the Strategic Cosmopolitan." *Transactions of the Institute of British Geographers* 28 (4): 387–403.

Modak, Frida. 2001. "Introducción: La gran interrogante." In *11 de septiembre de 2001*, ed. Frida Modak, 3–4. Buenos Aires: Grupo Editorial Lumen.

Moeller, Susan D. 1999. *Compassion Fatigue: How the Media Sell Disease, Famine, War and Death*. New York: Routledge.

Moeller, Susan D. 2004a. *Media Coverage of Weapons of Mass Destruction*. Center for International and Security Studies at Maryland.

Moeller, Susan D. 2004b. "A Moral Imagination: The Media's Response to the War on Terrorism." In *Reporting War: Journalism in Wartime*, ed. Stuart Allan and Barbie Zelizer, 59–76. London: Routledge.

Mohanty, Sachidananda, and Homi Bhabha. 2005. "Towards a Cultural Citizenship." *The Hindu*, July 3.

Moisy, Claude. 1997. "Myths of the Global Information Village." *Foreign Policy* 107:78–88.

Mokhiber, Russell, and Robert Weissman. 2003a. "Too Much." *Common Dreams News Center*, February 26. http://www.commondreams.org.

Mokhiber, Russell, and Robert Weissman. 2003b. "Christian Fundamentalists to Produce Iraqi News." *AlterNet*, May 2. http://www.alternet.org.

Monastersky, Richard. 2005. "Congressman Demands Complete Records on Climate Research by 3 Scientists Who Support Theory of Global Warming." *Chronicle of Higher Education*, July 1.

Monbiot, George. 2003. *The Age of Consent: A Manifesto for a New World Order*. London: Flamingo.

Monmonier, Mark. 1999. *Air Apparent: How Meteorologists Learned to Map, Predict and Dramatize Weather*. Chicago: University of Chicago Press.

Mooney, Chris. 2004. "Blinded by Science." *Columbia Journalism Review*, November/December.

Mooney, Chris. 2005. "Some Like it Hot." *Mother Jones*, May/June: 36–49.

Morgan, Kevin, and Adrian Morley in association with Powys Food Links, The Soil Association, and Sustain. 2002. *Relocalising the Food Chain: The Role of Creative Public Procurement*. The Regeneration Institute, Cardiff University.

Morris, Bob. 2003. "'Hi, I'm your Waiter, and this is Reality'." *New York Times*, May 11.

Morris, David. 2003. "Genetic Resistance." *ABCNews.Com*, July 15. http://www.abcnews.com.

Morrow, Lance. 1996. "The Religion of Big Weather." *Time*, January 22: 72.

Mosco, Vincent. 2004. *The Digital Sublime: Myth, Power, and Cyberspace*. Cambridge, MA: Massachussetts Institute of Technology Press.

Moses, Lucia. 2003. "What's in a Deadline?" *Editor & Publisher*, March 25.

Mosisa, Abraham T. 2002. "The Role of Foreign-Born Workers in the U.S. Economy." *Monthly Labor Review*, May: 3–14.

Mother Jones. 2003. "News." *MotherJones.com*. March 25.

Mouffe, Chantal, ed. 1992. *Dimensions of Radical Democracy: Pluralism, Citizenship, Community*. London: Verso.

Mouffe, Chantal. 1993. *The Return of the Political*. London: Verso.

Mowlana, Hamid. 2000. "The Renewal of the Global Media Debate: Implications for the Relationship between the West and the Islamic World." In *Islam and the West in the Mass Media: Fragmented Images in a Globalizing World*, ed. Kai Hafez, 105–18. Cresskill: Hampton Press.

Mukhia, Harbans. 2002. "Liberal Democracy and its Slippages." *Economic and Political Weekly*, January 19.

Mullen, Megan. 2002. "The Fall and Rise of Cable Narrowcasting." *Convergence* 8 (1): 62–83.

Mullen, Megan. 2003. *The Rise of Cable Programming in the United States: Revolution or Evolution?* Austin: University of Texas Press.

Mullen, Megan. 2004. "Food Network: U.S. Cable Network." In *Museum of Broadcast Communications Encyclopedia of Television*, 2nd ed., ed. Horace Newcomb, 893–94. New York: Fitzroy Dearborn.

Mullen, Megan. 2005. "Television's Gated Communities." *Flow: A Critical Forum on Television and Media Culture* 2 3.

Multichannel News. 1999. "New York—Food Network's." July 12: 66.

Multichannel News. 2003. "Rethinking Food TV." November 24.

Multichannel News. 2005. "Blizzard Helps Weather Blanket Jan. 22 Nielsens." January 31: 10.

Murdock, Graham. 1997. "The Re-Enchantment of the World: Religion and the Transformations of Modernity." In *Rethinking Media, Religion, and Culture*, ed. S. M. Hoover and K. Lundby, 85–101. London: Sage Publications.

Murdock, Graham. 2005. "Public Broadcasting and Democratic Culture: Consumers, Citizens, and Communards." In *A Companion to Television*, ed. Janet Wasko, 174–98. Malden: Blackwell.

Murphy, Gael. 2005. "The Guards are Sleeping." *AlterNet*, May 2. http://www.alternet.org.

Murphy, Sophia, Ben Lilliston, and Mary Beth Lake. 2005. *WTO Agreement on Agriculture: A Decade of Dumping*. Minneapolis: Institute for Agriculture and Trade Policy.

Murray, Susan, and Laurie Ouellette. 2004. "Introduction." In *Reality TV: Remaking Television Culture*, ed. Susan Murray and Laurie Ouellette, 1–18. New York: New York University Press.

Murrow, Edward R. 1958. Speech to the Radio-Television News Directors Association, Chicago, October 15.

Muschamp, Herbert. 2004. "The New Arcadia." *New York Times*, August 29: 224.

Nader, Ralph. 2003. "MSNBC Sabotages Donahue." *Common Dreams News Center*, March 3. http://www.commondreams.org.

Nahdi, Fuad. 2003. "Doublespeak: Islam and the Media." *openDemocracy*, April 3. http://www.opendemocracy.net.

Nairn, Tom. 2003. "Democracy & Power: American Power & the World." *openDemocracy*, January 9, 16, and 23; February 4 and 20. http://www.opendemocracy.net.

Nakai, Katosha Belvin. 2003. "When Kachinas and Coal Collide: Can Cultural Resources Rescue the Hopi at Black Mesa?" *Arizona State Law Journal* 35:1283–1330.

Nandy, Ashis. 1998. *Exiled at Home*. New Delhi: Oxford University Press.

The National Academies. 2005. *Understanding and Responding to Climate Change: Highlights of National Academies Reports*.

National Environment Research Council. 2005. "Bleak First Results from the World's Largest Climate Change Experiment." January 26.

National Public Radio. 1995. "Who Watches the Weather Channel and Why?" *Morning Edition*, September 7.

National Weather Association. 2005. "NWA History." http://nwas.org.

Naureckas, Jim. 2004. "POWs on TV a War Crime?" *EXTRA!Update*, February: 1.

Naureckas, Jim. 2005. "*Newsweek* and the Real Rules of Journalism." *EXTRA!* July/August: 11–13.

Navasky, Victor. 2002. Forward to *Journalism after September 11*. by Barbie Zelizer and Stuart Allan, eds. London: Routledge.

el-Nawawy, Mohammed, and Leo A. Gher. 2003. "Al Jazeera: Bridging the East-West Gap Through Public Discourse and Media Diplomacy." *Transnational Broadcasting Studies* 10.

Negra, Diane. 2002. "Ethnic Food Fetishism, Whiteness, and Nostalgia in Film and Television." *Velvet Light Trap* 50:62–76.

Nestle, Marion. 2002. *Food Politics: How the Food Industry Influences Nutrition and Health*. Berkeley: University of California Press.

New Straits Times. 2003a. "Case for Global Alternate Media." October 18: 14.

New Straits Times. 2003b. "Full Interview with Dr Mahathir." April 6: 2.

New York Times. 1990. "A Campus Forum on Multiculturalism." December 9: 5.

New York Times. 2000. "Hispanic and Asian Populations Expand." August 30: A16.

New Yorker. 2001. "Battle Stations." December 10.

News Today. 2005. "Junk the Junk Food." February 24.

Newell, Peter. 2001. "Environmental NGOs, TNCs, and the Question of Governance." In *The International Political Economy of the Environment: Critical Perspectives*, ed. Dimitris Stevis and Valeire J. Assetto, 85–107. Boulder: Lynne Rienner.

Newport, Frank, and Joseph Carroll. 2003. "Support for Bush Significantly Higher Among More Religious Americans." *Gallup Poll Analyses*, March 6.

Newsweek. 2004. "Perspectives." July 5: 21.

Nichols, John. 2003. "Many Americans Follow War on BBC." *Madison Capital Times*, May 9.

Nichols, John, and Robert W. McChesney. 2003. "FCC: Public Be Damned." *The Nation* 276 (June 2): 5–6.

Nichols, John, and Robert W. McChesney. 2005. "Bush's War on the Press." *The Nation* 281 (December 5): 8–9.

Nisbet, Erik C., and James Shanahan. 2004. *MSRG Special Report: Restrictions on Civil Liberties, Views of Islam, & Muslim Americans*. Media & Society Research Group, Cornell University.

Nixon, Rob. 2005. "Our Tools of War, Turned Blindly Against Ourselves." *Chronicle of Higher Education*, February 18: B7–B10.

Non Resident Indians Online. 2001. "Dual Citizenship for People of Indian Origin." January 26. http://nriol.com.

Norris, Pippa, and Ronald Inglehart. 2003. "Public Opinion Among Muslims and the West." In *Framing Terrorism: The News Media, the Government, and the Public*, ed. Pippa Norris, Montague Kern, and Marion Just, 203–28. New York: Routledge.

O'Malley, Pat. 2001. "Discontinuity, Government and Risk: A Response to Rigakos and Hadden." *Theoretical Criminology* 5 (1): 85–92.

O'Neill, Molly. 2003. "Food Porn." *Columbia Journalism Review* 5.

Observatoire de la Finance and the United Nations Institute for Training and Research. 2003. *Economic and Financial Globalization: What the Numbers Say*. New York: United Nations.

Ocampo, José Antonio. 2005. "Globalization, Development and Democracy." *Items and Issues* 5 (3): 11–20.

Office of the United States Trade Representative. 2001. *The President's 2000 Annual Report on the Trade Agreements Program*. Washington.

Oliver, Raymond. 1969. *La Cuisine: Secrets of Modern French Cooking*, trans. and ed. Nika Standen Hazelton with Jack van Bibber. New York: Tudor.

Olsson, Karen. 2002. "The Shame of Meatpacking." *The Nation* 275 (September 16): 11–16.

OMB Watch. "Congressional Report Uncovers Chemical Security Risks Throughout the Country." 2005. *OMB Watcher* 6, no. 14.

On the Media. 2002. "Did 9/11 Change Foreign News?" National Public Radio, March 9.

Ong, Aihwa. 1999. *Flexible Citizenship: The Cultural Logics of Transnationality*. Durham: Duke University Press.

Ortiz, Jon. 2005. "Fans Hold Court on Skullcaps, NBA's Culture Clash." *Sacramento Bee*, January 29: A1.

Osborn, Andrew, and Brown, Paul. 2002. "Dutch Cabinet Resigns over Srebrenica." *Manchester Guardian Weekly*, May 1.

Ottosen, Rune. 2004. "Mr. President: 'The Enemy is Closer than You Might Think'." In *U.S. and the Others: Global Media Images on "The War on Terror,"* ed. Stig A. Nohrstedt and Rune Ottosen, 107–29. Göteborg: NORDICOM.

Palast, Greg. 2003a. *The Best Democracy Money Can Buy: An Investigative Reporter Exposes the Truth About Globalization, Corporate Cons, and High-Finance Fraudsters*. New York: Plume.

Palast, Greg. 2003b. "Hugo Chavez is Crazy!" *AlterNet*, June 25. http://www.alternet.org.

Parameswaran, Radhika. 2006. "Military Metaphors, Masculine Modes, and Critical Commentary." *Journal of Communication Inquiry* 30 (1): 42–64.

Paramio, Ludolfo. 2002. "Sin Confianza no hay Democracia: Electores e Identidades Políticas." In *Globalización, Identiday y Democracia: México y América Latina*, ed. Julio Labastida Martín del Campo and Antonio Camou, 25–42. Mexico: Siglo Veintiuno Editores.

Parekh, Bhikhu. 2000. *Rethinking Multiculturalism: Cultural Diversity and Political Theory*. Basingstoke: Palgrave.

Parekh, Bhikhu. 2001. "Reporting on a Report." Keynote Address to the Political Studies Association of the United Kingdom.

Parekh, Bhikhu, Stuart Hall, and Tariq Modood. 2000. "In Response." *Journal of Ethnic and Migration Studies* 26 (4): 734–37.

Parenti, Christian. 2004. "Al Jazeera Goes to Jail." *The Nation* 278 (March 29): 20–23.

Parker, Philip M. 1995. *Climatic Effects on Individual, Social, and Economic Behavior: A Physioeconomic Review of Research Across Disciplines*. Westport: Greenwood Press.

Patagonia. 2004. http://www.patagonia.com.

Paterson, Chris. 2005. "They Shoot Journalists, Don't They?" *AlterNet*, February 15. http://www.alternet.org.

Paterson, Matthew. 1996. *Global Warming and Global Politics*. London: Routledge.

Payne, Kenneth. 2005. "The Media as an Instrument of War." *Parameters: US Army War College Quarterly*, Spring: 81–93.

Pearce, Richard, and Maria Hansson. 2000. "Retailing and Risk Society: Genetically Modified Food." *International Journal of Retail & Distribution Management* 28 (11): 450–58.

Pelikan, Jaroslav. 2005. "General Introduction: The Press as an Institution of American Constitutional Democracy." In *The Press*, ed. Geneva Overholser and Kathleen Hall Jamieson, xvii–xxiv. Oxford: Oxford University Press.

Pellow, David Naguib, and Lisa Sun-Hee Park. 2002. *The Silicon Valley of Dreams: Environmental Injustice, Immigrant Workers, and the High-Tech Global Economy*. New York: New York University Press.

Pépin, Jacques. 1996. *Jacques Pépin's Kitchen: Cooking with Claudine*. San Francisco: KQED Books & Tapes.

Perkins, John. 2004. *Confessions of an Economic Hit Man*. San Francisco: Berrett-Koehler.

Peterson, Christopher. 2004. "Preface." *Annals of the American Academy of Political and Social Science* 591:6–12.

Petrini, Carlo. 2001. *Slow Food: The Case for Taste*, trans. William McCuaig. New York: Columbia University Press.

Petrini, Carlo. 2002. "Slow Down: The Return to Local Food." *Demos Collection* 18:25–30.

Pew Center for Global Climate Change. 2002. *Pew Center Analysis of President Bush's February 14th Climate Change Plan*.

Pew Charitable Trusts. 2002a. *Return to Normalcy? How the Media Have Covered the War on Terrorism*.

Pew Charitable Trusts. 2002b. *Public's News Habits Little Changes [sic] by September 11*.

Pew Fellowships in International Journalism. 2002. *International News and the Media: The Impact of September 11*.

Pew Forum on Religion & Public Life. 2004a. *The American Religious Landscape and Politics, 2004*.

Pew Forum on Religion & Public Life. 2004b. *Religion and the Environment: Polls Show Strong Backing for Environmental Protection Across Religious Groups*.

Pew Global Attitudes Project. 2005. *American Character Gets Mixed Reviews*.

Pew International Journalism Program. 2002. *America and the World: The Impact of September 11 on U.S. Coverage of International News*.

Pew Internet & American Life Project. 2002. *One Year Later: September 11 and the Internet*.

Pew Internet & American Life Project. 2003a. *The Internet and the Iraq War*.

Pew Internet & American Life Project. 2003b. *Consumption of Information Goods and Services in the United States*.

Pew Internet & American Life Project. 2004. *Faith Online*.

Pew Research Center. 2005. *Trends 2005*.

Pew Research Center for the People & the Press. 2002a. *What the World Thinks in 2002: How Global Publics View: Their Lives, Their Countries, America*.

Pew Research Center for the People & the Press. 2002b. *Among Wealthy Nations . . . U.S. Stands Alone in its Embrace of Religion*.

Pew Research Center for the People & the Press. 2003a. *Polls in Close Agreement on Public Views of War*.

Pew Research Center for the People & the Press. 2003b. *Different Faiths, Different Messages*.

Pew Research Center for the People & the Press. 2003c. *Views of a Changing World June 2003*.

Pew Research Center for the People & the Press. 2003d. *Strong Opposition to Media Cross-Ownership Emerges Public Wants Neutrality and Pro-American Point of View*.

Pew Research Center for the People & the Press. 2003e. *Broad Opposition to Genetically Modified Foods—Modest Transatlantic Gap*.

Pew Research Center for the People & the Press. 2004a. *A Global Generation Gap: Adapting to a New World*.

Pew Research Center for the People & the Press. 2004b. *Mistrust of America in Europe Ever Higher, Muslim Anger Persists*.

Pew Research Center for the People & the Press. 2004c. *Religion and the Presidential Vote*.

Pew Research Center for the People & the Press. 2004d. *Trouble Behind, Trouble Ahead? A Year of Contention at Home and Abroad. 2003 Year-End Report*.

Pew Research Center for the People & the Press. 2005a. *Global Opinion: The Spread of Anti-Americanism*.

Pew Research Center for the People & the Press. 2005b. *The Internet and Campaign 2004*.

Phillips, Peter. 2005. "Big Media Interlocks with Corporate America." *Mediachannel.org*, June 27. http://www.mediachannel.org.

Piccalo, Gina. 2004. "The Pitch That You Won't See Coming." *Los Angeles Times*, August 22: E1, E26.

Pilger, John. 2003. "We See Too Much. We Know Too Much. That's Our Best Defense." *Independent*, April 6.

Pinter, Harold. 2005a. "Art, Truth and Politics." *Guardian*, December 8.

Pinter, Harold. 2005b. "Art, Truth and Politics." Nobel Lecture – Literature 2005. http://nobelprize.org/nobel_prizes/literature/laureates/2005/pinter-lecture-e.html.

Plato. 1972. *The Laws*, trans. Trevor J. Saunders. Harmondsworth: Penguin.

Polan, Dana. 2001. *Jane Campion*. London: British Film Institute.

Polanyi, Karl. 2001. *The Great Transformation: The Political and Economic Origins of Our Time*. Boston: Beacon Press.

Political Economy Research Institute. 2004. *The Misfortune 100: Top Corporate Air Polluters in the United States*.

Pollard, Jason. 2003. "Common Entrance Exams." *Index on Censorship* 32 (2): 70–81.

Pollitt, Katha. 2001. "Victory Gardens?!" *The Nation* 273 (November 19): 10.

Porges, Seth. 2003. "Bush 9/11 Admission Gets Little Play." *Editor & Publisher*, September 19.

Porterfield, Jim. 1999. "Pépin's Hands-On Cuisine." *Hemispheres*, October: 149.

Portes, Alejandro. 2001. "Introduction: The Debates and Significance of Immigrant Transnationalism." *Global Networks* 1 (3): 181–93.

Post, Diahanna L. 2005. "Standards and Regulatory Capitalism: The Diffusion of Food Safety Standards in Developing Countries." *Annals of the American Academy of Political and Social Science* 598:168–83.

Postfarm. 2004. "Fuck the Weather Channel." 2004. http://postfarm.net.

Postrel, Virginia. 1999. "The Pleasures of Persuasion." *Wall Street Journal*, August 2.

Postrel, Virginia. 2003. *The Substance of Style: How the Rise of Aesthetic Value is Remaking Commerce, Culture, and Consciousness*. New York: HarperCollins.

Power, Michael. 2004. *The Risk Management of Everything: Rethinking the Politics of Uncertainty*. London: Demos.

PR Newswire. 1999. "Scripps October Revenues Increase 8.7 Percent." November 8.

PR Newswire. 2001. "The Weather Channel Delivers Afghanistan Weather On-Air and Online." November 13.

Preuss, U. K. 1998. "Migration—A Challenge to Modern Citizenship." *Constellations* 4 (3): 307–19.

Program on International Policy Attitudes and Knowledge Networks. 2003. *Misperceptions, the Media and the Iraq War*.

Program on International Policy Attitudes and Knowledge Networks. 2004a. *Americans on Climate Change*.

Program on International Policy Attitudes and Knowledge Networks. 2004b. *Americans on Globalization, Trade, and Farm Subsidies*.

Program on International Policy Attitudes and Knowledge Networks. 2004c. *Americans and Iraq on the Eve of the Presidential Election.*

Program on International Policy Attitudes and Knowledge Networks. 2004d. *US Public Beliefs on Iraq and the Presidential Elections.*

Program on International Policy Attitudes. 2005. *Overwhelming Majority of Americans Favors US Joining with G8 Members to Limit Greenhouse Gas Emissions.*

Project for Excellence in Journalism and Committee of Concerned Journalists. 2000. *A Question of Character: How the Media Have Handled the Issue and How the Public Has Reacted.* Pew Charitable Trusts.

Project for Excellence in Journalism. 2002. *The War on Terrorism: The Not-So-New Television News Landscape.*

Project for Excellence in Journalism. 2005. *The State of the News Media: An Annual Report on American Journalism.*

Public Citizen. 2001. "Nuking Food: Irradiation Raises Safety Concerns." 21 (1): 13.

Purcell, Mark. 2003. "Citizenship and the Right to the Global City: Reimagining the Capitalist World Order." *International Journal of Urban and Regional Research* 27 (3): 564–90.

Putnam, Robert D. 2000. *Bowling Alone: The Collapse and Revival of American Community.* New York: Simon & Schuster.

Putnam, Robert D. 2001. "A Better Society in a Time of War." *New York Times*, October 19.

Quaccia, Jon. 2004. "Big Business and Labor Working Hand in Hand." *Alternative Press Review*, August 12.

Radelet, Steven. 2005. "Think Again: U.S. Forcign Aid." *Foreign Policy,* February. http://www .foreignpolicy.com.

Raines, Howell. 2002. Forward to *Out of the Blue: The Story of September 11, 2001 from Jihad to Ground Zero,* by Richard Bernstein and the Staff of *The New York Times.* New York: Times Books.

Rajagopal, Arvind. 2002. "Violence of Commodity Aesthetics." *Economic and Political Weekly*, January 5.

Rampton, Sheldon, and John Stauber. 2003. *Weapons of Mass Deception: The Uses of Propaganda in Bush's War on Iraq.* New York: Jeremy P Tarcher/Penguin.

RAND Corporation. 2005. "RAND Study Links Higher Prices for Fruits and Vegetables to Excess Weight Gain Among School Children."

Randle, Quint, and Jeremy Mordock. 2002. "How Radio is Adapting Weather to the Web: A Study of Weather Strategies on Local News/Talk Radio, Television, and Newspaper Home Pages." *Journal of Radio Studies* 9 (2): 247–58.

Raphael, Chad. 2004. "The Political Economic Origins of Reali-TV." In *Reality TV: Remaking Television Culture*, ed. Susan Murray and Laurie Ouellette, 119–36. New York: New York University Press.

Raphael, Chad, Lori Tokunaga, and Christina Wai. 2004. "Who is the Real Target? Media Response to Controversial Investigative Reporting on Corporations." *Journalism Studies* 5 (2): 165–78.

Ravo, Nick. 1999. "Clint Youle, 83, Early Weatherman on TV." *New York Times*, July 31: B7.

Rawls, John. 1971. *A Theory of Justice.* Cambridge, MA: The Belknap Press of Harvard University Press.

Raynolds, Laura T. 2003. "Forging New Local/Global Links through Fair Trade Agro-Food Networks." In *Globalization, Localization, and Sustainable Livelihoods*, ed. Reidar Almås and Geoffrey Lawrence, 57–68. Aldershot: Ashgate.

RCR Wireless News. 2005. "Weather Channel Launches Video Service with Sprint PCS." March 21: 18.

Reiter, Ester. 1996. *Making Fast Food: From the Frying Pan into the Fryer*, Second ed. Montreal: McGill-Queen's University Press.

Rendall, Steve. 2003. "Dissent, Disloyalty & Double Standards." *EXTRA!Update*, May–June.

Rendall, Steve, and Daniel Butterworth. 2004. "How Public is Public Radio?" *EXTRA!* May–June: 16–19.

Rendall, Steve, and Tara Broughel. 2003. "Amplifying Officials, Squelching Dissent." *EXTRA!Update*, May/June.

Rensi, Edward H. 1995. Forward to *Opportunities in Fast Food Careers*, by Marjorie Eberts, Margaret Gisler, and Linda Brothers, eds. Lincolnwood: VGM Career Horizons.

Reporters sans Frontières. 2003. www.rsf.org.

Reuters. 2003a. "Al Jazeera Banned from NYSE Floor." March 25.

Reuters. 2003b. "Search for WMD Finds 'Bomb' on Internet." July 4.

Revkin, Andrew C. 1999. "Gaze Deeply into My Eye." *New York Times*, September 17: B1, B9.

Revkin, Andrew C. 2001. "Weather Forecasters Look Ahead, Far Ahead." *New York Times*, November 13: F1.

Revkin, Andrew C. 2003. "Experts Fault Bush's Proposal to Examine Climate Change." *New York Times*, February 26.

Reynolds, Amy, and Brooke Barnett. 2003. "This Just in . . . How National TV News Handled the Breaking 'Live' Coverage of September 11." *Journalism & Mass Communication Quarterly* 80 (3): 689–703.

Reynolds, Mike. 1999. "Sports and Weather are Ops Favorite Viewing." *Cable World*, February 1.

Reynolds, Mike. 2003. "Local Weather Forecast: Enhancements Due." *Multichannel News*, December 15: 8.

Reynolds, Paul. 2005. "White Phosphorous: Weapon on the Edge." *BBC News Online*, November 16. http://news.bbc.co.uk.

Rich, Andrew, and R. Kent Weaver. 2000. "Think Tanks in the U.S. Media." *Harvard Journal of Press/Politics* 5 (4): 81–103.

Rich, Frank. 2004. "It was the Porn that Made Them do It." *New York Times*, May 30.

Rich, Vera. 2003. "The Price of Return." *Index on Censorship* 32 (3): 82–86.

Richmond, Ray. 2005. "'Super Size Me' Star Cooks Food for Thought." *Hollywood Reporter*, June 14–20: 15.

Rieder, Jonathan. 2003. "Getting a Fix on Fragmentation: 'Breakdown' as Estimation Error, Rhetorical Strategy, and Organizational Accomplishment." In *The Fractious Nation? Unity and Division in American Life*, ed. Jonathan Rieder, assoc. ed. Stephen Steinlight, 13–54. Berkeley: University of California Press.

Rifkin, Jeremy. 2002. "The World's Problems on a Plate." *Guardian*, May 17.

Ritzer, George. 1993. *The McDondaldization of Society: An Investigation into the Changing Character of Contemporary Social Life*. Thousand Oaks: Pine Forge Press.

Roberts, Les, Riyadh Lafta, Richard Garfield, Jamal Khuhairi, and Gilbert Burnham. 2004. "Mortality Before and After the 2003 Invasion of Iraq: Cluster Sample Survey." *The Lancet* 364:1857–64.

Robertson, Craig. 2003. *"Passport Please": The U.S. Passport and the Documentation of Individual Identity, 1845–1930*. PhD diss., University of Illinois.

Robinson, Piers. 2004. "Researching US Media-State Relations and Twenty-First Century Wars." In *Reporting War: Journalism in Wartime*, ed. Stuart Allan and Barbie Zelizer, 96–112. London: Routledge.

Robinson, Piers, Robin Brown, Peter Goddard, and Katy Parry. 2005. "War and Media." *Media, Culture & Society* 27 (6): 951–59.

Rodgers, Jayne. 2003. "Icons and Invisibility: Gender, Myth, 9/11." In *War and the Media: Reporting Conflict 24/7*, ed. Daya Kishan Thussu and Des Freedman, 200–12. London: Sage Publications.

Rodriguez, Roberto, and Patrisia Gonzales. 1995. "Cultural Idea for Citizenship is Catching on." *Fresno Bee*, May 15: B5.

Rogers, Daniel. 2002. "McDonald's to Rethink Brand Messages in UK." *Marketing*, October 17: 1.

Rogers, Patrick. 2001. "Drawing the Line." *People*, July 23: 50.

Roker, Al. 2002. "Weather Whiners." *New York Times*, April 7: CY15.

Romano, Allison. 2004. "Wants a Bigger Slice." *Broadcasting & Cable*, September 6: 10–12.

Rondinelli, Dennis A. 2002. "Transnational Corporations: International Citizens or New Sovereigns?" *Business and Society Review* 107 (4): 391–413.

Roosevelt, Franklin Delano. 1937. "Second Inaugural Address."

Rorty, Amélie Oksenberg. 1995. "Rights: Educational, not Cultural." *Social Research* 62 (1): 161–70.

Rosaldo, Renato. 1994. "Cultural Citizenship and Educational Democracy." *Cultural Anthropology* 9 (3): 402–11.

Rosaldo, Renato. 1997. "Cultural Citizenship, Inequality, and Multiculturalism." In *Latino Cultural Citizenship: Claiming Identity, Space, and Politics*, ed. William V. Flores and Rina Benmayor, 27–38. Boston: Beacon Press.

Rosen, Jay. 2002. "September 11 in the Mind of American Journalism." In *Journalism after September 11*, ed. Barbie Zelizer and Stuart Allan, 27–35. London: Routledge.

Ross, Andrew. 1991. *Strange Weather: Culture, Science and Technology in the Age of Limits*. London: Verso.

Rotzer, Florian. 2003. "The World is What the Media Reports." *Telepolis*, January 7.

Rousseau, Jean-Jacques. 1975. *The Social Contract and Discourses*, trans. G. D. H. Cole. London: J. M. Dent.

Roy, Anupama. 2001. "Community, Women Citizens and a Women's Politics." In *Community and Identities: Contemporary Discourses on Culture and Politics in India*, ed. Surinder S. Jodhka, 239–59. New Delhi: Sage.

Roy, Arundhati. 2001. "The Algebra of Infinite Justice." *Guardian*, September 29.

Roy, Arundhati. 2004. "Do Turkeys Enjoy Thanksgiving?" *OutlookIndia.com*, January 24. http://www.outlookindia.com.

Runnymede Trust Commission. 2000. *The Future of Multi-Ethnic Britain*. London: Profile.

Rusciano, Frank Louis. 2003. "Framing World Opinion in the Elite Press." In *Framing Terrorism: The News Media, the Government, and the Public*, ed. Pippa Norris, Montague Kern, and Marion Just, 159–79. New York: Routledge.

Ruskin, Gary, and Juliet Schor. 2005. "Junk Food Nation." *The Nation* 281 (August 29): 15–17.

Rutenberg, Jim. 2003. "Newspapers: Words Reflect Changing Report." *New York Times*, March 25.

Saad, Lydia. 2003a. "Americans Foresee Energy Shortage within 5 Years." *Gallup News Service*, March 13.

Saad, Lydia. 2003b. "Public Balks at Obesity Lawsuits." *Gallup News Service*, July 21.

Said, Edward. 2001. "We all Swim Together." *New Statesman*, October 15: 20.

Said, Edward. 2003a. "The Other America." *Al-Ahram*, March 20–26.

Said, Edward. 2003b. "Blind Imperial Arrogance: Vile Stereotyping of Arabs by the U.S. Ensures Years of Turmoil." *Los Angeles Times*, July 20.

Sanbonmatsu, John. 2001. "Letter." *New York Times*, October 25.

Sanders, Lisa. 2005a. "McDonald's Unveils Global Ad Campaign Aimed at Children." *Advertising Age*, March 8.

Sanders, Lisa. 2005b. "Global Ad Spending to Rise 6% in 2006." *Advetising Age*, December 5.

Sandford, Alasdair. 2005. "French Row Over Charity Pork Soup." *BBC News Online*, December 23. http://news.bbc.co.uk.

Sarat, Austin. 2001. *When the State Kills: Capital Punishment and the American Condition*. Princeton: Princeton University Press.

Sardar, Ziauddin, and Merryl Wyn Davies. 2002. *Why do People Hate America?* Cambridge: Icon Books.

Sarlo, Beatriz. 2001. "Ser Argentino: Ya nada Será Igual." In *Imaginarios de Nación: Pensar en Medio de la Tormenta*, ed. Jesús Martin-Barbero, 47–53. Bogotá: Ministerio de Cultura.

Sattar, M. G. 2001. "Responses to Franck Amalric." *Development* 44 (4): 12.

Saunders, Edward M., Jr. 1993. "Stock Prices and Wall Street Weather." *American Economic Review* 83 (5): 1337–45.

Scardino, Albert. 2005. "Sun Sets on US Broadcast Golden Age." *Guardian*, March 9.

Schatz, Roland. 2003. Forward to *Media Wars: News at a Time of Terror*, by Danny Schechter. Lanham: Rowman & Littlefield.

Schechter, Danny. 2003a. "The Media, the War and our Right to Know." *AlterNet*, May 1. http://www.alternet.org.

Schechter, Danny. 2003b. *Media Wars: News at a Time of Terror*. Lanham: Rowman & Littlefield.

Schechter, Danny. 2005a. "Independent Press was a Target in Iraq." *Media Channel*, February 28. http://www.mediachannel.org.

Schechter, Danny. 2005b. "Fighting for the Op-Edisphere." *TomPaine.com*, April 9. http://www.tompaine.com.

Schechter, Danny, and Aliza Dichter. 2003. "The Role of CNN." In *Media Wars: News at a Time of Terror*, by Danny Schechter, 46–50. Lanham: Rowman & Littlefield.

Schell, Jonathan. 2003. "The New American Order." *The Nation* 277 (July 7): 7.

Schell, Jonathan. 2005. "Faking Civil Society." *The Nation* 280 (April 25): 6.

Scherer, Glenn. 2004. "The Goldy Must be Crazy." *Grist Magazine*, October 27. http://www.grist.org.

Schiller, Herbert I. 2000. *Living in the Number One Country: Reflections from a Critic of American Empire*. New York: Seven Stories Press.

Schillinger, Liesl. 1999. "Ming's Thing: How to Become a Celebrity Chef." *New Yorker*, November 15: 60–67.

Schlesinger, Arthur, Jr. 1991. *The Disuniting of America*. Knoxville: Whittle Direct Books.

Schlesinger, Arthur, Jr. 2003. "Today, it is we Americans who Live in Infamy." *Los Angeles Times*, March 23.

Schlesinger, Philip, Graham Murdock, and Philip Elliott. 1983. *Televising "Terrorism": Political Violence in Popular Culture*. London: Comedia/Marion Boyars.

Schlosser, Eric. 2001. *Fast Food Nation: The Dark Side of the All-American Meal*. Boston: Houghton Mifflin.

Schmitt, Eric. 2005. "New U.S. Commander Sees Shift in Military Role in Iraq." *New York Times*, January 16: 10.

Schonfeld, Reese. 2002. "Artful Dodging: TV Accounting Methods." *Electronic Media*, July 22: 10.

Schrambling, Regina. 2004. "Julia Child, the French Chef for a Jell-O Nation, Dies at 91." *New York Times*, August 13.

Schudson, Michael. 1998. *The Good Citizen: A History of American Civic Life*. Cambridge, MA: Harvard University Press.

Schudson, Michael, and Susan E. Tifft. 2005. "American Journalism in Historical Perspective." In *The Press*, ed. Geneva Overholser and Kathleen Hall Jamieson, 17–47. Oxford: Oxford University Press.

Schweder, Richard A., Martha Minow, and Hazel Rose Markus. 2002. "Introduction: Engaging Cultural Differences." In *Engaging Cultural Differences: The Multicultural Challenge in Liberal Democracies*, ed. Richard A. Schweder, Martha Minow, and Hazel Rose Markus. New York: Russell Sage Foundation. 1–13.

Seabrook, John. 2000. "Selling the Weather." *New Yorker*, April 3.

Seaford, Helen. 2001. "The Future of Multi-Ethnic Britain: An Opportunity Missed." *Political Quarterly* 72 (1): 107–12.

Sedgwick, Eve Kosofsky. 1990. *Epistemology of the Closet*. Berkeley: University of California Press.

Sehgal, Rashme. 2003. "State Secrets." *Television Asia*, May: 33.

Sen, Amartya. 1996. "Freedom Favors Development." *New Perspectives Quarterly* 13 (4): 23–27.

Senate Committee on Commerce, Science and Transportation Hearings. 2005. February 2.

Sexton, Sarah, Nicholas Hildyard, and Larry Lohmann. 2005. "We're a Small Island: The Greening of Intolerance." *The Corner House*.

Shafer, Jack. 2003. "POW TV." *Slate*, March 24. http://www.slate.com.

Shafir, Gershon. 1998. "Introduction: The Evolving Traditions of Citizenship." In *The Citizenship Debates: A Reader*, ed. Gershon Shafir, 1–28. Minneapolis: University of Minnesota Press.

Shah, Sudhir. 2002. "Not Much Gain in Dual Citizenship." *Economic Times New Delhi* (February 10): 13.

Shandler, Geoff. 1999. "Weather Report." *New Yorker*, July 19: 30–31.

Shapiro, Michael J. 2001. *For Moral Ambiguity: National Culture and the Politics of the Family*. Minneapolis: University of Minnesota Press.

Sharkey, Jacqueline E. 2003. "The Television War." *American Journalism Review*, May.

Sharma, Amol. 2003. "Come Home, we Need you." *Far Eastern Economic Review,* January 23: 28.

Sharma, Devinder. 2005. "Tsunamis, manglares y economía de mercado," trans. Felisa Sastre. *Rebelión*, January 14. http://www.rebelión.org.

Shaw, Randy. 1999. *Reclaiming America: Nike, Clean Air, and the New National Activism*. Berkeley: University of California Press.

Shea, Christopher. 2003. "The Last Prejudice?" *Boston Globe*, July 27: E1.

Shellenberger, Michael, and Ted Nordhaus. 2004. *The Death of Environmentalism: Global Warming Politics in a Post-Environmental World*.

Sherman, Paul, and Bill Vann. 2002. "The Pennsylvania Mine Rescue and the Human Cost of Coal." *World Socialist Web Site,* August 3. www.wsw.org/articles/2002/aug2002/mine-a03_prn.shtml.

Shils, Edward. 1966. "Mass Society and its Culture." In *Reader in Public Opinion and Communication*, 2nd ed., ed. Bernard Berelson and Morris Janowitz, 505–28. New York: Free Press; London: Collier-Macmillan.

Shiva, Vandana. 2000. *Stolen Harvest: The Hijacking of the Global Food Supply*. New Delhi: India Research Press.

Shiva, Vandana. 2002. *Water Wars: Privatization, Pollution, and Profit*. Boston: South End Press.

Shiva, Vandana. 2005. "Lecciones del tsunami para quienes menosprecian a la madre tierra." *Rebelión*, January 15. http://www.rebelión.org.

Shpiro, Shlomo. 2002. "Conflict Media Strategies and the Politics of Counter-Terrorism." *Politics* 22 (2): 76–85.

Shuman, Michael H., and Merrian Fuller. 2005. "Profits for Justice." *The Nation* 280 (January 24): 13–22.

Siegel, Tatiana. 2005. "Climate Control." *Hollywood Reporter*, July 12–18: S-6.

Silberstein, Sandra. 2002. *War of Words: Language, Politics and 9/11*. London: Routledge.

Siller, Bob, Ted White, and Hal Terkel. 1960. *Television and Radio News*. New York: Macmillan.

Simpson, John. 2005. "One of the Best." *BBC News Online*, August 8. http://news.bbc.co.uk.

Sistek, Scott. 2005. "So You Want to be a Meterologist?" *Komo 1000 News*. http://www .komotv.com.

Skocpol, Theda. 2003. "Social Provision and Civic Community: Beyond Fragmentation." In *The Fractious Nation? Unity and Division in American Life*, ed. Jonathan Rieder, assoc. ed. Stephen Steinlight. Berkeley: University of California Press. 187–205.

Skocpol, Theda. 2004. "The Narrowing of Civic Life." *American Prospect*, June: A5–A7.

Slow Food. 2003. *All About Slow Food* http://www.slowfood.com.

Smith, Chris. 2003. "A Spurious 'Smoking Gun'." *Mother Jones*, March 25. http://www .motherjones.com.

Smith, Dow. 2003. "TV News Networks Better Cure their Myopia." *Newsday*, May 6.

Smith, Lynn. 2005. "Weather is Their Only Business." *Los Angeles Times*, September 24: E1, E22.

Smith, Tom W., and Seokho Kim. 2004. *The Vanishing Protestant Majority*. National Opinion Research Center General Social Survey Report 49.

Smith-Spark, Laura. 2005. "Death of a 'TV Dinner' Salesman." *BBC News Online*, July 21. http://bbc.news.co.uk.

Smithsonian National Museum of American History. 2002. "What's Cooking?"

Smolkin, Rachel. 2003. "Are the News Media Soft on Bush?" *American Journalism Review*, October/November.

Smulyan, Susan. 1994. *Selling Radio: The Commercialization of American Broadcasting 1920–1934*. Washington: Smithsonian Institution Press.

Sólociencia. 2004. "Forum 2004: El poder educativo de la television contra los cyclones." June 4. http://www.solociencia.com.

Solomon, Norman, and Reese Erlich. 2003. *Target Iraq: What the News Media Didn't Tell You*. New York: Context Books.

Solomon, Norman. 2001a. "When Journalists Report for Duty." http://televisionarchive .alexa.com/html/article_ns2.html.

Solomon, Norman. 2001b. "Media War without End." *Z Magazine*, December. http:// zmagsite.zmag.org/curTOC.htm.

Solomon, Norman 2004. "How the News Media Stopped Worrying and Learned to Love Rumsfeld." *ZNet*, August 26. http://www.zmag.org/weluser.htm.

Sontag, Susan. 2002. "How Grief Turned into Humbug." *New Statesman*, September 16.

Soros, George. 1997. "The Capitalist Threat." *Atlantic Monthly*, February.

Sousa, Lisa. 2002. "Alternative Media Break Information Blockade." *Media File* 21 1.

Spang, Rebecca L. 2002. "On the Menu: Why More Choice isn't Better." *Demos Collection* 18:51–58.

Spanish Newswire Services. 2003. "Chile-Indigenas: Relator de la ONU se reunira con indigenas chilenos." July 18.

Spanish Newswire Services. 2004. "Foro Cultural: Ministra Espanola dice que la cultura es pilar para el desarollo." June 30.

Spigel, Lynn. 2001. *Welcome to the Dreamhouse: Popular Media and Postwar Suburbs*. Durham: Duke University Press.

Sports Illustrated. 1994. "We Noticed the Other Day that the Weather Channel has Signed on." October 31: 11.

Sproat, D. Kapura. 1998. "The Backlash Against PASH: Legislative Attempts to Restrict Native Hawaiian Rights." *University of Hawaii Law Review* 20:321–73.

Srinivas, Katta. 2002. "A Question of Citizenship." *Indiainfo.com*. http://www.indiainfo.com.

Stamler, Bernard. 2001. "The Weather Channel's New Campaign Aims for Viewers who Aren't Climate 'Fanatics'." *New York Times*, May 15.

Stanley, T. L. 2004. "Rocker Sammy Hagar Builds a Marketing Empire." *Advertising Age*, September 27.

Steinberg, Jacques. 2003. "Weblogs: Facts are in, Spin is out." New York Times, March 25.

Stephenson, Peter H. 1989. "Going to McDonald's in Leiden: Reflections on the Concept of Self and Society in the Netherlands." Ethos 17 (2): 226–47.

Sterling, Bruce. 1995. Heavy Weather. New York: Bantam.

Stevens, Jacqueline. 1999. Reproducing the State. Princeton: Princeton University Press.

Stevenson, Deborah. 2004. "'Civic Gold' Rush: Cultural Planning and the Politics of the Third Way." International Journal of Cultural Policy 10 (1): 19–31.

Stevenson, Nick. 2003. "Cultural Citizenship in the 'Cultural' Society: A Cosmopolitan Approach." Citizenship Studies 7 (3): 331–48.

Stewart, David. 1999. The PBS Companion: A History of Public Television. New York: TV Books.

Stiglitz, Joseph. 2002. "The Roaring Nineties." Atlantic Monthly 290 (3): 75–89.

Strange, Niki. 1998. "Perform, Educate, Entertain: Ingredients of the Cookery Programme Genre." In The Television Studies Book, ed. Christine Geraghty and David Lusted, 301–12. London: Arnold.

Streeter, Thomas. 1996. Selling the Air: A Critique of the Policy of Commercial Broadcasting in the United States. Chicago: University of Chicago Press.

Striffler, Steve. 2002. "Inside a Poultry Processing Plant: An Ethnographic Portrait." Labor History 43 (3): 305–13.

Struck, Doug. 1999. "Kamikaze Cook-Off." TV Guide, November 13: 32–33.

Sturken, Marita 1998. Desiring the Weather: El Niño, the Media, and Californian Identity. Los Angeles: Southern California Studies Center, University of Southern California.

Sturken, Marita. 2001. "The New Weather. Dramatic, Global, and Geeky." Chronicle of Higher Education, July 13: B4.

Suellentrop, Chris. 2003. "Al Jazeera: It's Just as Fair as CNN." Slate.com, April 2.

Summerfield, Susan. 2003. "Culinary Resources: Cookery and Culinary History Web Sites." C&RL News, November.

Surowiecki, James. 2004. "The Risk Society." New Yorker, November 15: 40.

Sutcliffe, Bob. 2003a. A More or Less Unequal World? World Income Distribution in the 20th Century. Working Paper Series 54. Amherst, MA: Political Economy Research Institute.

Sutcliffe, Bob. 2003b. "Wealth of Experience." Index on Censorship 32 (2): 42–51.

Tafoya, Sonya. 2004. Shades of Belonging. Washington: Pew Hispanic Center.

Taiara, Camille T. 2003. "Spoon-Feeding the Press." San Francisco Bay Guardian, March 12.

Taibo, Carlos. 2003. "Hegemonía con Quiebras." In Washington Contra el Mundo: Una Recopilación de Rebelión.org, ed. Pascual Serrano, 23–32. Madrid: Foca.

Taiwan News. 2004. "Yu to Propose 5 Fresh Policy Goals Today." September 17.

Talvi, Silja J. A. 2005a. "Alls or Nothings." In These Times, October 24: 10.

Talvi, Silja J. A. 2005b. "Funding the Fundies." In These Times, November 21: 10.

Taylor, Lucy. 2004. "Client-Ship and Citizenship in Latin America." Bulletin of Latin American Research 23 (2): 213–27.

Taylor, Lynne. 1996. "Food Riots Revisited." Journal of Social History 30 (2): 483–96.

Teague, Peter. 2004. Forward to The Death of Environmentalism: Global Warming Politics in a Post-Environmental World, by Michael Shellenberger and Ted Nordhaus.

Technological Horizons in Education Journal. 1998. "Weather Channel Wants you to Look at the Sky." November 1: 49.

Teh, Lydia. 2005. "Much Variety for Cookery Show Fans." The Star, June 29.

Teinowitz, Ira. 2005a. "Food Advertising Pushed into Harsh Spotlight." Advertising Age, March 15.

Teinowitz, Ira. 2005b. "Senator Mocks Food Industry Efforts to Monitor Ads." Advertising Age, March 16.

Teinowitz, Ira. 2005c. "Food Industry Braces for Two-Day FTC Hearing." Advertising Age, July 13.

Teinowitz, Ira, and Stephanie Thompson. 2005. "Children See Less TV Food Advertising in 2004 Than in 1977." *Advertising Age*, July 14.

Television & New Media. 2002. 3 2.

Tempest, Matthew. 2004. "Brown Pushes 'Choice' Agenda." *Guardian*, September 27.

Tewksbury, David. 2003. "What do Americans Really Want to Know? Tracking the Behavior of News Readers on the Internet." *Journal of Communication* 53 (4): 694–710.

Thelen, David. 2000. "How Natural are National and Transnational Citizenship? A Historical Perspective." *Indiana Journal of Global Legal Studies* 7: 549–65.

THINK. 2002. "Schemes: World Cultural Center." www.rvapc.com/schemes/wcc/.

Thio, Li-Ann. 2002. "Battling Balkanization: Regional Approaches toward Minority Protection beyond Europe." *Harvard International Law Journal* 43:409–68.

Thomas, John D. 2002. "For the 'Weather-Engaged,' Manna from Heaven." *New York Times*, April 28: 2.

Thomas, Morley K. 1971a. "A Brief History of Meteorological Services in Canada Part 1: 1839–1930." *Atmosphere* 9 (1): 3–15.

Thomas, Morley K. 1971b. "A Brief History of Meteorological Services in Canada Part 2: 1930–1939." *Atmosphere* 9 (2): 37–47.

Thomas, Morley K. 1971c. "A Brief History of Meteorological Services in Canada Part 3: 1939–1945." *Atmosphere* 9 (3): 69–79.

Thompson, Stephanie. 2005. "Tyson Foods Launches Faith-Friendly Marketing Campaign." *Advertising Age*, December 6.

Thrupkaew, Noy. 2005. "The Not-So-Happy-Meal." *American Prospect*, June 28.

Thussu, Daya Kishan. 2003. "Live TV and Bloodless Deaths: War, Infotainment and 24/7 News." *War and the Media: Reporting Conflict 24/7*, ed. Daya Kishan Thussu and Des Freedman. London: Sage Publications. 117–32.

Thussu, Daya Kishan, and Des Freedman, eds. 2003. Introd. to *War and the Media: Reporting Conflict 24/7*. London: Sage Publications.

Tienda, Marta. 2002. "Demography and the Social Contract." *Demography* 39 (4): 587–616.

Time International. 1993. "The Week United States: Are We at 500 Channels Yet?" May 17: 15.

Times Union Albany. 2000. "Exhibition Kitchen to be Named for Julia Child." April 5.

Timms, Dominic. 2005. "Al-Jazeera's English-Language Team Takes Shape." *Guardian*, March 4.

Tiryakian, Edward A. 2003. "Assessing Multiculturalism Theoretically: *E Pluribus Unum, Sic et Non*." *International Journal on Multicultural Societies* 5 (1): 20–39.

Toufe, Zeynep. 2002. "Let them Eat Cake." *EXTRA!Update*, November/December.

Traugott, Michael W., and Ted Brader. 2003. "Explaining 9/11." In *Framing Terrorism: The News Media, the Government, and the Public*, ed. Pippa Norris, Montague Kern, and Marion Just, 183–201. New York: Routledge.

Tripathi, Salil. 2003. "Powers of Transformation." *Index on Censorship* 32 (3): 125–31.

Trombley, Mark A. 1997. "Stock Prices and Wall Street Weather: Additional Evidence." *Quarterly Journal of Business and Economics* 36 3.

Tryhorn, Chris. 2003. "When are Facts Facts? Not in a War." *Guardian*, March 25.

Tugend, Alina. 2003. "Pundits for Hire." *American Journalism Review*, May.

Tumber, Howard, and Marina Prentoulis. 2003. "Journalists under Fire: Subcultures, Objectivity and Emotional Literacy." In *War and the Media: Reporting Conflict 24/7*, ed. Daya Kishan Thussu and Des Freedman, 215–30. London: Sage Publications.

Turkel, Studs. 2003. "In Bed with Bush." *In These Times*, October 30.

TVyVideo.com. 2003. "Los sistemas de información meteorológica. Pronóstico: variado." June.

Tyndall Report. 2003. *On Aftermath of September 11*.

UCLA Center for Communication Policy. 2002. "Study by Internet Project shows E-Mail Transformed Personal Communication after September 11 Attacks."

UN-HABITAT. 2003. "The Challenge of Slums." October 1.

UNESCO Institute for Education. 1999. *Cultural Citizenship in the 21st Century: Adult Learning and Indigenous Peoples.*

UNESCO. 2001. *Déclaración Universal de la UNESCO Sobre la Diversidad Cultural.*

United States Department of Health and Human Services. 2005. *Executive Summary: The President's New Freedom Initiative for People with Disabilities: The 2004 Progress Report.* http://www.hhs.gov/newfreedom/.

United Nations Development Programme. 2004. *Human Development Report 2004: Cultural Liberty in Today's Diverse World.* University of Delaware. 2005. "Food on TV: An Introduction."

UPI NewsTrack. 2005. "Weather Channel Faces Age Bias Lawsuit." January 6.

U.S. Congress. House. *Homeland Security Act of 2002.* HR 5005. http://frwebgate.access .gpo.gov/cgi-bin/getdoc.cgi?dbname=107_cong_bills&docid=f:h5005enr.txt.pdf.

Von Bella, Douglas A. 2003. "Bureaucratic Responsiveness to the News Media: Comparing the Influence of *The New York Times* and Network Television News Coverage on US Foreign Aid Allocations." *Political Communication* 20 (3): 263–85.

Van Creveld, Martin. 1999. *The Rise and Decline of the State.* Cambridge: Cambridge University Press.

van Ham, Peter. 2001. "The Rise of the Brand State: The Postmodern Politics of Image and Reputation." *Foreign Affairs* 80 (5): 2–6.

van Zoonen, Liesbet. 2005. *Entertaining the Citizen: When Politics and Popular Culture Converge.* Lanham: Rowman & Littlefield.

Vasudevan, Ravi S. 2001. "An Imperfect Public: Cinema and Citizenship in the 'Third World'." In *Sarai Reader 01: The Public Domain,* 57–68. Delhi: Sarai.

Veder, Robin, and James Rodger Fleming. 2001. "Yesterday's Forecasts." *Cabinet Magazine* 3.

The Vegan Research Panel. 2005. *Discovering 21st Century Vegans.*

Velvel, Lawrence R. 2004. "Introduction." *The Long Term View* 62:3–18.

Venegas, Juan Manuel. 2003. "¿Yo por qué?, insiste Fox; ¿qué no somos 100 millones de mexicanos?" *La Jornada,* August 2: Política 3.

Venturelli, Shalini. 2000. *From the Information Economy to the Creative Economy: Moving Culture to the Center of International Public Policy.* Washington, DC: Center for Arts and Culture.

Vidal, John. 2004. "Meat-Eaters Soak Up the World's Water." *Guardian,* August 23.

Vigoda, Eran, and Robert T. Golembiewski. 2001. "Citizenship Behavior and the Spirit of New Managerialism: A Theoretical Framework and Challenge for Governance." *American Review of Public Administration* 31 (3): 273–95.

Von Moltke, Konrad, and Atiq Rahman. 1996. "External Perspectives on Climate Change: A View from the United States and the Third World." In *Politics of Climate Change: A European Perspective,* ed. Tim O'Riordan and Jill Jäger, 335–45. London: Routledge.

Vonnegut, Kurt. 2004. "I Love You, Madame Librarian." *In These Times,* August 6.

Vonnegut, Kurt. 2005. "Your Guess is as Good as Mine." *In These Times,* December 19: 39, 40.

Wade, Robert Hunter. 2003. "The Invisible Hand of the American Empire." *openDemocracy,* March 13. http://www.opendemocracy.net.

Wallach, Lori, and Patrick Woodall/Public Citizen. 2004. *Whose Trade Organization? A Comprehensive Guide to the WTO.* New York: New Press.

Wallerstein, Immanuel. 1989. "Culture as the Ideological Battleground of the Modern World-System." *Hitotsubashi Journal of Social Studies* 21 (1): 5–22.

Wallerstein, Immanuel. 2003. *The Decline of American Power: The U.S. in a Chaotic World*. New York: New Press.

Warneke, Ross. 2003. "This Many Cooks Make Quite a Broth." *The Age*, October 9.

Warner, Gerald. 2000. "British Identity Threatened by Phony Race Relations Industry." *The Scotsman*, October 15: 20.

Washington File. 2003. "Time Frame Unknown but Regime's End Clear, Rumsfeld Says: Interview on CBS's *Face the Nation* with Bob Schieffer and David Martin." March 23.

Wasko, Janet, ed. 2005. Introd. to *A Companion to Television*. Malden: Blackwell.

Waters, Mary C. 2003. "Once Again, Strangers on our Shores." In *The Fractious Nation? Unity and Division in American Life*, ed. Jonathan Rieder, assoc. ed. Stephen Steinlight, 117–30. Berkeley: University of California Press.

Watson, Alison M. 2004. "Seen but not Heard: The Role of the Child in International Political Economy." *New Political Economy* 9 (1): 3–21.

Watts, Michael J. 2000. "The Great Tablecloth: Bread and Butter Politics, and the Political Economy of Food and Poverty." In *The Oxford Handbook of Economic Geography*, ed. Gordon L. Clark, Maryann P. Feldman, and Meric S. Gertler with the assistance of Kate Williams, 195–212. Oxford: Oxford University Press.

Weather Channel. 1998. "About Us." http://www.weather.com/aboutus/.

Weather Channel. 2000. http://www.weather.com/interact/chat/.

Weather Channel. 2001." About Us: The Weather Channel Backgrounder." http://www.weather.com/aboutus/marketing/press/cable/backgrounder.html.

Weather Channel. 2003. "The Weather Channel Position Statement on Global Warming."

Webster, Frank. 2003. "Information Warfare in an Age of Globalization." In *War and the Media: Reporting Conflict 24/7*, ed. Daya Kishan Thussu and Des Freedman, 57–69. London: Sage Publications.

Webster, James G. 2005. "Beneath the Veneer of Fragmentation: Television Audience Polarization in a Multichannel World." *Journal of Communication* 55 (2): 366–82.

Weed, William Speed. 2004. "Television Meterologist." *Popular Science*. http://www.popsci.com.

Weiner, Jennifer. 2001. *Good in Bed*. New York: Washington Square Press.

Weinstein, David. 2004. *The Forgotten Network: Dumont and the Birth of American Television*. Philadelphia: Temple University Press.

Weisman, Steven R. 2005. "Under Pressure, Qatar May Sell Jazeera Station." *New York Times*, January 30.

Wells, Matt. 2003. "ITC Tackles Fox News Bias Claims." *Guardian*, May 8.

Westcott, Kathryn. 2005. "Pressure Builds for US Climate Action." *BBC News Online*, February 14. http://news.bbc.co.uk.

Westheimer, Joel. 2004. "Introduction." *PS: Political Science & Politics* 37 (2): 231–34.

Westheimer, Joel, and Joseph Kahne. 2004a. "Educating the "Good" Citizen: Political Choices and Pedagogical Goals." *PS: Political Science & Politics* 37 (2): 241–48.

Westheimer, Joel, and Joseph Kahne. 2004b. "What Kind of Citizen? The Politics of Educating for Democracy." *American Educational Research Journal* 41 (2): 237–69.

Whitaker, Brian. 2002. "US Thinktanks Give Lessons in Foreign Policy." *Guardian*, August 19.

Whitehead, Colson. 2001. *John Henry Days: A Novel*. New York: Doubleday.

The White House. 2002. *The National Security Strategy of the United States of America*. September 17. http://www.whitehouse.gov/nsc/nss.html.

The White House Project. 2005. http://www.thewhitehouseproject.org/research.

Whiten, Jon. 2004. "Bad News from Iraq?" *EXTRA!Update*, February: 3.

Whiten, Jon. 2005. "'The World Litle Noted': CBS Scandal Eclipses Missing WMDs." *Extra!* March/April: 7.

Wikipedia: The Free Encyclopedia. 2005. "Weather Forecasting." http://en.wikipedia.org.

Wildweather.com. 2002. "Meteorologist of the Month." April/May.

Wilkinson, Marian. 2003. "POWs Vanish Amid War on Nasty Images." *Sydney Morning Herald*, March 25.

Williams, Juliet A. 2001. "The Personal is Political: Thinking through the Clinton/Lewinsky/Starr Affair." *PS: Political Science and Politics* 34 (1): 93–98.

Williams, Raymond. 1983. *Keywords: A Vocabulary of Culture and Society*, revised ed. New York: Oxford University Press.

Wilson, Kris. 2002. "Forecasting the Future: How Television Weathercasters' Attitudes and Beliefs about Climate Change Affect their Cognitive Knowledge on the Science." *Science Communication* 24 (2): 246–68.

Wilson, Robert. 2004. *The Vanished Hands.* Orlando: Harcourt, Inc.

Wilson, Woodrow. 2005. "The Study of Public Administration." In *Communication Research and Policy-Making*, ed. Sandra Braman, 61–84. Cambridge, MA: MIT Press.

Wind, Gregory. 2004. "Climate Control: Forecast: Weather Data is More Local and Precise." *Broadcasting & Cable*, March 22: 17.

Winocur, Rosalía. 2002. *Ciudadanos Mediáticos: La construcción de lo publico en la radio.* Barcelona: Editorial Gedisa.

Winthrop, Robert. 2002. "Exploring Cultural Rights." *Cultural Dynamics* 14 (2): 115–20.

Wolf, Martin. 2000. "When Intervention Treads on Individual Freedom: The Runnymede Trust's Report on Multiculturalism Raises more than the Issue of whether Britishness is Racist." *Financial Times*, October 16: 31.

Woodward, Will. 2005. "Jamie Oliver Turns on Sainsbury's." *Guardian*, March 8.

World Economic Forum. 2004. *Global Governance Initiative Annual Report 2004.*

World Trade Organization. 2003. *World Trade Developments in 2001 and Prospects for 2002.* Geneva.

Wright, Angus, and Wendy Wolford. 2003. "Now it is Time: The MST and Grassroots Land Reform in Brazil." *Food First Backgrounder* 9 2.

Wright, Micah Ian. 2003. *You Back the Attack! We'll Bomb Who We Want! Remixed War Propaganda.* New York: Seven Stories Press.

Wucker, Michele. 2005. "The Perpetual Migration Machine and Political Power." *World Policy Journal* 21 (3): 41–50.

Wyatt, Edward. 2003a. "New Issues as Hearings Address Rebuilding." *New York Times*, January 13.

Wyatt, Edward. 2003b. "Panel Makes Unexpected Choice for World Trade Center Site." *New York Times*, February 26.

Yates, Michael D. 2005. "A Statistical Portrait of the U.S. Working Class." *Monthly Review* 56 (11): 12–31.

Young, Iris Marion. 1990. "Polity and Group Difference: A Critique of the Ideal of Universal Citizenship." *Feminism and Political Theory*, ed. Cass R. Sunstein, 117–41. Chicago: University of Chicago Press.

Youngers, Coletta. 2003. "The U.S. and Latin America after 9-11 and Iraq." *Foreign Policy in Focus Policy Report.* June. http://www.fpif.org.

Yúdice, George. 2002. *El Recurso de la Cultura: Usos de la Cultura en la Era Global.* Barcelona: Editorial Gedisa.

Zacharias, Usha. 2001. "Trial by Fire: Gender, Power, and Citizenship in Narratives of the Nation." *Social Text* 69:29–51.

Zachary, G. Pascal. 2000. "A Philosopher in Red Sneakers Gains Influence as a Global Guru." *Wall Street Journal*, March 28: B1, B4.

Zbar, Jeffery D. 2001. "Careful Segmenting Puts Weather on the Map." *Advertising Age*, April 16: S4.

Zea, Leopoldo. 2001. "De la Guerra Fría a la Sucia." In *11 de septiembre de 2001*, ed. Frida Modak, 5–10. Buenos Aires: Grupo Editorial Lumen.

Zelizer, Barbie, and Stuart Allan. 2002a. "Introduction: When Trauma Shapes the News." In *Journalism after September 11*, eds. Barbie Zelizer and Stuart Allan, 1–24. London: Routledge.

Zelizer, Barbie, and Stuart Allan, eds. 2002b. *Journalism after September 11*. London: Routledge.

Zerbisias, Antonia. 2003. "The Press Self-Muzzled its Coverage of Iraq War." *Toronto Star*, September 16.

Zerbisias, Antonia. 2005. "Colleagues Under Fire but U.S. Media Mute." *Toronto Star*, March 8.

Zernike, Kate. 2004. "Lawyers Shift Focus from Big Tobacco to Big Food." *New York Times*, April 9: A15.

Ziccardi, Alicia, ed. 2003. *Planeación Participativa en el Espacio Global: Cinco Programas Parciales de Desarollo Urbano en el Distrito Federal*. Mexico: Universidad Nacional Autónoma de México.

Zinn, Howard. 2003. Introd. to *Target Iraq: What the News Media Didn't Tell You*, by Norman Solomon and Reese Erlich. New York: Context Books.

Zinn, Howard. 2004. "An Occupied Country." *The Long Term View* 6 2:88–91.

Žižek, Slavoj. 2002. *Welcome to the Desert of the Real! Five Essays on September 11 and Related Dates*. London: Verso.

Zorach, Rebecca. 2003. "Insurance Nation." *Boston Globe*, March 9: D2.

INDEX

TOBY MILLER is Professor of English, Sociology, and Women's Studies, and Director of the Program in Media & Cultural Studies at the University of California, Riverside. He is the editor of two journals: *Television & New Media* and *Social Identities*, and the author of *Sportsex* (Temple).